MORALITY AT THE MARGINS

Morality at the Margins

YOUTH, LANGUAGE, AND ISLAM IN COASTAL KENYA

SARAH HILLEWAERT

FORDHAM UNIVERSITY PRESS

New York 2020

Visit us online at www.fordhampress.com.

Library of Congress Cataloging-in-Publication Data

Names: Hillewaert, Sarah, author.
Title: Morality at the margins : youth, language, and Islam
in coastal Kenya / Sarah Hillewaert.
Description: New York : Fordham University Press, 2020. |
Includes bibliographical references and index.
Identifiers: LCCN 2019028489 | ISBN 9780823286515
(hardback) | ISBN 9780823286508 (paperback) |
ISBN 9780823286522 (epub)
Subjects: LCSH: Muslim youth—Kenya—Lamu
Island—Social conditions—21st century. | Social
change—Kenya—Lamu Island. | Swahili language—
Kenya—Lamu Island. | Nonverbal communication—
Kenya—Lamu Island. | Lamu Island (Kenya)—
Social conditions—20th century.
Classification: LCC HQ799.8.K42 L36 2020 |
DDC 305.386970967623—dc23
LC record available at https://lccn.loc.gov/2019028489

Printed in the United States of America
22 21 20   5 4 3 2 1
First edition

To the people of Lamu

CONTENTS

I listened to the call to the afternoon prayer as I sat at the front of the Tundani Mosque and realized it would be one of the last times I would hear the mix of voices reminding people to pray resound over Lamu's rooftops. The *adhan* had been one of my favorite aspects of life in Lamu, especially the call to the early morning prayer. Waking the town's residents from their sleep, a first call would break the nightly silence. And then a second call would start, and then a third, and a fourth, until all of Lamu's forty-two mosques would remind sleeping residents to get up and pray. Soon after, you could hear the shuffling of feet in the dusty streets, of men silently making their way to the neighborhood mosque. And as the sun rose quickly, the town woke up; voices grew louder as children were urged to get ready for school, as men gathered on the *baraza* to enjoy some Arabic coffee, as people hurried to the jetty to catch a boat to the mainland. Recordings of Quran recitation played from neighborhood shops where savory breakfast snacks were sold. And Lamu's many donkeys noisily reminded their owners to feed them. While there were no cars on Lamu, motorcycles had recently been introduced to the island, and I wondered how those loud bikes would alter the early morning scene I had come to appreciate so much.

My thoughts were interrupted by the sound of men entering the mosque, downstairs from where we were sitting. While Lamu women habitually do not pray in the mosque, a few places of worship reserved the upper floor for women to organize lectures or other events. I fixed my *hijab*. Its silky material had slipped back and caused some hair strings to pop out. I liked the goldish color of this scarf because it matched the gold details of the bright pink dress I was wearing. "*MashaAllah,*" my host mother had mumbled when I appeared from my room, back at the house. Praising God, she approved of my outfit and dapped my wrists and dress with *mafuta mazito*, with sweet, heavy perfume oil. "*Tosha!*" That's enough! I had objected, reminding her that we still had to walk to the mosque. I didn't want the perfume to smell too strongly as we were sure to pass by *baraza* or stone benches where men habitually relax. At the mosque, she attached a *kikuba*—a jasmine-flower broach—to my dress, the beautiful smell penetrating my nose. *Oudi* was burning, and the prayer area slowly filled with a mist of incense smoke. I was nervous. We sent out invitations for the prayer event a few days earlier. That morning, we cleaned the upper floor of the mosque, ordered crates of soda, and made packages of savory snacks that would be distributed at the end of the prayer. I couldn't help but wonder how many women would attend. Noticing my uneasiness, my host mother smiled. "People will come," she reassured me and reminded me that many women would first pray at home, then prepare the afternoon tea for their family, and only then come to the mosque.

It was the day before my departure from Lamu in June 2010. The event was a *dua* or prayer in the neighborhood mosque to bid farewell to the women who had welcomed me into their homes over the last three years, and to ask for their prayers as I traveled back to the United States. I had been reluctant to organize the *dua*. I did not want to make a big deal out of my departure, nor did I want to interfere with other social gatherings that were undoubtedly taking place at the same time. But my host mother (and other women of the family) had insisted: I could not leave without allowing them to pray for me.

About half an hour following the afternoon prayer, women started to trickle in until the mosque's upper level was almost full. I smiled as I recognized friends and women who had become like family, even before they removed their *ninja* (facial veil).[1] In the secluded space of the mosque, many women took off their black *buibui* to reveal the colorful dresses they wore underneath the black garments that had concealed clothing and bodily shape. As I watched them arrive, I reflected upon my time in Lamu and how my view of the town and its residents had changed over the course of three years. When I first arrived on the island, I struggled to recognize women and viewed their coverings as anonymizing, as concealing not only bodily appearances but also identity and personality. I had been surprised when male interlocutors told me they recognized their sisters, wives, or, in some cases, girlfriends from afar. Many times, female acquaintances had to "flash" me when they encountered me on Lamu's streets. Realizing I did not recognize them, they would glance left and right to assure nobody was too close by, then quickly lift their veils up and down to reveal their faces for only a second. As I was about to return to America, I thought about how I learned to recognize my friends by the plethora of distinguishing features I now identified in their appearances— details in *buibui* designs, ways of wearing the facial veil, movements, hand gestures, bodily shapes, or distinguishing eyes. I could hardly believe that, at some point, I had been blind to the signs of social class, piety, urbanity, flirtation, conservative demeanor, or individuality carried in these women's appearances.

I first arrived in Lamu six years earlier, in the company of my mother and sister. Our travels through Kenya had lead us to this island town described in travel guides as a place "where time stood still." The proprietor of our hotel in Mombasa had urged us to visit Lamu, depicting it as a remote town without motorized transportation, known for its donkeys, and made up of limestone mansions that reminded visitors of its cosmopolitan past. While I had been to Kenya many times before, conducting research in Nairobi, I had never made it to Lamu. During my first visit, I became fascinated by the island's transoceanic past and its seeming present-day seclusion. I wondered what it was like to be young in Lamu and returned to the island two summers later to start my research.

Having reached the end of my fieldwork, I looked at Lamu quite differently. While I still recognized the idyllic nature of the town and its history, I also knew it was a place troubled by its economic and politically marginalized position; a town wondering about the future of its youth and fighting the increasing use of alcohol and drugs, the rising HIV/AIDS rates, and the growing imposition of "outsiders" and "land grabbers." I had also come to know the stories attached to the alleys, walkways, and corners of Lamu. I learned about the significance of smiles, gazes, and tones of voice. I understood the subtle meaning of different times of day and nuances in greetings. And I had come to understand both the opportunities and threats that locals saw in the changes affecting their town—in tourism, aid organizations, or the construction of an international port.

I also learned about the importance of trust in this Swahili community and about local ideologies surrounding the inappropriateness of revealing too much about oneself or one's family. Swahili communities like Lamu, while hospitable to visitors, are reserved when it comes to welcoming people into their homes and lives. Opening one's house to someone (and thus exposing them to the everyday life of the family) is considered an *amana*—a trust that assumes a commitment from the one with whom information is shared, a vow not to violate the confidence instilled in you. I struggled with this awareness as I wrote this book, trying to find an appropriate voice with which to narrate my experiences while also respecting the trust people had given me. During the writing process, I often thought back to that day in the mosque in 2010, when Lamu women came to bid me farewell, and contemplated whether my depictions of everyday life in Lamu did justice to the respect and trust they had given me.

Middleton (1992) has long underlined the importance of "the private" in Swahili communities, discussing how ideologies of the public and private distinction inform cultural values of, for example, respectability and honor (1992, 187). Thompson and Stiles (2015) and Thompson (e.g., 2015a, 2017b) equally highlight ideologies of secrecy along the East African coast, particularly when it comes to intimacy, relationships, and sexuality. Susan Hirsch (1998), however, contemplates what such ideologies of privacy, trust, and secrecy entail for the ethnographer working in Swahili communities. When ruminating on her study of Swahili women's participation in Islamic courts in Mombasa, she notes the ethical dilemma faced by anthropologists working along the East African coast and points to "the awkward fit between the Swahili ideology of concealing personal matters and the goal of obtaining and writing about 'inside knowledge'" (Hirsh 1998, 14). Hirsch wholly captures my moral deliberations when she remarks that ethnographers "to the extent that [they] expose the tensions underlying multiple relations of power in Swahili society, particularly by describing them ethnographically . . . threaten to break community norms by narrating problems that—according to Swahili cultural ideals—are best left unremarked" (Hirsch 1998, 14).

This ethnography is, in a way, a product of my own process of moral self-positioning, of trying to find an objective yet respectful voice with which to write about life in contemporary Lamu. I am aware, however, that I still run the risk of revealing issues that are considered best left unspoken, at least in public. To protect the anonymity of my interlocutors and thus safeguard the trust they instilled in me, all names in this book are pseudonyms, unless noted otherwise. Contextual information that could reveal anyone's identity is either omitted or altered. At times, I slightly change biographical information to further conceal a person's identity; this can include, for example, details about family structure or employment. Because of ethnographic importance, relevant details with regard to status or ethnicity remain unchanged (see also Meneley 1996, 4).

My reflections on the implications of writing a book about Lamu, however, are informed by more than Swahili ideologies of trust. I was warned early on about the difficulties I could face when conducting research in Lamu. Before I left for the field in 2007, a colleague reminded me of Lamu residents' negative response to the work of anthropologists who had researched the island before me. I was told, for example, that Mohammed El Zein (1974) passed away shortly after the publication of his study on religious symbolism in Lamu. Rumor had it that a powerful Swahili curse was pronounced after the release of his book, for some Lamu residents disapproved of its conclusions and disseminating of information that had been shared with him in confidence. While there was, of course, no evident connection between the book release and his death, people (Lamu residents and fellow academics) pointed to this rather "strange" coincidence. Lamu residents had been equally disturbed by subsequent ethnographies on the lives of young women in Lamu or the town's history of slavery. I was told, for example, that ethnographers had shared photographs of (unveiled) Lamu women, without these women's consent. As a colleague pointed out, the anthropologists in question had all changed field sites following the criticism they received.

Throughout my stay in Lamu, residents related to me their encounters with these anthropologists. I was never sure whether these stories were meant as a warning or as proof of scholarly interest in Lamu and thus the (historical) significance of the town. These stories, however, were often followed by a series of questions: about my background, my family, my reasons for conducting research. The fact that my study did not have one clear-cut question (for example, I did not just study the local Swahili dialect, kiAmu) but rather focused on a series of processes made interlocutors a bit apprehensive. While they understood that I conducted research on language change, they often did not comprehend why I attended community meetings on, for example, drug abuse in Lamu. This suspicion resulted in me being less comfortable taking fieldnotes in public and in my being reluctant to take photos in town or at events. I relied on a research assistant to take pictures and I later asked professional photographers to use their photos in the book. I resorted to not recording my conversations with interlocutors, only using my voice recorder when working with research assistants, who would lead the interview.

The distrust aroused by my taking photos or using a recorder was also related to another challenge to my research. After the 1998 bombing of the American embassies in Nairobi and Dar Es Salaam, and especially after the 2002 bombing of an Israeli hotel in Mombasa, the Lamu Archipelago had become a target of investigations by international security forces, including the CIA. This reached a climax when investigators discovered that Fazul Mohammed, the brain behind the 1998 and the 2002 bombings, had lived and married in the community of Siyu, one of the towns located in the Lamu Archipelago (see also Prestholdt 2011). Following this discovery, investigations in the Lamu area intensified and several locals were arrested and questioned (Prestholdt 2009). The United States responded to these events by training Kenyan Maritime Police in a facility in the Lamu Archipelago through the State Department's Antiterrorism

Assistance program and by installing a Maritime Security and Safety Information System along the coast through the Combined Joint Task Force-Horn of Africa (Prestholdt 2011, 11). Such military activity was counterbalanced with investments in local development efforts and humanitarian assistance programs (like USAID). While the aid was much needed (and welcomed) in Lamu, it also caused residents to be suspicious of the intentions of aid workers and, by extension, of all foreigners residing in their town. It came as no surprise to hear that I was suspected of being an undercover CIA agent. Some locals were quite forthcoming about their suspicions and blatantly asked me if I was a spy. At one point, I was summoned by the head of the CIPK (Council of Imams and Preachers of Kenya), who politely questioned me about my reasons for being in Lamu.

Yet my research was also constrained, in less dramatic ways, by aspects related to status, gender, and age. During my initial visits to Lamu, my encounters with locals had been limited to interactions with the young men who worked at Lamu's seafront. Making a living in the tourism industry, these youth (also known as "beach boys") were "cultural brokers"— the intimate, friendly connection between the Western tourist and the "mysterious" local culture. When I returned to Lamu for research purposes, I mistakenly assumed these young men would introduce me to mothers, sisters, and wives. I quickly learned not only that they were reluctant to do so, but also that my habit of spending time with these young men in the hopes of advancing my research was counterproductive.

While Lamu has long grown accustomed to tourism, there remains a relatively clear separation between Lamu residents and tourists. Unless they own or rent one of Lamu's stone houses, travelers generally spend their time along the town's main street or seafront, avoiding the labyrinth of alleys. Male youth working in the tourism industry were tolerated because they entertained foreigners who brought economic revenue to the island, yet the young men's conduct was frowned upon. Their open interactions (and romantic relationships) with Western women as well as their dreadlocks or smoking habits were often criticized. Newly arrived in Lamu, I was advised by employees of the National Museums of Kenya (where I established my initial research contacts) that spending time with these young men could result in residents viewing me as just another *mzungu* or Western tourist who had fallen for the charms of the beach boys.

I therefore began to avoid the seafront and tried to engage with community groups and aid organizations (connections facilitated by museum staff). These groups relied on young volunteers and thus provided opportunities to spend time with local youth (other than the beach boys).

Through this volunteer work, however, I encountered a specific section of Lamu youth—generally high school or college-educated, unmarried, and often rather progressive. Not only did I have little contact with other young people, such as young women who spent their time at home, I also encountered few parents. While museum staff introduced me to a few elders, I soon realized these were older residents to whom all researchers were referred and who had prepared a standard narrative about Lamu and its history. Cultural norms, however, prevented me from approaching other male residents. Women from the former upper classes generally remained home, and I was unlikely to be introduced to them, even by relatives who I had met in community organizations. This hesitancy to introduce me to family members was partly due to suspicion of researchers in Lamu, but it was also related to the ideologies of privacy in Swahili communities; doors to the home were not easily opened, especially not by the former merchant elites. My initial interactions were mostly with Bajuni women deriving from the surrounding islands in the Archipelago, who were somewhat less concerned with privacy and spent more time outside the home. Other early interlocutors included employees of the National Museums of Kenya, who were familiar with researchers and quite quickly invited me to their homes or offered to discuss my research interests.

As time progressed, however, I expanded my networks and was slowly integrated into the social life of Lamu. Looking back, I realize it was my growing mindfulness of details of comportment and a developing understanding of *heshima* or respectability as it relates to age, gender, and social class that enabled a gradual shift in my social standing. My ability to display consideration of respect and respectability within my everyday verbal, material, and bodily practices allowed more shielded Lamu residents to accept me into their social circles (but not necessarily their homes). This did not happen overnight though, and I often needed explicit instructions on proper comportment.

During the first month of my research, for example, I asked advice from an acquaintance who worked for the Lamu Museum. I had moved into an apartment in Mkomani, on the historically upper-class side of Lamu, and was eager to establish connections with my neighbors. I had decided to start by offering a greeting as I walked past their house. Using the Islamic *assalaam aleykum*, I hoped to distinguish myself from the tourists who lodged in the same house as me. My greetings, however, were received with silence several times. "Why won't they greet me back?" I asked. With an amused expression, my friend first asked about whom I was greeting and when and where I was greeting them. When she realized

I was referring to a group of neighborhood elders who socialized after the morning prayers, she chuckled. She noted that enthusiastically smiling at elder men and offering them an Islamic greeting, while evidently not being Muslim (although I wore long skirts, I had not yet started covering) would not evoke a response. While she acknowledged that I was only trying to be friendly, she proposed I approach things differently the next morning. She suggested I cover my head with a scarf and walk past the gathering with some distance, without making eye contact with the men. I could then softly but audibly ask *"Habari zenu?"* (How are all of you?). This way, she told me, I would show respect for the *baraza* and its members while also acknowledging the Islamically important social connection between neighbors. I followed her advice and received the first greeting from my neighborhood *baraza* the next day.

I smile as I recount these early exchanges because several of those *baraza* elders became and still are close acquaintances. I also came to view these interaction norms as self-evident and now shake my head as I recollect my initial obliviousness to them. I describe them here, not to suggest some kind of naivety on my end, but rather to underline the explicitness with which I was instructed on seemingly minor details of comportment and the difference some of this advice made. In other words, notions of what constitutes respectable conduct to whom and in which context, rather than unspoken, were quite readily available for Lamu residents to discuss. Indeed, my first months in Lamu were replete with instructions from interlocutors as they advised me on how to integrate myself into Lamu society as a respectable individual: turn off music when hearing the call to prayer, cover your hair while in public, sit with your neighbors when they have lost a family member. I learned to avoid the male-dominated seafront and grasped the respectability that lies in using Lamu's alleys rather than main roads. I was instructed on how to properly greet men, women, and children. I was taught to read and use many of the material and verbal signs that inform social relations, status, and life in Lamu and came to understand how people constitute themselves as particular kinds of moral individuals through a series of bodily practices (Abu Lughod 1986, 5). It was precisely through receiving such coaching about proper conduct that I acquired insights into navigating everyday life and social expectations in Lamu (Meneley 1996, 4). At the same time, however, my understanding and eventual appropriation of such markers of social identity were informed by changes in my personal life as well.

Over the course of my stay in Lamu, residents ascribed different social positions to me—tourist, researcher, welcomed guest, close friend, fellow

Muslimah, adopted family member. Ethnographers who worked in Muslim-majority field sites often remark that one is not fully recognized as "a proper social being" unless one shares with community members the Muslim faith (Meneley 1996, 3). An adherence to Islam has, indeed, always been central to being recognized as "Swahili," yet in contemporary Lamu many residents place more emphasis on others' respect for local (Islamic) values than on a conversion to Islam. I was often told that some Euro-American expatriates showed more consideration for local norms than some immigrants from the surrounding islands who shared a Muslim identity with people from Lamu.

While interlocutors enquired about my faith, few of those conversations were followed by overt encouragements to convert. People supported me when they learned I was fasting during the month of Ramadan, for example, but did not assume this meant I was going to become Muslim. Especially those friends who knew I was learning about the religion for personal reasons, rather than for academic purposes, never asked if I would convert. When I later asked a friend why this had been the case, she smiled, looked a bit perplexed, and reminded me that "there is no compulsion in religion." She told me that all she could do was lead by example and hope her lifestyle would inspire me.

My conversion to Islam during my stay in Lamu did not come with a marked shift in social status. I had started covering my hair soon after my arrival and because of my frequent socializing with local women I began wearing a *buibui* or black cloak a few months into my fieldwork. My conversion thus did not come with clearly visible signs, and most people asked about it only upon seeing me participate in devotional practices. While my social status did not noticeably change, people's behavior toward me often did (for example, some men refrained from shaking my hand). Moreover, my own comportment and particularly my expectations of others' interactions with me (especially men) shifted meaningfully. I relied on the guidance I received from (female) interlocutors as I tried to negotiate a new social position and perform a particular kind of piety. My journey as a Muslim convert is therefore intricately connected with my experiences in Lamu. It forms part of the background of which readers should be aware when reading this book, as my own journey provided insights into the significance of everyday behaviors for the negotiation of changing social relations and positionalities.

I do not, however, suggest that people's shifts in behavior toward me were based only on the knowledge that I had converted. On the contrary, the exchanges I discuss earlier in this preface occurred before my conversion to Islam. Rather, it was my growing embodiment of behavioral norms and my progressive association with specific Lamu families that resulted in others' changing attitudes toward me. I arrived in Lamu as a young, unmarried woman and had opted to live alone, to allow a freedom of movement I assumed was needed for fieldwork. Both those factors, however, impacted my social standing. Respectable young Lamu women would never live alone and unmarried girls generally do not attend women's social events, such as weddings and funerals. At twenty-eight, however, I was older than the average Lamu bride and, while they did not necessarily approve, acquaintances understood my choice to live by myself. Neighbors and friends, however, frequently invited me to eat or stay with them, and I soon was associated with two families in particular.

This affiliation came with new responsibilities. As they welcomed me into their homes, these families also expected me to uphold their reputation and thus act according to their *heshima* or respectability. If I acted inappropriately, this would reflect negatively on them as well. At the same time, however, these families attributed a somewhat ambiguous position to me as they recognized that not all rules of proper behavior applied to me. For example, they acknowledged my need to be out for most of the day as part of my fieldwork. Daughters of those same families, however, were often chastised for taking too long to return home after school. Precisely my mindfulness of this tension—of simultaneously occupying an insider and outsider status—made me aware of how to use everyday practices to perform this balancing act. As I moved through town, I was conscious of the routes I walked, the people I interacted with, and my overall comportment, knowing my behavior was being observed. At the same time, my ambiguous position prompted some people to deviate from local norms when interacting with me, testing which (inappropriate) greetings they could use or simply assuming that certain norms did not apply to me. On several occasions, male friends would offer to accompany me through town, something unthinkable for local women (unless for professional purposes or if the man was a relative). In those instances, I was intensely aware that my response to them—how I negotiated these potentially transgressive behaviors—reflected on me as well as on my host family.

I elaborate on the different considerations I made while living in Lamu because it highlights the complexity of social relations and rules of conduct in this community. No behavior remains unobserved in Lamu, a rule that applied to me just as much as it did to local young women. My own feelings and experiences are incorporated into the stories I tell, not as some decorative flourish (Behar 1996, 14), but because I consider them vital to understanding the arguments made and the social world described (Anderson 2006).

The discussions in this book focus on the everyday; they reveal the complexities of life in present-day Lamu and the seemingly mundane practices through which residents of the island come to terms with the changes impacting their community. I have tried to accurately represent the political and social issues that concern Lamu residents, but also recognize that I tell a particular story about their perceptions of these changes. Rather than a mere factual account of the contemporary social composition of Lamu and the historical, political, and economic causes underlying its changed social geography, I document how waAmu—people who perceive themselves as the rightful residents of Lamu—respond to this altered social context. And I recognize that this narrative could have been told in many different ways.

Lamu has always been a highly stratified society where urban merchant elites distinguished themselves as pious, civilized, and socially autonomous in relation to local non-elites and nonlocals. In the past, their social position was maintained through performances of a particular kind of respectability, entailing (among others) notions of consumption, proper social interaction, and displays of modesty. Not static, this relative status and the norms that informed it have been redefined in relation to what these elites were best able to live up to (in terms of, for example, economic status or religious education). As Meneley (1996) noted for the class-ideologies of Zabidi elites in Yemen, the correctness and moral authority of waAmu's social life was persuasive to themselves as well as to non-elites and others who moved to Lamu. To a certain extent, their lasting insistence on the superiority of their lifestyle (and the outside "threats" to it) remains convincing, to themselves and to foreign researchers. Within present-day Lamu, however, their social and moral authority is increasingly contested.

In this book, I explore how a previously hegemonic ideology of morality, civility, and social status is challenged and redefined in the face of contemporary change. I thus do not tell an uncorrected elite story but instead document how challenges to a relationally defined social hierarchy leads Lamu residents to reflect upon, imagine, and redefine their ideas of belonging and associated notions of morality. The voices of those in relation to whom former elites define themselves are not entirely absent. Opinions of local non-elites are represented to illustrate how notions of morality are reconceptualized, but also to show how residents of Lamu are jointly positioning themselves against the Kenyan nation. At the same time, the voices of other groups against whom Lamu residents are defining themselves are not present. Perspectives of Kikuyu residents or Euro-American expatriates undeniably form an important angle from which to explore the questions raised in this book. Yet, that would constitute a different project altogether.

Throughout this preface, I referred to research assistants, interlocutors, and friends who aided and advised me during fieldwork. For my more formal research, I mostly relied on two male research assistants—Omari Hassan, who was in his twenties, and Mwalim Baddi, who was in his mid-fifties at the time and who passed away quite unexpectedly as I finalized this book.[2] He is sorely missed. Both of these men worked with researchers before (mostly historians and anthropologists) and were familiar with the practices of academic fieldwork. Their experience aided me in better understanding and navigating Lamu residents' apprehension toward some of my research interests. As I proposed interview questions, they often suggested different ways to approach a particular topic. I also relied on Mwalim Baddi and Omari to tackle some of the gendered challenges I faced. While I could more easily conduct interviews with women, it was difficult for me to approach Lamu men. Both Mwalim Baddi and Omari conducted interviews with men from different ages and social backgrounds (generally in my presence, but with them asking the questions). Their familiarity with Swahili cultural norms assured the success of many interviews that would otherwise have been stilted and little informative.

Following interviews, we always sat down on the rooftop of my house to listen to the recorded interactions and discuss topics that came up or questions that remained unanswered. Having picked up on my interest in details of language use, Mwalim Baddi and Omari would point out dialect use, code-switches, or changes in intonation as we listened to the recordings. Often, those comments on *how* interviewees spoke (rather than what they spoke about) brought to the fore the value of interactions that had, at first, appeared of little interest. The same accounts for those research assistants who transcribed interviews. I mostly worked with a female high-school graduate and a male college graduate and had instructed them to transcribe interviews as they occurred, urging them to use nonstandard orthography whenever applicable. While apprehensive at first, both transcribers became fascinated with interviewees' language use and the challenge to accurately represent the use of local vernaculars (rather than resort to Standard Swahili spelling). We often discussed transcription methods and orthographic choices. Yet these interactions equally sidetracked to discuss the themes addressed in the interviews—contemporary youth, religion, social change, norms and values. The conversations with my research assistants often drove home the ideological connections between language use (and broader communicative practices) and notions of morality in the Lamu community. These rooftop discussions remain some of the most fascinating and academically stimulating conversations I had during my time in Lamu. I am indebted to these research assistants and recognize their invaluable contributions to this book.

MORALITY AT THE MARGINS

Introduction

"*Muko hadir?*" Are you (pl.) present? The commanding voice of Ustadh Taha resonated through the prayer hall of the mosque. Amplified by loud-speakers, his question blared over the rooftops of nearby houses, reaching women who were hastily preparing food as the time for the sunset prayer was approaching. It was Ramadan 2008, and Taha, a young but well-versed imam, was delivering his daily lecture to men gathered in one of Lamu's biggest mosques. The seemingly evident connections he made between quotes of Islamic scripture and depictions of the local context, colored by expressions in the local Swahili dialect and urban slang, kept his audience engaged.

Talking to me about his Ramadan lectures, Taha later explained that he attracted a diverse, mostly young crowd. Apart from the few elders re-laxing in the corner, the mosque was usually filled with *madrasa* students who had spent the day studying Quran, beach boys who had cut their dreadlocks as a symbolic gesture for the start of Ramadan, unemployed high school graduates, and a few businessmen who had closed shop for the day. Escaping the afternoon heat and eager to pass the time until the break-ing of the fast, these young men—Shia and Sunni alike—came to the mosque to hear the imam speak. My friend Maryam's voice recorder was placed visibly on the imam's pulpit, enabling us—Maryam, a few of our friends, and I—to listen to the sermon later that evening.

Ustadh Taha was highly respected among Lamu's younger generation, yet he differed from the youth gathered before him. Eloquent, provocative, politically engaged, and well educated in religious scripture, the imam was locally held by young and old alike to be one of the few figures who could inspire Lamu youth to bring positive change to the island. The imam himself, through his verbal and nonverbal practices, reflected Lamu's historical and contemporary exposure to a multiplicity of global influences: While his use of kiAmu, a local dialect of Kenya's national Swahili language, indicated his belonging to Lamu's former merchant elites, his fluent Arabic reflected the religious education he received abroad, and the English words he inserted demonstrated his familiarity with urban discourses and youth slang. His light skin color testified to his ancestors' Yemeni origin, while the black *kilemba* (turban) on his head was a symbol both of Omani influences and of Taha's adherence to the Shiite sect of Islam in a predominantly Sunni town.

The young people in Taha's audience, however, would not immediately describe their imam as cosmopolitan. On the contrary, his refusal to learn English, his insistence on speaking kiAmu, and his persistence in wearing a *kanzu* (white robe) differed from the eagerness with which many of his audience members incorporated *tabia ya kizungu* or Western practices—jeans, shorts, the occasional dreadlocks, and a frequent shifting between kiAmu, kiBajuni, Standard Swahili, and English.[1] But while some of these young men chewed the addictive and stimulant *miraa* leaves,[2] occasionally smoked a joint, and had girlfriends waiting for them in Lamu's narrow alleys, they held Taha in high regard. This respect was enforced by the imam's ability to combine an adherence to religious and cultural traditions with a realistic and straightforward approach to the contemporary struggles of young Lamu residents—his recognition of increasing unemployment, of political and economic marginalization, of longing for development and westernization, of rising drug and substance abuse, and of the challenges all of these pose to religious observance and the preservation of local norms and traditions. Taha's sermon that day spoke directly to this struggle by asking not only whether Lamu residents were present within the physical space of the mosque, but also whether they were morally present and physically engaged in the processes of development the community so desperately needed.

Muko hadir? Nyinyi mnadhani mtaingia peponi sampuli hizi?
Mnavyoishi hiyau? Kulala kwenye magodoro mkiamka mkipidjwa na
mafeni, mkiketi barazani, mkipidja mastori, mkisagiwa, mkivuta
bhangi? Yaani sampuli hizi ndo waIslamu wa kwenda peponi? Ikiwa
hesabu zenu ni hizo, futani. Ikiwa hatutaki ku(athiriwa) hatutaki
chochote, hakuna maendeleo. Mwenyezimungu atayazengeya kwa
wengine, la budha. Na ndio wao waingilia sasa. Tuko wapi sisi?

Are you (pl.) present? Do you all think you will enter heaven this way?
The way you are living now? Sleeping on mattresses, as you wake up
while the fans are blowing, as you are sitting on the *baraza*, as you are
sharing stories, as you are chewing *miraa*, as you smoke marijuana? Is
that how Muslims enter heaven? If that is your calculation, forget it. If
we don't want to be affected, if we don't want [to do] anything, there is
no development. And God will give it [development] to others. And
those are the ones who are arriving now. Where are we?

According to Taha, *maendeleo* (development) did not consist of having elec-
tric fans, nor should young Lamu residents confuse wearing baggy pants
and smoking marijuana with signs of modernity and progress. This pre-
occupation with material details of so-called development and young
people's fixation on appropriating Western practices, the imam argued, signaled youth's misunderstanding of what development and progress ought
to entail. At the same time, however, Taha warned his audience that elders
were mistaken if they believed that resisting change and persisting in local habits, such as conversing on a *baraza*, gave them the moral high ground.
While such leisurely practices were previously indicative of Muslim residents' respectability and high social class, Taha highlighted that such laid-
back lounging on a stone bench equally entailed a failure to live up to
religious obligations in present-day Lamu. According to him, the refusal
to critically engage with change had resulted in Lamu's contemporary marginalized position; it had left space for "others" to come in and take advantage of the opportunities God had intended for Lamu residents, "and
those are the ones who are arriving now." Referring to the increasing influx and permanent residence of mainland (Christian) Kenyans and Euro-
American expatriates in Lamu, Taha reminded his audience that they would
be held accountable as Muslims for how they (failed to) take responsibility
for the well-being of their town. Being a good Muslim, according to Taha,
was then about being a good Lamu resident, and one's religious obligations
therefore entailed simultaneously moral and political responsibilities.

Maendeleo (progress and development), *(tabia) za kisasa* (modernity), *kwenda na wakati* (lit., going with the times), and, particularly, what each of these notions entail frequently formed the focus of discussions among residents of Lamu, a small town located on an Indian Ocean island by the same name, situated at Kenya's northern edge. From its thirteenth-century foundation until the nineteenth century, this Swahili town was at the center of the Indian Ocean trade network, connecting the east coast of Africa to the Arabian Peninsula, the Persian Gulf, and the Indian subcontinent. The white limestone merchant mansions that continue to characterize the old part of Lamu are a lasting testimony to the town's historical prosperity and cosmopolitanism. The merchant elites who governed this town at the time were global consumers who took pride in displaying their transoceanic interconnectivity by, for example, incorporating Arabic, Portuguese, Hindi, and Gujurati vocabulary in their language use or by displaying paraphernalia from across the globe in their houses. These *waungwana* elites claimed distinction from, and supremacy over both local non-elites (including slaves) and mainland Africans on grounds of primary settlement, Arab genealogy, economic wealth, and an adherence to Islam (and thus forming part of the transoceanic Muslim world). While racialized through its emphasis on Arab descent, these differences were predominantly phrased in moral terms as they distinguished themselves on grounds of civility, respectability, and belief in God; they were *waungwana* (noblemen) as opposed to mainland *washenzi* (savages).

Beginning in the mid–nineteenth century, however, the island became increasingly peripheralized in relation to the formation of centers in Europe and mainland East Africa. The moment of decolonization and Lamu's incorporation into the Kenyan nation (1963) entailed the island's submission to a mainland, Christian-majority government and later (in the 1980s) introduced economic neoliberalism and new discourses on development and modernity. These processes placed Lamu within the national and global periphery and increasingly challenged local understandings of civility, urbanity, and cosmopolitanism (Bayat and Herrera 2010; Comaroff and Comaroff 2001; Hanson and Hentz 1999). Now depending on tourism and fishery rather than on transoceanic trade for their economic survival, Lamu residents (and Kenya's coastal Muslims in general) perceive themselves as second-class citizens, ruled by upcountry Christians who marginalize them in both economic and political terms by, for example, withholding structural investments, limiting educational opportunities, obstructing Muslims' ability to obtain national identity cards or land title deeds, and by condoning drug abuse and trafficking in the region (Kresse 2010, 74).

At the same time, Lamu's changed geopolitical and economic position opened the door to a new kind of migration to the island. While the town historically developed through continuous interactions with and integration of overseas "others," present-day newcomers are attracted not so much by Lamu's success as a center of trade or Islamic scholarship, but rather by the marginalized position of the town and its inhabitants. People from the Kikuyu ethnicity, one of Kenya's biggest and politically dominant ethnic groups, occupy the majority of governmental and administrative positions and control the town's agricultural market. People of the Meru ethnicity supply the much-loved and addictive *miraa* and their small stores (also known to secretly sell alcohol) are present on almost every corner in town. Maasai flock to Lamu to work as watchmen for Euro-Americans, the latter now owning property on Lamu Island and managing large parts of the town's tourism industry.

Whereas people from Lamu heretofore distinguished themselves as civilized and cosmopolitan in opposition to the Kenyan mainland, these new residents and mainland Kenyans often portray them as backward and underdeveloped. When asked why they are hired over local residents, for example, Kikuyu highlight their diligence and hardworking mentality, while waAmu just "sit on benches." For Euro-American residents, Lamu is a town where "time stands still," their presence, in a way, posing a paradox, since tourism is meant to provide economic revenue and development yet simultaneously depends on the preservation of the island's unspoiled nature and its appeal to tourists' imagination of the exotic and the "oriental" (Walley 2004).

Other changes, however, form a different range of challenges for Lamu residents. While marginalized as Muslims by a Christian-majority government, residents of the Kenyan coast have recently become the focus of international campaigns against religious extremism following a range of terrorist attacks, including the bombing of the US embassy in Nairobi in 1998, attacks on a beach hotel and airplane in Mombasa in 2002, the siege on Nairobi's Westgate mall in 2013, the deadly bus attacks in Mpeketoni (Lamu County) in 2014, the Garissa University massacre in 2015, and most recently, the 2019 Nairobi DusitD2 complex attack in which twenty-one people lost their lives. Despite Muslim communities' condemnation of these events, tensions between the Kenyan government and Muslims increased significantly over the last two decades. Raids of mosques in Mombasa, random arrests of (mostly young) male Muslims (including arrests in Lamu Town), and suspicious murders of Muslim clerics have become part of life along Kenya's coast.

These transformations meaningfully altered everyday life within coastal Muslim communities, including Lamu, and significantly challenged residents' self-understandings. In the sermon with which I started this Introduction, Taha's call for his listeners to reconsider their behaviors in relation to both their accountability before God and the needs of their community included an appeal to reexamine the meanings of respectability, civility, and modernity, given the challenges residents now face—as inhabitants of Lamu and as Muslims in present-day Kenya.

Until about fifty years ago, sitting on one of Lamu's many *baraza* while sipping Arabic coffee was an embodiment of social status, respectability, and urban flair. Now, local youth frequently depict this practice as outdated, whereas mainland Kenyans or Euro-American expatriates view it as an example of laziness (see Figure 1). The elders on the *baraza*, however, scoff at the young Lamu men who walk by sporting dreadlocks and wearing T-shirts with slogans such as "Spanish Sex Instructor"—clothes

Figure 1. Elder men and youth on Lamu's main square. Photograph by Eric Lafforgue.

brought to them as a gift by the Western tourists with whom they work (see Figure 2). Yet these are the same young men who gathered in the mosque to listen to Taha and whose work with tourists enabled them to provide for their families. Whereas in the recent past, women's seclusion was indicative of high social status and religious piety, going to college now represented development, financial wealth, and an overall modern attitude. Although young women's educational success was generally evaluated as a positive change that would contribute to the well-being of the Lamu community, secular education and employment also enabled young women to openly interact with men, thereby challenging previously dominant views of respectability and modesty that informed social life on the island.

The guiding question in Taha's sermon thus enquired about much more than listeners' mindfulness of God; it urged them to contemplate the connection between their physical and spiritual presence in relation to these rapid transformations. The issue for Lamu residents was not only how to be morally responsible—how to achieve pious lifestyles in the face of secularization—but also what it means to be a morally responsible person in present-day Lamu, as neither the *baraza*-sitting elder nor the *miraa*-chewing youth formed a model of moral personhood in contemporary society. In such a context, what do civility (*uungwana, ustaarabu*), respectability (*heshima*), development (*maendeleo*), and modernity (*kisasa, kwenda na wakati*) mean? Indeed, what does a morally responsible, religiously informed engagement with development—which Taha appeared to call for—look like?

Ustadh Taha delivered his *khutba* against the backdrop of the ethnic violence that erupted in Kenya following the 2007 national elections, but he also spoke to more recent events in the community; he referred to Kikuyu residents' construction of churches in the predominantly Muslim town, for example, and to the collapse of a house that had killed a playing child. Many considered these events strikingly representative of Lamu's altered geopolitical position and the gloomy future that lay ahead; they formed a visible confrontation with Lamu residents' political, economic, and religious disenfranchisement. The physical dilapidation of the town's architecture, once the hallmark of Lamu's cosmopolitan centrality, and the actual danger it formed for the town's children appeared strangely iconic of Lamu's moral decay and the risks it posed to the younger generation. While residents worried about access to good education and health care, or about drug abuse and HIV/AIDS, there was also a larger concern about what these changes signified for altering moral dispositions. For a town that for centuries distinguished itself from the African mainland as urban and cosmopolitan but that is now poor and marginalized in relation to the Kenyan

Figure 2. "Spanish sex instructor" T-shirt. Photograph by Eric Lafforgue.

mainland, the question is not whether or not they desire *maendeleo* but rather what development entails in contemporary society.

This book offers an ethnographic exploration of everyday life on Lamu Island and examines what happens when narratives of self-positioning change: What happens when signs of civility, respectability, and cosmopolitanism come to be read as indices of remoteness, backwardness, or religious radicalization? In such a context what do "development" or "piety" entail? And what implications do these changes in shared signification have for everyday interactions, self-fashionings, and conceptions of appropriate conduct? If the white robe that previously signaled respectability, piety, and social status could now potentially be read as a sign of conservative, radical Islam or traditionalism, how does one present, for example, a pious, modern self?

I explore these questions by documenting the discursive and embodied production of difference; I examine the seemingly mundane practices through which Lamu residents negotiate what it means to be a "good Lamu resident" in contemporary Kenya. Specifically, I chronicle the deliberations of the meanings and appropriate semiotic mediation of the ideological distinctions at the heart of Lamu Muslims' self-understandings, including notions of civility, respectability, and piety. I discuss how this is talked about—how Lamu residents discursively contemplate and redefine their views of distinctiveness in relation to a range of others, including other Lamu residents, mainland immigrants, and the Kenyan state—but also how such altered understandings of difference are mediated within seemingly minute details of everyday comportments, including in language use, modes of dress, gestures, and movements. Phrased differently, I pay close attention to discourse (and the ideologies expressed in them) but also look at how those ideas and ideologies play out in everyday life.

This is therefore a book about signs—signs of social change, respectability, transgression, piety—and particularly about *which* verbal and material forms function as signs, of what, to whom, and when. Rather than just focus on "Islam," "modernity," or "morality," this ethnography shows how these abstract concepts and people's understandings of them are differently mediated within practice and become tangible as signs within everyday social interactions. Most important, however, I ask what happens within everyday exchanges, and associated evaluations of self and other, when the shared recognition of signification fails—when individuals do not or differently recognize material practices as signs of, for example, piety or social transgression. How does this potential ambiguity of signs—this semiotic confusion—impact negotiations of social relations and positions;

how does it affect ethical self-fashionings; and how does it inform reconceptualizations of moral values such as "piety"?

I focus specifically on what these questions entail for Lamu youth, who
most evidently face the challenge of negotiating newly emerging social positions as critical, modern, Muslim residents of Lamu. Young people can
be seen vividly in this ethnography as they make conscious and distinct
life choices in response to their complex relations and loyalties to local traditions, a changing economy, an ambiguous and often problematic relationship with the postcolonial state, an increasing presence of foreigners,
and globalizing Islam. The stories I tell show how not all young Muslims
in Lamu chose the same strategies or follow the same path; yet all try to
find a way to position themselves in a manner that reconciles their desires
for development with their particular understandings of religious norms
and local values and their conceptualization of Lamu's position within
Kenya. Instead of analyzing young Muslims' supposedly conflicting simultaneous engagements with Islamic revival and Western modernity, I explore how Lamu youth claim newly emerging social positions and, indeed,
political stances by strategically embodying particular social norms while
renegotiating others. Rather than see resistance to local notions of modesty, respectability, piety, or femininity, I identify a particular agency in
young people's calculated inhabiting of certain norms and in their everyday deliberation of the proper mediation of others. For Lamu youth, the
question is not necessarily whether one ought to be respectable or pious,
but rather what respectability and piety can and should entail given, on
the one hand, Lamu's marginalized position and the kinds of development the town needs, and on the other, the (political) significance of
Islam and tradition to Lamu residents' distinctive identity.

The focus of my analysis is therefore not the everyday socialization of
morality; I am not so much interested in whether and how Lamu youth
are instructed on how to be a proper Muslim and how they come to embody particular social norms (Fader 2009, 35). Rather, I focus my analysis
on the everyday challenging of such socializations in response to a rapidly
changing world. I demonstrate how beliefs about language, the body, and
material practice in complex and meaningful ways are shaped by and respond to changes at different scales of society. In doing so, I embed the
analysis of often-ignored, supposed micro-level interactions within broader
political processes and draw attention to the social forces that produce the
constraints and possibilities through which people live their everyday lives
(Van der Veer 2008). The question of piety for Lamu residents, for example, is not just directed inward toward the development of a particular

spiritual or pious self; rather this ethical self-fashioning is always also projected outward, "directed at a network of *other* bodies" at different levels of society (Selim 2010). By drawing attention to this inherent sociality of embodied practices, I not only demonstrate the intersubjective and dialogic nature of meaning-making processes but also ethnographically illustrate that projects of personal cultivation can function as political projects as well (Van der Veer 2008). By reconceptualizing how one can embody piety, seen as a core aspect of Lamu residents' distinctive identity, young people are not only positioning themselves toward elders, they are also taking a political stance in a national context where they perceive themselves to be marginalized as Muslims. Similarly, when Taha urges Lamu residents to reconsider what it means to be respectable in contemporary Lamu, he phrases this as a moral responsibility, but one that is informed by the political and economic circumstances in which Lamu residents (as Muslims) find themselves. It is in this renegotiation of distinctive values, such as respectability, in the face of change that the political significance of the everyday lies.

Morality at the Margins therefore offers a linguistic anthropological approach to discussions of ethical self-fashioning and everyday Islam. Through a focus on verbal and material details of seemingly mundane interactions, it provides novel ways to understand young Muslims' attempts to wed notions of piety with desires for certain kinds of modernity (Deeb 2006, 2015), but also meaningfully situates this within a particular political context. Rather than focus either on a conscious turn toward pious lifestyles (Hirschkind 2006; Janson 2013; Mahmood 2005) or on the supposed ambivalences in the everyday lives of young Muslims (Deeb 2009; Harb and Deeb 2013; Marsden 2005; McBrien 2009; Schielke 2009, 2015), I document the seemingly small and often-ignored negotiations of moral personhood that occur in daily exchanges. These fleeting moments pass by quickly and can be easily overlooked, and yet they represent some of the most vital points through which larger scale transformations touch down concretely in community life, and by which they receive local inflection and resonance. I thus draw attention to how ostensibly mundane practices are informed by but also respond to broader societal shifts and cannot be dissociated from more obvious political or moral claims. The everyday choices young people make are therefore not straightforwardly motivated by either a striving for virtuous Islam or desires for a Western-style modernity; rather, they are shaped simultaneously by concerns for religion, respectability, tradition, development, and political and economic marginalization. In the sermon that opens this Introduction,

Taha appeared to call for such a morally responsible and politically motivated engagement with development. His inquiry into the *presence* of his
audience, after all, did not just refer to their physical attendance in
mosque, but also (and most important) to their spiritual awareness of a
presence with God that ought to motivate their everyday practices, including the ways they perceived of, oriented to, and engaged with *maendeleo* (development).

The Moral Implications of a Conversation with God

"*Muko hadir?*" Taha repeated his query once more as he further wove together a complex spatiotemporal framework for his audience. The exchange
on which the imam based his hour-long sermon might seem sparse, but it
was in fact intensely and densely spatiotemporal, discursively connecting
different physical locations and times of day to individuals' moral states.
Through the question-answer structure Taha appeared to be locating himself and his audience in ordinary space-time—an ongoing conversation in
the physical location of the mosque—yet he also expressed a moral stand-
point. It was through this dialectic between the recognizable real-world
space-time of the mosque (and Lamu more broadly) and the moral space-
time of accountability to the Divine that the full significances of the exchange emerged.

The rhetorical question that structured the imam's sermon was striking because the notion *hadir* is Arabic rather than a word commonly used
in the Swahili language. *Hadir* can be translated as "present," as Taha explained to his audience. In modern Arabic, he elaborated, people use *hadir*
in response to a teacher when she is taking attendance. For example, when
she calls out "Muhammad!" the student will respond "Hadir!" literally
meaning "Present!" or "I am here!" By asking his audience whether they
were truly *hadir* or present, Taha therefore appeared to suggest that God
had previously called out to this audience and that they had responded: *hadir*, we are present. Taha questioned, however, whether they were conscious of the moral responsibilities this response had entailed.

In the Islamic tradition, *hadir* carries a signification beyond taking attendance; it is linked to the concept of *hudur*, or a believer's presence with
God. Religious scholars explain the concept of *hudur* as a spiritual awareness of one's existence *before* God, distinct from a mere consciousness of
God's omnipresence. While one might recognize that God is always
nearby, believers generally do not fully experience or comprehend their
own presence—and thus accountability—before and with God; we are in

a way veiled from Him. The ultimate goal of believers, Islamic scholars propose, is to achieve a state of *hudur*—a continuous awareness of one's presence with God that informs one's everyday practices (e.g., Chittick 1989; Sands 2006; Saritoprak 2017).

When inquiring whether his audience was *hadir*, Taha therefore was not questioning their attendance in the mosque; rather, he was asking about his audience's presence with, and willingness to oblige God.[3] It was this inextricable connection between individuals' God-consciousness and their everyday moral obligations that informed Taha's critique toward what he perceived as Lamu residents' superficial concerns for development.

> Sisi, kwanzia mimi ninayenena, na nyinyi mnaosikia, na walioko mskitini na wasikuweko hapo mskitini. Kila mmoya ana majukumu kuhusu kujibu maswali mbe ya mwenyezimungu. Nnini maana ya mada hii? Shahadat-ul ummah. Ummah uwe HADIR. . . . Uko wapi ummah? Iko wapi ayat la mwenyezi mungu? Muko hadir? Tuko hadir? Hatuko hadir.

> We, starting with me who is speaking, and you who are listening, and those who are in the mosque and those who are not in the mosque. Everyone has the responsibility to answer questions in front of God. What does that mean? The witnessing of the *ummah* [religious community], that the *ummah* is PRESENT. . . . Where is the *ummah*? Where are the verses/signs of God? Are you present? Are we present? We are not present.

According to Taha, the knowledge that each of them will have to one day account for their actions before God and, especially, the awareness that they are never not "in front of God" ought to inspire a concern for the town's well-being and an active *and* morally responsible engagement with its development and governance. Such participation (and thus physical presence) ought to be motivated, not by a desire for personal wealth or power, but precisely by the ubiquitous awareness of believers' accountability before and obligation to the Divine. Quoting from the Quran, he reminded his audience, "He is with you wherever you are" (57:4). The problem, Taha stated, is that we are no longer with Him; we have forgotten the moral implications of our response to His call.[4]

By listing recognizable locations and encounters that are imbued with moral value (such as conversing on a *baraza* or chewing *miraa*), Taha made his audience aware of their choices, the consequences of their actions, and of their moral responsibility as agentive-subjects. Through this focus on ordinary practices, the imam emphasized, not only that Lamu residents

had individual agency, but also that the physical positions and practices resulting from their choices were inescapably moral stances; that these were
inseparable (Keane 2011, 2016; Lambek 2010). Indeed, Taha presented his
audience's conduct as "an object of thought [for them] to question it as to
its meaning, its conditions, and its goals" (Foucault 1997, 117).

According to the imam, being a "good Muslim" in present-day Lamu did
not consist solely of striving toward religious devoutness; rather, it included
everyday decisions with regard to how one wants to participate in change,
motivated simultaneously by one's mindfulness of God and one's awareness
of the community's (politically and economically) marginalized position.
When Taha maintained that adopting Western practices ought not be motivated by a yearning to be like the West, but should rather be inspired by
one's desire and capacity to contribute to and change the Lamu community,
he made claims about agency that drew upon a particular moral narrative of
modernity (Keane 2007, 49). This moral narrative, however, differed meaningfully from scholarly opinions that suggest that modernity goes hand in
hand with dissociation from religion (Fader 2009, 2–3).

The Moral in Modernity

"Modernity" has often been viewed, in both media and academic discourses, as a kind of unilinear and inevitable historical advancement
through which human beings are progressively liberated from false beliefs,
traditions, and fetishes; emancipated, the "modern" subject depends on
their own rational ideas about self-fulfillment rather than upon religion
or tradition. More significantly, the West is often viewed as the quintessential example of such modernization process whereby disenchantment
and secularization are generally viewed as preconditions for Western-style
modernity. Webb Keane (2007, 48) signals the highly moral tone of such
takes on modernity. In these narratives, he points out, modernization does
not just concern technological, economic, or medical advancements, but
above all, is about a particular understanding of self-mastery and, indeed,
human agency. Individuals who are "modern" express their own free will,
rather than follow dogmatic prescriptions that curb expressions of individuality. Conversely, individuals who continue to rely on, for example, religion are viewed as displacing their agency onto false traditions or gods
and are considered premoderns or antimoderns (Keane 2007, 6–7).

Such narratives of modernity are therefore often normative because they
formulate expectations about what a modern person ought to be. The mor-
alization of modernity lies precisely with the fact that people are expected to

become this particular kind of modern subject, whereby not doing so is viewed as an ethical failing that forms a threat to both the individual and the entire society (Keane 2007, 2016). One only needs to think of popular media discourses that blame religion—and Islam in particular—for the rise of violent terrorism and for terrorists' blind following of supposedly dogmatic religious rulings. Similarly, modernity and modernization are often portrayed as the answer to Muslim women's submission to and deliverance from patriarchal norms and religious chains.[5] Such views tend to situate Islam (and religion more broadly) in the realm of tradition and opposed to modernity, which is seen as generated by nation-building, secularization, and modernization.

Critiques of such Western-centered views of modernity have now multiplied, and anthropologists have cautioned against the tendency to analyze discussions of modernity in terms of Western notions of moral autonomy, self-realization, and secularization (e.g., Mahmood 2005). Because such a moral narrative of modernity is frequently at the heart of Western denunciations of Islam, with forms of "political Islam" or "Islamism" being viewed as the "quintessential other, the anti-modern antithesis to the supposedly secular West" (Deeb 2006, 4), many studies have come from the anthropology of Islam, with much attention being paid to what "being modern" means to Muslim subjects themselves. Scholars like Saba Mahmood (2005), Charles Hirschkind (2006), and Lara Deeb (2006) have argued that modernity—and the individual agency it implies—does not depend on a denouncing of religion, but can rather consist of a conscious turn to piety, of a conscientious commitment to spiritual progress, in addition to technological development. Studying Muslim women's participation in Egypt's piety movements, Saba Mahmood (2005) argued, for example, that self-realization and ethical self-fashioning can lie in a purposeful submission to a higher power rather than in a Western-conceived expression of a "free will," and everyday practices such as praying are then a crucial part of creating an (inner) pious disposition.

While such discussions were innovative because they challenged Western-centered approaches to modernity and agency, objections to a sole focus on pious Muslims soon followed: Surely not all Muslims live pious lifestyles, nor are all consciously striving toward increased piety. Can we really present this search for piety as a unilinear process, whereby moral subjects unproblematically move away from an earlier lifestyle to a new, pious one? What do we make, for example, of young men in Egypt who fast and pray for the month of Ramadan but celebrate Eid—the religious holiday that marks the end of the fast—by smoking, drinking, and watching pornography (Schielke 2009; Schielke and Debevec 2012)? Within such a framework, how do we make sense of young Muslims' struggles to pray or their "relapses" into frivolous lifestyles after previously having committed to a life of piety (e.g., Janson 2013; Marsden 2005; Schielke 2009, 2012, 2015)?

While these critical voices agreed that studies of morality ought to focus, not on rules and prohibitions, but on how individuals negotiate and practice moral personhood in everyday life, they objected to the sole focus on individuals' conscious (and continuous) cultivation of a virtuous self. Calling attention to the ambiguities and double-standards in young Muslims' lives—to what some called the "failure" of everyday living—the ensuing interest in "everyday Islam" took ambivalences (such as the combination of praying and drinking) as its starting point and focused on "conflicts, ambiguities, double standards, fractures, and shifts as the constitutive moment of the practice of norms" (Schielke 2009, 37–38). While many Muslims might commit to different kinds of ethical self-fashioning, and while they might contemplate what "correct" Islamic practice entails in contemporary societies, scholars of everyday Islam argued that this was "only one part of what effectively is a new kind of sociality" (Soares and Otayek 2007, 11).

I take from these studies an emphasis on lived Islam as it intersects with a range of other social fields and concerns that inform the lives of contemporary Muslim youth. I refrain, however, from describing young Muslims' simultaneous engagement with both spiritual and technological progress as an "alternative" modernity (Masquelier 2009). Using a qualifier like "alternative" to refer to the modern dispositions of practicing Muslim youth seems to imply that there is a "normal" modernity that is still considered secular rather than religious in relation to which these young Muslims' behaviors need to be explained. Depicting Muslim youth's less pious lifestyles as consisting of "inconsistencies" similarly appears to suggest that one somehow still expects believers to strive toward the embodiment of a particular kind of normative Islam, which these youths "fail" to do when they drink beer or have romantic relationships. It also seems to reproduce some kind of artificial distinction between religious practice and the secular world (Fader 2009). Studying lived Islam, however, entails paying attention to subjects' ongoing, everyday negotiations of what it means to "be Muslim" in a specific sociocultural context, with all its concomitant political, social, and historical meanings (Deeb 2015).

To Taha, being a "good Muslim" in contemporary Lamu involved much more than fasting in Ramadan or praying the five compulsory prayers; it also comprised active concern for and involvement in the development of the town—something the young and older men in his audience *both* failed to do, according to the imam. For Taha, moral uprightness then extended beyond a question of religious piety, to include an individual's social activism and political stance. Indeed, the sermon that has formed the ethnographic thread throughout this Introduction was directed at an audience many of whom might be considered as, in one way or another, "failing" to strive for Islamic piety. Some of the young men present in the mosque smoked, drank alcohol, or had girlfriends. While he was aware of this and while these practices were considered *haram* or impermissible, Taha did not focus on them when questioning his audience's accountability before God. On the contrary, while he critiqued young people for being preoccupied with the appropriation of Western practices (dress styles, musical preferences, drinking habits), he equally criticized older Lamu residents for seemingly aimlessly sitting on their *baraza*.

One of Taha's audience members, for example, was Jamal—a young man who worked in Lamu's tourism industry and who frequently appropriated "un-Islamic" practices in an attempt to appeal to Western tourists: He grew dreadlocks, wore shorts, smoked marijuana, organized beach parties, and sometimes drank alcohol. Condemned for his behavior by other Lamu residents, Jamal defended his practices to me as mere occupational tools, strategically used to charm tourists and secure an income to provide for his family in an otherwise grim economy—in itself, one could argue, a moral good (Chapters 3 and 5). But while Jamal's Islamic practice could be described as inconsistent, he considered himself Muslim—with room for improvement, but practicing and fearful of Allah nonetheless. During the month of Ramadan, he cut his dreadlocks, fasted, assiduously attended to his prayers, and listened to sermons in the mosque. He would set intentions to uphold these practices upon completion of the holy month and when unable to do so he would seek forgiveness from Allah upon lighting his first joint (see also Schielke 2009). At the same time, however, these "beach boys" were often the first to suggest they would be willing to fight for the rights of Muslims in a country they perceived as increasingly hostile to Islam. Young men like Jamal most closely resemble the young Muslims that have formed the focus of discussions on everyday Islam, their everyday comportment appearing quite ambiguous as they wed *haram* practices with explicitly proclaimed adherences to and defenses of Islam. Yet for these young men, as for Taha, being a "good Muslim" extended beyond questions of religious observance, to include respect for local traditions (and pride of their Lamu identity) as well as political consciousness (Chapters 4 and 5).

Similarly, young women like Maryam—my friend who recorded Taha's sermon and with whom I later listened to it—considered themselves observing Muslims. Maryam prayed, fasted, paid alms, intended to go for Haji, provided for her extended family, and educated herself about Islam by recording sermons or watching Peace TV. And like the young women in Lara Deeb's (2006) work, she viewed educating herself and striving toward professional development to be an essential part of her being a "modern" Muslim; her spiritual and technical striving were mutually supportive. In fact, Maryam saw her professional development and her work at an aid organization as a religious obligation, much as Taha argued in his sermon. At the same time, she often told me that young Lamu women tended to forget that they were young Muslims *in Lamu*; that their contemporary access to education, employment, and global Islamic discourses had made them oblivious to what it meant to be a good Muslim in this specific community (Chapters 4 and 5). "Respecting yourself and your family is more important to being a good Muslim than knowing that, according to religious rulings, women are allowed to eat on the street," Maryam once told me upon seeing young women eat roasted corn on Lamu's main square, a practice locally considered inappropriate for respectable women.

Taha, Jamal, and Maryam all considered themselves—in one way or another—to be pious, modern, and Muslim. They differed, however, in what each of these denominators entailed and how these ought to be expressed within everyday practice. Yet all of these individuals, and people like them, continuously encounter one another in everyday life and (sometimes) struggle to get their self-presentations accepted. In other words, the practices through which an individual constitutes oneself as a particular kind of person—as pious, upright, modern—are not solely focused inward, but are always also directed at a range of others, situated at different levels of society. These audiences evaluate observed practice, and through their judgments equally situate themselves as particular kinds of individuals—as devout, progressive, conservative. These assessments, however, are not without consequence but rather inform people's future presentations of self. In other words, projects of ethical self-fashioning are both intersubjective and dialogic.

Understanding the importance of "the everyday" thus requires the recognition that moral norms and everyday practices, rather than separate, are co-constituted and continuously negotiated in relation to one another (Deeb 2015, 95–96). Indeed, understanding the complex entanglements of ethical selfhood, everyday practice, and (religious or secular) norms requires attending to the seemingly mundane practices, vocabularies, and bodily gestures that are (un)consciously adopted in processes of ethical self-formation (Fadil and Fernando 2015). This includes attention to the intersubjective and dialogic nature of these processes as well as the social fields of power within which they take place. Linguistic anthropology, with its focus on how multiple levels of interaction link to and signify through (ideological) connections to others on different societal scales, is particularly well situated to contribute to such new considerations of self-fashioning and its contextual intricacies.

This book examines these complex intersections by looking at everyday interactions—from explicit discussions about social change, to seemingly ordinary exchanges between Lamu residents, to young women's dress styles and movement through town—to demonstrate how the everyday choices individuals make entail ethical judgments and negotiations of moral personhood in relation to normative Islam as well as broader sociopolitical processes. I thereby ethnographically document how understandings of virtue ethics—like piety or respectability—are continuously negotiated through everyday practices, and how new social positions can gradually emerge from such quotidian deliberations.

In this book, one will find little explicit discussion of what youth in Lamu—and Lamu residents in general—consider to be normative Islam. Rather, the conversations and debates I analyze reveal that Lamu residents' primary concern lies with the transformations their community is undergoing and the perceived concomitant moral deterioration of the island's younger generation. I focus my analysis on how social change and associated notions of piety, respectability, or transgression become tangible as signs within everyday interactions. Not only do I look at how mundane practices offer the potentiality of signification—how details of interaction can become inscribed with meaning—but I also consider how such signs can be strategically used in presentations of self and evaluations of others. To fully understand this, we need to take into account the workings of what has been called *semiotic ideologies*—of the ways in which words, material forms, and practices acquire meaning in a particular social context (Keane 1997, 2003).

Ideologies and the Reading of Signs

The notion "semiotic ideologies" refers to material forms, their signifying capacity, and the ideologies by which they are taken to have moral implications. Stated differently, while words, material forms, or practices exist as objects of experience, they have no meaning in and of themselves; they are assigned meaning only through experiences of them. As Charles Peirce underlined in his tripartite theory of the sign, a sign functions as a sign only if some group perceives it as a sign. For example, someone's pronunciation of English only becomes a sign of their social background—as British, Kenyan, or "immigrant"—to someone in a specific social setting. Nobody in Britain, for example, would note that their friend is speaking with a remarkable British accent. It becomes a "British" accent only outside of the UK. More important, such identifications frequently come with particular moral judgments—someone with a "French" accent might be evaluated as sophisticated, whereas someone who is perceived to have an "immigrant" accent might be judged as less educated. Such evaluations are informed by ideologies—by particular socially situated assessments of aspects of language—rather than by anything objectively present in an individual's language use.

Similarly, a piece of cloth covering a woman's hair is in essence just that (a piece of cloth); it becomes a "headscarf" and thus acquires meaning as a religious symbol or a sign of modesty only to someone familiar with a particular social and religious framework. There is nothing inherent in the scarf itself that makes it "modest" or "pious." At the same time, the cloth worn as *hijab* can extend its meaning beyond a sign of piety to include political resistance in a context where religious head coverings are prohibited. Moreover, nuances in the manner of wearing a veil can be invisible to some, while highly meaningful to others (for example, Khabeer 2016; Lewis 2015a, 2015b; Renne 2013). In the context of Lamu, the color, length, or style of head wrappings are important signs through which young Muslim women express their modern, urban, or conservative demeanors. Yet these signifiers comprised within the scarf are invisible to the tourist who visits Lamu. To draw upon an earlier example, eating in public is not in itself a sign of moral transgression, nor is it necessarily an indicator of decreased piety. In fact, a tourist would make nothing of the young Lamu woman eating an ice cream along the town's seafront. For that same young woman, eating an ice cream in public can be a sign of her urban and modern disposition. Other Lamu residents, however, can evaluate this practice as a moral transgression and a sign of the young woman's impropriety (Chapter 3 and 5).

Readings of material forms as signs are therefore always situated within a specific context and have a particular moral value. Moreover, the ideological readings of material forms are never just opinions about material objects; they are always also opinions about the people who use them (Keane

2007, 16). Finally, ideological evaluations are never stable. Of course, particularly ideologies can become seemingly naturalized and taken for granted, even though they serve the interests of a particular (dominant) group or class; they can become hegemonic (Gramsci 1971; Williams 1977). But precisely because material practices exist as objective forms, they can also become objects of reflection. Especially in moments of social change, taken-for-granted ideas can become explicitly reflected upon and reevaluated. Material forms can even become a source of moral anxiety when their previously seemingly stable meaning is no longer self-evident. The established moral reading of material forms—the shared semiotic ideologies—can thus shift, particularly in contexts of social transformation.[6]

This book centers on an investigation of the intersection of morality and semiotic practice, or the semiotic ideologies surrounding practices that reveal the social embedding of verbal and nonverbal communication, and the ways in which moral interests work to produce them. I attend to how metapragmatic frames, or concepts that guide interpretations of everyday practices, shape the moral evaluations of interactions and provide participants with an awareness of opportunities for and limits to (strategic) negotiation. This approach allows me to connect practices that constitute daily encounters such as details of talk, dress, and movement to other scales and domains of social life, or what linguistic anthropologists refer to as different "orders of indexicality" (Silverstein 2003). This focus on situated moments of negotiation provides insight into the ideological processes through which different semiotic forms come to signify and the ongoing nature of such meaning-making processes.

Lamu forms a particularly interesting locale to explore this social embeddedness of verbal, material, and bodily practices as signs and their use in individuals' everyday negotiations of social relations and positionalities. Its ethnographic context offers an opportunity to examine precisely how attention to the workings of semiotic ideologies can provide novel insights into how projects of ethical self-fashioning are shaped by and respond to different social fields of power. I previously highlighted that Lamu was and continues to be a highly stratified society, whereby former merchant elites distinguish themselves from others based on claims to civility, respectability, and religious observance. These distinguishing virtues were importantly mediated within verbal, material, and bodily practices, as elites, non-elite locals, and nonlocals were evaluated and situated on the social ladder based on assessments of their comportments within everyday interactions. Moreover, as a center of trade and scholarship that dealt with the continuous influx of outsiders, minute details of behavior have always been central to valuations of individuals' status as local or guest.

Present-day transformations, however, have challenged the supremacy of the former merchant elites and the hegemonic nature of the behavioral ideologies through which they defined themselves and others. Not only has Lamu become a more religiously and ethnically diverse place, newcomers to the island no longer necessarily recognize the moral authority of the former elites. Moreover, the geopolitical position of Lamu itself has meaningfully changed and has impacted the way Muslim residents of the town—elites and non-elites alike—position themselves toward the Kenyan nation. In other words, social norms of civility or respectability and their proper mediation within practice are locally redefined while simultaneously remaining central to conceptualizations of Lamu in opposition to the Kenyan government.

To fully comprehend these tensions and how they play out in daily interactions, and thus to grasp the social and political significance of the everyday in Lamu, a further situating of the town is needed. To Lamu residents, the history of the region supports their claims to a status distinct from mainland Kenyans and the town's settlement history continues to inform lasting insistences on local social divisions as well. Of course, these are situated, ideological readings of historical facts. Insight into historical settlement patterns and how these shaped the formation of a particular social hierarchy and a (now contested) hegemonic ideology of respectable conduct, however, will allow for a more contextualized reading of ideological discourses analyzed in subsequent chapters. In addition, it provides an essential background against which to understand the highly politicized insistences on cosmopolitanism, respectability, and Islam in Lamu residents' present-day conceptualizations of self.

Situating Lamu

Lamu Old Town forms the urban epicenter of the Lamu Archipelago, an island group comprising seven islands, the best known of which are Faza, Kiwayu, Lamu, Manda, and Pate Island (see Figure 3). Each of these islands is home to several villages, most of which were historically important city-states and trade centers. Towns like Takwa (now in ruins), Shanga, Pate, and Siyu are believed to be among the earliest Muslim settlements in the area with remains dating back to the eighth century (Chittick 1974; Horton and Middleton 2000). Currently inhabited towns include Lamu, Shela, Matondoni, and Kipungani on Lamu Island; Pate, Siyu, Shanga, and

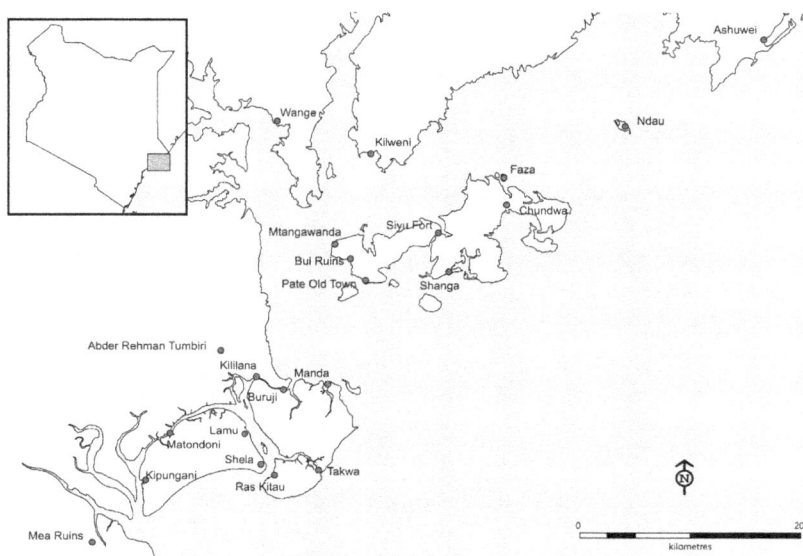

Figure 3. The Lamu Archipelago. National Museums of Kenya, Directorate of Antiquities Sites and Monuments.

Rasini on Pate Island; and Kiwayu village on Kiwayu Island. With its population of approximately 20,000 people, Lamu is the largest and most densely populated region of the archipelago and is its administrative center.[7]

When exactly the town of Lamu was founded is unclear. The *Khabar al-Lamu* or Lamu Chronicle claims that Lamu originated as early as the seventh century (Hichens 1938). The town's oldest mosque, the Pumwani Mosque, however, dates only from 1370 (Abungu and Beckwith 2009). Historical documents first mention Lamu in 1441, when the Arab writer and traveler Abu-al-Mahasini relates his encounter with a *qadi* (Muslim judge) from Lamu in Mecca. Portuguese records make note of a Portuguese warship that arrived at the island in 1505 to claim tribute from its rulers. Portuguese dominance of Lamu lasted for approximately 180 years, threatened only briefly by a Turkish fleet (Horton and Middleton 2000; Middleton 1992, 2004; Romero 1997).

Lamu's "golden age" began at the end of the seventeenth century. Omani Arabs ousted the Portuguese and Lamu prospered for the next 150 years. Because a *yumbe* council of elders ruled the town as a republic, the Omanis only loosely controlled Lamu. And after having defeated rival city-states Pate and Mombasa, Lamu became the dominant port on the East African coast and a center of religious education, poetry, politics, arts, and crafts. A reliance on protection from the Sultan of Oman, Sayyid Said, against the Pate-Mombasa alliance, however, made the island group part of the Zanzibar commercial network. This entailed active participation in the international slave trade, Lamu's elites themselves becoming exporters of slaves (Glassman 2004; Pouwels 1991).[8]

When the British arrived at the East African coast in the late nineteenth century, Lamu was still a rather successful port city. The rule of Bargash bin Said (the son of Sayyid Said) allowed the coastal strip to retain an element of independence throughout the colonial period, enjoying the status of protectorate rather than colony. But like other coastal towns, Lamu experienced increasing British pressure to reduce its active participation in the East African slave trade. The growing suppression of slavery left Lamu's merchant elites and landowners without the labor supply needed to maintain their field plantations and these elites suffered irremediable economic setbacks. The town's economy gradually weakened with the building of the Uganda Railroad and the transfer of the colonial capital from Mombasa to Nairobi after the completion of the Railroad in 1901. When legal emancipation was imposed in 1907 Lamu's economy was already in decline with its merchant elites on the brink of poverty—a condition that persisted almost without interruption until after World War II (Cooper 1980, 1990; Glassman 1991; Romero 1997; Ylvisaker 1979).

Uungwana and *Ustaarabu*: Social Hierarchy and Moral Hegemony

While archaeological data has revealed the distinctly African roots of Swahili populations,[9] most chronicles that recount the history of Swahili city-states claim a dual ancestry, linking the rulers of the towns both to African and to Arab lineages. Lamu's origin myth is even stronger in that stance, clearly distinguishing the town's first inhabitants from the African mainland (Coppola 2018; El Zein 1974). The *Khabar al-Lamu* speaks of two exclusively Arab settlements, one composed of traders from Damascus, Syria (Coppola 2018; Hichens 1938).

The Chronicle suggests that these first settlers were initially unaware of each other's presence as they established residence on separate sides of the island—Hidabu on the southern edge, and Vuyoni on the northern edge, locations still known to and identifiable by Lamu residents today. A battle allegedly ensued between residents of these two settlements following their first encounter, and the resulting division between victors and defeated laid the basis for Lamu's social hierarchy. According to the *Khabar Al-Lamu*, the newly united town was divided into two different groups living in separate wards—Zena and Suudi—and endogamy was imposed. This division between Zena and Suudi formed the basis for subsequent civil and military organization as the leaders of these two moieties rotated in taking up civic office, and the army was divided into two regiments (Middleton 2004; Ranger 1975).

The Chronicle thus explains why all groups that arrived following the settlement of these supposed Syrian and Arabian merchants—be they Omani traders, Yemeni settlers, or immigrants from the surrounding islands—were incorporated into a strict social hierarchy in which patrician families or *wenyeji* remained distinct from *wageni* or guests, aided by residence in different wards and restrictions to intermarriage. Whereas newcomers' genealogy, level of Islamic education, and economic wealth determined their prestige and assigned them a position on the social ladder, they were never considered *wenyeji* or fully local (Allen 1993; Romero 1997; El Zein 1974).

The *Khabar al-Lamu*, like many chronicles, was written long after these historical events took place and formed a retrospective justification for social hierarchy structures (Coppola 2018). This particular chronicle was composed in 1897 by Shaibu Faraji bin Hamid al-Bakariy al-Lamuy at the request of the *wali* of Lamu, Abdallah bin Hamid. This timeframe, at a moment of important shifts in the town's economic and political configurations, implies a need for a historical grounding of authority structures, and the historical accuracy of chronicles like these is therefore questionable.[10] These narrations nevertheless form part of Lamu's discursive history and are recounted until today as a justification for the town's topography as well as its (now significantly redefined) social structure (El Zein 1974).

While archaeological evidence reveals that all Swahili city-states were complicated, culturally variegated spaces,[11] chronicles like the *Khabar al-Lamu* enabled patrician clans to claim distinction from and supremacy over both mainland Africans and later immigrants on grounds of original settlement and Arab pedigree. As mentioned earlier, these distinctions were phrased in moral terms as *wenyeji* (patrician clans) distinguished themselves from *wageni* (guests) on grounds of civility, respectability, and belief in God; they were *waungwana* (noblemen) as opposed to mainland *washenzi* (savages).

Washenzi translates as "savages" or "stupid, ignorant ones." The notion suggests not only ignorance and ill manners but also a lack of religious education (Bromber 2006). *Washenzi* generally referred to non-Muslim mainland residents and (non-Muslim) newcomers to the island, the latter occupying the bottom of the social ladder (Pouwels 1987). The non-Muslim culture of the Kenyan interior was therefore considered the antithesis of the embodiment of patrician clans' *uungwana* or nobility (Glassman 2004, 736). Belonging to the *uungwana* social class entailed being wise and urban, displaying "purity, honor, trustworthiness, and courtesy, as well as knowledge of the world that comes only from belief in God" (Middleton 2004, 4). While social standing therefore derived in part from wealth and genealogy, it also was believed to be a moral status to which all could aspire.

This terminology of being upper class, and the ideologies that informed it, shifted in the nineteenth century from an emphasis on *uungwana* or nobility to *ustaarabu* or Arabness, in line with the changes in social and political authority. Shifts in power caused Omani Arabs to become privileged over local coastal elites, and Arabness—in terms of language use, modes of dress, as well as skin color and overall appearance—became a sign of high social status. The ideological essence of these concepts, however, remained similar, referring to overall respectful conduct (McMahon 2006, 200). An adherence to Islam was equally important in shaping this worldview as it provided the patrician clans with the notion that they were "connected more with their trade partners and coreligionists overseas than with their cultural cousins of the near interior" (Glassman 2011, 24). Combined, this worldview resulted in distinct material practices with prestige assigned to all things associated with the Arabian Peninsula, including modes of dress or the use of Arab clan names.

This distinction between noblemen and savages meaningfully informed the relationship, not only between Lamu's patrician elites and mainland Africans but also between these *wenyeji* and their slaves or *watumwa*. Although Lamu was not actively engaged in the slave trade until the early nineteenth century, its merchant elites did own slaves. House slaves often resided in the downstairs galleries of merchant mansions, while the slaves working on the elites' farms lived in daub-and-wattle huts on Lamu's outer edge, an area that came to be known as Langoni. Located at the outskirts of town, this was a part of Lamu where traders temporarily resided as they awaited the monsoon winds to sail back across the Indian Ocean. As traders settled more permanently and as the slave population grew, Langoni became more clearly opposed to Mkomani, its population being distinct from newcomers and slaves. The temporary huts in Langoni differed sharply from Mkomani's stone mansions and movement between the two sides of town consisted only of slaves who went to their masters or returned home for the night (Eastman 1988; El Zein 1974; Romero 1986, 1997).

What shaped the relationship between the merchant elites and their slaves was not a notion of absolute property, but precisely the ideological distinction between those who, from the perspective of the upper classes, were believed to possess the characteristics of either *uungwana* (nobility) or *ushenzi* (savagery), and by ideologies surrounding how this distinction manifested in material practices, employment, and racial traits (Chapter 3).[12] Slaves straddled this social and ideological boundary between noblemen and savages in different ways, and the distinction was much more of an ambiguous continuum than is sometimes presumed. Slaves were often able to integrate themselves into society as respectful (and later as free) individuals by mimicking their masters' *heshima* and appropriating material practices that signaled this embodied respectability. For example, after emancipation in the early twentieth century, former slave women (who were not allowed to cover under slavery) appropriated upper-class covering practices to integrate themselves within Lamu society as free individuals.[13]

An evident challenge to the distinction between noblemen and slaves came with the arrival of Habib Saleh (Al Jahadmy) in the 1880s, a Sayyid from the Comoros but with ties to Hadramaut in Yemen, who defied the local prohibition on religious education for slaves (Bang 2003, 2014, 2018; El Zein 1974). Upon his arrival in Lamu, Habib Saleh opted to reside in Langoni's slave quarters rather than live on the Mkomani side of town, where he had been offered a residence. From his small hut, he began teaching religion to local slaves and introduced them to honoring the Prophet through maulid celebrations—commemorations of the birth of Prophet Muhammad, that is. While causing controversy at first, Habib Saleh soon received support from leading Hadrami families and was offered a piece of land to build a mosque. The Riyadha Mosque became a center of religious education, attracting students from across Africa and the world. Lamu's annual, international renowned maulid celebrations commemorate Habib Saleh up until today.

The events surrounding Habib Saleh's arrival were indicative of deeper shifts within Lamu's social hierarchy.[14] While the patrician elites were still in control, different waves of migration in the late nineteenth and early twentieth centuries increasingly challenged both their religious authority and their economic supremacy with immigrants of Oman and Yemen becoming politically and economically powerful. While still considered *wageni*, these immigrants gradually managed to incorporate themselves into

Lamu's social structure and came to be considered noblemen or *waung-wana*. Precisely their ability to adhere to and appropriate patrician clans' notions of respectable conduct (meaningfully informed by Arab lineage and wealth as well) aided their integration into the higher echelons of Lamu society. In contemporary Lamu, these more recent immigrants are considered waAmu, "true" Lamu residents distinct from Bajuni immigrants living on the Langoni side of town.

I elaborate on Lamu's history of immigration and slavery before independence, and particularly on the ideologies that determined integration into and social status within the Lamu community to highlight that the town's social hierarchy and the distinctions it was based on have never been stable or unchanging (Wynne-Jones 2018). Indeed, Pouwels (1984, 248) underlined that Swahili communities throughout their history faced the challenge of maintaining order and unity while continuously experiencing the influx of large numbers of immigrants. What enabled a sense of stability, however, was precisely the hegemonic nature of merchant elites' ideology of belonging and ideal comportment. While not always uncontested, strategically displayed respectable conduct formed an important technique for newcomers to negotiate changing social status even beyond the abolition of slavery (Fair 2001; Glassman 2011; Iliffe 2005; McMahon 2006).

In today's Lamu, the topographical distinction between Mkomani and Langoni remains, with different stereotypes about the neighborhoods' inhabitants infiltrating daily interactions. Political organizations, youth groups, and soccer teams continue to be divided along these geographical and social lines and even seating arrangements at weddings reflect the divide that continues to exist between Mkomani's patricians and the "guests" residing in Langoni. While until a generation ago, marriages across the divide were controversial and exceptional, nowadays young people's connections appear to cross the partition more often, encouraged by shared schooling but also by broader societal shifts that challenge the moral authority (and high social status) of former elites.

These changes to Lamu's social geography are tied to the island's position within an independent Kenya. Indeed, the previously hegemonic understanding of merchant elites' social and moral supremacy and these distinctions' mediation within verbal and material practices were progressively challenged following the end of British colonialism. At the same time, however, contestations to Lamu residents' rightful belonging to Kenya and the island's perceived marginalization by the Kenyan government increasingly resulted in the equation of "Lamu" with "Muslim." Locally significant social distinctions among Lamu residents are thereby erased in opposition to the Kenyan mainland, and distinguishing characteristics as respectable or cosmopolitan are discursively ascribed to all residents rather than only former merchant elites. Present-day contemplations on what it means to be a "good Lamu resident" and the meanings of associated notions of respectability, civility, and cosmopolitanism therefore need to be understood, not just in relation to the preceding history of social stratification, but also in connection to contemporary debates surrounding Lamu's belonging to and position within contemporary Kenya.

Lamu in an Independent Kenya

The East African coast's status as protectorate under British colonialism had important implications in the debates leading up to Kenya's independence in 1963. Having always distinguished themselves from the African hinterland, coastal inhabitants were not willing to subject themselves to the rule of a Christian-majority government based in Nairobi. As the negotiations about an independent Kenya developed, so did the calls for coastal autonomy and even independence. Arab leaders and waSwahili who feared political domination by mainland Africans set up the Mwambao or "coastline" movement, an organization that demanded coastal autonomy. Divisions within the movement, however, never gave Mwambao the political strength to push for autonomy or independence. When Zanzibar withdrew its support, and with the British eager to rid themselves of an increasingly problematic colony, the coastal strip saw itself integrated into a newly independent Kenya, with the maintenance of a limited amount of privileges such as the use of Islamic courts for Muslim family and inheritance law (Brennan 2008).

The Mwambao movement, and its later political revival in the Islamic Party of Kenya and the more progressive Coast Peoples Party, revealed the deep cleavages between the coastal strip and upcountry Kenya (Ray 2018; Salim 1970; Smart 2017; Willis and Gona 2012). During the struggle for independence and Mwambao's demands for autonomy, religion and genealogy were played out as unresolvable differences between these two parts of what was a new nation. Whereas Swahili communities on the islands and in towns along Kenya's coast suggested their Islamic lifestyle made it impossible for them to be ruled by a Christian government, coastal Africans used immigrant history to argue that "Arabs" had no claim to land or political participation (Prestholdt 2014). These complaints and objections did not disappear after 1963, and many of the waSwahili's fears have proven to be grounded. In the conclusion to his discussion of the Mwambao movement, James Brennan argues:

> The subsequent domination of Kenya's government by upcountry Christian politicians of KANU has displaced coastal Muslims not only from local political offices . . . but also from huge tracts of valuable rural land and urban property. . . . Political patronage has increasingly determined land access since the 1980s, deepening the coast's squatter problem and raising broader tensions between coastal squatters and upcountry immigrants. . . . Feeling is widespread that the upcountry has, since independence, lived parasitically off of the coast. Given this sharp sense of coastal dispossession, memories of mwambao will likely continue to shape future claims and debates. (Brennan 2008, 858–59)

Brennan's prediction could not have been more accurate. As a new constitution was negotiated in 2010, the position of Kenya's Coast Province and the role of the Islamic courts became a heavily debated topic once again. More importantly, the new constitution resulted in a revival of the "mwambao" sentiment along the coast and a newly organized Mombasa Republican Council (MRC) gave voice to new demands for autonomy (Smart 2017; Willis and Gona 2012; Marshall and Kiriama 2018). The MRC focused its secessionist demands on disputes over land ownership, on the perceived unequal allocation of wealth, jobs, and educational facilities between the coast and upcountry Kenya, and on conspiracy theories about the government's intentional distribution of drugs along the coast (Willis and Gona 2012). While not consisting solely of coastal Muslims, the Kenyan government was suspicious of the MRC and justified repressive actions in terms of its anti-terrorism campaign. Rather than link the MRC and its demands to Kenya's history of slavery and colonialism, the government associated the movement with the Somali Islamist terrorist organization Al-Shabaab (Botha 2014, 4; Marshall and Kiriama 2018, 573). Looking at the MRC's self-presentation on social media, Willis and Gona, however, underline that the MRC intentionally appeared to appeal to "a multiracial ideal of coastal identity that is cosmopolitan and at ease with technology" (2012, 69).

While seemingly focused on Mombasa, the MRC's demands found much support in Lamu, where claims to a distinct cosmopolitan (though much less multiracial) identity similarly featured in secessionist discourses. Indeed, the tensions between the Swahili coast and mainland

Kenya appear exacerbated in Lamu, where senses of marginalization are intensified due to the island's remote physical location and the evident (economic) decline that followed the incorporation into the Kenyan nation. Whereas the position of Lamu's merchant elites had already significantly weakened under British colonialism, independence had important economic, political, and social implications for life in the archipelago. And Lamu residents could link these shifts quite evidently to the arrival of a new group of immigrants to the region.

Kenya's first president, Jomo Kenyatta, assured that members of his own ethnic group—the Kikuyu—were assigned to government positions throughout the country, including to Lamu. In addition, he assigned property to landless Kikuyu, whose farmland had been claimed by colonial settlers, as part of the Kenyan government's settlement schemes in 1976 and onward. In Lamu County, Kikuyu were allotted land around Lake Kenyatta, approximately fourteen miles removed from the island, where they were to labor on a new cotton plantation and received support for agricultural development. The new settlement carried the name Mpeketoni and soon developed into a successful town. Present-day Mpeketoni is a large settlement with a population almost twice the size of Lamu Town (estimated at 30,000) and healthcare and educational facilities far better than those found in the archipelago.

The success of Mpeketoni is a thorn in the side of many Lamu residents due to questions surrounding unequal land-right allotments (and the allocation of title deeds), uneven government support for education and health care, and increasing political authority (through its rapidly growing population). Moreover, Kikuyu inhabitants progressively migrate to Lamu to sell their produce on the town's market. The majority-Christian Kikuyu are therefore a political, economic, and social force in Lamu, often competing against and winning over Lamu residents in bids for political office and thus increasingly claiming authority over them. Many view these new residents of Lamu as "emblems of upcountry domination of the coast" and of the government's intentional marginalization and underdevelopment of the Lamu Archipelago (Smart 2017, 436).

Mpeketoni's prosperity contrasts sharply with Lamu's continuing economic decline. Following independence, residents had to rely on fishery and international tourism as the government imposed restrictions on mangrove cutting, preventing former merchant elites to continue their transoceanic trade. As a result, many former merchant elites left Lamu in search of economic alternatives. Having sold their houses to Euro-American expatriates, many upper-class families now live in Mombasa and Malindi, and large Swahili immigrant communities can be found in Canada and the UK. While former elites living in Lamu run local businesses and continue to profit from their farmlands, their economic revenue is limited and many depend on remittances from family members elsewhere. In recent years, an increasing number of young male Lamu residents travel to the Gulf to work as labor migrants in the hospitality industry. While reluctant to accept these kinds of employment in Kenya (refusing to work in the service of others), they invoke their families' historical transoceanic connections with the Arabian Peninsula as a reason to "return" and take up employment there.

Lamu's tourism was thriving and successful until the late 1990s, with the tourism industry providing significant income through hotels, restaurants, and tourist excursions. While many former upper-class families owned hotels, young men (mostly, but not exclusively, of the Bajuni ethnicity) worked with tourists either as tour guides or dhow operators, taking tourists on sailing trips through the lagoon. This form of employment was profitable until tourism started to decline following the bombings of the Kenyan and Tanzanian embassies in 1998, and continued to decrease after the violent 2007 elections and subsequent terror attacks along the coast. The previously successful tourism industry resulted in several young men marrying Euro-American tourists and moving to their spouses' home countries. Forming part of Lamu's diaspora, these men support family living in Lamu and invest in local realty for family members or to rent to the occasional tourist.

Lamu residents associate the town's marginalized position and the present-day precarity of life on the island to the incorporation in an independent Kenya. Invoking conspiracy theories and highlighting the government's increasing imposition, they discursively construct current transformations as unprecedented and threatening (Chapter 1). The presence and continuing arrival of mainland Christians is not only viewed as a challenge to the local social structure and political autonomy, but also as a threat to an Islamic lifestyle and the moral values that inform life in Lamu. In response, Lamu residents increasingly voice a more unified Lamu identity, structured around notions of *uungwana* and claims to embodied characteristics of respectability and cosmopolitanism (Chapter 1). Political movements like the MRC find support as Lamu residents echo the secessionist movement's accusations of land grabbing, unequal job allocations, educational deprivation, and other conspiracy theories.

Scholars have struggled to understand the seeming paradox between, on the one hand, Swahili communities' documented cosmopolitan and integrative past and, on the other hand, the strong political, nativist claims that developed at independence and continue to inform political life along East Africa's coast (Glassman 2014).[15] This proliferation of seemingly racial or ethnic identities in supposedly fluid and integrative Swahili communities, however, makes more sense when cosmopolitanism itself is seen as a nativist discourse and a political tool, whereby membership to a transnational Arab elite distinguishes Swahili upper-classes from slave descendants, the African mainland, and Arabs (Glassman 2014, 235). Instead of mistaking contemporary claims to cosmopolitan identities as illustrative of the Swahili coast's integrative past, these discourses ought to be viewed as political claims warranting analysis (Glassman 2014, 233).

Rather than claim only cosmopolitan identities, coastal residents in Kenya, however, also progressively identify and organize themselves as "Muslims" in the public sphere (Kresse 2010, 73). This increasing significance of a distinctly Muslim identity needs to be understood in relation to Swahili communities' situatedness in the margins of both the postcolonial state and the global Muslim *ummah* (Kresse 2010). Kenya's coastal Muslims view themselves as second-class citizens, ruled by upcountry Christians, while simultaneously being aware of their peripheral position in the Muslim world. Although residents of the Swahili coast pride themselves in their longstanding connections with the Arabian Peninsula and an early adherence to Islam, they are simultaneously conscious of their inability to speak Arabic, their disadvantaged economic position in relation to the Gulf and the Middle East, and an identification as African by their Arab counterparts (Kresse 2010, 74). This double-peripheral position importantly informs coastal residents' conceptualizations of their Muslim identity and how it is enacted in everyday life.

These situated (ideological) meanings of cosmopolitanism and Islam form the background against which to understand the seemingly mundane projects of self-fashioning that form the focus of this book. When young women in Lamu endeavor to establish a position as righteous and professional, for example, they are not merely responding to elders' expectations of virtuous femininity; they are also positioning themselves in relation to the Kenyan state. While the previously discussed historical and political background highlights the local significance of social norms and associated verbal, material, and bodily practices, it simultaneously draws attention to the potentially shifting meanings of such embodied practices. Young people in particular are conscious of the fact that locally significant social distinctions are increasingly erased in translocal perceptions of Lamu residents. Claims to transoceanic lineages or cosmopolitan dispositions through verbal or material practices, for example, are now easily read by government security forces as signs of Islamist extremism and potential affiliation with Al-Shabaab. Lamu youth are therefore faced with the challenge of addressing Lamu's need for development while also recognizing the political significance of upholding local norms of respectability and piety.

By examining how these different orientations and loyalties are negotiated in everyday practice, I show that young people in Lamu, like African youth more broadly, do not just react to particular situations such as poverty or political exclusion; they are also shaping the terms of debate surrounding the issues that affect their lives, and they are creating and distributing messages to define themselves in an altered social reality.

The Everyday Lives of African Youth

Public discourse on globalization and rapid social change has often depicted youth as "one of the great challenges of the twentieth century" (Honwana and de Boeck 2005, ix). Across the globe young people's practices have become "occasions for moral panic" (Austin and Willard 1998, 1). Pronouncements such as these or generalizing statements like "the problem of youth today," however, reify the concept of "youth" and erase the larger social concerns that motivate such arguments. In the process, "youth" itself becomes the issue and turns into "a metaphor for perceived social change and its projected consequences, and as such it is an enduring locus for displaced social anxieties" (Austin and Willard 1998, 1).

Nowhere is the perception of youth as a "lost generation" more acute than in Africa, where young people are depicted either as perpetrators and victims of social and political conflict or as dupes in the globalization of culture (see, for example, Abbink and van Kessel 2005; Beckerleg 1995; Durham 2000; Honwana 2012; Honwana and de Boeck 2005). Such pessimistic views are fueled by discussions of African youth's desperate endeavors to confront the restructurings of global capital that render daily life ever more precarious (Honwana and de Boeck 2005). From Angola to Lamu, there exists a profound sense of anxiety, an apparent crisis in the conditions of social reproduction caused by neoliberal policies and market orthodoxies (Bissell 2005; Comaroff and Comaroff 2001; Ferguson 2006; Hanson and Hentz 1999; Hodgson 2011; Weiss 2004). Add to this rising concerns about poverty and hardship, migration, HIV/AIDS, the break-down of the family, violence, and gangs and the negative image of youth in contemporary African societies is complete. Globalization and social change, while offering new (positive) opportunities to African youth, have generally been discussed in relation to these crisis-related issues: child soldiers (Honwana 2006), AIDS orphans (Dahl 2009, 2014; Dane and Levine 1994), child trafficking (Dottridge 2002), female genital cutting (Gosselin 2000), extremist ideologies and terrorism (Hansen 2016), and sexual abuse of children and sex tourism (Richter, Higson-Smith, and Dawes 2004).

One then rightly wonders how to write about youth in Africa "without falling back on the bleak picture of crisis, crime and violence" and do justice to the positive resourcefulness of African youth that has so often been erased within Africanist discourse (Abbink and van Kessel 2005, 2). The response within academic literature has been an approach that focuses on African youth as inventive and resilient subjects, whereby young people's voices are taken seriously. This resulted in a range of studies that looked at the creativity with which youth appropriate and adapt global practices, making them inherently local. Eileen Moyer (2004, 2005), for example, discusses the popularity of the Rastafari movement in Dar Es Salaam to demonstrate how global cultural flows were strategically localized, rather than blindly appropriated. Speaking directly against the moral and civic panic that exists around youth in Africa, Mamadou Diouf's (2003) study of the Setal movement in Dakar looks at African youth and public space in the postcolonial context to demonstrate how young people can positively react against the political context within which their position is defined.[16]

Using a problem-centered approach, these studies recognize and document African youth's agency to react to social crises or to localize global cultural flows.[17] These are, however, often discussions *about* youth rather than considerations that approach young people on their own terms (see also Janson 2013). What has been lacking within African (and Islamic) studies is a detailed analysis of young people's day-to-day interactions and their diverse considerations as they endeavor to reposition themselves within a rapidly changing society.[18]

Linguistic anthropological studies in African contexts have focused on the political economy of language (Irvine 1989), processes of entextualization (Spitulnik 1996), gendered claims to power and agency through discursive strategies (Billings 2013; Gaudio 2009; Hirsch 1998; Thompson 2015a, 2015b, 2017a; Stiles and Thompson 2015), linguistic deliberations of ethnic and religious identities (McIntosh 2009; Gaudio 2009), or narratives surrounding social ills like HIV/AIDS (Black 2012). However, there is little scholarship that analyzes young people's everyday practices and how these relate to the interactional management of social transformations.

By documenting young people's discourses about social change, as well as the semiotic practices through which they negotiate new youthful positions, this book takes a step toward filling this gap in both African studies and linguistic anthropology. A detailed analysis of young people's everyday practices, and the moral implications of the choices they make in terms of self-presentations, provides insight into youth's considerations as they position themselves in relation to religious, political, or traditionalist discourses. As I will show, residents of Lamu—young and old alike—evaluate everyday interactions as primary indices of social change and moral shifts. The detailed analysis of interactional practices and their ideological evaluation then provides insights into how young people manage encounters, maintain relationships, and negotiate new subject positions, as well as the sociopolitical processes that shape such deliberations. I suggest that youth never just reject or respond to local contexts; orienting toward a multitude of ideological discourses, they create new social niches that differently reflect their specific orientation to political debates, religious norms, local traditions, and notions of modernity.

I approach the category of "youth" as a discursive formation (Foucault 1976), as a social category shaped by unequal relations of power, authority, and respectability within the traditional society. In a community faced with shifts in moral authority, however, Foucault's "points of contestation" within such discursive formations become increasingly evident: Young Lamu residents in different ways contest their belonging to such discursively constructed categories and renegotiate what youth can or cannot do in present-day society. Such a view of youth then allows for an analysis of the agency of young people, their semiotic practices, and how they deal with the social and political forces that determine the conditions by which they are identified; it provides empirical concreteness to Foucault's phenomena of "contestation."

When writing, I use the term "youth" to refer to the social category of people defined as such by locals—*kijana* (pl. *vijana*) as distinguished from *mtoto* (child). This notion broadly refers to a group of people between the ages of eighteen and thirty-five (see also Abbink and van Kessel 2005). Locals' demarcation of this category of young people, or their conceptions of the age grade to which youth belong, is determined partly by the legal understandings of youth (imposed by the Kenyan government and the legal age at which young people are allowed to obtain an identity card) and partly by shifting conceptions of social responsibilities. I was told that *zamani* (in the past or before) youth stopped being *vijana* when they were married, when they were able to take up the responsibilities as husband or wife. Yet with changes in marital practices and because of a deteriorating economy, this category of youth has shifted as well. Even if they marry young, young people are not always able to provide for their family and reside with in-laws. Socially they are therefore still considered *vijana*. This shifting understanding of the age brackets of youth is not exclusive to Lamu but is a phenomenon found throughout the African continent (e.g., Abbink and van Kessel 2005; Janson 2013; Weiss 2009).

Many locals, however, remarked that the notion *kijana* was not as straightforward as a simple bracketing of the ages 18–35. Within Lamu (and possibly the broader Swahili coast and other African societies), everyone is considered *kijana* in relation to their elder. My assistant, who was around fifty-five years old, was referred to as *kijana* by the seventy-year-old man he interviewed. Such shifting or flexible conceptions of "youth" importantly hint at the local, context-bounded understandings of authority and status that will feature prominently in this book's discussion of changing social relations.

Chapter Overview

The first section of the book mainly focuses on discourses: on how discourses circulate and are taken up within everyday interactions, but also on how ideologies gain shape through and are expressed within these discursive practices. By identifying particular linguistic and semiotic ideologies and discussing how these are informed by interlocutors' situated views of past and present, I show how Lamu residents link observed everyday practices to social category belonging, and thus how social identities emerge or are challenged within interactions. The second half of the book shifts its focus to more explicitly look at young people's everyday verbal, material, and bodily practices, which are informed by and respond to the previously discussed ideologies and through which they position themselves as particular kinds of young Lamu residents.

Chapter 1 focuses on Lamu residents' contemplations on life in present-day Lamu. Particularly, I show how opinions on the transformations this town is currently undergoing cannot be separated from interlocutors' situated view of the past and the social hierarchy that previously informed life in the town. To understand fully the significance of these evaluations, I discuss the importance of *heshima* or respectability as a moral code that both shaped social relations within Lamu and distinguished the town's inhabitants from mainland residents. In particular, I explain how respectable conduct and social distinctions were evaluated and maintained through verbal and material practices as well as spatial boundaries. I also highlight, however, how and why a previously hegemonic understanding of respectability is increasingly challenged and redefined in present-day Lamu. This chapter not only offers the moral vocabulary with which to understand ideological discourses discussed in subsequent chapters; it also provides insights into how notions of belonging are mediated within seemingly ordinary practices.

Chapter 2 looks at the moral and political meanings of language within the context of Lamu. Building upon insights provided in Chapter 1, I consider how seemingly minute details of language become imbued with political meanings and moral values, and how this in turn shapes Lamu residents' everyday language use. I describe how the local dialect, kiAmu, came to be stigmatized in relation to the national language, Standard Swahili, but also how elements of this dialect only became distinctive and meaningful in response to the government-enforced imposition of the standard language. An analysis of discourses that evaluate young people's language use highlights the significance of accents and intonations as signs of political, social, and moral standing.

Chapter 3 asks how the discourses on sociopolitical change, morality, and belonging analyzed in the foregoing chapters, shape and inform the discursive evaluations of Lamu's younger generation and their everyday material and verbal practices. We see the social category of "youth" materialize as either enslaved to their longing for Western modernity (with explicit comparisons of youth to slaves) or as the *dot com* generation that has access to a range of possibilities previously unreachable for their parents. The analysis of these discourses shows how differently positioned social actors read and evaluate verbal and nonverbal practices and link them to newly emerging social categories. Such readings of material signs and their explicit incorporation into evaluations of youth hint at how young people are able to strategically use details of dress, smell, gaze, or stride in the presentation of self. It is precisely to such tactic self-fashionings that the last two chapters turn.

Chapter 4 follows young people and their interactional practices in a variety of environments, examining how they differently present themselves, depending on context and audience, by strategically drawing upon a broad linguistic repertoire. We see how Lamu youth use linguistic tactics to negotiate new social positions and take political stances, but also how a moral narrative of modernity can be linked to or mediated within such verbal practices. The chapter raises the question of intentionality and reception and asks whether young people's strategic self-positionings are always successful and what the implications of such indeterminacy are.

Nonverbal communication, while never separate from verbal interactions, has a distinct value in Lamu. Because verbal exchanges (especially with the opposite gender) could carry implications for someone's respectability, people frequently rely on nonverbal communication to converse while in public. Moreover, seemingly minute behavioral details, including nuances in dress styles or bodily movements, historically played an important role in everyday life in Lamu, as these signs allowed distinctions between local or guest, patrician or newcomer. Chapter 5 therefore looks at how material practices and the moving body are implicated in the negotiation of change and the emergence of new social positionings. It examines how young men and women in Lamu differently use material and bodily practices to gradually redefine norms of proper conduct and status. We follow two individuals in their everyday engagements: a young female professional accused of immoral conduct and a beach boy who becomes a local politician. Each uses different means to negotiate a respectful position within the Lamu community.

The epilogue reflects upon the changes Lamu has undergone since 2010. In particular, I contemplate the wider sociopolitical field that informs the seemingly mundane practices on which the book focused. I ask how the strategic use of verbal and nonverbal signs, as well as their readings, have further changed in light of recent terrorist attacks, government interventions, and newly imposed development schemes. While a thread throughout the book, the epilogue most explicitly contemplates how self-fashioning is always also a positioning against others, including the international focus on Lamu as a place where terrorists might come from.

In the book, three interludes provide poetic reflections on life in contemporary Lamu. In Swahili communities, verse was used historically to voice social and political critiques and poets today continue this tradition. Moreover, Lamu has always been a literary center, its dialect (kiAmu) being renowned as a language of poetry and praise. The poetic interludes provide readers with Lamu inhabitants' own musings on the issues addressed, in a medium authentic to this region. The first poem is a conversation between an elder and a youth, as they both contemplate the moral state of their community. Written in the voice the Swahili language, the second poem reflects on language change and asks coastal residents why they are abandoning their mother tongue. A third poetic interlude addresses Lamu residents and urges them to strive for development, while simultaneously remaining true to and conscious of their cultural traditions and moral values. All three poems were written and provided by Ustadh Mahmoud Ahmed Abdulkadir, one of Lamu's most renowned contemporary poets. Each poem is preceded by a short explanation of his reasons for writing the poem and the message he is trying to bring across. Research assistants helped with the translation of the poems into English, which were subsequently approved by the poet himself.

Mila Yetu Hufujika
(Our Traditions Are Being Destroyed)

MAHMOUD AHMED ABDULKADIR

Composed in December 2008, this poem captures the poet's reflections on contemporary life in Lamu. It does so through the voices of an elder and a young man (indicated by E and Y respectively), who speak to each other through Swahili *majibizano*, or poetic dialogue.

The poem addresses young people's growing forsaking of respectful conduct, as reflected in their language use and appearances, and speaks to the increasing substance abuse among Lamu youth, including the financial repercussions these addictions have. The poet subtly incorporated Quranic references to remind his audience of the Islamic warnings against some of the trends depicted in the poem. The young man's last words, for example, resemble a Quranic verse that reminds youth not to speak up against their parents and warns them of the Day of Judgment. As in the Quranic verse, the young man refutes the warning and denies the coming of the Last Day.[1]

[E]
Lahaula
By God

Yetu mila
Our traditions

Kwa jumla
Overall

Mambo yameharibika
Everything is ruined

Na lugha zimegeuka
And languages have changed

Sana zimevurujika
Things have perished

[Y]
Unanni
What's the matter

Kitwatini
Your head is down

Yambo gani
What is it

Mno umesikitika
You're incredibly sad

Na matozi hukutoka
And tears are falling

Kubwa mno lilotuka
This big thing that occurred

[E]
Huyaoni?
Haven't you noticed?

Tamaduni
Our culture

Duniyani
This world

Au hufanya dhihaka?
Or are you joking?

Zetu zimezofujika
Has been destroyed

Kheri mtu kuondoka!
Better to leave it now!

[Y]
Lipigeni?
What is it

Kaburini
To be in the grave

Kwa yakini
For certain

Lilokupa kushutuka?
? That has shocked you so much?

Ukatamani kufika
Is what you long for

Maisha umeyachoka!
You are tired of life!

[E]
Mato huna
Don't you have eyes

Masikiyo kadhalika?
Or ears for that matter?

Huyaona
Haven't you seen

Ziyoja zinazotuka
These terrifying things

Wasichana
Our girls

Nusu tupu huzunguka
Walking around half-naked

[Y]
Shukrani
Thank you

Yakupasa kutamka
For expressing your worries

Hisabuni
Keep in mind

Nasi sasa huwangika
We are in charge now

Yazamani
Things of the past

Sinafuu kuyashika
We need not cling to

[E]
Ulanisi
Sinful things

Ndiwo munaoutaka
Is what you desire

Nanajisi
And impurity

Huzinya mukiipaka
With feces you smear yourselves

Kwa kuasi
Through disobedience

Muhuri mumepijika
You have been branded evil

Mafahali
Grown-up men

Mikili wa meisuka
Braid their hair

Nazipuli
And earrings

Wamevaa kadhalika
They wear like women

Hayya mbali
Let alone this

Na dini wameepuka
They have also abandoned the religion

Wamezama
They sunk deep

Mno wameghafilika
Completely neglectful

Yalomema
Morality

Maadili wameruka
They have forsaken

Nakusoma
And studying

Kwetu kumezoroteka
We have abandoned

Hatudini
Unaware of religion

Duniya metuponyoka
Yet the world is not with us either

Tuyangani
We are straying

Nipopo huninginika
Like bats, we hang aimlessly

Masikini
We are poor people

Huzidi kufukarika
Only becoming poorer

Tumevuwa
We have removed

Vazi lakuhishimika
The attire of respect

Tumekuwa
We have become

Kama piya huzunguka
Purposeless, just going round and round

Twaondowa
We spend carelessly

Akiba watu huweka
While others save

Hata lugha
Even our language

Yetu imetuponyoka
Has been stolen from us

Huigaga
We speak it in a stammer

Hushindwa kuitamka
We can no longer pronounce it

Kwa kusaga
By chewing khat

Wengi tumefilisika
Many of us are bankrupt

[Y]
Ewe babu
Oh grandfather

Nimekukanya komeka
I have to stop you here

Kwa sababu
Because I can see

Nakuona wapuzukwa
You are speaking nonsense

Siajabu
It's no wonder

Akili imekuruka
You clearly have lost your mind

Unenayo
What you talk about

Niyazamani kumbuka
Is from a time long gone

Sasa hayo
Nowadays

Hakuna wakuyataka
Nobody wants those things

Kwa kiliyo
Just by crying

Mai hayatozoleka
Water won't be scooped

Tuwateni
Leave us alone

Tutende tunayotaka
To do what we want

Nyinyi kwani
After all

Siyotena wahusika
It no longer concerns you

Kaburini
In the grave

Ndipo pakupumzika
Is where you ought to rest

[E]
Masikiyo
From your ears

Sisi huwatowa taka
We tried removing dirt

Mutendayo
Your sinful acts

Mawi metusa mipaka
Have passed their limits

Siku hiyo
One day

Mutakuya kukumbuka
You will remember

[Y]
Siku gani
Which day

Siku isiyokufika
A day that will never come

Ndanganuni
It is a fictitious story

Zatangu nyaka na nyaka
Told for years and years

Hatuwoni
Yet we do not see

Alokufa kufufuka
The dead resurrecting

[E]
Chakuvunda
What's destined to perish

Sikweli huziwilika
Cannot be avoided

Kitapanda
It will get wrecked

Mwamba kikisa kwandika
Once it hits the rock

Menishinda
I have been defeated

Ni kheri mimi kashuka
It's better I alight

CHAPTER I

"This Is Lamu": Belonging, Morality, and Materiality

On a warm afternoon in 2008, a small group of men had gathered on one of several stone benches located alongside Lamu's seafront. Some were dressed in long white robes; others donned a traditional wraparound skirt, and most of them wore an embroidered hat or *kofia*. While sipping Arabic coffee, they observed the bustle at Lamu's seafront: people going home after a day's work, boats arriving from Kenya's mainland loaded with travelers from Malindi or Mombasa, *mashua* (traditional wooden sailing boats) returning from a day at sea, carrying either a load of freshly caught fish or, more often, Euro-American tourists who had gone sailing. The men quietly commented on what they observed—on familiar faces returning from travels to the city, on the appearance of people walking by, on fishermen's catch of the day.

These kinds of informal gatherings or *baraza* form an integral part of life along the Swahili coast.[1] Meeting on stone benches that can be found throughout Swahili towns, elder men gather after the early morning and afternoon prayers to enjoy some coffee and engage in lively discussions. Historically, men's ability to gather on a *baraza* was a sign of elite status and class membership; a successful tradesman could refrain from labor and instead engage in debates concerning the governance of the town. To this day, adult men often belong to a specific *baraza*, determined by neighborhood residence, lineage, and social class. These gatherings and the respectability of its members equally enforce respect from passersby. When walking in front of a *baraza*, young men generally pause their conversations and greet the gathering with an audible *assalaam aleykum*. Lamu women usually change their route when they notice a *baraza* assembly on their path. If an alternative road is not available, women tend to halt their conversations and lower their gazes (or cover their faces) until they have passed the bench.

I did not fully understand women's reluctance to walk in front of a *baraza* until one day my friend Maryam and I had to visit a store located not far from such popular gathering place. When we walked past, the men halted their conversation, and I could feel their observing gaze. Noticing my uneasiness, Maryam whispered: "Just imagine they are flower pots!" She later explained that walking in front of a *baraza* invites men to look at you: You make yourself available to their gazes. Smiling or glancing at the men, even if a mere expression of discomfort, would suggest their attention was desired. Maryam told me she managed her uneasiness—and thus maintained her respectability—by not acknowledging the men's presence: Flowerpots just sit there; they don't notice you, they don't stare at you, and you do not need to recognize them.

While a sign of respect for the *baraza* members, observing these (generally unspoken) rules equally imparted respectability on the young women and men walking past and was indicative of their own social status and class membership. In the past, not everyone was equally capable of upholding such norms of respectability. Because they could not rely on housemaids to run their errands, for example, poor women or former slaves often had no choice but to appear in public and avail themselves to men's gazes. In present-day Lamu, however, young people and newly arrived immigrants seemed to increasingly transgress such behavioral rules. It was not always evident whether this disregard was out of necessity, obliviousness, or intentional defiance. When asked about their behavior, some Lamu youth claimed urban or progressive attitudes. Others offered their professional employment as a justification, suggesting their job required fast movement; they simply did not have time to avoid a *baraza*. Lamu residents' judgments of nonlocals' behaviors, however, were often quite negative. Immigrants from the Kikuyu and Meru ethnicities were seen as unabashedly ignoring these social norms, while Euro-American tourists and expatriates living in Lamu Town were believed to just be oblivious to norms of respectability.

My female friends would chuckle or suck their teeth in disapproval when they observed (or heard about) scantily dressed tourists walking right in front of a *baraza*. On more than one occasion, friends would tell me about a respected Lamu elder who promptly left the *baraza* upon observing a female tourist walk by in hot pants and a tank top. Five minutes later, he allegedly returned with a wraparound cloth and friendly urged the woman to cover up, for the sake of her own respectability just as much as his own.

That afternoon in 2008, conversations were few on this particular bench along Lamu's seafront. Watching people walk by, Mwalim Baddi—my research assistant, who regularly attended this bench—used the silence to inquire about the *baraza* members' views on life in contemporary Lamu. Observing a few beach boys anchor their sailing boat after returning from a snorkeling trip with three American tourists, he asked whether the men thought life in Lamu had changed. Did it differ from their childhood? The *baraza* members were quick to respond and suggested that there was a stark difference between *hivi sasa* (nowadays) and *hapo zamani* (the past). Young people, so they argued, had lost *heshima* or respectability; their appearance, language use, and general comportment showed little consideration for the norms of deference that used to inform everyday interactions. When asked what caused this change, a few of the men referred to young people's use of mobile phones, satellite TV, and the influence of secular education.

The *baraza* members' response then appeared to echo complaints from elder generations the world over, voicing nostalgia for a past when young people were respectful and upright, and with modern technology being identified as the main culprit for corrupting the younger generation. One elder, however, agitatedly disputed these initial responses. Life in Lamu had changed, he suggested, not because of technological innovations but because of the increasing presence and permanent residence of *wageni* or guests—immigrants from Kenya's mainland, but also tourists and expatriates. Having patiently listened to the elder's tirade, directed at these "guests" but also at Lamu youth who increasingly appropriated these newcomers' practices, a (relatively) younger *baraza* member carefully interjected a well-known saying, attempting to offer an alternative view: *"Ama 'hiyo ndiyo Amu atakao nae'?"* "This is Lamu, whoever wants to can come"?

Often used by Lamu residents to underline their hospitality and the island's historical appeal to explorers, traders, and travelers, this proverb suggests that visitors have always been welcome in Lamu, and once they arrive, they simply do not want to leave again. Interlocutors explained that the saying referred to the historical, magical appeal of island life and its cosmopolitan status, based on a combination of geographical location, Swahili culture, and especially the hospitality of Lamu residents.[2] The man's interjection insinuated that instead of being a new phenomenon, the arrival and permanent residence of newcomers was the continuation of a historically desired trend that had always shaped the culture of and life in Lamu. The elder's reaction was quick and sharp.

> Haikwambiwa kwa hayo! Waliambiwa ndooni hapa, mwangalie utamaduni wa kiAmu, atakao nae, kwa kandu na makofia. Hatukuwa na uchafu. Sasa ni zijembe wapidja wale. Amu imekuwa hiyau. Nyani mwenye kuya tena sasa? Mwenye haya? Mwenye dini yake? Kuya kuona. . . . Wamesokota nye humtambui ni binadamu. Je, ilikuwa Amu katika miyaka khamsini? Ilikuwa hunuka asmini Amu bwana.

> It was never said in those terms! They were told to come here and experience the culture of Lamu, and want/desire that, the *kanzu* (white robe) and the *kofia* (embroidered hat). There was no dirt. Now they [newcomers] are beating the drums. This is what Lamu has become. Who comes nowadays? With *haya* (modesty)? With *dini* (religion)? Who comes and experiences. . . . They plait their hair [have dreadlocks], one cannot even recognize that it is a human being. Was Lamu like this in the fifties? It smelled like jasmine in Lamu, my friend.

When listening to the recorded discussion, I noted the agitation in the elder's voice; he almost sounded insulted when offering his interpretation, or rather contextualization, of the often quoted saying. Hospitality and residence on the island had never been categorical, he strongly advised. Rather, Lamu residents' welcoming demeanor and the integration of *wageni* into Lamu society had always been conditional upon guests' acceptance of and adherence to local values of modesty and religiosity. What infuriated the elder was not the arrival of newcomers, but rather their disregard for local moral values—for the behavioral expectations tied to *heshima* (respectability).

A silence fell over the group of men as each reflected upon the implications of the elder's clarification of a proverb believed to capture Lamu's historical status as a cosmopolitan and urban center of trade, travel, and Islamic scholarship. After all, this specific interpretation suggested that, just as the island's geopolitical position had shifted, so had the moral and political authority of its inhabitants.

Complex intersections of societal structure and status, notions of morality, and material practice historically informed and continue to shape life in Lamu. Residents justify distinctions between "us" and "them" at different levels of society through ideological discourses of social differentiation that focus on others' perceived moral dispositions. As we will see, socioeconomic shifts increasingly undermine a previously hegemonic view of respectability or *heshima* and its mediation within bodily and material practices, enabling challenges and redefined claims to moral personhood and status. Untangling these junctures is no easy feat, particularly because of the fractal recursive nature of these discourses and the ideological erasures that accompany them (Irvine and Gal 2000). Whereas all Lamu residents distinguish themselves as being more respectable than mainland and Euro-American newcomers, similar distinctions based on embodied *heshima* continue to exist within Lamu society where former elites and Bajuni immigrants now each perceive one another as lacking (particular kinds of) respectability.

By discussing how time, space, and material practices are imbued with moral value, this chapter historicizes and links local understandings of morality, materiality, and social status. Rather than the historical accuracy of claims made in interluctors' evaluations of life on the island, I am interested in the ideologies that inform them. While I highlight the importance of historical events and how these continue to shape the present, I am particularly mindful of how the present shapes the readings and imaginings of the past.[3] The discourses analyzed here are those of Lamu residents (waAmu and waBajuni) as they position themselves in relation to "others"— to mainland newcomers in Lamu Town, to Euro-American expatriates, and to the Kenyan government. At the same time, the historical view of *heshima* laid out in this chapter is the one established, promoted, and maintained by Lamu's former merchant elites. Contemporary contestations over the true meaning, importance, and proper mediation of *heshima* are at the heart of the everyday negotiation of moral value, social relations, and notions of belonging that form the focus of this book. Insights into these tensions show that debates surrounding change in present-day Lamu cannot be understood as separate from either shifts on socioeconomic and political levels or a metapragmatics of personhood, that is, how the entire sense apparatus is conceived of and ideologically linked to the moral state of the individual and their position on the social ladder.

It Used to Smell like Jasmine in Lamu

"It smelled like jasmine in Lamu, my friend." Opposing Lamu's supposed present-day pollution to a former purity, typified by the sweet smell of jasmine filling the town's streets, the elder concluded his agitated response to the invocation of historical hospitality as an explanation for the town's present-day social diversity. Rather than a reference to the actual fragrance or stench of the town, the elder spoke to a loss of cultural refinement within and the moral deterioration of the Lamu community, a demise he perceived as resulting from Kenyan independence and Lamu's reluctant incorporation into a new nation. His concluding statement, however, not only expressed nostalgia for the past; it also voiced a political stance that drew upon ideological connections between moral value, material culture, and notions of belonging.

Jasmine is an important signifier of Swahili culture. Brides and grooms are garlanded with jasmine and roses at weddings, and most households aim to have jasmine growing in their garden so as to sprinkle unopened jasmine blossoms on pillows to scent slumber and dreams (Issa 2012). Women frequently burn incense to impregnate houses and clothing with a deep, sweet smell. Incense and perfume are equally an integral part of religious events and rituals, with spaces and clothing being permeated with fragrances. Lamu residents place a high cultural value on creating an olfactory rich environment, considering it a sign of sophistication and refinement. While linked to devotional practices and Islam, it also calls upon the coastal residents' historical transoceanic connections with Arabia (where much of the incense is imported from). Scent is then not merely part of adornment or self-decoration; it is "central to rituals, status, social interactions, territorial distinctions and solidarity" (Boswell 2008, 296). The seemingly mundane practice of perfuming oneself can therefore signal individual intention and social relations, but also social and political position. The opposite is also true; references to a supposed loss of olfactory refinement signify more than actual smells. The elder's use of a metaphor of fragrance and its contemporary loss entailed a political stance, expressing a disintegration of a community where *wageni* or "outsiders" increasingly control public space and the behaviors within it (see also Boswell 2008). Indeed, this elder *baraza* member was not the only one who opposed purity to pollution when reflecting upon, respectively, Lamu's seemingly prosperous past and its contemporary state.

"*Hapo zamani na sasa ntafauti*! The past and now are different!" Rukia sipped her steaming hot chai while she looked me intently in the eyes. In the silence that followed, she seemed to reflect upon how to explain to this young researcher the distinct difference she observed between the Lamu of her youth and the town as it was today. We were sitting in Rukia's one-room house, located in Lamu's Langoni neighborhood. I had found myself a comfortable spot on the traditional, woven Swahili bed that was pushed against the wall. Rukia sat opposite me, on the single chair available. On the table was a plate with *sambusa* and *bhajia* that her grandson had dropped off. Leaning my back against the wall, knees pulled up, I enjoyed the snacks and took notes as Rukia spoke.

A few days earlier, one of the staff members of the Lamu museum had introduced me to Rukia. Knowing I was interested in different perspectives on life in contemporary Lamu, he told me she would have interesting stories to tell. Originally from Siyu, one of the surrounding islands in the archipelago, Rukia moved to Lamu as a young girl. And despite having lived in town for the majority of her life, her kiSwahili was still distinctly of the Siyu variety (which she proudly pointed out during our first interview), and she often "translated" to the local kiAmu dialect to assure I understood her fully. Rukia was highly respected in Lamu. She would often tell me about her family, who belonged to the *waungwana* upper class in Siyu and originally derived from Yemen. Having moved to Lamu shortly after Kenyan independence, her father had hoped to attain prosperity through fishing and trade but never acquired much wealth. Sitting in her cramped home in Langoni, the area of town where immigrants historically settled, Rukia would continuously emphasize that, despite their poverty, her family always maintained their *uungwana* elite status through the display of their respectability in language use, modes of dress, and general comportment. That respectability, she argued, is now lost on the younger generation.

> Zamani kulikuwa na heshima. Mila imepunguwa. Mila ya zamani na sasa ntafauti. Tafauti yake ni matamshi ya kuzungumza. Wakizungumza wazungumza maneno machafu. Watu wa zamani walikuwa wakizungumza maneno ya heshma, lakini sasa watu wazungumza maneno machafu.

> In the past, there was *heshima* (respect/respectability). *Mila* (customs) have decreased. The *mila* (customs) from the past and now are different. The difference lies in the way of speaking. When they talk, they speak dirty words. People in the past used to speak *ya heshima* (respectfully) but now people speak dirty words.

Rukia's initial response surprised me. Observing the poverty she lived in, I had expected her to voice concerns about the declining economy and government restrictions on fishery, for example. Yet she phrased her view of change in Lamu in moral and not political or economic terms. And much like the elder on the *baraza*, who recalled the smell of jasmine in Lamu during his childhood, Rukia noted an opposition between the historical purity of Lamu Town versus its contemporary dirtiness. Like the elder, she thereby referred, not just to a physical pollution, but also and especially to a moral impurity as displayed in individuals' everyday interactions. In our subsequent encounters, Rukia would use every opportunity to further elaborate on this view of change: Young girls passing by, the shouting of young men in the alley outside her house, or even the material of a cloth, all evoked reflections upon Lamu's altered social context and particularly the moral condition of its inhabitants.

Hivi sasa na hapo zamani, ntafauti; it must have been the sentence I heard the most during my three-year residence on Lamu Island (see also Caplan 2004). Whether I spoke to elderly women who reminisced about their childhood, to parents who discussed raising children in contemporary Lamu, or to young Lamu residents who contemplated their lives on the island, whether these were Lamu's former merchant elites or people deriving from the Bajuni islands, all appeared to agree on the opposition between a vaguely delineated, glorious past and a grim present. And while the past was differently described as either a time of economic wealth, political authority, or cultural significance, all interlocutors agreed that *heshima* (respectability) was the defining distinction between the past and the present. Their contemplations suggested that "respect" structured everyday life in the past as it informed language use, appearances, and overall comportment. In present-day Lamu, a growing disregard for *heshima* in everyday interactions was identified as the main indicator of the overall deterioration of the community. The perceived cause of such indifference, however, was not a generational shift, but rather the growing presence of newcomers whose arrival had been facilitated by unprecedented economic and political change and who were disinterested in integrating themselves into a social hierarchy structured around notions of respectability.

While Lamu residents' reflections upon life on the island might present the past as stable and harmonious, the town experienced significant and rapid changes throughout its history (as was outlined in the Introduction). The current historical imaginings—of harmonious social coexistence and unambiguous signs of moral character and social class belonging—are then, in part, nostalgic reinterpretations of the past, informed by contemporary discontents and informative of speakers' position in the landscape of the present. Discussing colonial nostalgia in Zanzibar, William Bissell (2005) suggests we analyze this kind of nostalgia not as a form of fraught history but rather as a social practice that expresses individuals' stances toward contemporary struggles. The plurality of nostalgic discourses, he argues, can provide an understanding of people's differing social and ideological orientations toward the contemporary context, particularly through an analysis of their selective use of signs from the past to frame the present (Bissell 2005, 216–18). In other words, the practices interlocutors identify as lacking *heshima*—which aspects of behavior and especially whose comportments are pinpointed as disreputable—are not mere nostalgic recollections on previous moral uprightness but also entail political stances that comment upon individuals' rightful belonging to and social position in Lamu.

An analysis of discursive evaluations of life in present-day Lamu, and the different forms of nostalgia that permeate them, therefore not only offers insights into why Lamu residents conceptualize change in moral terms; *what* they identify as signs of change—which details of language use, dress, bodily comportment, or indeed smell—also reveals altered understandings of "belonging to Lamu." Such changing ways of thinking about a new collective self—about what it means to be "from Lamu" but also who can count as a Lamu resident—are neither wholly inherited nor wholly invented but are being refashioned in part from old discursive materials, in part from translocal discourses, in part from newly imagined narratives (Glassman 2011, 22). Indeed, Lamu residents' focus on a loss of *heshima* as *the* sign of contemporary social change cannot be fully understood outside of a historical context in which the *wenyeji* patrician elites distinguished themselves from both newcomers (*wageni*) and slaves (*watumwa*) based on differential respectability.

The moral states Lamu's upper classes historically ascribed to the different groups that made up the town's social hierarchy—*uungwana* (nobility), *ushenzi* (barbarity), and *utumwa* (enslavement)—intimately linked assessments of social status and rightful belonging with notions of refinement and its opposite. These, in other words, were highly moralized appraisals that were semiotically mediated in "modes of dress, comportment, spiritual practice, architecture, employment type and even linguistic terminology and accent" (Benjamin 2014, 136). As such, evaluations of status and belonging were deeply embedded in considerations of self-comportment, with notions of embodied respectability meaningfully shaping unequal social relations.

At the same time, however, upper-class claims to *heshima* (respectability) as a sign of social status were fully dependent on oppositional distinctions; any pretensions to embodied "sophistication" or "civilized" behaviors were contingent on "having others as contrastive foils, *washenzi* (savages), the unwashed, those fresh off the boat and unfamiliar with coastal norms, Kiswahili and the Muslim *umma*" (Bissell 2018, 593). Precisely these op-positional distinctions (and their spatial, architectural, and material med-itation and reproduction) are contested within contemporary Lamu, with new voices offering alternative readings of material forms as signs of laziness (rather than respectability) or backwardness (rather than sophis-tication). Lamu residents, and the former elites in particular, respond to those voices and their increasing imposition when they complain about a lack of *heshima*, when they reconceptualize the conditions for hospitality, or when they object to the present-day stench of the town.

These intersections of material practice, moral personhood, and notions of belonging, and particularly the changes they are undergoing within con-temporary Swahili societies have hardly been explored ethnographically. Yet, precisely (contestations over) the proper semiotic mediation of status and moral dispositions make questions of belonging and social identity within present-day Swahili communities so fascinating. An in-depth dis-cussion of Lamu's social hierarchy is not the focus of this chapter. How-ever, an understanding of the hegemonic ideology that historically informed self-other evaluations, and particularly its mediation in material practices and spatial structures, is needed to fully comprehend present-day nostal-gic discourses and their focus on fragrance, modes of dress, language use, and movement as signs of change.

Understanding Heshima: Defining Respect and Respectability

Previous studies of life in Swahili towns suggest that claims to respectable conduct, more so than notions of an ethnicized identity, permitted the *we-nyeji* ruling families to continuously distinguish themselves from new-comers and slaves. This notion of respectability can be summarized in the concept of *heshima*, an all-encompassing term describing a Swahili moral code (Iliffe 2005; Kresse 2009; McMahon 2006; Saleh 2004). *Heshima* can be loosely defined as "having dignity and honor"; it means displaying an awareness of how to properly extend courtesy and esteem to others and thus includes a conception of appropriate social interaction (McMahon 2006).[4] An individual's position on Lamu's social hierarchy was endorsed based on observed everyday comportment or on how intersections of wealth, genealogy, and moral disposition were mediated in lived practice—from dress to employment and accent: "a mungwana was a person who dressed in a certain way, ate certain foods, earned his livelihood in certain ways, attended to his prayers assiduously, lived in certain types of houses, behaved in certain ways in public, and above all, spoke the vernacular Swahili well" (Pouwels 1987, 73).

Heshima was also linked to understandings of leisure and labor. Because wealth partly determined social status, a nobleman's ability not to engage in labor also imparted *heshima*. This respectability, however, did not derive merely from not working, and an important distinction existed between "leisure" and "laziness" (McMahon 2006, 208). Laura Fair describes how in Zanzibar Town men's leisure time spent on the *baraza* socializing and disseminating news was "an essential element of community membership" (Fair 1997, 236). In contrast to laziness, leisure could then be defined as "both non-obligated activities . . . and activities that involve fulfilling social obligations, such as membership of an association or visiting relatives" (Martin 1995, 7; quoted in McMahon 2006, 208). While noblemen demonstrated their *heshima* by not working, someone who was considered lazy would still have less *heshima* than a hardworking person (McMahon 2006, 208).[5]

Lamu's social hierarchy, however, did not always focus exclusively on respectful conduct. Rather, it shifted from an emphasis on racialized belonging to economic wealth and subsequently to everyday displays of respectability in accordance with transformations in the town's socioeconomic composition, particularly at the end of the nineteenth century (see the Introduction). As they progressively lost prestige based on genealogy and political and economic power, Lamu's patrician elites increasingly emphasized *heshima* as a distinguishing factor of their noble status and authority. The primary criterion for social status attribution was then no longer what a person *did* but what a person *was*, emphasizing virtue and religiosity (Iliffe 2005, 5). Precisely this shift from a nobility of rank to a nobility of character provided the merchant elites with a means to retain their high social status in a changing social context (Appiah 2010; Iliffe 2005).

This new focus on noble character had important implications for life in Lamu. While viewed as an inner quality of the individual, the family as a whole possessed *heshima* (see also Porter 1998). The responsibility to uphold social standing therefore rested with all family members.[6] This resulted in an overall increase in public monitoring, with individuals' behaviors becoming subject to scrutiny and control. Upper-class men were expected to display respectful behavior, and notions of proper conduct comprised, for example, appropriate greeting styles and language use, respecting norms of hospitality, proper dress (for example, wearing a *kanzu* or *kikoi*), and not eating in public (Caton 1986). Women's covering and seclusion in particular became a matter of social prestige (Gower, Salm, and Falola 1996). Indeed, the separation between men and women in communities like Lamu is a much more recent phenomenon, introduced at the beginning of the twentieth century, rather than an established religious practice, as it is often portrayed to be (Askew 1999). The current discursive construction of a time where women lived segregated and protected their virtue is therefore a reflection upon a recent past rather than an accurate depiction of "historical times."

Gender segregation became an important indicator of class status because seclusion was not equally available to everyone. High-class women increasingly avoided public or open spaces, such as streets and markets, and generally remained inside the house, relying on housemaids to run errands. This did not mean that elite women did not have a social life. Making use of *wikio*—closed walkways connecting houses above the streets—or rooftops, they regularly visited family and friends and lead active social lives (Gensheimer 2018) (see Figure 4). If upper-class women did leave the house using the street, they only did so after the sunset prayers while covered by a *shiraa* and accompanied by slave girls. This covering consisted of two sticks holding up pieces of cloth—a tent-like construction—under which women walked (see Figure 5). After the abolition of slavery, women

Figure 4. A Lamu alley with a *wikio*, or walkway. Photograph by Sarah Hillewaert.

Figure 5. Demonstration of traditional *shiraa*. Photograph by Ashikoye Okoko.

carried their own *shiraa* and young children or family members would accompany them.

Notions of respectable behavior (and associated social status attribution) were thus meaningfully linked to material practices. Different locales within town, however, were also imbued with moral value, with conduct at Lamu's harbor area being distinct from behavior in the interior of the town, for example. The moral geographies of different neighborhoods or streets, and the boundaries between them, allowed for the monitoring of public conduct of respected families as well as newcomers. In other words, spatial divisions at different levels of Lamu society—ideological boundaries between different areas within town and segregations within the Swahili house—facilitated the regulation of a social hierarchy structured around *heshima*. Moreover, an awareness of spatial divisions' ideological value facilitated the presentation of self and the evaluation of others.

Degrees of Separation: Spatial Boundaries as Moral Values

Spatial structure played a historical central role in Lamu residents' conceptions of self and evaluations of others. As the Introduction laid out, Lamu Town was an urban milieu broadly structured by its dual and oppositional division into two neighborhoods, each tied to a series of ideological and material contrasts: "Arab" versus "African," stone structures versus daub-and-wattle houses, rich versus poor, free men versus slaves, representing both a spatial and social order (Bissell 2005; Hillewaert 2018). Discussing the politics of conversion in colonial East Africa, Derek Peterson similarly describes the importance of space and spatial boundaries as a source of moral knowledge in a range of communities throughout Eastern Africa. He argues that spatial divisions—walls, fences, screens— organized human sociability and formed a guide to respectful behavior (2012, 17). More than mere boundary markers, physical features like fences enabled the separation of intimate from public relations, and regulated subjects' comportment within these different spaces. Privacy, honor, and architecture were meaningfully linked in communities like the Luo, the Kikuyu, the Masaai, and the Swahili, whereby reputation building was "a cooperative discipline," requiring people to monitor their appearances and to conduct themselves with reserve (Peterson 2012, 17–19).

This central, regulating role of spatial and ideological boundaries within the social life of Lamu residents has not gone unnoticed by historians, archaeologists, and even architects conducting research in the Lamu Archipelago.[7] Emphasizing separation as a central social organizing principle, Prins (1971) proposed that Lamu's division into the two main residential areas of Mkomani and Langoni (and previously Zena and Suudi) reflected a dual principle central to the town's social hierarchy and political management rather than being the mere result of historical settlement patterns. Other descriptions of Lamu focus on the gendered nature of spatial separations and underline the distinction between male open, public spaces and female closed, domestic spaces (Allen 1979; Fuglesang 1994; Middleton

1992). Studies of Swahili architecture similarly highlight the importance of spatial partitions in Lamu's stone houses for the maintenance of privacy and the regulation of social interaction (Allen 1979; Donley-Reid 1982, 1987, 1990; Gensheimer 2018; Ghaidan 1975; Kamalkhan 2010; Wynne-Jones 2013).

In present-day Lamu, however, a range of people increasingly crosses these physical and ideological boundaries due to social, political, and economic shifts. Young women leave the house for studies or work, new immigrants settle where they can find a home to their liking, impoverished families alter the structural layout of their home to accommodate more people or rent out rooms. These changes not only complicate moral judgment and status evaluations for observers, but they also challenge the hegemony of the previously dominant understanding of *heshima* and its mediation within practice.

Contemporary Lamu, for example, remains divided into two distinct neighborhoods: Mkomani and Langoni. This division is a historical one and echoes the distinction between Zena and Suudi reported in Lamu's origin myth. In the past, wealthy patrician elites resided in Mkomani, and (former) slaves, temporary guests, and recent immigrants lived in Langoni. This geographical division then also entailed an ideological moral opposition; the "civilized" *waungwana* were distinct from the "unrefined" *washenzi* living in Langoni. The dual organizing principle of this geographic and social separation was also reflected in competitions between, for example, Lamu's soccer teams, bands, and dance groups, whereby each team represented one of these two neighborhoods (Ranger 1975). While today it is no longer the case that only former merchant elites reside in Mkomani, and while newcomers or immigrants from surrounding islands no longer are destined to settle in Langoni, the geographical division retains an ideological significance to Lamu residents (see also Heathcott 2013).

In present-day Lamu, Mkomani continues to be known as the upper-class, quiet, respectful, and less-crowded neighborhood, whereas Langoni is occupied mainly by immigrants from Lamu's surrounding islands and is famous for its hustle and bustle, its multitude of businesses, and its never ending coming and going of a wide array of people. "Life in Langoni is 24/7," I was often told. For residents of Mkomani, and especially for women, a visit to Langoni is a "journey." One does not merely go for a walk and end up on the Langoni side of town; it is a destination often explicitly stated and justified: "I am going to Langoni to visit this particular store or visit a distant relative." For many Langoni residents, going to Mkomani is equally exceptional. Yet transgressions of spatial boundaries are nevertheless happening more frequently due to social, political, and economic changes. Youth from Mkomani attend schools located on the Langoni side of town. Some former elites are only able to afford a house in Langoni, whereas waBajuni might opt to rent or buy an apartment in Mkomani. Newcomers to the island, such as Kikuyu, on the other hand, are often oblivious to or could not care less about these historical distinctions tied to social class and genealogy and settle where it suits them best.

While movement between the different areas of town has thus become more frequent, and while (elite) women no longer live in *purdah*, another set of spatial divisions facilitates the public monitoring of (one's own and others') behavior in present-day Lamu. Specifically, there are moral values associated with the two streets that run parallel through Mkomani and Langoni, as well as the maze of backstreets that typifies both neighborhoods. The first street—*usita wa pwani* or the seafront—is a male-dominated area, always crowded with porters unloading boats, elder men sipping coffee on a *baraza*, idle young men looking for something to do, and tourists wandering around. Parallel to the seafront runs *usita wa mui* or Lamu's main street, a crowded avenue with stores located alongside it. A third area consists of the town's backstreets, a labyrinth of tiny alleys in both neighborhoods.

A woman's choice between strolling down the town's seafront (see Figure 6) and walking along Lamu's main street or opting for the quiet backstreets is meaningful. The use of the alleys provides anonymity and limits encounters with other residents, whereas walking along the seafront entails being seen mostly by men. Lamu's main street is a busy, mixed-gender space. A woman's choice between these different routes is not neutral, but rather makes a statement about social class, origins, piety, and the notion of respectability she adheres to. While fifty years ago an unaccompanied upper-class woman would have violated norms of appropriate conduct by walking via Mkomani's backstreets by herself, her current walking via these narrow alleys entails an attempt at maintaining a social status structured around a formerly hegemonic notion of *heshima*. Some young Bajuni women, on the other hand, might view walking along the seafront as a claim to a modern or urban demeanor and a clear defiance of previously taken-for-granted understandings of respectability. The ideological value of social space in Lamu is thus gradually being redefined to accommodate changing moral values and social hierarchies.

Like the division between Mkomani and Langoni, these three parallel running areas can be viewed as determining different degrees of intimacy, informing social control, and placing different limits on social interaction.

Figure 6. Lamu seafront. Photograph by Eric Lafforgue.

Precisely the semiotic value of the town's spatial layout—the meanings as-cribed to neighborhoods and streets—enables observers to link individu-als' physical location at a certain time of day to their social status, respectability, and moral personhood. At the same time, an awareness of (previously) dominant ideological understandings of places and times al-lows individuals to strategically rely on these as tactics in presentations of self. An individual's route and behavior when walking these different paths are therefore crucial means to assess, reproduce, or challenge understand-ings of respectability and social status.

A third and final set of spatial divisions that historically informed and reproduced a particular hegemonic view of *heshima* can be found in the ar-chitecture of Swahili stone houses, as these exemplify degrees of separa-tion that regulate interaction at the most intimate level.[8] Facades of former merchant elites' stone mansions are generally windowless, shield-ing wealth, women, and private lives from the eye of the passerby. This lack of windows and the thickness of walls prevent any sound from in-side the house to be heard outside on the streets. These blank, high walls are interrupted only by house entrance porches, flanked by *baraza*, open-ing into the house through a monumental doorway—the door, its richly carved frame, and the size of its lock being the only outside signs of the family's wealth; the bigger the door and the greater the lock, the more prominent the family (Aldrick 1990; Kamalkhan 2010; Gensheimer 2018). This door generally opens up to a wall or a staircase that prevents outsiders from seeing the inside, family life. The outside stone benches fulfill an important social function, since these allow the men of the house to entertain casual visitors without having to invite them inside the house, accommodating the importance of hospitality as well as the need for privacy and limits to visibility.

A Swahili stone house's interior generally consists of an open courtyard and three or four parallel spaces or galleries. The first space functions as a sitting area where close friends and family are entertained. While being intimate, it is also recursively the most public—most similar to the *baraza*. The second space is the children's sleeping area, while the third forms the parents' private quarters. The fourth, most back area (*ndani*) is a space kept for either giving birth or for accommodating someone's last hours. The doors to these different galleries are often though not always strategically misaligned to prevent visibility from one section into the other, blocking visitors' view of the parents' quarters or more intimate spaces (see Figure 7).

These mansions often had an additional high wall located next to the wall that blocked the view from the entrance. Between these two dividers was a narrow space where the women of the house could stand to answer visitors knocking on the door, if the men of the house were not home. It is said that the hollow, narrow space altered the sound of a woman's voice, such as to protect her respectability. A part of her appearance that should be covered out of dignity or modesty—an aspect of her *'awrah*—a woman's voice was not supposed to be heard loudly by strangers (through shouting or singing, for example). The echo of the narrow space was said to alter and thus "cover" a woman's voice, when responding to a visitor knocking on the door.

Ghaidan (1975) describes this layout of Swahili stone houses as an "intimacy gradient," ranging from the most public *baraza* to the most intimate space of life and death. In many ways, the Swahili stone houses formed an iconic representation of the merchant elites' hegemonic notions of respectable conduct. As a "structuring structure" (Donley-Reid 1990), the houses' architecture mirrored and produced (ideological understandings of) social categories of individuals, ranging from the most distant outsider to the most protected (female) intimate (Wynne-Jones 2013, 762). At the same time, however, these stone structures acquired their value as "civilized" and "respectable" only in contrast to the "barbarian" daub-and-wattle huts that comprised Langoni.

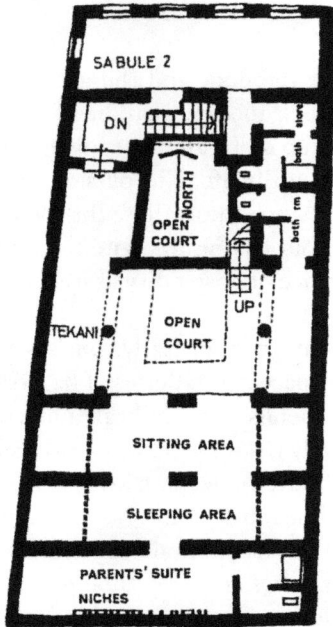

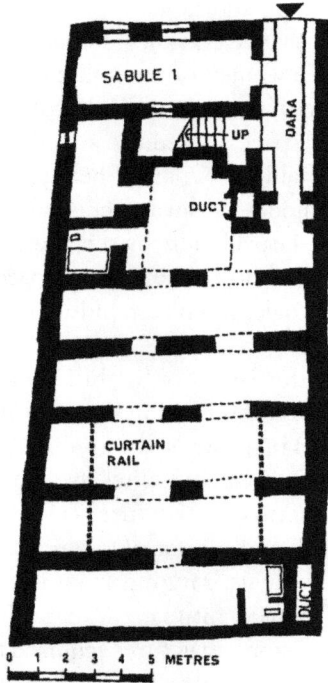

Figure 7. Layout of a Lamu house. From Ghaidan (1975).

Historically, houses in Langoni never had a layout similar to Mkomani's mansions as residents generally lived in one- or two-room huts. Merchant elites' notions of *heshima* were therefore impossible to uphold. Even in present-day Langoni, new houses are not built following the old architectural principles, even if their owners are wealthy. Residents now claim to build "modern," "Western-style" stone houses that are more convenient than the often dark, windowless galleries of the historical mansions. Opting for a layout consisting of, for example, a sitting room, kitchen, and several bedrooms, however, also means that previously hegemonic notions of respectability are difficult to adhere to. Depending on its structure, noises from inside the house are easily heard on the street and front doors frequently open up to the home's main living space, where one could easily catch glances of (uncovered) women. The lack of a front porch makes it difficult to entertain visitors outside and male guests are much more easily invited inside the home. On the Mkomani side of town, on the other hand, former elites often struggle to upkeep their stone houses and either sell them to Euro-American expatriates or divide the galleries up into separate rooms to house more people. The contrastive distinctions between the architecture of these two neighborhoods, and their "structuring structures" are therefore increasingly challenged and redefined.

Despite these present-day changes, the detailed overview of spatial divisions at different levels of Lamu society paints a visual picture of how spatial boundaries historically enforced the merchant elites' hegemonic notion of proper conduct and enabled the maintenance (and reproduction) of a social hierarchy based on *heshima*. These ideologically loaded locales, however, were meaningfully produced by time as well, in terms of both their historical significance and the very real influence time has on the interpretation of an individual's actions. The time of day one encounters someone permits judgments about the appropriateness of their presence at that particular location, but the rhythm or pace of the activity an individual engages in also avails a set of evaluative judgments—the slowness of a young woman's pace, the length of her greetings, and the speed of her speech are all subject to appraisal and allow for judgments of the individual's *heshima* and moral personhood.

These different spatial and temporal divisions form a semiotic expression, a material form, of an ideological link between morality, belonging, and social status (Hirsch 1998). Indeed, these embodied ideologies of space and time form part of what Bourdieu (1984) called a *bodily hexis*—a complex of words, gestures, postures, and movements charged with social meaning and value and indicative of one's position on the local social ladder. An individual's ability and willingness to understand, maintain, and respect those boundaries and regulations previously reflected their social status and moral character, and a particular kind of belonging to the Lamu community; it situated them on Lamu's social (and, indeed, topographical) map.

In contemporary Lamu, many continue to consider a woman's ability to display modesty and avoid less intimate spaces (like *pwani*, the seafront) as determinative of her *heshima* and social status. A young woman is viewed as having *heshima* when she is able to maintain particular boundaries of intimacy—to refrain from playing with a man's senses through gaze, smell, or voice. At the same time, however, and as was alluded to throughout this chapter, sociopolitical and economic shifts progressively challenge both what these boundaries are and to what extent upholding them remains a sign of respectability. Just as a man's sitting on a *baraza* is no longer necessarily a moral good, so is a woman's staying at home no longer an indisputable sign of her uprightness. Indeed, a single mother who leaves her house to work and provide for her family is arguably more respectable. Walking in front of a *baraza* can then still be considered as lacking *heshima* because it avails a woman to the male gaze, yet observers' attention now lies with *how* she passes in front of this bench, looking for other embodied signs that could provide information about her pious or defiant intentions.

As boundaries are crossed and redefined and as new material practices are introduced, however, the social equilibrium structured around a particular hegemonic notion of *heshima* is being challenged as well. While Lamu's social structure was contested and reshuffled in the past, newcomers to the island previously had a vested interest in incorporating themselves into a social order controlled by merchant elites and shaped partly by descent, partly by economic wealth, and partly by displays of virtue and respectability. Yet contemporary *wageni* (guests)—immigrants from surrounding islands in the archipelago, mainland newcomers, as well as Euro-American expatriates—do not necessarily seek integration into this particular social hierarchy and bring with them other practices that conflict with previously hegemonic understandings of proper conduct. These transformations do not just cause another reshuffling of the social hierarchy; they challenge the very meanings of *heshima* and the social order it informs. With Islam at its core, this renegotiation of respectability entails questions of social status, but also importantly concerns views of religious piety and Islamic virtue. And whereas non-elite Lamu residents might challenge previous elites' understanding of what *heshima* ought to look like, newcomers like mainland Christians from the Kikuyu ethnicity are considered a threat to an Islamic lifestyle that informs notions of respectability. All of these shifts, however, are perceived to be a consequence of Lamu's integration into an independent Kenya.

Lamu residents' focus on *heshima* and its loss in contemporary discourses of social change thus refers not only to an actual loss of respect among youth; it also speaks to shifts in an (ideological) social structure in which the *waungwana* (noblemen) are at risk of becoming *watumwa* (slaves)—or worse, *washenzi* (savages)—by forsaking their norms and values in favor of an adherence to nonlocal, non-Islamic, and often Western practices. *Heshima* can therefore be considered a "multiplex sign" (Briggs 1988): an ideological notion that both refers to and indexically calls upon a whole social and political system, an entire social order associated with the past (Hill 1998, 266). Talking about a loss of *heshima* in present-day Lamu not only signifies, for example, impolite language use among the town's younger generation; it also refers to the disappearance of complex sets of social roles, material practices, and sociopolitical perspectives. At the same time, however, these challenges to a hegemonic ideology determined by former merchant elites creates new opportunities for those previously situated at the lower end of Lamu's social hierarchy (Comaroff and Comaroff 1991). Given these shifts in social structure and moral authority, I now return to residents' contemplations on life in present-day Lamu, and specifically to their discursive reconceptualizations of what it means to be "from Lamu" today.

Proverbs and the Discursive Reconceptualization of Self-Other Relations

Talking about notions of identity among East Africa's coastal residents, historians have frequently depicted Swahili towns as "plural societies" (Furnivall in Brennan 2012), a portrayal that recognizes the diversity of East Africa's coastal culture but that underlines the tranquil coexistence of different social groups within it. Scholars were often baffled by the fluid and indeterminate identification of coastal populations.[9] In the 1960s, for example, Prins (1961) wrote that inhabitants of Lamu rarely thought of themselves as belonging exclusively to any one racial or ethnic category (a person was never Swahili and nothing else), and observed that individuals constantly crossed and straddled what outsiders (and colonial administrators) perceived to be racial or ethnic boundaries. This notion of ethnic fluidity was partly motivated by Lamu Town's continuous incorporation of different groups of newcomers—from Oman, Yemen, Shiraz, India, and Portugal—and partly based on residents' own shifting identifications throughout coastal history. While newcomers' position within Lamu's social hierarchy depended on their adherence to and embodiment of local expectations toward respectful behavior, and although notions like *ustaarabu* were indeed racialized, these evaluations remained—to a certain extent—fluid rather than rigid or based on supposedly inherent traits.

In short, there never existed a clearly delineated "Lamu ethnicity." While one might live in Lamu, one's social identities were differently determined by genealogy, social class, neighborhood residence, religious practice, and displays of respectability. For example, someone might identify as *mwenyeji* (an original inhabitant of Lamu), but also as *muungwana* (someone with *heshima*), as *mwArabu* (Arab), *mSwahili* (a Swahili), *muIslamu* (a Muslim), and so forth. While these categories overlap, explicit identification with any one of them depended on context and interlocutor. The *baraza* elder whose contemplations on life in contemporary Lamu opened this chapter, however, appeared to suggest that belonging to Lamu had never been unconditional and that there had existed clearly defined expectations for newcomers to be recognized as Lamu residents.

Before a fellow-*baraza* member interrupted him, the elder had rebutted others' suggestions that new technologies were negatively impacting life in present-day Lamu and had corrupted the town's younger generation. Offering an extensive critique of the Kenyan government and its migration policies, the elder argued that newcomers' disrespect for local moral values was the main reason for rapid social change. The elder provided lengthy examples of government administrators' ineptness, tribalism, and laziness and thereby established an iconic-like relation between these newcomers' outward, everyday practices and their inward moral condition, identifying both as a cause for Lamu's current disarray. He did not decry the arrival of mainland immigrants only on grounds of political domination or economic disenfranchisement. Rather, the elder judged and condemned newcomers on moral grounds: They were untrustworthy, insincere, and undisciplined. Indeed, the terminology the elder used to depict the behavior of mainland Kenyans resembled the terms with which Swahili patrician clans in the past referred to their slaves, who likewise were thought incapable of honoring the values of Swahili culture and civility.[10]

As his spirited critique came to an end, the elder pondered why all Kenyans now felt the need to come to Lamu. Lamu surely belonged to Kenya, but did Kenya not have thirty-eight provinces? Did he have an equal right to move to another part of Kenya, like Kisumu, for example? In response to this rhetorical question the other *baraza* member had uttered

"Hiyo ndiyo Amu, atakao nae"—"This is Lamu, whoever wants to can come"—suggesting that migration, the arrival and permanent residence of newcomers, had always formed an integral part of life in Lamu. The proverb implies that the moral value of hospitality is at the heart of "being from Lamu." The elder's response, however, argued that Lamu residents never meant the saying to be an open-ended invitation, welcoming whomever arrived on the island to stay permanently. Instead, there had been clear conditions to residence on the island. In certain ways, then, the elder's reaction appears to contradict the foregoing historical discussion of the town's social hierarchy as seemingly rigid but effectively fluid and diverse, with newcomers gradually being integrated into the town's social structure and this structure's changing over time.

In his response, the elder drew upon the historical distinction between *uungwana* (nobility) and *ushenzi* (savagery) and reflected upon a time when newcomers valued and respected the moral authority of Lamu's patrician elites. He did not present these moral conditions as attainable dispositions, but rather spoke of them as inherent characteristics, thereby giving his rebuttal a more explicit racialized tone. Discursively linking individuals' moral conditions, not only to their appearances, but also to territory, culture, and language, the elder's argument, in fact, seemed informed by contemporary discourses on ethnic identity in postcolonial Kenya. Although drawing upon the ideological understandings of *uungwana* and *ushenzi*, he did so to reject the fluid and hospitable Lamu identity invoked by the proverb and thereby drew clear lines around what it meant to be— and become—an inhabitant of Lamu. Indeed, his statement appeared to echo arguments raised by the Mwambao movement that strove for autonomy of the Kenyan coastline around Kenyan independence.

While seemingly nostalgic in its depiction of historical Lamu as a clean and morally upright town, the elder's argumentation was therefore highly political and cannot be fully understood separate from the rising tensions surrounding land rights and discussions about political recognition at the Kenyan coast in 2008. While exhibiting a continuation of dominant ideologies on similarity and difference, the elder linked the moral values that inform these distinctions to an increasingly polarized conception of clearly delineated and territorialized identities. By connecting his critique of Lamu's current condition to Kenya's political context, the elder's statement proposed a reevaluation of what it means to be "from Lamu" in contemporary Kenya.

Because the *baraza* has always been a space for political and philosophical debates, it maybe should not come as a surprise that discussions on life in present-day Lamu were quite political. What interests me in these discourses, however, is not so much that social changes are linked to political transformation, because they are. Rather, what fascinates me is that notions of rightful belonging, historically defined by situated perceptions of moral uprightness, are increasingly talked about as rigid, inherent, and tied to territory. *Uungwana*, rather than a moral quality that can be achieved and on the basis of which someone can be incorporated within the community, is now discursively constructed as an inherent quality of all Lamu residents, who are always already presumed to be Muslim. The social diversity within Lamu Town and, indeed, the fluid social hierarchy based on complex and shifting intersections of genealogy, wealth, race, and respectable conduct are thereby discursively erased. More importantly, internal differentiations—local disagreements between former merchant elites and, for example, Bajuni residents about what constitutes respectability, who embodies it, and how it ought to be mediated in practice—are similarly erased in discourses that oppose Lamu to the Kenyan mainland, presenting a supposedly recognizable and clearly delineated "Lamu identity." And while this elder phrased his arguments in a nostalgic discourse, reminiscing on a childhood during which Lamu smelled like jasmine, similar sentiments were expressed in distinctly different spaces, by much younger Lamu residents.

Not long after I discussed the *baraza* debate with my research assistant, I noticed on my Facebook newsfeed the same proverb to which the elder had responded so agitatedly. In fact, I encountered it twice, although the second occurrence took a slightly different formulation. Facebook had become increasingly popular during my three-year residence in Lamu. With smartphones and data packages becoming more affordable, Lamu youth increasingly joined social media platforms and often had friend networks that extended well beyond Lamu, including people living in Mombasa, Nairobi, the United Arab Emirates, Britain, Europe, and North America. In addition, Facebook groups had become quite popular among Kenya's coastal youth, and new groups were created quite frequently, often focused on cultural conservation, religious practice, or politics. But Facebook also was a means for residents of Lamu who had moved abroad to stay connected with friends and family at home and to reminisce about life on the island.

The status update that caught my attention appeared to be part of such nostalgic reflection. Having just returned to London after a visit to her hometown, a young woman updated her profile status to "*hiyo ndiyo Amu, atakao nae,*" meant to express how much she missed Lamu. While she had left, she was longing to return. She thus called upon the popular meanings of the saying: The hospitality of Lamu residents causes one to never want to leave again. The status update received a long list of responses, mostly from young people currently living on the island. The majority of reactions, however, were posted in response to the initial comment on the original status update:

Siku hizi watu husema "hii ndiyo Amu, ina wenyewe." Msemo umepitwa na wakati.

Nowadays people say "this is Amu, it has its owners." The proverb has been passed by time.

Contrary to the *baraza*-elder, this Facebook user did not clarify or contextualize the proverb to explain to the young woman its correct usage and its inapplicability to contemporary newcomers. Rather, the author offered a reformulation of the saying, which they considered more befitting to the contemporary context: What defines Lamu nowadays is not its hospitality but locals' sense of ownership and rightful belonging. The author did not recall historical conditions for Lamu residents' openness, but rather explicitly claimed possession of Lamu Town and thus effectively expressed a changed moral attitude of its inhabitants—a shift from hospitality to territoriality. In fact, the implications of replacing *"atakao nae"* (whoever wants to, can come) with *"ina wenyewe"* (it has owners/original inhabitants) run much deeper than a mere claim to ownership.

The phrase *"ina wenyewe"* is a political slogan that derives from the Tanzanian and Kenyan struggles for independence. It was used to oust the British colonizer and to strive for freedom of the Swahili coastal strip, including the battle for an independent Zanzibar. This reformulation of the well-known proverb therefore carried significant political implications, with historical hospitality being replaced with a call for political action and even separation (of Lamu, from Kenya) (see Figure 8). The discursively constructed notion of a Lamu identity, based on moral uprightness as an inherent quality, which we saw emerge earlier from the elder's argumentation, was now explicitly politicized and territorialized, replacing even more evidently the notion of a fluid, incorporative identity that determined life in Lamu in the past.

The call for political action, constructed around references to historical battles for independence from Kenya, took an even more categorical tone in a third reformulation of the proverb I encountered. It was 2009, and Lamu's annual Cultural Festival was about to commence. Initiated in 2001, following the town's recognition as a UNESCO World Heritage Site, the festival is described as "a celebration of both the past and the

Figure 8. Graffito: *"Hii ndiyo Amu. Ina wenyewe."* (This is Lamu. It has its owners.)
Photograph by Sarah Hillewaert.

future, and the beliefs and traditions that are the heart and soul of the
Lamu community."[11] The weeklong festivities display the cultural diversity of Lamu Town, exhibiting dances, foods, and dress styles from the different social groups living on the island and are meant to attract both
national and international tourists. A few days before the start of the festival, I noticed that one of my interlocutors, a young man of approximately
twenty-three, had updated his Facebook status to *"hiyo ndio Amu atakao
nae,"* thereby signaling the approaching start of the yearly celebrations and
welcoming (inter)national visitors to the island. Over the years, the proverb had been printed on banners, flyers, and T-shirts to evoke both Lamu
residents' hospitality and the town's cosmopolitan heritage that formed the
focus of the festivities. The Facebook status thus was not really remarkable; the reactions it received were. The following was one of them:

> My friieeend! Hutosha! Wamezie kuya, mui umeyawa. Kumekua
> kuteleeee, mpaka sisi tumekua ni wageni. Sasa ni "HINI NDIYO AMU
> FANYENI MWENDEZENU"

> My friend! Enough already! They already came and the town is full.
> There are too many, to the point where we ourselves have become the
> *wageni* (guests). Now it is "THIS IS AMU NOW HURRY UP AND GO HOME"

Contrary to the elder's earlier reinterpretation of the saying, this explicit, emphatic reformulation of the well-known proverb did not stipulate the conditions under which people were historically welcome to stay in Lamu. And while the author echoed the rejection of the original proverb's contemporary relevance found in the previously discussed reformulation, this sentence invoked territoriality and ownership even more explicitly. Reminiscent of anti-immigrant, nationalist discourses, this particular contribution to the Facebook post argued that Lamu residents ought to claim possession of their town and refuse to welcome new immigrants. It turned the original saying on its head, expressing a shift from hospitality to hostility. Lamu having reached its hosting capacity, guests now threatened to overtake the locals as owners of the town. Indeed, the author of the post warned Lamu residents that they as *wenyeji* or original inhabitants were at risk of becoming *wageni* or guests. According to this author, "*hiyo ndiyo Amu,*" this is Lamu, was no longer meant to call upon a sense of hospitality or historical diversity. Rather, it ought to inspire *wenyeji*, the original inhabitants, to expel newcomers.

Much like nationalist discourses, this notion of territoriality and rightful ownership was further enhanced by the author's linguistic performance. Implicitly linking territory, language, and cultural identity, the author wrote their contribution entirely in the distinctly recognizable local dialect, kiAmu. Words such as *wamezie* and *hini* as well as phonetic features like the /y/ in *umeyawa* identify the author as *wenyeji*, as an "original" inhabitant of Lamu Town. In fact, some of the words (like *mui*) would be considered archaic. While young people selectively incorporate details of the vernacular in their online practices, writing entire contributions in kiAmu seldom occurs (Hillewaert 2015). This author's remark therefore stands out because they are taking a stance through their writing practices. Through this nonstandard orthography, the author identifies themselves as mwAmu—as *mwenyeji* and even as *muungwana*—but simultaneously challenges what these social categories ought to stand for in present-day Kenya. Informed by translocal discourses, language, culture, and territory are linked to notions of authenticity and rightful belonging, and thereby appeal to a seemingly clearly defined and shared understanding of what it means to be "from Lamu" in contemporary Kenya.

Conclusion

The discussions on Lamu's seafront *baraza* and on Facebook were strikingly similar, despite the very different spatiotemporal locations and participatory frameworks of the interactions. While each nostalgic in their own right (invoking notions of historical cleanliness, cosmopolitanism, and authority), the narratives were also meaningfully shaped by local and transnational discourses on dispossession, citizenship rights, and the postcolonial state. The analysis of these discourses showed that claims to *heshima* and the supposed loss thereof in contemporary Lamu are not mere nostalgic reflections, but also important political tools. Much as "cosmopolitanism" can function as a nativist discourse (Glassman 2014; see also the Introduction), so can discursive invocations of moral personhood and its identification in observed practice play a central role in claims to rightful belonging and accusations of imposition.

At the same time, however, the discourses analyzed here erased the voices of those social groups whose presence these individuals are reacting against. While not interacted with or integrated into the conversation, all interlocutors referred to the presence of mainland Kenyans (mostly from the Kikuyu and Meru ethnic groups) and Euro-American tourists or expatriates. Many of the discourses examined, however, also spoke about Lamu's youth and their behaviors. The discursive redefinitions of self-other relations analyzed in this chapter are precisely the backdrop against which we ought to understand ideological evaluations (and judgments) of Lamu youth. Present-day reconceptualizations of what it means to be "from Lamu" not only draw rigid and clearly defined distinctions between the previously more fluid categories of "Lamu inhabitant" and "guest"; they also already entail condemnations of those who are seen as straddling these boundaries. As they endeavor to negotiate newly emerging subject positions, young Lamu residents are thus particularly vulnerable to moral judgments. Indeed, the morally responsible engagement with change—the moral presence—Ustadh Taha called for in the Introduction to this book is not a social position readily available to young people, nor is it equally accessible to all. As we will see, the semiotic embeddedness of *heshima*, though increasingly contested, entails that young people's renegotiations can easily be viewed as moral transgressions. And because societal change is perceived as a consequence of government imposition, alleged indiscretions can easily be evaluated as signs of political orientation as well.

The next chapter zooms in on precisely this point: on the political implications of the seemingly mundane and of details of language use in particular. Whereas appropriate social interaction has already been highlighted as essential to an individual's embodied *heshima*, ideological evaluations of such everyday practices are equally informed by discourses on political marginalization, economic deterioration, and global Islam. Just as residents' conceptualizations of belonging shift in relation to observed outcomes of supposed macro-sociological processes, so do appraisals of individuals' linguistic practices and the associated assessment of their moral disposition. As we will see, seemingly minute details of language have historically carried important social meanings in Lamu, and these significations are constantly redefined, reimagined, and reinvigorated in relation to contemporary processes of change. Precisely this semiotic sensitivity of linguistic detail enables youth to strategically use language in the negotiation of newly emerging social positions.

CHAPTER 2

Dialects of Morality

In December 2013, shortly after moving to Toronto, I attended my first Swahili wedding in the city. A few weeks earlier, a friend of a friend had introduced me to a young Kenyan-Canadian woman named Sauda, who soon invited me to the women-only event. She had told me that the Swahili community in Toronto was quite large and insisted I meet women from Lamu and Mombasa living in the city. Arriving at the wedding hall, I glanced at the many unfamiliar faces. Sauda quickly walked over, greeted me warmly, and then grabbed my hand to introduce me to her friends. "Auntie Zahra!" Sauda called one of the women who were busily conversing. "This is my friend Sarah, she just moved to Toronto but used to live in Lamu." The woman's face lit up when she saw me. "It is you!" she proclaimed loudly, "you're the girl from the video!" Surprised as I was, I smiled and nodded my head. Zahra enthusiastically grabbed my arm and pulled me along as she introduced me to the women present. "Look!" she declared every time. "It's the girl from YouTube!"

In early 2008, about a year into my fieldwork, an employee of the National Museums of Kenya introduced me to a reporter from KTN, one of Kenya's national television networks. He told the reporter that I was a scholar who researched young people's language use, and particularly the gradual loss of the Swahili vernaculars spoken in the Lamu Archipelago. "But listen to the way she speaks kiSwahili," he said with an amused tone of voice. At the time, I did not understand what he meant. While I knew my kiSwahili had become fluent during my time in the field, I was not fully aware of the extent to which I had acquired the local vernacular, kiAmu, in terms not just of vocabulary but also of distinctive pronunciations, intonation, and even hand gestures that often accompany speech. I agreed to be interviewed about my research, and the fifteen-minute interview was aired a couple of weeks later, right after the kiSwahili evening news. I was in Mombasa at the time and was unaware of the interview's being broadcast. The next day, people recognized and addressed me on the street and complimented my fluency in kiSwahili. This continued for several weeks. The interview was aired numerous times again and the video appeared on YouTube, where it received approximately 50,000 hits. In the years that followed, that same video circulated on Whatsapp and Facebook. Even in 2019, more than ten years after it first aired, people continue to send me the interview via social media. It was this video to which Zahra referred when she first saw me at that wedding in Toronto.

What is so interesting about that interview, and why does it keep resurfacing? I often ask my friends when the video appears, once again, on my Facebook feed. Surely, I am not the only *mzungu* (white person) who speaks kiSwahili? My friends tend to smile and say that while some *wazungu* might speak kiSwahili, very few speak kiAmu, the vernacular from Lamu. Moreover, they said, my intonation and body language were very much "kiAmu." Those details—the fully embodied appropriation of the vernacular—caught people's attention more than the mere fact of my speaking kiSwahili, my friends suggested.

Still, people's positive responses to the video had baffled me even when I was living in Lamu. Young people I interviewed often told me they disliked speaking dialects like kiAmu; they blamed the predominance of vernaculars in Lamu for their low performance in school, where Standard Swahili is the norm. Many youth also explained how they avoided speaking kiAmu when traveling to cities like Mombasa or Nairobi. Not wanting to be ridiculed as sounding backward for speaking a vernacular from an area that is now often perceived as remote and underdeveloped, they described how they often switched to Standard Swahili or to kiMvita— the variety of kiSwahili spoken in Mombasa. Being the language taught in schools, Standard Swahili signaled young people's education (and countered stereotypes of underdevelopment), whereas the use of kiMvita demonstrated their familiarity with an urban context. Some young people, however, expressed a preference of kiMvita over Standard Swahili, as the Mombasa vernacular distanced them from Lamu without having to adhere to the (Christian) government-imposed standard. Not all youth, however, shared this view. While a minority, some young people explained that they insist on speaking kiAmu when traveling to the mainland, despite the stereotypes they often encountered. To them, speaking kiAmu was a matter of pride of and respect for their cultural heritage, but also of taking a stance toward and distance from the Kenyan government. Nonetheless, even some of these youth agreed that Standard Swahili was "correct" language use, as opposed to the "incorrect" vernaculars. Young people's linguistic practices, however, were informed by much more than mere notions of correctness in relation to the standard.

When I first arrived in Lamu, I knew little kiSwahili and had little grasp of the different vernaculars and language varieties that made up Lamu's linguistic landscape. My friends in Nairobi had warned me that coastal people spoke "difficult" kiSwahili and that interacting with people from Lamu would undoubtedly distort my knowledge of Sheng, the urban youth language spoken in Nairobi (and other major cities of Kenya). Because I had previously conducted research on Sheng, I spoke the urban youth language quite well, although my friends often pointed out that my vocabulary had become rather dated.[1] The flipside was that my knowledge of Standard Swahili had diminished significantly, and I struggled not to insert Sheng (or English) into my conversations.

During my first weeks in Lamu, I therefore frequently apologized for my broken or deficient use of kiSwahili to the young men with whom I interacted at the time. Friendly and approachable, the beach boys who hung out at the seafront had formed my initial link to the Lamu community. I often inadvertently greeted them using Sheng or incorporated English verbs in kiSwahili grammar. For example, I would say *nitacome* instead of *nitakuja* when I told someone I would join them later. Much to my surprise, these young men refuted my claims to a lack of kiSwahili proficiency. On the contrary, they praised my language use. When they noticed my confusion, they clarified that they were the ones who didn't speak proper kiSwahili, since they used "outdated" or "incorrect" dialects and had only limited knowledge of the standard language, let alone Sheng. They ought to learn from me, they suggested laughingly. And while they appeared to be joking, I somehow became these young men's reference for translations of song lyrics and words that were introduced through popular media or travels to Mombasa and Nairobi. I struggled, however, to follow their conversations. During my first months on the island, I often did not fully understand my interviewees, who then made an attempt to speak "proper" kiSwahili or "translated" from the dialectal variety they spoke.

As time went on, I gradually learned to speak kiSwahili more fluently, consciously leaving out English vocabulary and urban jargon. And I progressively began to distinguish the different varieties of kiSwahili so often referenced by Lamu residents: distinctions in vocabulary and pronunciation between the local kiAmu dialect and the kiBajuni varieties from the surrounding islands, or the distinctly different intonation associated with kiMvita. I began to recognize people who came from Nairobi based on their use of either Standard Swahili or kiBara, a variety of kiSwahili spoken by mainland Kenyans (Bryan 2017; Wald 1985). Most important, however, I started to grasp the social meanings with which these language varieties were imbued and began to understand the role seemingly minute linguistic differences played in forming social relations, presenting oneself, and evaluating others.

These opening anecdotes speak to the social and political significance of linguistic and broader semiotic details in the everyday interactions of Lamu residents. They also illustrate, however, the situatedness or social embeddedness of linguistic competencies and evaluations of them. What it means to speak a language is not a given. Instead of being set in stone, assessments of fluency and value depend on who is doing the speaking, who is doing the evaluating, and the spatiotemporal embeddedness of the interaction. While we—the women in Toronto, the beach boys, the people watching KTN evening news, users of the Internet, my friends in Nairobi, and I—all spoke kiSwahili, the value attributed to the different kinds of kiSwahili we all spoke depended on the context in which the evaluations occurred. My friends in Nairobi had considered my knowledge of Sheng inadequate, yet the young men at Lamu's seafront evaluated my use of the urban youth language positively and even appropriated some of the vocabulary I used. My use of Sheng to greet elders when walking along Lamu's backstreets, only a couple of streets removed from the seafront, however, was considered neither admirable nor valuable. Similarly, my friend Maryam found my initial use of Sheng hilarious as she endeavored to explain to me how rude, inappropriate, and "mainland-ish" I sounded. Residents of Mombasa and, later, Toronto evaluated my use of kiAmu positively, both because of the rarity of the occurrence and because of the national broadcasting of a *mzungu* speaking an otherwise devalued kiSwahili vernacular, rather than the mainland-imposed standard language. Those same Mombasa residents, however, would poke fun at a young man speaking the

dialect of Lamu while in the city, calling him backward and unsophisticated. And although my friends in Nairobi thought I spoke Standard Swahili quite well before leaving for Lamu, residents of Lamu Island found my
kiSwahili proficiency to be lacking. At the same time, both my use of Sheng
and kiAmu would have been considered deficient forms of kiSwahili within
official contexts—in a classroom, for example, or when submitting a piece
of writing to Taifa Leo, a kiSwahili newspaper.

I provide this account of my own experiences to illustrate both the complexity of young Lamu residents' linguistic repertoires and the social
meaningfulness of language, and particularly of linguistic detail, within
the context of Lamu. Lamu residents not only recognize a range of local
vernaculars, but they also attribute different values to what institutions
(such as schools or government offices) consider inadequate deviations from
the kiSwahili standard. As this discussion demonstrates, however, these
ideologies are neither homogenous nor hegemonic. While a standard language ideology—the view of the standardized form of kiSwahili as "better" or "more correct" and thus more valuable—is spreading quickly among
the younger generation through education and administration, a political
consciousness also progressively ascribes value to local vernaculars. Within
the Lamu Archipelago itself, different vernaculars are associated with distinct social groups and with Lamu's social hierarchy. Just like nostalgic discourses and the signs of social change they emphasize are indicative of a
speaker's social and ideological positions toward the contemporary context, so do language attitudes and the details of linguistic practice on which
they focus entail processes of social differentiation as well as moral and
political stance-taking.

Multiple, often conflicting ideologies inform Lamu youth's everyday linguistic practices, but they equally affect how others evaluate these practices within local and translocal contexts. The anecdotes recounted thus
far exemplify how language varieties can be valued and devalued within
different, situated interactions (Blommaert 2010) and therefore speak to
the long-accepted understanding within linguistic anthropology that languages do not simply exist "out there." Rather, they are ideological objects
whose very definitions are invested with social, political, and cultural interests (Blommaert, Collins, and Slembrouck 2005; Gal and Woolard 2001;
Haviland 2003; Irvine 1989; Irvine and Gal 2000; Schieffelin, Woolard,
and Kroskrity 1998; Silverstein 1979; Kroskrity 2000).

To this understanding of languages as interactionally and ideologically
constructed and evaluated, this chapter adds the notion of moral value; it
addresses how people imbue language varieties with notions of morality

and uprightness. Within the context of Lamu, knowing how to speak and when to use or avoid particular varieties become signs of the speaker's *heshima* or respectability and thus their moral disposition. The previous chapter described displays of *heshima* within everyday interactions as a determining factor in the attribution of social status in Lamu. I thereby emphasized physical appearances and the appropriation of upper-class consumer habits, but I also made mention of language use and accent as part of the semiotic toolkit residents use in presenting themselves and evaluating others. The young man who responded on Facebook to the well-known proverb that formed the focus of Chapter 1, for example, did so by writing distinctly recognizable kiAmu. While this use of the vernacular identified him as mwAmu and while it reflected his *heshima* within the local context, he also risked being ridiculed as backward by other, nonlocal Facebook users. At the same time, however, his language use clearly identified him as coming from the Lamu Archipelago, a region increasingly viewed by the government as an area where political and religious extremists might come from. One can then ask how evaluations at different levels of society impinge upon young people's language use and how they shape Lamu youth's everyday negotiations of newly emerging social positions.

Understanding the historical and sociopolitical processes through which nuances in language acquired social meanings provides insights into how everyday social interactions can become part of individuals' moral and political vocabulary. Linking Lamu residents' notions of incorrect or appropriate language use to the town's (changing) social hierarchy and to the island's relation to the Kenyan mainland (see Introduction and Chapter 1) reveals the remarkable semiotic potential of language varieties and linguistic detail. It provides insights into language attitudes as affects, as situated responses to processes of disenfranchisement whereby a clearly defined and sufficiently distinct vernacular is central to claims to a redefined (ethnolinguistic) identity. At the same time, however, I place these locally situated discourses in relation to other evaluations, of vernaculars as incorrect, as archaic and backward, as associated with extremist (political or religious) ideologies.

The detailed discussion of Lamu's linguistic landscape that follows forms an essential background to understanding the various considerations young people make in everyday interactions and the central role linguistic practices play in the negotiation of a particular kind of moral presence as a "good" young, modern Muslim in contemporary Lamu. A question that will emerge is precisely how young Lamu residents use language to negotiate newly emerging social positions when faced with scalar and often conflicting ideologies. At the same time, one might ask how residents of Lamu evaluate young people's linguistic practices, given the strong language ideologies discussed here.

Lamu's Linguistic Landscape

In Lamu Town, six different varieties of kiSwahili are used next to the standard language.[2] In addition, kiMvita (also known as kiMombasa, the dialect of Mombasa), English, and Arabic can be heard and seen to different extents throughout the town. International tourism brought languages such as Spanish, French, and different varieties of English (such as American, British, or Australian English) to the island. In addition, immigration from Kenya's mainland increasingly introduces other ethnic languages, like Kikuyu, to Lamu's linguistic landscape. Young people in Lamu encounter and use these language varieties in different ways and to different extents in their day-to-day lives.

Standard Swahili, for example, is the language of instruction in primary education and Lamu children are expected to speak and write Standard Swahili when attending school. The majority of media—be it the national broadcasting corporations, print media, or radio stations like BBC World—equally use Standard Swahili. The popularity of Tanzanian music also exposes young Lamu residents to Standard Swahili through popular culture. In addition, all government administration uses either English or Standard Swahili. Inhabitants of Lamu therefore encounter the standard language when watching the evening news, reading a newspaper, consulting a textbook, filling out official forms, or listening to music.

Lamu residents speak English with different degrees of fluency, access to the language being determined by disparate contact with secular education, new forms of technology (including satellite TV, Internet, and cellular phones), or Euro-American tourists. This process of differential acquisition creates important register effects; the "kind" of English people speak becomes indicative of their educational and social background. In colonial East Africa, contact with English (as the language of the colonizer) was strategically constrained by regulating access to education and by encouraging the use of vernaculars (like kiSwahili) in official communication. Restricted to the higher echelons of colonial society, English became the language of political, social, and economic progress. When reaching independence in 1963, Kenya appropriated colonial language policies and retained English as the medium of instruction in education, kiSwahili becoming a compulsory school subject only in 1981 (Chimerah 1998;

Ogechi 2003; Whiteley 1969). The status of English as a prestige language was further reinforced through its use in government, judiciary, and other official contexts.

In Lamu, children hardly use English within daily interaction. The only context where they are expected to display active knowledge of English is within school walls, and while schoolgoing youth use the language daily, their ability to communicate in English remains rather limited. This contrasts with the English of Lamu youth whose families sent them to secondary schools in Mombasa or Nairobi, for example, and who often continue their studies at the college level. When walking through Lamu, one can nonetheless notice snippets of English: stores advertise their products in English (next to kiSwahili and Arabic), American song lyrics are painted on walls, and local theaters announce the newest movies using English. Locals, both men and women, are devout soccer fans, and the logos of Manchester United, Arsenal, or Manchester City can be found throughout the town (see Figure 9). In short, access to media technology together with the presence of Euro-American tourists and expatriates have made English somewhat common in Lamu and encounters with the language are not restricted to the school environment or administrative context. Few Lamu residents, however, speak the language fluently, and even those who do generally do not use it frequently in everyday interactions.

Figure 9. Soccer graffiti on a Lamu wall. Photograph by Sarah Hillewaert.

Language contact is not new to the Lamu Archipelago; on the contrary, kiSwahili is itself an example of longstanding language borrowing along the East African coast and across the Indian Ocean (see, for example, Nurse and Spear 1985; Walsh 2018). Still, locals experience the current context, shaped by encounters with Standard Swahili and English, as one of unprecedented language change and loss. Throughout my fieldwork, Lamu residents (and particularly elders) lamented the loss of dialect diversity. And while young people acknowledged the historical significance of local vernaculars, they blamed education, popular media, and travel for their diminishing familiarity with the dialects and their frequent switching to Standard Swahili, English, or urban variants of kiSwahili.

These discourses on language loss echoed the narrations of moral transformation discussed in Chapter 1. Indeed, these previously analyzed discussions about social change often focused on the altered linguistic practices of Lamu youth as a sign of young people's changing moral conditions. Lamu residents (both young and old) spoke about the past as a time when language varieties were clearly distinct and, importantly, valued and respected. Such nostalgic reflections not only recounted this linguistic history to reminisce about the island's glorious past; they also ascribed meaning, value, and a distinct status to language varieties like kiAmu.

I do not intend to discuss here to what extent the Lamu vernacular was linguistically distinct from, for example, kiMvita or kiShela and how much of the dialect is currently disappearing. Linguists have previously documented the Northern Swahili Dialects (e.g., Nurse and Hinnebush 1993), as they are formally called, and kiAmu's historical status as a literary language is unquestioned (e.g., Vierke 2011, 2014). Rather, I am interested in Lamu residents' discursive emphasis on kiAmu's historical distinctiveness and suggest we should see this as an affective stance, as an ideological position informed by the same process of cultural, political, and religious anxiety that animates Lamu's cultural production more general. Residents of contemporary Lamu assess observed language change in relation to discursively recounted historical distinctions and attribute different moral values to individuals' perceived maintenance or dissolving of such linguistic boundaries. Indeed, the discourses analyzed in what follows will reveal possible creative adjustments to kiAmu, emphasizing distinctions or alterations that might make kiAmu more "like itself"—reinvigorating, elaborating on, or even exaggerating its differences from mainland varieties.[3] This present-day awareness of and insistence on the dialect's particularity is thus not some form of fraught history but should rather be understood as a way of defending a broader set of (ideological and moral) conventions against the onslaught of the standardized language and, especially, the government that imposes it. In other words, Lamu residents' views on language change are never only about increasing language contact or diversity, but always already encompass attitudes toward politics, ethnicity, race, and religion.

The "Dialects" of the Lamu Archipelago

"KiSwahili" was spoken along the East African coast as early as the tenth century, but up until the creation of Standard Swahili under colonial rule, the language existed only in a range of what are now considered dialectal variations (see also Irvine 2008). KiAmu, kiMvita, and kiBajuni, for example, were recognized, distinct variants of kiSwahili, each linked to important city-states along the East African coast (Bakari 1985; Mazrui and Shariff 1994; Nurse and Hinnebusch 1993; Nurse and Spear 1985; Stigand 1915; Walsh 2018; Whiteley 1969). Today, kiSwahili vernaculars remain important within local contexts, but they are not recognized as distinct varieties (and thus mother tongues) at the national level. Within the Lamu Archipelago, residents use and emphasize the distinction between six varieties of kiSwahili: kiAmu, kiShela, kiMatondoni, kiPate, kiSiyu, and kiBajuni, each associated with different settlements on the islands. Jointly, these language varieties are known as the Northern Swahili Dialects (Nurse and Hinnebusch 1993; Nurse and Spear 1985).

The contemporary significance and local insistence on the separate status of these varieties of kiSwahili need to be understood in relation to the region's history. Specifically, each of the Northern Swahili Dialects is associated with previously prosperous city-states located in the Lamu Archipelago. Each of these city-states dominated trade in the region at one point in history and the historical, political, and economic rivalry between them is well documented. The shared memory and nostalgic recollection of these different pasts ensures the lasting emphasis on distinct social identities and the linguistic differences believed to represent them.

Of the Northern Swahili Dialects, kiAmu is arguably the best known. While Lamu's economic and political power indisputably aided kiAmu's historical fame, it was its status as a language of poetry that resulted in its recognition along the East African coast. With a stable written form and established poetic conventions, kiAmu was a famous literary language that was in use as early as the fifteenth century (Harrow 1991; Knappert 1979; Mazrui 2007; Vierke 2011, 2017; Zhukov 2004). Epic poems like the *Hamziya* (1652) and *Al-Inkishafi* (1749; see Figure 10), for example, were

Figure 10. Handwritten manuscript by Muhammad bin Abubakar bin Umar al-Bakariy of Lamu, 1910. From Ibn Nasir and Hichens (1939), courtesy of Sheldon Press, London.

written in the kiAmu dialect, using Arabic orthography.[4] Although these texts were written in the late seventeenth and early eighteenth century, Knappert comments on the perfection of style and argues that for such writing conventions to exist there must have been a tradition of writing epics in Arabic script, perhaps dating to a century before the writing of *Hamziya* (Knappert 1999, v; see also Vierke 2014, 320). Clarissa Vierke similarly comments on the longstanding written literary tradition in the Lamu Archipelago. In her discussion of Swahili *tendi*—one of the major poetic genres in kiSwahili—Vierke underlines Lamu's prominence as a cultural and literary center in the nineteenth century and kiAmu's status a "prestige dialect associated with the literary field" (Vierke 2011, 307). Poets from Mombasa and Tanga, for example, appropriated features of the dialect for stylistic reasons, a trend Mazrui (1992) refers to as "Lamuisms" (Vierke 2011, 307; see also Biersteker 1996). Until today, Lamu is celebrated for having skilled poets, the majority of whom continue to write their poetry in kiAmu rather than Standard Swahili and many of whom use Arabic script rather than Roman orthography.

The status of kiBajuni as a distinct dialect is equally undisputed, and linguists have gone as far as to suggest that the Bajuni ought to be considered a separate "ethnolinguistic unit."[5] With its 20,000 speakers, kiBajuni is the widest spoken of the Northern Dialects, a status historians attribute to the Bajuni tribes' previously strong position along the Kenyan and Somali coasts (Nurse 2011).[6] This historical status, together with an economically and politically marginalized position in contemporary Kenya and Somalia, resulted in an increasing sense of ethnic identity among the Bajuni, as separate from other Swahili-speaking residents of the Lamu Archipelago. People who identify as Bajuni progressively underline the status of kiBajuni as a distinct variety of kiSwahili, detached from other vernaculars such as kiAmu, or as a different language altogether. Organizations such the Shungwaya Welfare Association or websites like bajuni.com focus on the preservation of Bajuni linguistic and cultural practices.

This call upon a distinct identity is supported by a governmental recognition of Bajuni as one of the forty-three ethnicities of Kenya, in contrast to "Swahili" or "Amu," for example, who are not acknowledged as ethnic groups and who are required to identify as Bajuni (or Kenyan-Arab) in order to obtain a national identity card. The contemporary political and administrative recognition of waBajuni affects their position within Lamu Town, where they previously occupied a lower social position as recent immigrants or refugees. WaBajuni's (renewed) claims to historical and cultural authority and authenticity therefore progressively challenge Lamu's social hierarchy, and particularly waAmu's claims to primary settlement and embodied *heshima*. Debates on language loss and change within Lamu cannot be separated from these shifts in the town's social stratification.

While all of the Northern Swahili Dialects continue to be associated with different towns located within the Lamu Archipelago, these Swahili vernaculars are now also all spoken within Lamu Town as a consequence of migration to the urban center of the archipelago. Whereas this resulted in increased contact between these vernaculars, the majority of Lamu residents (including immigrants from surrounding islands) proclaim to uphold dialect boundaries. Although such claims to dialect maintenance are questionable from a language contact viewpoint, several factors contribute to these assertions. One of these is Lamu's previously discussed topography, whereby newcomers to Lamu historically settled in the Langoni area of town, whereas the *wenyeji* or merchant elites predominantly lived in the neighborhood of Mkomani. The spatial and ideological boundary between Mkomani and Langoni then increasingly also entailed a language boundary. KiBajuni, kiPate, and kiSiyu were predominantly spoken in Langoni, whereas kiAmu was mostly heard in Mkomani. Among Lamu's younger generation, however, this boundary is becoming increasingly porous as young people across the social divide go to the same schools and forge friendships. While still aware of the differences among and social meanings attached to the different local varieties of kiSwahili, Lamu youth are familiar with, appropriate, and differently use a range of dialect features.

KiMombasa: Historical Competition and Contemporary Appeal

Located along the coast about 220 miles from Lamu, Mombasa is an important port city that contributes considerably to Kenya's economy. A successful city-state in the past, Mombasa also played a significant role in the history of the Swahili coast and had a long-standing rivalry with Lamu. Mombasa's current economic success, however, contrasts sharply with Lamu's deteriorated condition, and Lamu inhabitants' resentment over this "victory" is evident in the sometimes-tense relationship between inhabitants of both towns. Like kiAmu, kiMvita was renowned in the past and was used to write poetry and praise, including the famous *Muyaka* poem (Abdulaziz 1979). Because of the economic and political power of Mombasa and the prominence of kiMvita as a literary language, this variety of kiSwahili was long proposed as the variant on which Standard Swahili ought to be based. Early descriptions of the kiSwahili vernaculars considered kiMvita to be evidently distinct (Krapf 1882; Stigand 1915) and its separate status was equally recognized in later linguistic studies (Driever 1976; Nurse and Spear 1985).

Lamu residents suggested to me that kiMvita, while still distinct from Standard Swahili, was now most recognizable by its melodious or "singing" intonation, its distinct phonology and morphology having been lost because of the exposure to and influence of the standard language. When people from Lamu suggest that Mombasa residents are no longer capable of speaking "true" kiMvita, however, they make judgments not only about factual language change but also about these residents' moral conditions. Having preferred urbanization and economic prosperity to cultural (and religious) preservation, residents of Mombasa were said to have forgotten and devalued cultural practices (and identities), with language at its core. Lamu elders and parents therefore lamented young people's increasing fondness of "kiMombasa" (a more popular reference to the present-day form of kiMvita) over kiAmu, as it suggested a (moral) superiority of the former. And while elders would emphatically tell me they did not change their language use when traveling to cities like Mombasa or Nairobi, many young people admitted to using kiMombasa when traveling to the city. As highlighted earlier, they argued that the urban dialect made them appear developed, cosmopolitan, and more attractive (see also Hillewaert 2015).

I elaborate on the different, locally recognized, varieties of kiSwahili spoken in Lamu Town and their ideological evaluations because these linguistic distinctions play a central role in young people's everyday interactions. Because of the long-standing, often tense, historical relations between previously prosperous city-states along Kenya's coast, language use has always been a primary index of not just geographical origins but also genealogy, wealth, and social status. As Chapter 1 already underlined, these categories cannot be separated from judgments of respectability and morality. I previously emphasized that evaluations of an individual's *heshima* were based on judgments of outward appearances, norms of interaction, as well as language use and accent. A nobleman or *muungwana* knew how to properly interact and spoke the local dialect well. Newcomers to the island were then not only judged based on what they looked like but also on how they sounded, being evaluated by seemingly minute details of intonation and pronunciation that revealed the visitors' background and status. It is therefore not surprising that discourses on social change and the perceived associated moral transformation of the community frequently take young people's language use as the prime example of deteriorating moral conditions. Such judgments, however, are also informed by the increasing imposition of Standard Swahili and the devaluation of dialectal varieties at the national level (see also Wald 1985).

Standardization of Swahili: A Colonial Project

When the British arrived at the East African coast in the late nineteenth century, they encountered kiSwahili as a widely spoken lingua franca with a long-standing literary tradition. The language, however, in different ways defied the colonizers' ideological understanding of what a (standard) "language" ought to be. For example, there did not exist one single or "unified" Swahili language in precolonial East Africa (Peterson 2006); the range of dialectal varieties contradicted Herderian language ideologies that prescribed that a people (and a nation) ought to be defined and united by one, "coherent" language. In addition, the presence of an extensive literary tradition, combined with successful centers of trade and Islamic scholarship challenged explorers' preconceptions of the African continent (LaViolette and Wynne-Jones 2018; Mazrui 2016; Ray 2018). The written tradition, with its Arabic orthography and focus on Islamic virtue, was consequently seen as foreign to the local context (Mazrui 2016; Topan 1992; Vierke 2014; Wald 1985).[7] Mazrui (2016, 17–18) emphasizes that it was precisely the presumed Islamicity of the Swahili language—partially reflected in the language's extensive borrowing from the Arabic language—that worried missionaries and colonial educators. Conversion to Christianity and the purging of all "foreign" elements were considered a necessity to restore the "natural condition," and to subsequently allow Africans to become truly civilized, colonial subjects (Broomfield 1930, 1931; Roehl 1930). This "purification process" or "dis-Arabizing" (Mazrui 2016) entailed a switch from Arabic to Roman orthography, the replacement of Arabic vocabulary with "African" concepts, and the establishment of one standard language in which the Bible could be translated (Irvine 2008; Mazrui 2016; Topan 1992; Vierke 2014; Wald 1985). The result was to be "a pure, noble—if the expression is permitted—rebantuized Swahili" (Roehl 1930, 199, quoted in Mazrui 2016, 19). While Gerald Broomfield objected to Roehl's call for a non-Arabic Swahili, arguing it was a "contradiction in terms," Reverend Dr. Johann Ludwig Krapf considered a switch to Roman script essential to the missionary project, believing Arabic orthography would sustain and facilitate Islamic influences (Mazrui 2016, 20).

While a concern for missionaries, standardization and "dis-Islamizing" of kiSwahili was equally important to the British colonial project (Mazrui 2016; Topan 1992). Colonizers were in need of an effective means to communicate with their colonial subjects and a linguistic medium that would aid economic transactions; a lingua franca like kiSwahili could facilitate that. The language's Arabic orthography, its lexical borrowings from Arabic, and its dialectal variations, however, alienated colonizers and prevented a much-needed (linguistic) control over administration and education—elements vital to creating and maintaining symbolic power (Fabian 1986). With no unified language at hand, standardization of kiSwahili became a matter of both "political and practical urgency" (Peterson 2006, 8).

This writing and reworking of African vernaculars like kiSwahili allowed missionaries, linguists, and entrepreneurs to envision their particular imagined communities, thereby often creating rather than documenting ethnic or tribal groups (e.g., Irvine 2008; Peterson 2006). Contrary to Leonard Bloomfield's (1933) view of the standardization process as a natural step in a language's development, there was nothing organic about the standardization of kiSwahili under colonial rule. The standard language had to be designed, constructed, and purified—a task assigned to East Africa's Interterritorial Language Committee in 1930, involving actors with varying and sometimes clashing interests and points of view. This committee determined not only the Swahili variant on which the standard was to be based but also the language's "correct" phonemic structure and its spelling and grammar rules.

The standardization process itself was largely driven by the United Mission to Africa, headquartered in Zanzibar, and spearheaded by Gerald Broomfield (1930, 1931) and Edward Steere (1919). Both had written grammars on the Swahili language, were proponents of the language's re-Bantuization, and proposed the Zanzibari dialect to form the basis for a standardized kiSwahili. These linguists were challenged, however, by the Church Missionary Society, headquartered in Mombasa and supported by Ludwig Krapf (1882) who championed the use of kiMvita. Whiteley (1969) recounts the struggle between these two camps and suggests that it was Zanzibar's prominence as a political and economic center (and thus practical rather than linguistic reasons) that eventually formed the determining factor in the Committee's decision (see also Chimerah 1998).

There was nothing inevitable or intrinsic to the Committee's decisions regarding the spelling system or vocabulary of what was to become Standard Swahili (Peterson 2006, 11). Rather, the standardization process enabled missionaries to purge Arabic from the Swahili language and represent their own interests. Minutes from the Committee's meetings suggested that, for example, the unnecessary introduction of Arabic words and expressions, where equally good and expressive Bantu words existed, would create difficulty and confusion for mainland speakers (Mazrui 2016; Peterson 2006). Ignoring the functionality of distinctive aspirations, implosives, and consonant clusters, thinking them imports from Arabic, the committee eliminated these features in the new spelling system, creating a language and an orthography that many mother tongue speakers considered inadequate.[8] Khalid (1977), for example, illustrates the lexical confusion caused by this "purification" of kiSwahili by discussing the orthography of the words for "river" and "pillow," both rendered as *mto* in Standard Swahili orthography. In the vernaculars, the words are distinguished by (non)aspiration of the voiceless stop /t/. Khalid (1977) suggests that the erasure of distinctive aspiration in Roman orthography and subsequent loss in pronunciation causes "the Swahili [to] laugh when he hears the European, or his African pupil, or even a mother-tongue speaker of the Zanzibari lingua franca, assert that he rested his head on a river, or else that he went swimming in a pillow" (Khalid 1977, 168).[9]

Despite the missionary reports and academic reviews that underlined the Interterritorial Language Committee's decisions as faulty and inadequate, Standard Swahili was implemented with little alteration in official circles and education. Alamin Mazrui (2016) discusses how this establishment of the new standard language and its Roman orthography through the missionary project and the colonial school system worried Muslim clerics, who objected to the perceived "dis-Islamization" of kiSwahili. Calling upon coastal Muslims to boycott Standard Swahili and the education system through which it was imposed, Muslim scholars argued that kiSwahili was "not pure except by its mixture with Arabic."[10] Mazrui marks the fascinating claim to linguistic purity in these objections to the newly standardized language, highlighting that purists generally argue for the removal of those words or idioms that are perceived to be linguistically "foreign." Yet here we see exactly the lauding of "a concept of purity based on (selective) hybridity—the mixture between the indigenous (Bantu) and the foreign (Arabic)—emphasizing once again the perceived centrality of Arabic and Islamic civilization in the construction of Swahili" (Mazrui 2016, 26). As will be discussed, we encounter similar ideologies of linguistic purity among some Lamu residents today.

When independence reached Eastern Africa, despite the many objections to the newly standardized language, Swahili became the national and official language in Tanzania and a national language (next to English) in Kenya, where it became an official language only in 2010. In Kenya and Tanzania, Standard Swahili is used in all printed literature, in (primary) education, and official government business, both written and oral (Wald 1985). The standardization of kiSwahili, then, could be considered a success when viewed in terms of a colonial project that endeavored to design a language that facilitated communication across different ethnic groups, or as a postcolonial project needing a language that was not tied to any one particular ethnicity (Chimerah 1998; Polomé 1967). At the same time, the implementation of this standard variety did not instill a sense of national unity among Kenyan citizens, as its usage remained associated with the Swahili coast (Chimerah 1998; Whiteley 1969). Moreover, mother-tongue speakers of kiSwahili never acknowledged the authority of its standard variety, and many continue to reject the standard language's imposition in both administrative and educational contexts. In many ways, kiSwahili then defies established understandings of notions such as "language," "dialect," or "mother tongue." The Swahili language refers to a set of linguistic practices that are recognizable as belonging to the same "unit," yet the elaborate diversity within it is simultaneously indicative of complex social identities on different levels of society. It thus defies conceptions of "ethnolinguistic units" in more than one way, something that is the case for many descriptions of African languages (Irvine 2008).

While the creation of Standard Swahili erased dialectal differentiation in official knowledge production, linguistic diversity on the ground continued to shape social interactions and relations. The institutionalized linguistic hierarchy—the linguistic regime of value—it was able to put in place, however, created a negative evaluation of linguistic diversity in relation to the standard: divergence from the imposed linguistic norm became iconic of speakers' lack of education or marginality (from the view of the center). The political recognition of a standard language and its associated functions in official contexts defined other languages or dialects in direct relation to it. While used to invoke or appeal to a national identity in postcolonial contexts, Standard Swahili therefore simultaneously created a state-endorsed inequality (Kroskrity 2000, 28). Artificial as standard language projects may be, their political impacts are real and significantly influence individuals' and communities' linguistic practices. Wald (1985), for example, observed how language attitudes among speakers of kiMvita shifted under influence of this ideology of the "monoglot standard" (Silverstein 1996) and noted how the standard language quickly came to be associated with economic prosperity. Such stances toward Standard Swahili are equally present in Lamu and inform young people's everyday linguistic practices. At the same time, however, this standard language hegemony (Silverstein and Urban 1996) is never total or complete, and objections to it are informed by historical consciousness and political orientations.

Stances toward Standard Swahili in Lamu

We have to refrain from using the term "*kiSwahili Sanifu*" to refer to Standard Swahili. *Sanifu* in Swahili means "the best" or "the most beautiful." The standard language is not the best variant of our Swahili language and this term should not be used to talk about this impoverished version of the language.[11]

It was November 2010, and I had just presented a paper at the inaugural research conference of RISSEA—the Research Institute for Swahili Studies of Eastern Africa—in Mombasa. I had focused my discussion on the influence of Standard Swahili on educational achievements of schoolgoing youth in Lamu, and a rather agitated discussion (in kiSwahili) unfolded quite quickly after I ended my presentation. Among the audience were elders from both Lamu and Mombasa, many of whom were respected poets and teachers. The majority of audience members, however, were university professors, authors, and other educators from Kenya's mainland and from Tanzania, many of whom spoke kiSwahili as a second language.

In response to my paper and my argument that the imposition of Standard Swahili undermined educational achievements of children in Lamu and contributed to dialect loss in the archipelago, attendees disagreed whether Swahili dialects ought to be recognized in school curricula and what then the status of kiSwahili Sanifu—the kiSwahili term for Standard Swahili—ought to be. Upon hearing the frequent use of the notion kiSwahili Sanifu, Mwalim Soud, a prominent resident of Lamu and a retired teacher, demanded the microphone. Visibly agitated, he reprimanded attendees (including me) for using the term kiSwahili Sanifu to refer to the standardized variety of kiSwahili. While he recognized the status of Standard Swahili in contemporary Kenya (and in Eastern Africa more broadly), he vigilantly objected to anyone calling it *sanifu*, which he translated into English as "correct" or "the best." Contrary to what the use of *sanifu* implied, Standard Swahili was not "the best" form of kiSwahili, so he claimed; it was merely functional.

Derived from Arabic, many people would translate *sanifu* as "constructed," rather than "the best" or "correct" and *kiSwahili sanifu* then literally means "the constructed Swahili language." However, in popular perception *sanifu* has often come to be associated with "the best"; when something is *sanifu* it is the most correct form and the norm against which vernaculars are evaluated as incorrect. Contrary to the previously discussed inability of the standard language to adequately represent the vernaculars, speakers of kiAmu or kiMvita have come to object to dialect use precisely because these do not adhere to standard language orthography. Wald (1985) aptly illustrates the fallacy of this ideology by describing how Mombasa youth object to the vernacular use of *ndoo* instead of the Standard Swahili *njoo* for the imperative "come!" The former, his interlocutors explained, is identical to the word for "bucket," and it therefore sounds quite ridiculous. Yet Wald points out that the two words are pronounced differently in kiMvita, whereby the consonant cluster in *ndoo* (come!) has a dental pronunciation, with the tongue touching the upper teeth, whereas *ndoo* (bucket) is pronounced alveolar. Standard language orthography, however, does not allow for this distinction and thus fails to represent the vernacular adequately. Young people's objection to words like *ndoo* based on notions of correctness, however, demonstrates the hegemonic nature of the standard language ideology and the authority of the educational system through which it was imposed. It was exactly this linguistic hegemony against which Mwalim Soud objected.

Following Mwalim Soud's remark, the debate at the conference got quite heated: Given the fact that Standard Swahili was a construct, what then constituted "Swahili literature"? Why did publishers refuse manuscripts written in, for example, kiAmu? Was it not ironic that mother-tongue speakers of kiSwahili could not produce "Swahili literature"?

Mwalim Soud was not alone in his critical stance toward Standard Swahili, nor were local intellectuals or poets the only ones who lamented the increasing domination of the standard. Indeed, many of my interviewees elaborated at length on the (semantic and grammatical) richness of kiAmu and its regrettable disappearance as a consequence of Standard Swahili's imposition. Although Lamu residents recognize Standard Swahili's official status, and thus its linguistic and social value (Bourdieu 1992), its imposition within media, administration, and education (to name but a few) is considered indicative of increasing, government-induced disenfranchisement and cannot be separated from broader discourses on societal (and moral) transformation. For inhabitants of Lamu, the imposition of Standard Swahili signifies much more than the looming disappearance of local dialects. These ideological connections between the imposition of the standard language and perceived government marginalization were most evident in discussions pertaining to the schooling system and orthography. In analyzing these discourses, it becomes evident that interlocutors' opinions on Standard Swahili were often just as much about Lamu residents' orientation to and the archipelago's integration into the Kenyan nation, as they were about linguistic quality or notions of correctness.

KiSwahili in the Educational System

When asked about the reasons why young people increasingly avoid speaking kiAmu or kiBajuni, Lamu residents were quick to refer to secular education. Schoolgoing youth along the coast, including the Lamu Archipelago, are administratively considered mother-tongue speakers of kiSwahili, yet students quite frequently obtain failing grades for this school subject. Parents and children alike explained that students often struggle to recognize distinctions between the "correct" standard they are expected to speak at school and the "incorrect" dialectal varieties they use at home. Teachers, however, spend little time instructing students on the standard language and its writing conventions, precisely because pupils are viewed as mother-tongue speakers. Seen as contributing to educational failure, vernaculars are therefore avoided by students and parents alike. These explanations, however, often also had a political undertone inasmuch as they linked educational policies to the postcolonial state, the supposed tribalism of the government, and the ensuing dispossession of coastal populations and Muslims in particular.

Consider, for example, Mohammed's reflections upon the increasing loss of kiPate among youth. The excerpt below derives from a lengthy discussion between my research assistant, Mwalim Baddi, and his close friend Mohammed, who had been reminiscing about the beauty of local dialects and particularly the distinctions between varieties such as kiAmu, kiPate, and kiSiyu. After having asked Mohammed to provide examples of kiPate, Mwalim Baddi (MB) had wondered why young people no longer used these dialects. Mohammed (M) was quick to respond, blaming the local schooling system and focusing his critique on the presence of schoolteachers from the mainland rather than from Lamu.

M. Ile shule ile, kuna somo la kiSwahili lakini kiSwahili chenyewe si cha Kipate. Si Kipate. Ndrio sasa hapo alipokuwa mwanangu husoma akawa hufeli kiSwahili. Chukaankuliwa na walimu hadi masta kulee. Kwa nini hawa ni waSwahili wakafeli kiSwahili? Nkamwambiya, naam ni lazima wafeli kiSwahili. . . . Sasa atakuya hapa mwalimu atakayemsomesha mwanangu kiSwahili atoka Meru. Mmeru atoka Meru, au ni Njaluwo wa kutoka Taita. Hoko waye hawaisi namna ya kiSwahili, wawe wamekiona kitabuni tu. . . . Kama alipachikana mwalimu wa kutoka nyumbani hafeli kiSwahili. Kosa lilikuwa ni kwa sababu mwalimu atakuya ni kutoka bara bwana. Tukula bwana, tukula ati chule. Sasa kukula nnini? [laughs]

MB. Si kiSwahili.

M. Sasa itachiziye asifeli na imeandikwa kwenye kichabu, ndo ashafeli. Kwa heri bwana!

M. That school over there, they teach kiSwahili but the kiSwahili taught is not kiPate. It is not kiPate. So when my child went to study he failed kiSwahili. So the headmaster called us. Why do they fail for kiSwahili and they are waSwahili? I told him, yes of course they fail for kiSwahili. . . . Now the teacher who will teach my child kiSwahili comes from Meru. A Meru from Meru, or a Jaluo from Taita.[12] They come here but they do not know the ways of kiSwahili, they just saw it in books. . . . If there had been a teacher from home, he [my child] would not fail kiSwahili. The problem is that the teacher is from the mainland. *Tukula*, my friend. *Tukula*, meaning let's eat (*tule*). What is *kukula*? [laughs]

MB. It is not kiSwahili.

м. Now how can he not fail kiSwahili if it is written in books like that. That is why he already failed [before he begun]! It's over my friend!

Mohammed recounted how he had been summoned to a school in Pate, following his son's failing of kiSwahili as a school subject. How is it possible, the teacher had asked him, that local students continue to fail kiSwahili despite the fact that they are mother tongue speakers of the language? Suggesting that the teacher implicitly accused his son of stupidity, Mohammed laughingly pointed out the irony of these allegations. His son failed kiSwahili not because he was incapable of speaking or writing the language, but because the kiSwahili taught in schools (and published in textbooks) was deficient and distorted. According to Mohammed, teachers themselves did not know what was true or correct kiSwahili because they derived from the mainland—being ethnically Jaluo or Meru—rather than from the coast, where kiSwahili had originated. Because of this, Mohammed suggested, the government sets local students up for failure even before they start their education.

Rather than examine the factual accuracy of Mohammed's claims, I instead underline Lamu residents' sense of misrecognition that underlies statements like these. Mohammed's last proclamation—"it's over"—refers not only to his son's failed education but also to the lost authority and (political) power of coastal residents. The institutionalized devaluation of local language varieties, together with the administrative authority of mainland newcomers cannot be dissociated from Lamu residents' perceptions of broader societal transformation analyzed in Chapter 1. The dispossession Mohammed sees in the institutionalized misrecognition of the local vernaculars mirrors, for example, elder *baraza* members' description of newcomers' ignoring of local norms of respectability and Lamu locals' loss of moral authority. Indeed, to many residents, the experienced loss of the vernaculars in favor of a distorted kiSwahili (or kiBara) spoken by mainlanders was iconic of the broader transformations the community was undergoing.

The teacher's supposed use of *tukula* rather than *tule*, considered a mistake by coastal residents but not necessarily by mainland speakers of kiSwahili, therefore concerns much more than a disagreement about correct grammar. Mohammed's example refers to a mistake often made by nonnative speakers of kiSwahili. The grammatical rule dictates that the verbal prefix indicating the infinitive (*ku–*) is dropped in one-syllable verbs, in the subjunctive. The verb "to eat" is *kula* and becomes *tule* in the subjunctive for "let's eat." Many speakers from Kenya's mainland, however, are either oblivious to this grammatical ruling or find forms like *tule* strange-sounding, and they retain the infinitive prefix "*ku–*," which then becomes *tukule* or *tukula*. To Lamu residents, the institutionalized acceptance of these ungrammatical forms is indicative of the speaker's authoritative position in contemporary Lamu, and Kenya more broadly. The educational system, the failing grades of local students, and everyday linguistic practices within Lamu's soundscape (where one progressively hears forms like *tukula*) become iconic of the increasing local imposition of the mainland (Christian) government and associated processes of political, economic, and moral disenfranchisement.

Placing such ideological evaluations of everyday language use in the context of our forgoing discussion about the nuances of pronunciation (such as the distinctive aspiration of /t/ in *mto*) and their contemporary erasure in Standard Swahili gives a sense of the ideological significance of linguistic detail in the context of Lamu. Subtle features of language use do not merely reference social group or ethnic identity; rather they are important indices of the speaker's identity as *mgeni* or guest (rather than *mwenyeji* or local) and associated political affiliations as well as moral conditions.

Discursive evaluations of the educational system, however, were not the only critiques Lamu residents voiced with regard to the imposition of the standard language and the resultant devaluing of local vernaculars. More evident political, religious, and moral stances were taken when rejecting standardized writing conventions.

WRITING SYSTEMS AND POLITICAL STANCES IN EVERYDAY INTERACTIONS

I believe it was about three months into my fieldwork when I stopped by the office of Maryam, who was rapidly becoming a close friend of mine, for a cup of tea and a chat. I had gotten accustomed to checking in on her, as my days were filled with (fruitlessly) trying to meet people and scheduling interviews. Our daily conversations over tea were not only welcome escapes from the stress and confusion of fieldwork; Maryam had also developed a keen interest in my project and frequently suggested people whom I might want to talk to or introduced me to people walking into her office. That morning, as I was about to leave, Maryam handed me a note. "I almost forgot," she said, "Ustadh Mahmoud asked me to give this to you."

Ustadh Mahmoud was a local imam to whom I had been introduced just a day earlier. Maryam had suggested several times I go see the imam because he was a respected Islamic scholar and a well-known poet. A strong proponent of kiAmu, he would definitely have interesting things to say about young people's language use, so she said. When I eventually found my way to the imam's small library, on the second story of his house situated on the border between Mkomani and Langoni, Ustadh Mahmoud had been welcoming and enthusiastic to hear about my research project. We had agreed I would come back the next day for a more extensive interview. I was therefore surprised to receive the note from Maryam.

I opened the paper and blankly stared at the neat, Arabic handwriting. Expressing my confusion to Maryam, I asked her if she could translate, since I did not speak or read Arabic. She glanced at the paper and laughed. "That's not Arabic," she said, "it is kiAmu." The note had merely confirmed our appointment that afternoon and when I arrived at his library later that day, I apologetically explained to Ustadh Mahmoud that I did not read Arabic script. "Well," he said smilingly, "if you want to know more about kiAmu, you better learn."

Ustadh Mahmoud was one of the few people I knew in Lamu who insisted on using Arabic orthography, particularly when writing his poems. While perfectly capable of using Roman script, he equally relied on Arabic orthography when taking notes in books, writing messages to his children (and to me), and sending letters to his former (European) students. Ustadh Mahmoud also insisted on speaking and writing kiAmu (even when traveling to Nairobi, for example, to deliver sermons there) and his poems frequently lamented the gradual loss of the dialect, thereby critiquing the increasing imposition of Standard Swahili. For Ustadh, this persistence in using the local vernacular was indicative of his Lamu identity, and indeed, his *heshima*. Always wearing a white *kanzu* and an embroidered *kofia*, even when traveling to Nairobi (and North America, for that matter), this sense of respectability was equally reflected in his appearance. During my fieldwork, I spent many hours in Ustadh Mahmoud's small library, discussing the origins, changes, and futures of the Swahili vernaculars.

When asked about his insistence on using Arabic script, Ustadh Mahmoud stated that Roman orthography had significantly deteriorated the Swahili language. Roman script's limited number of letters prevented the correct representation of important and functional phonemes that could be represented using Arabic script, so he argued. This inability to correctly write the language, he continued, resulted in an impoverished variant, which was now considered "the standard." I distinctly remember the first example through which Ustadh Mahmoud illustrated his view of the orthographic distortion of kiSwahili. "You know the kiSwahili word for *news*?" he asked me, in English. I confidently nodded and responded "*habari*." The imam smiled and responded that my answer illustrated his point exactly. The kiSwahili word for *news*, he reminded me, was derived from the Arabic خبر, and using Arabic script to write kiAmu allowed for the representation of the voiceless velar fricative /*kh*/ as part of the original loanword, effectively writing *khabari*. Standard orthography, however, insists on *habari*, using a voiceless glottal fricative, causing people to mispronounce the word and erase its Arabic origins. Ustadh Mahmoud suggested that erasures like these not only could create confusion in daily interaction, they also removed the historical importance of Arabic and Islam to the Swahili language.

In his argument, the imam echoed previously discussed scholarly opinions on the limitations of Roman orthography to adequately represent the Swahili vernaculars and the perceived dis-Arabizing or dis-Islamizing that was part of the standardization process (Khalid 1977; Lodhi 2003; Mazrui 2016; Topan 1992; Wald 1985). Yet, I found the particular example he provided to be of interest. Earlier mentioned objections to Roman orthography—the inability to distinguish between *mto* as "pillow" or "river," and between *ndoo* as "bucket" or the imperative "come!"—highlight phonetic distinctions that cannot be represented using Roman script. They thus justifiably speak to the limitations of Roman orthography to represent nuances in the Swahili vernaculars. Similarly, the missionary and colonial dis-Islamization of kiSwahili through the replacement of distinctly Arabic loanwords with supposedly more "African" concepts is historically documented (Mazrui 2016). Yet words like *habari*, while deriving from the Arabic خبر, could be said to merely have followed the regular integration of loanwords into Bantu language structures, losing the consonant /*kh*/ not present in the host language in favor of /*h*/.

Indeed, there is little evidence that waAmu historically pronounced it *khabari*. Clarissa Vierke notes that poets from Lamu incorporated Arabic lexemes in their poetry and integrated Arabic pronunciations in their manuscripts in order to approximate Arabic accentuation and articulation, thereby appealing to the language's status as a language of religion and education (Vierke 2011, 327; see also Seidel 1895, 12; Polomé 1967, 42). In addition to the use of the velar fricative /*kh*/ instead of /*h*/, Vierke also observes the uvular plosive /*q*/ being used rather than /*k*/. She emphasizes, however, that this orthography "does not need to echo the pronunciation of the poet-reciter" (2011, 327), but rather ought to be considered a literary device, distinct from waAmu's everyday language use. Similarly, in her study of the relations between Giriama and Swahili living in Malindi, Janet McIntosh (2009) notes diviners' use of Arabisms, such as glottal stops, in an attempt to sound Arabic or Islamic. McIntosh refers to the semiotic weight of such pronunciations—to the meanings their use carries within the interaction and their implications for claims to (religious) authority, and the ideologies that make these meanings possible (2009, 3). Yet she equally underscores that the use of Arabisms was part of a particular linguistic performance during divination, rather than individuals' habitual way of speaking.

Ustadh Mahmoud's insistence on using velar fricatives or uvular plosives in both spoken and written language is then neither entirely historically correct nor completely new or unfounded. By insisting on Arabisms like /kh/ and /q/ in their everyday linguistic practices, Lamu residents like Ustadh are making creative adjustments to kiAmu in order to make it more "like itself"—reinvigorating, elaborating on, and possibly exaggerating, its differences from Standard Swahili. Pronouncing it *khabari* is then not a nostalgic return to some archaic form; rather it communicates much about the speaker's understanding of what it means to be "from Lamu" in contemporary Kenya. It is precisely this semiotic weight of linguistic nuances— the ideological stances expressed through details of written and spoken language—that makes everyday linguistic practices central to discussions on the intersections of morality, politics, and everyday Islam in Lamu.

Let me elaborate on this point. Few people in contemporary Lamu are able to read "Swahili Arabic," since the majority has learned to read and write Standard Swahili in secular education and are only familiar with Arabic script through Quranic schools. Ustadh Mahmoud therefore often had to "translate" his writings, especially when they were published in local magazines or when they were read at public gatherings. One could attribute his insistence on using Arabic orthography to a nostalgic appeal to kiAmu's historical status as a language of literacy, to a certain stubbornness. I suggest, however, that this determination to use Arabic orthography, rather than being concerned with intelligibility or the aesthetics of the script, derived from the immediate (visual and audible) connection to Arabic and Islam it enabled. At the same time, Ustadh's orthographic practices (and his pronunciations for that matter) were not about an exclusive recognition as "Muslim" or "Arab"; rather, it was precisely about being "Amu" or "Swahili." In other words, Ustadh Mahmoud's scriptive and pronunciation choices intend to summon up, not just a Muslim identity in a majority Christian country, but precisely the Kenyan coast's historical relations with the Arab world. While appealing to a Muslim identity, contemporary uses of Arabic script or Arabisms in everyday language use are not just religious images, but they also appeal to a historical continuity that changes the very center of the author's or speaker's identity from the East Coast of Africa to the East Coast of Arabia. As discussed in the Introduction to this book, such claims to "local cosmopolitanism" (Ho 2002, 2006) are important political tools (Glassman 2014).

Arguments and orthographic practices like these, and their significance within everyday interactions, can only be fully understood in relation to the foregoing historical discussion of the standardization of kiSwahili and the different political and racial interests that motivated it. The increasing imposition of a standard language orthography caused concern, not only because of the ensuing linguistic changes but also because coastal residents experienced it as being associated with their increasing social, political, religious, and economic disenfranchisement in contemporary Kenya. Through their everyday appropriation of Arabisms, their insistence on using Arabic script, or in their dismissal of standard language writing conventions, Lamu residents reject much more than merely Standard Swahili; they object as much to the ideologies that shaped the standardization project and the power differentials implied in the subsequent standard language imposition. Ustadh Mahmoud's persistence in using the kiAmu dialect and Arabic orthography is then not a mere nostalgic effort, nor is it solely a metalinguistic statement that challenges the authority and validity of Standard Swahili; it entails an important political and moral stance and forms an orthographic expression of the redefined notions of belonging discussed in Chapter 1.

Everyday Language Use: Dialects of Morality

Up until now, this chapter has extensively focused on Lamu residents' language ideologies pertaining to Standard Swahili and its perceived impact on Swahili vernaculars and its speakers. Yet from the onset, I have also alluded to the fact that Lamu youth are increasingly abandoning local vernaculars in favor of the standard language or urban varieties of kiSwahili. How do we make sense of such shifts, given the strong negative opinions Lamu residents appear to hold about Standard Swahili? One could suggest that this is merely a generational shift, with the opinions analyzed previously being expressed mainly by elder Lamu residents rather than the younger generation. At the same time, however, Chapter 1 highlighted that negative views of the perceived moral transformation of Lamu were not limited to elders; Lamu youth equally lamented a loss of respect and particularly the increasing imposition of *wageni* or newcomers. In fact, it was Lamu youth who offered the strongest and most political reformulations of the proverb "*hiyo ndiyo Amu.*" How then do we bring such strong political stances in line with a language shift that adheres to a government-imposed standard language? And how does the avoidance of the vernaculars impact the perception Lamu residents have of the younger generation?

I previously mentioned that young people are hesitant to use local vernaculars because they view them as "incorrect" in relation to the standard. In other words, the standard language hegemony meaningfully informs schoolgoing youth's language use; they perceive local vernaculars to be valuable within the local context (linked to a particular sense of authenticity) but are convinced of the value, importance, and "correctness" of Standard Swahili as a language that "belongs to no-one in particular" (Woolard 2016). But there is more to it. Many Lamu youth will use (some) kiAmu or kiBajuni while in Lamu, but will shift away from the vernaculars when they are traveling to Mombasa and Nairobi. While these youth justify such shifts in terms of intelligibility (they argue that people from Nairobi simply don't understand kiAmu), they further admit that their reluctance to use kiAmu is mostly a result of other Kenyans' joking remarks when overhearing the vernacular. Lamu youth admitted that they simply didn't want to be ridiculed.

They frequently justified their avoidance of kiAmu and preference for kiMombasa when traveling to the city by referencing a sentence used by people from Mombasa when hearing someone speak one of the Northern Swahili Dialects: "*Ambacha ukucha punda uyao*" (see also Hillewaert 2015). Mombasa residents generally pronounce the sentence with a heavy or exaggerated kiBajuni accent, emphasizing the /*ch*/ sound, which many perceive to be characteristic of all vernaculars spoken in the Lamu Archipelago. In fact, the sentence emphasizes two distinguishing features—*ch* and *uyao*—to draw attention to and poke fun of those individuals who are believed to speak "like that"—all residents of the Lamu Archipelago. The feature "ch," however, is typical only of the kiBajuni dialect, not of kiAmu nor of other dialects from the region.[13] In both Standard Swahili and kiMombasa the sentence would be written (and pronounced) as "*ambata ukuta punda anakuja,*" and can be translated as "press yourself against the wall, because there is a donkey coming" (Figure 11). The warning—urging

Figure 11. Donkeys carrying burdens in Lamu's narrow streets. Photograph by Eric Lafforgue.

someone to make way for a donkey—is particularly out of place in a city like Mombasa, an urban center with broad streets, hectic transportation, and a complete lack of donkeys (Hillewaert 2015).

How can we understand the impact of this linguistic stereotype? In other words, what ideological processes allow residents from Mombasa to use this sentence as a joke (and a judgment) and why do Lamu youth take such offence, to the extent that they refuse to speak the vernacular? Which ideologies are at work here? Agha (1998) explains the functioning of linguistic stereotypes by highlighting how people ideologically link arbitrary features of speech to particular types of people, thereby formulating an association that (to them) seems self-evident and inherent—"all those people speak like that." In doing so, those linguistic features become easily recognizable signs of an individual's social identity and such ideologies thus simplify the sociolinguistic complexity that otherwise typifies everyday interactions. Judith Irvine and Susan Gal further elaborate on the workings of linguistic stereotypes (and processes of semiotic differentiation more broadly) and explain why such arbitrary links come to be viewed as intrinsic and natural (Gal 1995; Irvine and Gal 2000; Irvine 2001).

They describe three semiotic processes through which people select perceived qualities of language use and link these to perceived characteristics of social groups. *Iconization* refers to an ideological process through which individuals view a linguistic feature as an icon of a speaker's inherent nature—someone who speaks slow, thinks slow. *Erasure*, on the other hand, refers to individuals' erasing of linguistic differences to simplify sociolinguistic complexity—*all* of these people speak "like that" (thus removing an array of differences existing between members of a particular social group, as well as their similarities with those who are making the judgment). *Fractal recursivity* projects a distinction or opposition that exists at one level of society, onto another level—"they" are less sophisticated than "us," but within that supposedly unsophisticated group, you are likely to also find the same opposition between those who are more or less sophisticated. Of course, these processes cannot be understood outside of the social, historical, or political contexts in which they take place. In other words, iconic connections and the erasure of linguistic diversity are motivated and informed by the sociopolitical processes that gave rise to social differentiation in the first place.

In Lamu, we see these processes play out in the aforementioned linguistic stereotype. First, while evidently kiBajuni, residents of Mombasa shout the sentence at any speaker who is perceived to be from the Lamu Archipelago and thereby discursively *erase* the important social, historical, and linguistic diversity that typifies this island group. For waAmu, this stereotype is therefore particularly offensive, as they distinguish themselves from waBajuni based on notions of civility and respectability. Second, the incongruity between the utterance (urging someone to let a donkey pass by) and the reality of the context in which it is pronounced (in a city typified by loud motorized transportation) underlines the difference between the two historically rival cities, emphasizing Lamu's present-day marginal position as opposed to Mombasa's (economic) success. People from Mombasa use this sentence to underscore the "underdeveloped" state of present-day Lamu, but they also draw from particular language ideological perspectives because they link the dialect and those who speak it to the narrow streets and prevalence of donkey transportation, viewing all as outdated and underdeveloped. The perceived pristineness of the town is equated with the backwardness of the dialect, which is in turn considered iconic of the (moral) condition of its speakers (Hillewaert 2015).

The language ideologies that informed Mombasa residents' negative evaluations of the Northern Swahili Dialects, however, went beyond associations between geographical location, economic development, and the material practices of inhabitants. When asked about their aversion toward kiAmu, many young men from Mombasa were quick to describe the dialect as sounding too "soft," and by extension "too feminine," even when spoken by men. Similarly, Lamu residents who depicted the dialect and tried to explain to me its distinction from other Northern Swahili Dialects, like kiBajuni, often suggested that "*lafdhi yake ni laini*"—that the dialect's pronunciation was soft or smooth. They would simultaneously rub their thumb, index, and middle fingers together as if touching soft material. Instead of identifying one particular phonological feature (like "ch" or "*uyao*"), they depicted the material quality of kiAmu as a whole as soft, smooth, and gentle.

Many interviewees proposed that this perceived smoothness gave kiAmu a distinctly feminine quality. Some young men in Lamu therefore explained that, in addition to not wanting to be called backward and ridiculed, they avoided kiAmu when traveling to Mombasa because they did not want to be viewed as possibly homosexual. While they recognized the historical value of the dialect and acknowledged the importance of preserving it, they simultaneously argued that its usage did not seem appropriate for men in an urban context. This topic came up when my interlocutor Abdul and his friend Kassim were talking about their (lack of) pride of their Lamu origins.

Abdul was a twenty-two-year-old young man from an upper-class Lamu family who had recently returned to the island after having lived in Nairobi for several years. He had traveled to the capital to attend college but dropped out in his second year. He subsequently remained in Nairobi, hoping to find employment but eventually returned home to Lamu, where he worked in a family-owned store. Although he never complained about being in Lamu, Abdul struggled to adjust to life in the island town. He not only retained a more urban dress style (often wearing baggy jeans and sneakers) but also frequently used Sheng or Standard Swahili infused with English when speaking to his peers or to me. When interacting with family members, however, Abdul generally switched back and forth between kiAmu and kiMombasa.

Kassim was about twenty-three years old at the time of the interview and was visiting Lamu over the Christmas holidays. Kassim's parents were originally from Lamu and belonged to one of the prestigious patrician families. While they moved to Mombasa when Kassim was a child and had lived in the city ever since, the family visited Lamu quite often and stayed with Abdul's family when they were in town. When in Lamu, Kassim frequently expressed his aversion to these visits and complained about how boring he thought life in Lamu was: There was nothing to do, the streets were covered with donkey dung, and everything just happened too slowly. Time really did not pass in Lamu, he often sighed. The following exchange between Abdul (A) and Kassim (K) occurred shortly after Kassim had woken up and grumbled that sleeping was the best use of his time in Lamu. Abdul used the opportunity to question Kassim about his dislike of the town and reminded him that his family came from Lamu. The conversation quickly turned to language use.

Regular Standard: kiSwahili/kiMombasa
<u>Underlined</u>: kiAmu
Bold: English
Italic: Exaggerated kiMombasa

A: Ukija kama hapa Lamu, je waongea kiAmu ama hapana?

A: When you come here to Lamu, do you speak kiAmu or not?

K: Siwezi kuongea kiAmu!

K: I cannot speak kiAmu!

A: Kwa nini usiongei kiAmu na uko Lamu?

A: Why shouldn't you speak kiAmu and you're in Lamu?

K: Sipendi kwa sababu lafdhi yake.

K: I don't like it because of its pronunciation.

A: Kivipi hupendi? Ni aibu ama ni ya nini?

A: Why don't you like it? Is it shameful?

K: Ni aibu alafu enyewe ikakaa ka ya kisenge senge.

K: It is shameful and then it is like gay-ish.

A: Kivipi yani?

K: Kihanithi yani

A: *Huipendi hiyo lugha kabisa?*

K: Siipendi! kama wewe ni wa Lamu lakini mbona huongei kiAmu?

A: **Okay**, mi ni Mlamu siongei kiAmu?

K: **Yes**

A: **Okay**, mimi ni wa Lamu na naongea kiAmu, na saa hii naongea kiAmu.

K: Huongei kiAmu

A: <u>Hiyau hiyau</u>

K: Uwongo! Si sana kuongea kiAmu!

A: Uhm, na je wewe unaheshimu dini yako?

K: Naheshimu sana.

A: Lakini mbona mavazi yako unayovaa mara nyingi si ya kiIslamu?

K: Natoka kulala

A: Like, how?

K: Gay-sounding I mean.

A: *You don't like this language at all?*

K: I don't like it! Like you, you are from Lamu but why don't you speak kiAmu?

A: **Okay**, I am from Lamu but I do not speak kiAmu?

K: **Yes**

A: **Okay**, I am from Lamu and I speak kiAmu and now I am speaking kiAmu.

K: You are not speaking kiAmu.

A: <u>Like this like this</u>

K: Lies! You don't speak kiAmu often!

A: Uhm, and do you respect your religion?

K: I respect it very much.

A: But why are the clothes you wear often not Islamic?

K: I just woke up.

When Abdul questions Kassim about his ability to speak kiAmu, Kassim sharply expresses his unwillingness to use the dialect. He does not refer to the stereotypical depiction of the Northern Dialects as backward, but rather suggests that the vernacular—and by extension its speakers—have a "gay-like" quality. Although Abdul had not been speaking kiAmu, his subsequent shift to an emphasized use of kiMombasa following Kassim's depiction of the kiAmu dialect stands out. The shift does not go unnoticed and Kassim subsequently calls Abdul out on the contradiction between his line of questioning and his language use. To challenge

Kassim, Abdul inserts *hiyau*, a demonstrative that can be translated as "like this" and would take the form *hivyo* in Standard Swahili. A stereotypical word often used in jocular depictions of Lamu residents—people from Mombasa often compare its pronunciation to the sound a cat makes—it neither proves nor denies Abdul's knowledge and (regular) use of kiAmu.

When Kassim does not accept this switch to kiAmu, Abdul abruptly switches topics to question Kassim about his religious practice. Kassim follows this change of topic, seemingly acknowledging the signifying link between individuals' language use and their piety. When Abdul subsequently focuses his attention on Kassim's mode of dress, he connects language use and nonverbal material practice to the moral condition of his interlocutor. He thus seems to discursively link Kassim's dislike of kiAmu to his dress style and his orientation to Islam.

The example interestingly contributes to our understanding of young people's ambivalent position in contemporary Lamu, and particularly to how such inbetweenness informs young Lamu residents' shifting, mixing, and sometimes seemingly contradictory language use. While recognizing the historical and moral value of the dialect and while recognizing the imposition of Standard Swahili, Lamu youth's language use is equally informed by translocal discourses and stereotypes about the island. Their switching between and mixing of the language varieties then illustrate their everyday negotiation of multiple orientations—to the local context, religion, political debates, urban environments, and global discourses. The preceding example also shows how individuals' evaluations of language use are associated with the moral transformation they perceive the community to be undergoing. Most interestingly, however, is the example's illustration of the ideological processes through which people make these evaluations, how individuals link arbitrary qualities of speech to qualities of personhood in a way that they perceive to be inherent. According to Kassim, the feminine quality he identified in kiAmu is iconic of the feminine disposition of its speakers, which subsequently justified an evaluation of their sexual orientation.

Lamu youth who admitted to shifting away from the dialect recognized the soft quality of their mother tongue and did not object to an identification of this smoothness as "feminine." Yet to them, the depiction of the material qualities of kiAmu as feminine called upon or was iconic of kindness and religiosity. Many young men said they considered a girl who spoke kiAmu attractive, exactly because her language use signaled her moral condition as pure, sensitive, and conservative. A girl who spoke kiMombasa had an urban sophistication that was appealing, but was also presumed to have lost a quality of shyness, sensitivity, and religious devotion. While a girl from Mombasa was fun to flirt with, some suggested that Lamu girls were preferred marriage partners.

Lamu residents' awareness of linguistic stereotypes like these does not mean, however, that young men's avoidance of kiAmu was always evaluated positively (as performing a particular kind of masculinity, for example). While some youth explained their language shifts as a result of (business) travels to the mainland or work with nonlocals (therefore signaling their lucrative employment and thus a moral good), it was a supposed inability to "shift back" to kiAmu upon returning to Lamu that was perceived negatively. Other Lamu residents often viewed such failure (or inability) to use kiAmu within the local context as an (ideological) orientation away from Lamu. It not only implied particular political stances, but was also considered indicative of altered attitudes toward respectability, norms of interaction, and piety.

I elaborate on these linguistic stereotypes and Lamu residents' awareness of and responses to them, not only to contextualize young people's avoidance of the vernaculars, but also to draw attention to the signifying nuances comprised in language use. Although the use of kiAmu, or speech recognized as kiAmu, identified the speaker as coming from the Lamu Archipelago (thus retaining its reference to a particular geographical location), nuances and material qualities of speech permitted the attribution of a quality of personhood, of significance beyond the geographical.

This emphasis on nuances of speech and their potentiality for signification suggests that speakers can strategically mobilize a quality of speech to evoke a particular quality of personhood. In other words, speakers can intentionally use (or avoid) features of speech when claiming or negotiating particular identities or social positions, even when they don't speak the language fluently. Yet, as the foregoing discussion illustrated, the indeterminacy of audiences—the range of different people who might potentially overhear one's speech—and their possible different evaluations of language use make such everyday negotiations both challenging and interesting. The distinguishing features of kiAmu carry the potential to signify, but what they stand for is not a given. Inhabitants from Mombasa and Lamu recognize a material quality of the dialect—both identify its softness, for example—but what this softness represents is not agreed upon. Similarly, some distinguishing features of the Northern Dialects, such as "ch," "*hiyau*," or "*uyao*"—are recognized by people from both Lamu and Mombasa. What these features indicate about these speakers' personhood or moral condition, however, depends on the people doing the evaluating. This semiotic indeterminacy is important beyond the immediate context of interaction and is shaped by broader sociopolitical fields of power. For example, an individual's strategic use of Arabisms like /kh/ can be read as simply nonstandard, as valuing kiAmu, as a claim to Arab identity or religious authority, or potentially as a sign of extremist ideologies associated with the Mombasa Republican Council or Al-Shabaab. While linguistic presentations of self in everyday life are well documented (Goffman 1956), it is precisely the different scalar evaluations of such practices and the moral judgments that accompany them that will make the analysis of young people's everyday language use in subsequent chapters so fascinating.

Conclusion

Different historical, political, and social processes introduced different languages and situated ideological evaluations of these linguistic varieties to the Lamu area. Insight into such processes complicate our understandings of notions like "standard language," "prestige varieties," and "dialects" and reveal why language varieties like kiAmu or Standard Swahili can each be viewed as signaling either prestige or backwardness, respectability or lack thereof, depending on context and audience. In other words, regimes of language are not singular but can be multiple and conflicting.

Whereas historical or political processes determine which details of language use come to be viewed as meaningful, what these distinguishing features signify is dependent on both the audience and context of the speech act. Precisely because of the particular historical and political environment that gave rise to these distinctions, however, they never merely indicate geographical origins or notions of "authenticity." Rather, in the context of Lamu, nuances in speech are meaningfully associated with the moral personhood of the interlocutor. In the past, speakers' details of speech were perceived as indicating their status as *wenyeji* or *wageni* and the associated embodiment (or lack thereof) of particular notions of respectability. In present-day Lamu, nuances of pronunciation and intonation are signs of speakers' adherence to or orientation away from the local context or the Kenyan nation. Traces of Standard Swahili might signal the interlocutor's education level and travels to the mainland or could be viewed as indicative of their nonlocal origins; the incorporation of an intonation similar to kiMvita can indicate their urban demeanor or a sense of shame for their Lamu heritage; the retention of details of speech specific to kiAmu can signal *heshima* or a lack of education. The specifics of such assessments and the associated moral stance of the speaker depend on who is doing the evaluating and in which context.

As we have seen, however, languages and linguistic practices, while stigmatized, can also become important markers of identity, particularly in contexts where belonging is questioned or redefined. In other words, the most recognizable and stigmatized feature of a vernacular can become central to political stances and reconceptualizations of identity. This is precisely why the young man's orthographic choices in Chapter 1 were so important. When writing *"hiyi ndiyo Amu, fanyeni mwende zenu"* or "this is Amu, now hurry up and go home," he strategically used kiAmu and thereby disrupted standard language orthography. In addition to the explicitly stated, it is the semiotic weight (McIntosh 2009) of his linguistic and orthographic choices that made his contribution so meaningful. In doing so, the young man called upon virtually all the language ideologies highlighted throughout this chapter—rejecting Standard Swahili and its association with the Kenyan government as well as challenging popular stereotypes associated with vernaculars like kiAmu. By claiming the vernacular, and discarding the stereotypes, the young man took an explicit political stance. For Lamu residents, such linguistic choices often also entail a moral stance, one inseparable from claiming a Muslim identity and from being a "good Lamu resident" in contemporary Kenya.

The discussions in these first two chapters lead us to ask what these ideological evaluations of social transformation mean for Lamu youth. So far, I have alluded to young Lamu residents who increasingly cross social, linguistic, and ideological boundaries in a range of ways, crossings enabled or necessitated by the shifts being discussed: Children now attend schools in different neighborhoods with peers from different social and ethnic backgrounds, exposing them to Standard Swahili and English; young men and women travel to Mombasa or Nairobi for secondary education or college, introducing them to kiMvita, English, Standard Swahili, or Sheng; young women increasingly take up employment in public offices; economic pressures push young men to work in the tourism industry or travel to the Arabian Peninsula in search of employment; mobile telephony, social media, and pop culture enable communication across social, ethnic, and gender lines. As in many other contexts, young people are then ineluctably linked to the processes of change discussed so far. One might then ask whether the moral condemnations of such shifts equally entail a moral judgment of Lamu youth. In other words, how are young people viewed in contemporary Lamu? Are the changes discussed so far linked to a particular category of "youth" and are transformations therefore viewed as a mere generational shift? Or are historical social distinctions and associated notions of embodied respectability projected onto the younger generation? Linking the perceived moral transformation of Lamu (Chapter 1) to the strong ideological views about language use and linguistic change (Chapter 2), we will now explore how ideological discourses inform evaluations of Lamu youth and their everyday practices.

kiSwahili

MAHMOUD AHMED ABDULKADIR

In July 2003, Mahmoud Abdulkadir read an article in one of Kenya's national newspapers, reporting on the activities of a national committee in charge of the Swahili language. The poet was struck by the accompanying photo of the committee. "None of its members visibly looked Swahili," he recounts; none of the participants wore Swahili clothing or look like a Swahili person. Rather, all members appeared to derive from "upcountry" Kenya. Unsettled that no waSwahili were concerned with the Swahili language, he wrote this poem.

Written in the voice of the Swahili language, the poem asks waSwahili why they no longer value their language and why they left it in the care of others of non-Swahili origins. The poet reminds Swahili speakers of their mother tongue's value and historical significance and contests the idea that kiSwahili is a lingua franca that does not belong to any one ethnic group. The poem captures many of the ideologies discussed in the previous and subsequent chapters. The sentiments of historical significance and cosmopolitanism, and of contemporary disenfranchisement are clearly expressed through the voice of the Swahili language.[1]

Kunyamaa nimechoka
I'm tired of staying silent

Tanyamaa hata lini
How much longer shall I keep quiet

Wanangu huniepuka
My children are avoiding me

Kuwaona natamani
Yet I long to see them

Walobaki kunishika
Those who hold onto me

Siwangu niwawendani
Are not mine, but others' offspring

Mimi nimewatendani?
What have I done to you?

Mbona mwanipija zita?
Why do you wage a war on me?

Wangu mimi wadamu
Mine of blood

Wana wa Uswahilini
Children of Swahililand

Asili hawana hamu
They do not yearn at all

Yakuniyuwa ninani
To know who I am

Wame natiya kaumu
They left me to other people

Na wana wa majirani
And to the neighbors' children

Kosa langu kosagani?
What is my mistake?

Mbona hunijipa zita?
Why do you wage a war on me?

Mimi mamenu sitasa
I, your mother, am not barren

Wala sina punguwani
Nor do I have any defects

Nimezaa wa Mambasa
*I gave birth to children in
  Mombasa*

Nakungine zisiwani
And other Swahili islands

Nizee wanasiyasa
I gave birth to politicians

Naziyongozi wadini
And to religious leaders

Mafundi wa kulafani
To craftsmen of different arts

Namashujaa wazita
And to heroes in battle

Ndimi mamake Muyaka
I am the mother of Muyaka

Piya Mwengo Athumani
And also Mwengu Athumani

Na Zahidi kadhalika
Zahidi as well

Na wengi wake wendani
And many of his contemporaries

Ali Koti na Mataka
Ali Kuoti and Mataka

Walitoka matumboni
They came out of my womb

Inkishafi ngaliya
Look at the Inkishafi[3]

Ndipo takapo kweleya
Then you will understand

Nitungo zimesaliya
These verses have endured

Walozitunga ni nyani?
Who were their composers?

Na Malenga Wamvita
And Malenga wamvita[5]

Nyao walizifuwata
They followed in my footsteps

Nnabahani huteta
Nabahani criticizes[6]

Ndiye pweke uwandani
He is the only one

Bado kuzaa naweza
I can still give birth

Lakini mumenipuuza
But you have shunned me

Wangine meitokeza
Now others have emerged

Musamiyati kubuni
Creating vocabularies

Wote mbwa moya karini
All from one generation

Wa kawaa kama nyota
And they shone like stars[2]

Ukisome na kidani
And read the kidani[4]

Nikwambiyao mwendani
My friend, what I am telling you

Na hazifi asilani
And they will never die

Niwanangu walopita
My children who passed on

Napiya Chiraghudini
And Chiraghudini as well

Hawakukiri uduni
They never accepted inferiority

Lakini hufaliyani
But what is the use

Ingawa ameikita
Yet he stands firm

Siyakoma ukingoni
I have not reached the end

Mumeitowe fuwoni
You have abandoned me

Kunipangiya kanuni
To standardize me

Nyinyi uliponiwata
When you discarded me

Huliya kisikitika
I cry and grieve

Wengi wanaoandika
Those who contribute

Idhaani kadhalika
In the media as well

Wengi hawatoki pwani
Many are not from the coast

Changaliya jaridani
When I look in journals

Si wanangu ni wageni
Are not mine but strangers

Wapeka tungo ninyani
Who are ones that contribute?

Licha kuwa mbwamvita
Let alone from Mvita

Angaliya na zitabu
Look at the textbooks

Hazandikwi na Rajabu
They are not written by Rajabu

Njoroge ndiyo katibu
Njoroge is the author

Charo nawake wendani
Charo and his colleagues

Zisomweshwao shuleni
Being used in schools

Sisudi wala sishani
Neither by Sudi nor by Shani[7]

Ashishiyeo sukani
He holds the steering wheel

Nao nyuma hufuata
Behind they follow[8]

Hualikwa kongamano
When invited to conferences

Huona utungu mno
I am deeply hurt

Nahuziuma zitano
I bite my fingers

Wanangu mumeikhini
My children, you did injustice

Chenda hurudi ndiyani
I turn back before I arrive

Kuwa nyinyi siwaoni
Because I don't see you there

Lakini nitende nini?
But what can I do?

Mamenu mumeniwata
You abandoned your mother

Na huliya kwamatozi
I shed tears

Wanafundi wakibwezi
Students from Kibwezi

Changaliya mitihani
When I look at examination results

Nawakisumu ziwani
And from Kisumu at the lake

Ndiwo wanao barizi
They are the ones who lead

Mulotoka kwetu pwani
Students from the coast

Wafanyao utafiti
Those who do research

Waswahili ni katiti
The Swahili are few

Ninyani nimlaiti
Who is to blame?

Mimi hamuni thamini
You do not value me

Kiwasikiya hunena
When I hear others speak

Sarufi hakuna tena
There is no inflection

Nahata ladha hayana
No flavor in their speech

Sielewi hunenani
I don't understand what they say

Lau Muyaka tarudi
If Muyaka would return

Mwanangu itambidi
It would be necessary

Aete na mashahidi
And call witnesses

Nyute mwenda gerezani
You would all go to prison

Waliyoko kileleni
Who are on top

Muko tini hukokota
You are below holding the tail

Wadigirii zuwoni
For university degrees

Au hawapatikani
Or they are nonexisting

Mwenye makosani nyani
Who is at fault?

Mngine hamukupata
Yet you found none to replace me

Huniungonga moyoni
I feel disturbed at heart

Nahau naitamani
Yet I long to see Swahili grammar

Kama mashapu kanwani
Like tobacco in one's mouth

Huimba au huteta
Are they singing or fighting

Ae tena duniyani
To the world

Kwenenda mahamakani
For him to go to court

Waniyuwao yakini
Who know the truth

Kwa hatiya kuwapata
For what you did to me

Wallahi hamuna ghera
By God, you have no courage

Wala hamuna imani
Nor do you have faith

Hamuna lakuwakera
You are not ashamed

Kuwa hamuni thamini
That you don't value me

Mimi nikama mpwira
I am like a ball

Hutezwa uwandani
Being played on the playground

Hupijwa teke ndiyani
Being kicked in the street

Na kula anaepita
By every passer-by

Hata kwenye ushairi
Even in Swahili poetry

Waso wangu wamebuni
Those who aren't mine invented

Zilizo huru bahari
Free verse

Kwa kuoleza wageni
Imitating foreigners

Mimi hayo siyakiri
I cannot accept that

Si mashairi kifani
These are not proper poems

Hayo yote nikwa nini?
Why all this?

Hizo ni mbinu za zita
These are strategies for war

Hambiwa mwenyewe sina
I am told I belong to nobody

Hini niajabu gani?
How astonishing is this?

Huwae kakosa shina
How can I be rootless

Kawa na tandu yangani?
Yet have branches in the air?

Nyani alonipa ina
Who gave me my name

Alonandika ninyani?
And who wrote me down?

Kiwa siuswahili
If I'm not from Swahililand

Niwapi nilipopata
Then where did I come from?

Kuwa wengi huninena
That many speak me

Si dalili aswilani
Is not proof of lack of origins

Yakuwa wenyewe sina
Or that I have no owners

Kingereza hamuoni?
What about the English language?

Kunenwa *na wengi sana*
It is spoken by many

Kina na kwao shinani
Yet it has a clear ancestry

Pembe zote duniyani
In all corners of the world

Miziye haikukata
Its roots have not been cut

CHAPTER 3

"Youth" as a Discursive Construct

Tukisema ukweli utwana wakati hunu wa kwetu . . . twaweza
kusema kwamba uko utwana.

To say the truth, slavery in our time . . . we can say
that slavery exists.

A contemplative silence followed Hasan's statement. We were sitting in one of Lamu's seafront cafés, sipping a cold juice while enjoying the view of the lagoon. It was late afternoon, and the seafront was busy. Porters were unloading shipments that had arrived with the latest bus from Mombasa. Tourists wandered around, enjoying the view of the sunset while critically inspecting different cafés for an appealing evening meal. Two young men, sitting on one of the old cannons placed along the seashore, called out to a couple of young American women who were gallivanting by, dressed in tank tops and short skirts. Encouraged by the girls' smiles, the young men quickly jumped up and approached their potential customers for a sailing trip through the lagoon, eventually joining them in the restaurant next door. Two veiled young women strolled by, their open-design *buibui* fluttering behind them due to the strong sea breeze, and thereby revealing the tight jeans both of them wore underneath the black garment. Hasan smiled as he observed the activities on the seafront and reflected upon how to clarify his statement.

As I watched porters unload boats, carrying heavy bags of cement and blocks of limestone up the street, I had carefully enquired whether Lamu youth were still conscious of the town's slave history and whether this past continued to shape social relations. The porters' hard labor and their physical appearance—their faces covered with white dust from the cement and limestone, their clothing torn and dirty—had contrasted sharply with the appearance of other elder men, dressed in their impeccable white *kanzu*, who were conversing on a nearby *baraza*. To me, the distinction seemed to form a striking illustration of the social hierarchies that continued to shape life in the Swahili town.

My previous enquiries about Lamu's history of slavery, however, had been met with avoidance, from Hasan as well as from other friends and interviewees. They generally framed their reluctance to answer my questions in terms of the negative portrayals of Lamu in previous ethnographic studies as well as the unnecessary recollection of a history that supposedly was no longer relevant today. Whereas nobody denied the town's historical involvement with slavery, the explicitly voiced consensus appeared to be that slave descent or ownership was no longer a significant factor in Lamu's contemporary social fabric.

To my surprise, Hasan had now been quick to respond to my enquiry. His answer, however, was not quite what I had expected. His acknowledgment of the existence of "modern-day slavery" did not refer to the porters I had observed and who had prompted my question, but rather to Lamu youth. To Hasan, the idea of enslavement was invoked not by observing a particular kind of labor, but by the *heshima* or respectability displayed in an individual's comportment. Following a reflective silence, he pointed to the young Muslim women who had now paused in front of one of the many stone benches located along the seafront to readjust their *hijab*, revealing their hair in the process.

HASAN: Kuna msemo ambao kwamba husema mwata mila ni mtumwa. Mwata mila ni?

SH: Ni mtumwa.

HASAN: Ni mtumwa. Sawa siyo? Kwa hivyo, huko upande wa kwetu naweza kusema utumwa pia uko. Kwa sababu gani? Kwa sababu watu wengi wameata mila yao. Kwa mfano, nguo ambazo kwamba mabinti zetu wanazovaa siyo nguo ambazo kwamba wakati wa nyuma walikuwa wazee wetu walikuwa wakivaa. Saa hii wamekuwa wasichana wetu wameata mila yao ya kuvaa nguo vizuri kama inavyotakikana. Jambo kama hili waweza kusema mtu ni mtumwa kwa sababu ameata mila yake. Umeona, siyo?

HASAN: There is a proverb that says *whoever leaves his mila* (traditions) *is a slave.* Whoever leaves his *mila* is?

SH: Is a slave.

HASAN: Is a slave. Right? Thus, here in our context, I can say that slavery is also here. Why? Because many people have left their *mila*. For example, the clothes our young women wear, these are not the clothes that our elders used to wear. Now our girls have left their tradition of wearing proper clothes in a respectful way. In this case, you can say that the person is a slave because she has left her *mila*. You understand, right?

A thirty-year-old businessman claiming Yemeni ancestry and residing in Lamu's Mkomani neighborhood, Hasan had taken an interest in my research. Even during ordinary conversations, he would often call my attention to things he thought applied to my research interests, and he displayed a remarkable willingness and patience to explain to me why he held certain opinions. That day at the seafront was no different. While my own observations of heavy labor, low wages, and seeming social inequality had informed my enquiry about life in a postslavery society, Hasan's recognition of *utumwa* (slavery)[1] in contemporary Lamu was not driven by a shared understanding of possible exploitative labor relations within the town and the social stigma that I had assumed would be attached to such historical employment. Rather, his conceptualization of contemporary *utumwa* was informed by values of *heshima* and thus by assessments of individuals' moral states based on outward appearances—on their willingness to present and dress themselves in particular ways. According to Hasan, it was not the porters but the young women who were modern-day *watumwa* or slaves— not because of their employment, genealogy, or phenotypical traits, but rather because of their visible abandonment of local, respectful, and traditional practices in favor of *tabia ya kizungu*—Western habits—and the lack of *heshima* such behavior implied. Precisely this publicly displayed admiration and mimicking of nonlocal others' consumer habits, and the assumed moral servitude that accompanied this adoration, motivated Hasan's proverbial depiction of the young women as *watumwa*.

In a way, Hasan's remark echoed observations voiced earlier in this book—of the elder *baraza* member in Chapter 1, for example, who criticized young Lamu residents for appropriating disreputable habits of newcomers to the island (such as hairstyles), but also of Ustadh Taha in the Introduction. Taha had reminded his audience that Lamu residents shouldn't mistake development for the mere appropriation of Western material practices as this failed to live up to the morally responsible engagement with change demanded from them by their religion. Moral presence, the imam had suggested, entailed a God-conscious and selective engagement with those aspects of development that would aid the well-being of the Lamu community. As the foregoing chapters already outlined, however, which aspects of change or conservation were considered respectable and morally responsible rather than transgressive or backward was far from straightforward.

These ideological discourses of moral transformation and language change, both informed by perceived macro-sociological processes of dispossession and marginalization, meaningfully frame assessments of Lamu youth as well. In fact, certain sections of Lamu's younger generation are more vulnerable to moral condemnation precisely because social and economic changes have enabled or forced them to cross physical and ideological boundaries. A question that arises is then how youth in Lamu can negotiate a moral presence—a morally responsible engagement with development and change—given the ideological frameworks within which their behaviors are evaluated. Within a context of perceived societal moral deterioration, how are young people—as the demographic most intimately connected to social change—talked about? And how do youth themselves understand change, development, or conservation, and their participation in these processes?

Whereas "youth" often readily becomes "a metaphor for perceived social change and its projected consequences" (Austin and Willard 1998, 1), young people in Lamu are not categorically associated with change and/or moral deterioration. More than one social category of "youth" emerges from Lamu residents' discourses on social change, and more than one denomination captures young people's position in today's society. In other words, not all Lamu youth are equally subjected to evaluative, and often critical, discourses, nor do all observers assess young people in the same way.

In the ideological discourses analyzed in this chapter, youth emerge either as enslaved to their longing for Western modernity (with explicit comparisons of young people to slaves) or as the "dot com" generation that has access to a range of possibilities previously unreachable to my interlocutors. These evaluations, I argue, are not only shaped by residents' different social positions but also by shifting understandings of what respectable conduct or *heshima* ought to entail in contemporary Lamu. In representing these different voices, we see how a previously hegemonic ideology and its associated social hierarchy are increasingly being spoken against and thus overtly challenged by those who did not belong to the former merchant elites. Differently positioned social actors differently read and evaluate verbal and nonverbal signs and link them to newly emerging social categories. Importantly, however, young people's metapragmatic awareness of such situated evaluations can aid them in strategically using details of language, dress, gaze, stride, and spatiotemporal location in the presentation of self and, indeed, in the negotiation of a new kind of moral presence.

"Whoever Leaves Their Traditions Is a Slave"

The proverb "Whoever leaves their traditions is a slave" featured in many of my interviews and discussions with Lamu residents, old and young. To many, the saying appeared to adequately capture the disturbing moral state of Lamu residents, and of Lamu youth in particular. At the heart of these worries seemed to be a concern about a disregard for *heshima* in daily interactions, the most evident example of which was the willingness of Lamu youth to forego local norms of respectful dress and adopt others' consumer habits. In making the proverbial comparison between slaves and contemporary youth, interlocutors drew on a lineage of historical, local, and highly situated meanings of slavery. Just as the elder in Chapter 1 referred to moral values associated with *uungwana* (civility, nobility) and *ushenzi* (barbarity) to condemn the arrival of newcomers to the island, so did residents draw upon these historical social distinctions and their associated moral conditions to evaluate Lamu youth and their everyday practices.

The proverb to which Hasan referred, derives its meaning from the historical context in which *watumwa* straddled a boundary between barbarity and nobility (Eastman 1994). In an attempt to gradually integrate themselves into postslavery societies as free individuals, former slaves used to appropriate material and linguistic practices that were believed to represent *heshima* (Fair 1998, 2001). Yet it was in this abandoning of their habitual practices and traditions that their status as *watumwa* lay; in their desire to mimic the habits and standards of their former masters, they displayed their slave descent and thus failed to escape their stigmatized status (Glassman 1991). In contemporary Lamu, young people's increasing appropriation of nonlocal practices in exchange for those modes of behavior that were previously perceived to embody *heshima* motivates many residents, including young people themselves, to (proverbially) liken youth to slaves.

While the saying occurred frequently in discussions pertaining to Lamu's younger generation, it did not seem to refer to a newly emerging, single social category of "youth" as "slaves." In other words, not all young people were equally perceived as foregoing local norms of appropriate conduct in favor of others' consumer habits. Based on their differing engagements with "change" broadly conceived, specific segments of the Lamu community were seen to be more prone to such behaviors. At the same time, different opinions on who could be considered a contemporary slave suggest that there was no agreement on what an embodiment of *heshima* ought to entail in contemporary society: on what constituted respectful behavior, outdated traditions, or disrespectful engagements with change.

I already alluded to this uncertainty surrounding respectable conduct in the Introduction to this book, where Taha critiqued elders for seemingly aimlessly sitting on a *baraza* while the community needed an active, though morally responsible, engagement with change. Elaborating on Taha's call for moral presence, I explained how a moral narrative of modernity (Keane 2007) presents young people's pursuit of education, employment, and overall progress as a moral responsibility to produce a certain kind of "modern" self that can contribute to the general well-being of the Lamu community. Yet the foregoing chapters obviated that, in Lamu, there is not necessarily an agreement on what this working toward a "modern" self can or should entail. Elders especially have reservations as to what effects "progress" might have on an individual's moral condition, with the fear of Islamic principles being forsaken for an adherence to nonlocal, Western values. At the same time, however, these condemnations of change were always entangled with perceptions of an encroaching Kenyan state, intended on undermining Lamu residents' Islamic identities. More concretely, young people's attending higher education, for example, could be valuable to the development of the Lamu community, but at the same time obligated youth to participate in a secular and urban context, where they are exposed to Standard Swahili, to social norms different from those upheld in Lamu, and to the influence of the Kenyan government. To many, the moral in narratives of modernity then negatively implies a possible loss of moral values shaped by Islamic creed in favor of an orientation to Western norms and ideologies and a submission to a "foreign" government (see also Amidou 2009; Caplan 2009, 2011, 2013; Fuglesang 1994; Saleh 2004). And while the *baraza*-sitting elder might no longer be a model of moral conduct, his observing gaze and evaluative discourses are the context in which young people needed to negotiate a redefined moral presence.

Young women are often at the heart of these concerns (Beckman 2015; Fuglesang 1994; Thompson and Stiles 2015). Chapter 1 described how Lamu was (and continues to be) a highly stratified society where social status is assigned based on length of residence, family lineage, wealth, and honor, all of which are reflected in a person's observable display of respectability or *heshima* (Iliffe 2005; Kresse 2009; Hillewaert 2016; McMahon 2006; Saleh 2004). While the former merchant elites' moral code of respect is no longer hegemonic, it continues to structure life on the island and comprises important behavioral rules, including norms of appropriate social interaction and displays of *haya* or modesty (McMahon 2006). Historically, there existed an important gender distinction in this public attribution of social status based on displays of respectability. In the not so distant past, a man's status was mainly ascribed based on his public display of respectful conduct, whereas a woman's *heshima* rested in her ability to avoid the public eye. From the end of the nineteenth century until a few decades ago, Lamu women lived in *purdah*, and the ability to live in seclusion was itself indicative of social status (Askew 1999; Fair 2001). Only upper-class women could afford to uphold *purdah*, whereas (former) slave girls and lower-class women (often immigrants from surrounding islands) did appear in public, albeit covered.[2] The previously hegemonic notion of respectability was therefore very much associated with a particular group of Lamu residents—the patrician clans.

The contemporary emphasis on girls' participation in secular education and on young women's right and need to participate in the labor force brought women back outside onto the streets. Higher education now has become a sign of prosperity and economic wealth. Currently, many Lamu women work, shop, or visit friends in different parts of town, at any time of day (Hillewaert 2016). This visible presence, however, is precarious; it is subject to social scrutiny precisely because men outside of the immediate family can now observe women's behavior beyond the privacy of the home. This shift in the nature and extent of social surveillance introduced questions of social control and individual responsibility. And while the kind of public might have shifted, the previously hegemonic moral evaluation of women's observable behavior and its embodied respectability lingers. A sign of progress and modernity to some, women's participation in public life can equally be viewed as a potential transgression of social, spatial, and moral boundaries by others (see also Inoue 2007). One can then ask how young women in particular answer Taha's call for presence—for a morally responsible engagement with change and development—and how this question of presence intimately and tightly folds into questions of self-presentation.

Women in contemporary Lamu endeavor to navigate this contested field in different ways and through different means, including the strategic use of geographic space (see Chapters 4 and 5). By planning their movements through town, women exploit the ideological valuation of different physical locations to manage moral judgment of their public presence and thus the evaluation of their moral character. This expected awareness of the moral values ideologically associated with particular locales, however, also assumes individual responsibility: a young woman chooses where to walk (and to avoid or avail herself to particular kinds of gazes) and can therefore be judged based on individual intention and moral character. I do not mean to suggest that young women still willfully adhere to previously hegemonic notions of respectability and virtuous femininity, but rather that an awareness of possible judgments avails opportunities for strategic self-presentation. At the same time, however, an awareness of social expectations equally enables young women to blatantly challenge previously hegemonic ideologies of virtuous femininity associated with the former merchant elites. Some young women from Bajuni backgrounds, for example, quite intentionally use their public appearance to lay claims to shifting notions of *heshima*, informed by translocal discourses on education, progress, urbanity, or emancipation.

Young Women as Slaves

It was late afternoon in March 2008, shortly after the afternoon prayers. The sun was still blazing hot as Mwalim Baddi and I joined one of the *baraza* near Mkunguni, Lamu's main square separating the neighborhoods of Mkomani and Langoni. One of the busiest times of day, the men silently observed the hectic traffic of men, women, donkeys, and handcarts as they sipped their coffee and snacked on local sweets. Feeling uncomfortable joining the well-established and exclusively male space of a Swahili *baraza*, I remained quiet and tried to keep a respectable distance from the elderly men dressed in white *kanzu*. Usually a place of lively political or philosophical debates, I was certain the silence on the bench was due to my presence and hoped Mwalim Baddi would soon initiate a conversation. After a short while, Mwalim thanked the men for letting us join them and introduced me as the young woman who they had all seen around town, who came to Lamu to study language and cultural change. He clarified that he was helping me gather opinions on how life in Lamu had changed over the last few years, and explained that we would appreciate their views, as respected elderly residents. Mwalim Baddi's clarification of our presence was received with a few head nods and vocal confirmations. But the *baraza* was silent, and I wondered whether it would be better for me to just thank the men for their time and excuse myself. I carefully glanced at Mwalim, who subtly signaled for me to be patient.

The men continued to watch people walk by, and after what seemed like an eternity, one of the elder *baraza* members cleared his throat and gestured toward a group of young women who had just bought roasted cassava from one of the vendors nearby. As they continued their walk through town, the girls laughed audibly about something one of them had said and chatted while they consumed their snack. When the young women passed in front of the *baraza* where we were seated, a subtle but pleasant wave of incense and jasmine flowers reached us. I am not sure whether it was the seductive scent, their eating in public, their indistinct chattering, or a combination of all of these, but the man who had pointed them out sighed and remarked,

> Zamani huwezi kuzunguka barabani wamwona mwanamke kiBajuni au kiIslamu anayekula barabarani, wala kuna time fulani ikifika kwamba huwezi kuona wanawake kabisa. Sasa hiyau mpaka masaa sita za usiku unawaona wanawake barabani. Sasa kujivunia ana mila gani? Wanawake wetu wanatembea uchi, mambo ambayo si mila wala si katika dini yetu.

> In the past, you could not walk on the street and see a Bajuni or Muslim woman eating on the street, and there was a certain time when you could not see women at all. Now you can see women on the street until twelve o'clock at night. Now what *mila* (traditions) is she proud of? Our women are walking around naked, something that is not part of our *mila* (traditions) or of our *dini* (religion).

The man's comment, evoked by the young women's observable conduct, was responded to with much agreement from his fellow *baraza* members and resulted in a long discussion on young people's altering behaviors, with a particular focus on the changing attitudes of young women. I couldn't help but feel as if this focus on women's changed comportment was an indirect commentary on my presence at the *baraza* as well. Although I wasn't a Lamu resident, and while the norms of respectability did not equally apply to me as they did to young Lamu women, my presence at the bench did deviate from established norms and, to a certain extent, challenged the respectability of the *baraza* itself.

The entire conversation, however, had been triggered by the passing-by of three young women, engaged in what at first sight would appear to be an everyday activity—an afternoon stroll with friends, while eating a snack. However, different aspects of the young women's behavior—walking at a particular location (Lamu's main square, in front of a *baraza*), at a particular time of day (after the afternoon prayers), engaging in a particular activity (talking audibly while eating in public), displaying behavior that often is associated with more private spheres (eating but also having a particular scent), and seemingly without a specific purpose (strolling around instead of having a concrete destination)—were considered grounds for moral condemnation by their observers. Moreover, it allowed this audience to draw conclusions about other behaviors at other times—midnight walks—and thus to evaluate these girls as a certain *type* of people: women who had lost respect for local values in favor of supposed "urban" habits.

To the men on the *baraza*, this seemingly insignificant practice of an afternoon stroll was illustrative of the very focus of my research. Indeed, the elderly men considered the young women's behavior as stemming from the broader social, political, and economic changes that affected the community; the young women's particular public presence was considered iconic of the moral decline of the Lamu community. They did not criticize the young women for having gone on a walk per se; rather, the *baraza* members critiqued these women's choice of route together with their behavior for lacking modesty and showing disrespect to the men in front of whom they were passing. Precisely the young women's seeming obliviousness to or, indeed, possibly deliberate disregard of behavioral rules tied to *heshima* was considered illustrative of the moral condition of the community. The inability to know the young women's intent—whether their behavior was innocent and redeemable or a blatant affront—did not seem to impact the elders' evaluation. To these men, the "modern" attitudes the young women displayed did little to benefit or advance the community; it merely demonstrated an ideological hailing to the comportments of "others" and thus the pitfalls of social change.

Especially interesting are the words the elderly man used to depict the behavior of these girls and other women "like them." Although Lamu women generally do not leave the house unless fully covered—they wear the black *buibui* and a headscarf, and many cover their face with a niqab—the man described contemporary women's appearance as *uchi*. The kiSwahili word *uchi* literally means "naked," but it can also refer to being uncovered, exposed, and open. In all cases, however, it carries the negative connotations of a kind of nakedness, of shamelessness. The *baraza* members' emphasis on the nakedness of contemporary Lamu women does not necessarily suggest that women are removing the veil or leaving the house without a *buibui*. Rather, it signals women's changing physical locations and, particularly, their behavior within those locales. In fact, the evaluation of these young women as "naked" derives not only from possible resemblances with the behaviors of scantly dressed Euro-American tourists who are deemed oblivious to notions of respectful conduct, but also from similarities with the practices of historical slaves, who generally left the house uncovered, at different times of day. Thus, in addition to the iconicity of adopting practices of another group (nonlocals and mostly Euro-American tourists), young women are also framed as slavelike based on the presumed iconic resemblance between their conduct and that of historical slaves.

One might object that this is merely the voice of disgruntled former elites who struggle with the fact that not all Lamu residents endeavor to uphold their previously hegemonic behavioral norms, and with lower class residents now openly challenging their moral authority. Yet the elder on this specific *baraza* was from Bajuni background rather than from the patrician clans, and he would likely be considered a *mgeni* or guest by these former elites. And rather than refer to formerly pious behaviors of upper-class Lamu women, the elder's nostalgic reflection contrasted the youth's comportment with the historically virtuous appearance of Bajuni women. More than a frustrated response to a loss of elite moral and social authority, the evaluation of these youth's behavior therefore needs to be placed within a sociopolitical context of perceived dispossession and the encroaching presence of nonlocals whose behaviors young people are seen as appropriating. Rather than be condemned for ignoring a particular elite notion of uprightness, the young women are critiqued for forsaken moral norms that are seen to be at the heart of a distinctive Lamu identity and that separate Lamu residents from mainland Kenyans. Indeed, the elder's remark illustrates how residents can discursively erase local social distinctions informed by different notions of respectable behavior, when opposed to the Kenyan mainland.

At the same time, one could remark that the negative evaluations of youth and social transformation are again expressed by *baraza* elders—by the once authoritative, male voices that are now themselves increasingly being criticized for not contributing to development. One might then be tempted to write off these elders' nostalgic reflections as an example of generational discord; after all, where does one not find (grand)parents who complain about young people's lack of respect and their altered modes of dress? Of course, this is partially true, yet this doesn't make the elders' moral condemnations any less significant. *Baraza* in Lamu have not entirely lost their (moral) authority, and the judgments expressed by these elders meaningfully inform the self-evaluating frame of young people who endeavor to negotiate newly emerging social positions in contemporary Lamu, as will become strikingly evident in Chapters 4 and 5.

These depictions of young women as slaves, however, were not limited to elder men and were not just a matter of generational change. In this chapter's opening vignette, for example, Hasan equally referred to the Muslim girls at the seafront to explain to me his proverbial comparison between Lamu youth and *watumwa*. This association was not based exclusively on Hasan's assumptions about the young women's slave ancestry or on an observation of their phenotypical traits, as other debates on the lasting impact of slavery in contemporary postslavery societies might assume (see, for example, Cooper 1977; Eastman 1994; Kopytoff and Miers 1977). Nor did Hasan depict all young Lamu women as *watumwa*. Rather, the physical location and material practices of these specific girls—their presence at the seafront, in front of a *baraza*, together with their open-style *buibui*, tight jeans, and uninhibited interactions—motivated his evaluation of them as contemporary slaves.

In their conversations with me, young women often displayed awareness of their ambiguous position within contemporary Lamu, and of the different ways in which their public behaviors were read. Khadija, for example, was a young woman who held strong opinions about Lamu, and particularly about young people's responsibility to contribute to the wellbeing of their community. Belonging to a prominent and affluent Bajuni family, she was spending a year in Lamu after graduating high school and before starting college. During this time, Khadija decided to volunteer for an aid organization with an active youth section. The young volunteers frequently planned awareness-raising activities in town, focusing on a range of health issues (including the prevention of HIV/AIDS, malaria, or cholera). After one of those afternoon activities, the three of us—Khadija, my research assistant Omari, and I—sat down in a small office space along Lamu's main street where the volunteers had set up a cyber café. By attracting tourists and locals in need of Internet access, the volunteers hoped to raise money to reinvest in the office, to eventually provide an income generating activity for unemployed youth. Young men and women walked in and out of the workplace to inquire about upcoming activities, to greet their peers, and to spend time outside of the home, away from household chores.

As we sat down with a cup of chai, Omari inquired about Khadija's opinions on life in contemporary Lamu: Did she think life in the town changed significantly since, for example, her parents were young? Khadija followed her affirmative answer with a lengthy description of how young people's everyday behaviors had shifted, particularly in terms of language use and dress. When asked what she thought about these changes, she responded:

> Kulingana na ule msemo kwamba mwata mila ni mtumwa, sisi tumekuwa watumwa. Kwa sababu sisi tuna asili yetu, tuna mila zetu, tuna akhlaq zetu tulivofundishwa. Lakini kwa sababu sisi twataka kuwa wabora, twataka kuwaigiza ili twaona kama sisi ni wabora imebidi sisi kwa kiwango fulani tubadilishe mila zetu na kwa hivo tumekuwa sisi ndo watumwa.

> It is like that proverb that states that whoever leaves their *mila* (traditions) is a slave, we have become slaves because we have our *asili* (origins), we have our *mila* (traditions), we have our *akhlaq* (morality), and what we were taught. But because we want to be the best, we want to copy others such that we consider ourselves to be the best, it's necessary for us to change our *mila* (traditions) to a certain extent and thus we have become slaves.

Whereas Hasan had previously attributed the status of slavery to other youth, and to young women in particular, Khadija now used the same proverb to describe the moral state of "us"—of contemporary Lamu youth, including Omari and herself. Just like slaves in the past had appropriated upper-class patricians' consumer habits to be incorporated into Lamu society, so do young people now follow nonlocals' practices in the hope of being identified or recognized as being "like" them—modern, developed, "better." The embracing of these habits, Khadija suggested, indicates an acknowledgment of the desirability of nonlocals' social and economic position and, most important, of their moral values. Young people's obliviousness to or conscious disregard for local notions of respectful and civilized behavior therefore resembles the habits of *washenzi*. Like slaves in the past, youth are then viewed as mediating an opposition between *uungwana* as the ideal Swahili condition and *ushenzi* as the non-Islamic, foreign barbarian.

Khadija, however, did not stop there. She immediately elaborated on her comparison of contemporary youth to slaves, further framing her answer within discourses of development. Instead of attributing young people's state of enslavement solely to a blind hailing to translocal influences, she underlined that youth had a responsibility to distinguish between valuable traditions that ought to be preserved and outdated ones that prevent positive change.

Mimi ndo kama kioo cha jamii. Mimi ndiyo kama carrier. Nitabeba
hii information. Nipeleke next. Mimi ndo nitarelay hii information
kwengine. Lakini ikiwa mimi sasa nimeisahau information hii ama
mimi siitilii manaa, ama sioni kama ina faidha yoyote information
kama hii, siwezi kuipeleka mbee. Ijapokuwa kuna zile mila ambazo
lazima tuziate sabu kulingana na wakati kama huu ama kulingana na
maadili ya kibinadamu, mila nyingine lazima ziatwe.

I am thus like a mirror of the community. I am like a carrier. I will
carry this information. I will take it to [the] next [generation]. I will
relay this information elsewhere. But if I have now forgotten this
information, or I don't attribute meaning to it, or I don't see information like this has any value, I cannot take it forward. However, there
are some *mila* (traditions) that we ought to leave behind, considering
the times we are in, or considering the values of humanity certain *mila*
(traditions) have to be left behind.

Preempting possible condemnations of her own behavior—as a female
college student who was volunteering in a mixed-gender environment—
Khadija discursively linked the significance of respectful conduct, and thus
the preservation of *heshima* as an organizing principle in everyday life, to an
equally important engagement with change and development. In a way, she
explained precisely what a morally responsible engagement with development and change—Taha's call for "presence"—ought to entail for young
women in Lamu. While some Lamu residents might condemn young
people's (and particularly young women's) behavior as a state of enslavement, Khadija suggested that youth are capable of distinguishing between
those local practices that need to be preserved and those that are redundant,
old-fashioned, and prevent positive development. The well-being of contemporary Lamu and its future, Khadija suggested, lies in finding that balance. In her commentary, Khadija then implicitly spoke back to discourses
that equate young women and slaves. Instead of lacking *heshima*, women's
appearance and participation in public—their education, employment, and
activism—can be an integral part of much-needed development (and thus a
moral good in itself), if appropriate distinctions between outdated practices
(such as *purdah*) and valuable norms (such as modesty) can be determined.

This ambiguity as to what respectful conduct entails in contemporary
Lamu featured frequently in young people's discussions about their everyday lives, and their opinions on the practices of their peers. Sadiq,
for example, was a twenty-six-year-old man and an active member of
the volunteer group of which Khadijah also formed part. Single and

unemployed, Sadiq spent most of his days at the tiny office, managing the cybercafé and coordinating new activities for the volunteers. Highly opinionated, he had suggested several times he would be happy to speak to me about my research. When starting our interview, Sadiq strongly affirmed Omari's initial remark that Lamu had changed over the last several years. He quickly followed up with a lengthy, monologue-like narration, offering examples that, he believed, illustrated the moral decline of the community. One of these examples focused on young people's attitudes toward relationships and marriage:

> Sasa utakuta hizi ndroa zetu, zinakwendra, zinasambaratika. Maanake, kwa sababu ya utamaduni uliepukika. Utamaduni wa kizamani ulikuwa umefungana na dini kukwambia la ukweli. Na utamaduni ulikuwa na mila. Kama vile watu wa zamani wanavovaa wanawake shuga utaona ni kibandra kiyao. [laughs]

> [Sadiq and Omari continue to laugh (5.0)]

> Utaona ni kibandra kiyao. [laughs] Kumbe ni mtu yuwaja! Humuoni chochote! Ule ni utamaduni, lakini umeambatana na dini. Lakini sisi huku, tumeacha ule utamaduni, imekuwa sasa utamaduni kuuwacha, mpaka dini pia imeachika. Sasa hiyo ndrio tatizo kubwa.

> Now you will find that our marriages, they go, they fall apart. I mean, because *utamaduni* (culture) was avoided. *Utamaduni* from the past was tied to *dini* (religion) to say the truth. And *utamaduni* used to consist of *mila* (traditions). For example, in the past, the way women wore their abaya you would think it is a tent that is coming toward you. [laughs]

> [Sadiq and Omari continue to laugh for about 5 seconds]

> You would think a tent is coming. [laughs] Behold, it is a person who's coming! You can't see anything of her. That is *utamaduni* (culture)! But it is tied to *dini* (religion). But we, we have left that *utamaduni* (culture). *Utamaduni* has been left to such an extent that even *dini* has been left behind. Now that is a big problem.

Sadiq's overall argument appears to mirror that of the elder *baraza* men: the loss of respect for *utamaduni* or culture is linked to an increasing loss of religion and *mila* (traditions), resulting in the overall moral decay of the Lamu community. Like Hasan and the *baraza* elders, Sadiq considered young women to be iconic of this shift and, like the *baraza* elders, he contrasted present-day women's behaviors to the moral uprightness of Lamu women in the past. Yet, the manner in which Sadiq delivered his commentary reveals an alternative and, at times, seemingly contradictory stance toward the moral shift he is describing.

Sadiq focused his explanation of social change on the public appearance of Lamu women, comparing it to the historical use of the *shiraa*—a tent-like construction covering the entire body, held up by two sticks, previously used by upper-class women to leave the house (see Chapter 1). While offered as an example of the bygone moral uprightness of Lamu women, and thus meant to illustrate the regrettable loss of respectful modes of conduct, the image of the *shiraa* evoked uncontrollable laughter from both Sadiq and Omari. Rather than admirable and desirable, the image of women walking under tent-like constructions seemed humorous to both young men. Although Sadiq explicated and emphasized the importance of moral values like modesty and while he provided the example of the *shiraa* to illustrate how Lamu's traditional practices enabled the embodiment of values of respectability, the laughter simultaneously signaled a distancing from those traditions and suggested that this, in fact, would not be a desirable mediation of these norms in present-day Lamu.

Sadiq's opinion, while to a large extent echoing elders' concerns, also signaled ambivalence surrounding the moral good and its mediation within practice. In other words, while the importance of modesty, religion, and respectability is not questioned, how these values ought to be mediated in everyday practices is not as evident. The preceding example of the *shiraa* and the laughter it evoked, in a way, illustrates Khadija's argument that young people ought to differentiate the outdated from the valuable: while covering is important, the practice of *shiraa* is outdated. Sadiq and Khadija's reflections demonstrate that Lamu youth very actively contemplate how to reconsider norms of behavior in relation to the current needs of the community, and how that in turn informs what it means to be an upright Muslim in contemporary Lamu (and Kenya more broadly).

Contemplations like these interestingly show that Lamu youth are much aware of the evaluative discourses that are circulating within their community. In fact, their statements are highly interdiscursive—a range of different discourses inform and can be found within these reflections on life in contemporary Lamu and debates about what constitutes, in this case, respectable womanhood. Young people like Khadija are then always already speaking back to dominant or previously hegemonic ideologies of ideal behavior, recognizing their importance but simultaneously critiquing them by drawing upon translocal discourses on development, emancipation, and "correct" Islamic practice rather than upon traditions. Through this interdiscursivity—this simultaneous drawing on local and translocal discourses—these self-reflective, evaluative narratives uncover young people's ambivalent position within Lamu society; they display irresolute positions, as situated between respect for tradition and a longing for change, all the while keeping Islamic virtues as a concern. These ambivalences are not necessarily about "failures" to live up to normative Islam, but rather about what virtues like modesty and piety entail within this specific sociopolitical context—about how they ought to be mediated within everyday interactions. In fact, the linguistic and stylistic variation within these young people's narratives reveals the different "voices" (Bakhtin 1981; Hill 1995; Keane 2011) through which Lamu youth strategically endeavor to position themselves in everyday exchanges, and through which they gradually negotiate newly emerging social positions.

By "voice" I refer to the idea that our everyday interactions consist of different utterances, sounds, words, or registers that are habitually associated with a certain type of person or character. As Mikhail Bakhtin (1981) argued, novels and films are animated by having its characters draw upon particular voices and thus make recognizable to the audience the "types" of people they are to represent. Scholars of language have expanded the idea of "voice" to include the multiplicity of registers through which speakers animate everyday interactions—when we speak, we select a particular voice through which to present ourselves and represent others. Scholars have argued that such choice of voice has a distinctly moral character; precisely because it is a choice among options, speakers express a moral stance by selecting one representation over another (Hill 1995; Keane 2011). When I say that Lamu youth's everyday interactions are replete with different voices, I suggest that, by selecting particular discourses over others, they express different orientations toward the transformations the community is undergoing and thus position themselves and others as particular kinds of individuals. Rather than see the presence of multiple voices in these discourses as an internal struggle for the dominance of one of the moral positions they index (Hill 1995), this heterogeneous use of discursive resources enables young people to discursively enact (and partially negotiate) positions of ambivalence; it permits them to express and create moral spaces for positions of inbetweenness.

Beach Boys as Proverbial Slaves

The foregoing discussion of the moral condemnation of young women based on their outward appearances might lead us to assume a gendering notion of contemporary conceptualizations of "slavery" in Lamu or of the moral deterioration of the community. Indeed, many of the discourses I have analyzed thus far come from *baraza* discussions—exclusively male spaces where condemnations of young women's appearances, and particularly their movements in front of the *baraza*, are frequent. There is no equivalent for *baraza* for women (social gatherings in homes do not quite count as a *baraza*) and the evaluations that inform young women's attempts at redefining (public) respectability therefore often derive from the male gaze. An analysis of the discursive evaluations of youth in contemporary Lamu needs to be attuned to such gendered divisions in assessments and how these are based on differential spatial access, behavior, time (what are appropriate times to leave the house), and communicative modes.

While less the subject of *baraza* discussions, young men's behaviors were, however, also subjected to moral condemnation. When, during a recent field visit, I asked Ustadh Mahmoud (who we encountered in Chapter 2) whether young women, more so than young men, were vulnerable to the negative aspects of change, he strongly objected. The imam agreed that the changes for young women were more visible—through their public presence or their changing modes of dress, for example—but that young women also actively took advantage of the new opportunities available to them: they excelled in school, were eager to work, and were often actively involved in development programs. Young men, on the other hand, were much more likely to get caught up in the appeal of travels away from the island, for example, focusing their efforts on developing interactions with Euro-American tourists rather than education. In other cases, the economic decline of Lamu resulted in frustrations about an inability to provide, causing some young men to resort to drug and substance abuse. Ustadh Mahmoud argued that young women and men were *both* the focus of allegations of subjugation in present-day Lamu. In fact, young men's moral obligation to be the breadwinner placed them at a particularly vulnerable position for condemnation. Indeed, the macro-sociological shifts impacting the Lamu community played out very differently in the lives of young men and women; whereas the latter needed to negotiate their moral uprightness as they engage with a range of formerly unavailable (educational or economic) opportunities, the former were urged to defend their moral character when faced with unemployment and economic scarcity in a context where men are quite often still expected to provide.

Although he had not explicitly pointed them out, Hasan's proverbial condemnation of young people's conduct, for example, was equally applicable to another group of youth present at the seafront that afternoon. The "beach boys," or "dhow operators," as they prefer to be called, who had been hang-ing around the old cannons and who had called out to the American, female tourists were the focus of similar social judgments throughout my fieldwork. Wearing short pants (above the knee, showing part of the thigh),[3] T-shirts with the image of Bob Marley, and tricolored Rastafarian bracelets and necklaces, the young men sporting dreadlocks contrasted sharply with other men on the seafront—both with elders who habitually wore the white *kanzu* and with young men like Hasan who generally wore long pants or a *kikoi* and a *kofia* (Figure 12). More so than the young women wearing jeans under-neath their *buibui*, these young men's outward appearances reflected an adherence to outside influences and an ignoring of local expectations of re-spectful conduct. And while, in contrast to the girls, their physical presence on the seafront did not in itself cross the boundaries of *heshima*, Lamu resi-dents frequently evaluated the way these young men sat around as an unpro-ductive kind of idleness, lacking respectability, that contrasted with the leisurely conversing of the Swahili elders on the *baraza*.

Although seemingly less subjected to explicit moralizing discourses, beach boys are a stigmatized group within the Lamu community. Whereas young women are singled out as examples of impending moral decline, the young men on Lamu's seafront are often considered the epitome of the neg-ative outcomes of global influence and the ultimate embodiment of the

Figure 12. Lamu "beach boys," or dhow operators. Photograph by Jo Valvekens.

proverbial slaves in Hasan's statement. Although the young men themselves view their outward appearance and constant presence on the seafront as instruments in their attempts to appeal to tourists and thus strategic tools in their commercial endeavors, other community members consider the beach boys' practices to be directly indicative of an altered internal moral state. By discursively linking the young men's consumer habits to their desire to socialize with tourists, and the lack of *heshima* both of these are believed to entail, many Lamu residents relegate beach boys to the category of modern-day slaves. A recent public debate illustrates this point.

On April 16, 2014, a member of Lamu's county council who is a resident of the island proposed a motion to ban miniskirts, short shorts, and dreadlocks in the town. "Tourists come to behold our culture. If we dress up decently the way we do"—referring to the locally considered "proper" Islamic dress—"why shouldn't they emulate us if they really are interested in our culture?" she said, explaining the motivations for the motion. The council member further argued that "beach boys should equally respect the rules governing our culture." In response to objections that the motion would damage the local tourism industry, upon which Lamu depended for 70 percent of its income and in which beach boys played a central role, the council member and her supporters argued that culture ought to be upheld and respected by both visitors and locals (Kazungu 2014a, 2014b; Praxides 2014).

While the motion was not passed, mainly because of an opposing vote from nonlocal, Christian members of the council, the debate on the so-called dreadlock ban meaningfully speaks to the controversies and contradictions surrounding Lamu's beach boys and the role they play in the town's economy.[4] The motion and the support it received from within the Lamu community not only openly condemned the young men's outward appearances, they also placed their conduct on the same level as the behavior of *wazungu* or "white people" and the latter's disregard of Lamu's cultural and religious norms. Moreover, the motion dismissed the contributions dhow operators make to the economic survival of Lamu, and thus the framework of employment within which the young men's practices could be justified. Rather than be gainfully employed and contribute to the economic well-being of the community (in itself, one could argue, a moral good), these young men were considered to be idly waiting to entertain tourists. And their material practices were evaluated within this same framework of longing joblessness. As Hasan said: *Mwata mila ni mtumwa*. To Lamu residents such as the county council member, beach boys were a group of youth who placed pleasing others above their own norms and traditions, or rather they were willing to sacrifice their own moral values for the possibility of acquiring some economic revenue, and in making such servitude their daily occupation these young men were perceived to embody the proverbial slave.

My argument here differs somewhat from other academic discussions on the phenomenon of beach boys in the global South. One might assume that we need to understand the condemnation of beach boys in relation to other globally circulating discourses. That is, one might think that the Muslim community of Lamu deems beach boys to be morally problematic because of the notion of sex tourism that is so frequently linked to this phenomenon—as other academic studies propose (see, for example, Eades 2009; Herold, Garcia, and Demora 2001; Oppermann 1999; Ryan and Hall 2001). However, few of these studies have explored community perceptions of beach boys and their activities (but see Meiu 2015). Moreover, Lamu differs quite significantly from other localities where research on sex tourism has been conducted, such as Malindi or Mombasa in Kenya (Bergan 2011; Kibicho 2005) or the Gambia in West Africa (Brown 1992; Nyanzi et al. 2005), all of which are known destinations for sex tourists. While it may be the case that Lamu residents who criticize beach boys' behavior draw in part upon such broader circulating discourses, we cannot fully grasp the moral condemnation of these young men's occupation outside Lamu's historical context of *utumwa* and the moral values that shaped the society at the time.

As Muslim youth, beach boys, most of whom were born in Lamu Town, are considered integral members of the Lamu community, distinct from nonlocal, non-Muslim *wageni* and can thus never be fully considered *washenzi* or barbarians. Yet the markers of beach boy identity—their hairstyles, modes of dress, language use, and constant presence on the seafront—are differently read as strategic commercial tools and active scouting (by beach boys themselves) or as a shameless imitation of, and an idle waiting for foreigners (by other community members). The young men's hawking of seemingly useless services and their assumed insensibility to the religious and moral norms that should inform *waungwana*'s public conduct motivates many Lamu residents to draw parallels between the behavior of beach boys and that of slaves based on the elements of moral servitude it is seen to entail.

The comparison, however, is not solely motivated by the perceived abandonment of respectful material practices. The physical servitude and laziness that these young men's occupation is seen to embody equally defies norms of *heshima*. Beach boys' work is depicted as "labor that does not count" by using the ideological distinctions between *waungwana* and *washenzi*, and the respectful leisure and disrespectful idleness in which these groups respectively are seen to engage. While earning money could be constructed as a contribution to development, the question of employment or unemployment in the case of the dhow operators is not one of economic revenue or of contributions to the financial health of the community. It is a matter of morality and respectability. The ability to avoid submission to the whims of others continues to be indicative of one's *uungwana* or nobility and success as an employer rather than an employee. After all, in Lamu, employees would historically have fallen under the category of slaves. The view of "the beach boy" as contemporary slave thus entails a form of racialization, of discursively distinguishing the idleness of the African young man from the leisure of the Arab nobleman. In the elites' previously hegemonic ideology, the latter's relaxing on a *baraza* was a sign of success and imbued him with *heshima*, while the former's sitting was a sign of longing for servitude and encouraged comparisons to enslavement. Both are indicative of social class, moral standing, and racialized identity.

At the same time, beach boys (and sometimes their families) challenged the authority of such moral judgments, signaling broader economic transformations that are forcing Lamu residents to search for alternative or new sources of income. In order to make ends meet, former merchant elites are increasingly compelled to sell their homes to the Euro-American expatriates and tourists with whom the beach boys work. The latter, at least at some point, made much money in tourist trade, including earning commissions on house-sales as they introduced potential buyers to upper-class house owners. This difference in income generation, and the associated ability to provide for families, equally informs the strain between elite elders and beach boys. In other words, the criticisms of these young men, while informed by notions of Islamic virtue, are also shaped by anxieties surrounding economic revenue and authority. Indeed, one can ask who is more morally upright or a "better" Muslim in this case: the elder sitting on the *baraza* voicing opinions about social (and political) change or the young man hanging around at the seafront searching for employment, both equally idle but with different purposes. Precisely these contrasts progressively allow for a challenging of previously hegemonic notions of *heshima*, enabling residents like the beach boys to claim respectability on grounds other than those of former elites.

The young men working as dhow operators were well aware of the negative opinions many Lamu residents held of them. They similarly crafted their responses to such critiques (and my inquiries about them) in moral terms. In the current economic context, beach boys suggested, the tourism industry is often the most lucrative for young men who otherwise struggle to find a job. They thereby justified their self-fashionings and material practices as mere strategies—as tools used to appeal to tourists that could easily be left behind once the job was finished or once they changed employment. Being a "beach boy" was then not a lifestyle but rather a way of earning a living. The young men would provide examples of "retired" beach boys who had now married local women and were respected Lamu residents. They also emphasized how they tried to maintain their five daily prayers, or at least attend the Friday sermon. In addition, they would fast during the month of Ramadan and often limit their interactions with tourists during the holy month. Of course, these claims also need to be placed in context. While this argument had some validity when Lamu's tourism industry flourished (in the late 1980s and 1990s), the recent dip in tourist activity (following a range of terrorist attacks along the coast and international government's negative travel advisories for Kenya) makes such statements increasingly less credible.

What interests me here, however, is the response these young men offered to the condemnations of their behaviors and the moral tone their rebuttals took. The negative reactions to their comportment and employment, so the dhow operators proposed, mainly derived from the former merchant elites who had particular opinions on what respectable conduct ought to entail, notions they had historically been able to impose on others (based on their economic and political authoritative position). The young men suggested that the former elites were displeased with the challenges the beach boys (and people from Bajuni backgrounds who live in Lamu) posed, not to the reputation of the town, but to the hierarchy structures those formerly hegemonic norms were meant to uphold. The dhow operators quite explicitly questioned former elites' motivations for insisting on practices that were historically deemed respectable and indicative of *heshima*. For example, they suggested that patricians' insistence on gender segregation and limits to visibility and intimacy had little to do with respectability or moral uprightness, but rather was about masking these groups' true (non-Arab) origins. Referring to the historical view of *uungwana* or nobility that intimately linked Arab genealogy to respectability and social status, the beach boys suggested that these former elites were not Arab at all and that their claims to supremacy were therefore void.

The following conversation unfolded after I had asked a group of dhow operators, all between the ages of nineteen and twenty-five, about their lifestyle and the negative opinions other Lamu residents have of working with tourists. The conversation quickly turned to which group of residents most often critiqued the beach boys and the, sometimes tense, social relations between different segments of the Lamu community. The young men reminded me that, while some beach boys lived on the Mkomani side of town, the majority of them identified as Bajuni—as coming from one of the surrounding islands of the Lamu Archipelago—and lived in Langoni, the area of town where *wageni* habitually settled. In the eyes of the patrician families, they argued, residents of Bajuni descent always remained *wageni* and would never be considered fully local. And while interactions and friendships across the social divide—between *wenyeji* in Mkomani and *wageni* in Langoni— were common nowadays, the distinction remained significant, with patricians often claiming a higher social status based on particular understandings of *heshima* and their supposed inherent *uungwana* or nobility. The young men suggested, however, that some of the practices these families claimed to be essential to *heshima* had little to do with modesty and religiosity.

A: Sikia, ukienda kule, zizere zao huwaoni. Kwa sababu gani? Wako tofauti sana wao. Huwasita wale. Mila ya Pokomo, waPokomo safi. Umeona siyo? Weusi! Hata utashangaa ukiambiwa huyo bibi yake ni huyu.

A: Listen, when you go there, you do not see their elder women. Why? They are very different. They hide them. Pokomo traditions, pure Pokomo.[5] You understand, right? Black! You would even be amazed if you were told that she's his grandmother.

B: Kama rafiki yako ni kijoho, ukienda naye kwenye nyumba, we . . . usiingie ndani!

B: When your friend is kijoho[6] and you go to his house . . . You better not go inside!

C: Usiingie ndani, kabisa huingii.

C: Do not go inside, you won't get in.

D: Kendra kwao atafanya kivovote, afanye harakati yoyote ili akupate pale pale mlangoni.

D: When you go to their place, they will do no matter what, he will do anything to catch you there at the door.

E: Mbajuni amwambia "chwende zechu, ingia ndani msela."

E: A Bajuni says, "let's go home, go inside my friend."

F: Nyumbani hapa, wakati wowote nzee karibu.

F: Consider this your home; you are welcome anytime friend.

The young men proposed that, rather than a display of *heshima*, former elites' continued insistence on segregation—on shielding women from outsiders' eyes and therefore entertaining visitors on the outside *baraza*, rather than inside the house—was an attempt at upholding claims to Arab genealogy, despite the fact that some of their grandmothers were evidently from African descent. The dhow operators suggested that, in contemporary Lamu, true respectability did not lie in the strict monitoring of visibility and intimacy, but rather in welcoming visitors to one's home and entertaining them there. That kind of hospitality, they argued, is a true sign of *heshima* and moral uprightness.

While much less subtle and strategic, the young men's statements resemble Khadija's earlier argument: *heshima* as a moral value remains important in contemporary Lamu, but what constitutes respectable behavior is less evident. These young men challenged patricians' view of *heshima* as linked to specific forms of modesty and limits to interaction, and thereby equally contested a social hierarchy structured on claims to particular kinds of respectable conduct. At the same time, however, the beach boys' discussion obviates the complex intersections of ideological understandings of respectability and social status, race, and economic wealth.

As a previously hegemonic ideology, *heshima* thus remains a significant structuring principle on the basis of which Muslim residents of Lamu continue to be evaluated. Chapter 1 demonstrated that embodied *heshima* remains central to "being from Lamu," in opposition to disreputable newcomers and an encroaching Kenyan government. At the same time, social, political, and economic changes confront the previously hegemonic understandings of *heshima* and facilitate a gradual reconfiguring of local notions of social differentiation and hierarchy that it informed. Such challenging of respectability, development, and change—the ambivalent tension between these discourses—can equally be detected in the alternative discourses about young people's everyday practices, as discussed in the last section of this chapter.

We Call Them "Dot Com"

When Khadija previously recognized young people to be *watumwa* based on their longing for and appropriation of translocal practices (and thus recognizing some of the negative evaluations she was equally sub-jected to), she also underlined that an abandoning of some local traditions was necessary to allow for development. Describing young people's re-sponsibility to distinguish between outdated practices and required changes, while maintaining a respectful attitude, Khadija continuously switched between kiSwahili and English, thereby signaling her level of education to both Omari and me. When later analyzing this interview, Omari described Khadija as being "dot com." Unclear as to what he meant, I asked for clarification to which Omari replied that Khadija, while having *heshima*, believed that her education and expertise with modern technology (i.e., mobile phones, computer, the Internet) provided her with "special" knowledge that separated her from the average Lamu resident.

Long after this interview, I asked another young Lamu resident what "dot com" stood for. He suggested that the term was used to refer to young people who are familiar with and continuously use technology, including mobile phones and the Internet. But practically everyone owns a mobile phone nowadays, I responded. Does that mean that all young people are considered "dot com"? In other words, does the term "dot com" refer to a new generation or specific group of youth, distinct from their parents? (I had in mind a concept similar to *bluffeur* in Côte d'Ivoire, as discussed by Sasha Newell [2012].) When my friend immediately responded negatively to my question, I decided to look deeper into the meanings of "dot com" and specifically into when my friends and interviewees described a young person as "dot com" rather than *mtumwa*, for example. After all, both de-pictions referred to the appropriation of nonlocal practices, often linked to a particular notion of "westernization."

In one of the many streets of Lamu's Langoni neighborhood, among its many roadside stores, there was a middle-aged lady who sold popular snacks like *bhajia* (lentil fritters) and fried potatoes. As she sat on her doorstep daily, she would greet familiar faces and strike up conversations with cus-tomers. She would often wave down children playing on the street and fill their tiny hands with savory snacks. She did not make a living of this after-noon occupation; it merely was a nice way to keep busy and interact with people, so she told me. I often bought some of her crispy *bhajia* and some-times joined her on her doorstep to observe the hectic traffic of donkeys, *mikokoteni* (handcarts), and people passing on the street in front of her house. On one of those occasions, shortly after I first met her, I explained to her my research on life in contemporary Lamu, and particularly on young people's everyday interactions. About midway through my explana-tion, she interrupted:

Tunawaita ni dot com. Ushaona? Kuwa mtu ako na free. Mtu anaweza kujichagulia, mtu aweza kufanya lolote hata kama ni maskini.

We call them dot com. You understand? That a person has freedom. Someone can choose for themselves, they can do whatever they want, even if they're poor.

Contrary to previous explanations of the concept, this lady's use of "dot com" did not refer to young people's familiarity with technology, nor did it suggest a lack of respectability among the youth she perceived to be "dot com." To her, young people's altered practices did not signal enslavement to westernization, but rather entailed liberation from the social structures that historically determined life in Lamu. Whereas in the past, wealth, employment, religious education, and genealogy determined an individual's respectability and their associated social positions, transformations introduced through new media and secular education now brought about changes in social structures that availed to young people a broad set of opportunities; chances that had been inaccessible to her. An elderly lady coming from one of the surrounding Bajuni islands, her perspective spoke to how social structures were reproduced and challenged within contemporary Lamu, but equally illustrated how (nostalgic) reflections upon life in Lamu reveal distinctly different stances toward the community, and its younger generation in particular.

This *bhajia*-selling lady was not the only one whose views of Lamu youth shifted away from a lack of *heshima*, to an opinion of opportunity and innovation. Just like the observed lack of respect in linguistic and material practices previously formed the basis for an evaluation of young people as *watumwa*, so did particular modes of dress or talking motivate an evaluation as dot com. Sumaiya, for example, was a woman of about forty-five who lived in a neighborhood called Bosnia.[7] When discussing life in Lamu, and particularly the everyday behaviors of the town's youth, she specifically referred to their language use and stated the following.

Jamaa zetu wakionana wao kwa wao mara nyingi utaona huwa hawana ile ya kumwambia salaam aleykum na habari gani ama huyambo. Huwa lugha yao ni ile ya kidotkomu. Maanake mtu atakwambia vipi niaje na wao huyatukuliya kuwa ni salamu.

Our young men when they see each other you will often see they do not have the habit of saying *salaam aleykum* or *habari gani* or *huyambo* (how are you?). Their language is that of *ki-dot com* (the dot com

language). I mean someone will say *vipi, niaje* (yo, whassup) and they
view that as a greeting.

Whereas young people's linguistic practices were otherwise often referenced as the most evident examples for a loss of *heshima*, Sumaiya described
young people's greeting styles as *dot com*, as a way of speaking they use "*wao
kwa wao*," or among themselves. While recognizing shifts in linguistic
practices, she did not attribute those to a loss of respectability or a state of
enslavement. Rather, Sumaiya viewed these practices as merely distinguishing "a younger generation."

I encountered similar uses of "dot com" when people explained altered
styles of dress among youth. Salma, a mother of four, observed:

> Ni dot com sasa. We msichana utamwona mtu anavaa suruali, pengine
> mtu amevaa kitu imemkaa vizuri. Sasa na we utatamani, si ndriyo?
> Mbinadamu. Waona katika tv, waona generation imebadilika. Aah,
> nguo mzuri! Nimeiona katika TV! Wafuwata new generation mpya.

> It is dot com now. You as a girl, you will see someone who is wearing
> pants, maybe someone is wearing something that fits nicely. Now you
> will desire it as well, no? That's only human. You see it on TV, you see
> the generation has changed. Oh, beautiful clothes! I saw it on TV! You
> follow the new generation.

According to Salma, shifts in dress styles did not result from young girls'
disregard for local norms of respectability, nor were they indicative of a
degenerated moral state. According to her, the observed appropriations of
new styles and practices are a normal result of and human response to access to novel practices. While she did not necessarily approve of these
changes, and while she did not appropriate new styles of dress herself,
Salma considered young girls' altered appearances to be a normal part of
change—a comprehensible desire on their part to emulate the material
signs they encountered through TV's, phones, and computer screens.

A last example I want to share derives from a short discussion I had with
one of the older, upper-class men whom I came to know very well during
my stay in Lamu. While I never formally interviewed him, he would often
explain to me how the changes in Lamu disturbed him. These frustrations
did not specifically concern the practices of young people; rather his complaints about the increasing presence of *wageni* echoed other residents'
grievances, as discussed in Chapter 1. One evening, his youngest son came
home with a pair of jeans so baggy that the entire household burst out
laughing. Later that same night, I asked the father how he felt about his

son's changing habits. Otherwise talkative, he merely shrugged, smiled, and said:

> Sisi tunawaita dot com sasa. Wana baba, mama, na grandfool.

> We call them dot com now. They have a father, a mother, and a grandfool.

This is one of the few instances in which I encountered a use of "dot com" that hinted at a lack of respect among Lamu's younger generation. The grandfather, who was viewed as a source of wisdom and authority in the past, has now become a grandfool. This play on words not only suggested a lack of respect on the side of Lamu youth; it also importantly hinted at elders' lack of understanding of the current transformations. Within the present-day context, elders' wisdom has turned into foolishness. As in the previous examples, this use of "dot com" then referred to an increasing lack of control over youth; it recognized the possibility of a different orientation among young people that caused them not to adhere to, and incorporate the practices of the older generation.

I find the use of "dot com" fascinating for several reasons, not the least of which being the alternative it forms to discourses on change as moral disarray and young people as enslaved to their desires. Important, however, is that the young people described as "dot com" by Sumaiya and Salma most likely would be described as *watumwa* by other observers. This is not to say that people like Salma and Sumaiya did not consider *heshima* to be significant, nor does it mean that they viewed the young people about whom they were talking to be lacking *heshima*. Rather, it suggests that what constitutes *heshima* to them differed meaningfully from, for example, the *baraza*-sitting elders who critiqued young women for eating on the street. In addition, the reference to young people as "dot com" did not apply exclusively to young men or to young women, but rather it referred to young people as a somewhat distinct social category. It was not the case that young women were condemned as slaves for their appropriation of changing modes of dress, whereas young men were described as "dot com" based on their changing language use or use of technology. Indeed, these different assessments of young people's practices and their respectability were very much tied to social class distinctions and differential interpretations of previously hegemonic notions of *heshima*.[8]

Residing on the Langoni-side of town, the women who considered young people's changing appearances as part of "dot com" did not belong to Lamu's previous merchant elites. And like the beach boys, their opinions on young people's everyday practices indirectly challenged patricians' pre-viously hegemonic understandings of what *heshima* ought to entail. In contemporary Lamu, an individual's respectability continues to be evalu-ated based on modes of dress, employment, location of residence, move-ment, and language use and accent, but which details of these practices signal propriety rather than enslavement or backwardness is in flux. In other words, how respectful behavior is evaluated, or rather what is per-ceived to be respectful behavior, is meaningfully shaped by the social po-sition of the observer and is importantly redefined in relation to macro-sociological changes. Precisely in these discursive evaluations of young people's everyday behaviors do we see the reproduction of social di-viding lines in Lamu, and the differential translation of political and eco-nomic change into opportunities or challenges depending on the interlocutor. Depictions of young people as *watumwa* then not only con-demn the appropriation of global consumer practices, but also object to a changing social structure where Lamu residents living in Langoni are in-creasingly challenging the moral authority of former elites living in Mkomani.

Conclusion

The discourses analyzed in this chapter revealed shifting understandings of what morality and respectability entail in contemporary Lamu; for ex-ample, whether and especially which kind of employment, income gener-ation, or new opportunities (through education) can be considered upright and for whom. Such ideological perceptions of social change shape opin-ions on and evaluations of Lamu youth and their everyday practices. By examining these discourses, we see how ideological links between physi-cal locations, times of day, modes of behavior, linguistic practice, and per-ceived moral disposition enable the discursive construction or emergence of particular "types" of people. At the same time, however, interlocutors equally position themselves through their reading of others' practices. In other words, the links made between outward appearances and inward moral dispositions signal speakers' own social (and moral) positions—as disgruntled former elites, as pious but ambitious youth, as former lower class seeing opportunity in contemporary change.

Lamu residents have a strong sense of moral deterioration. As we have seen, this perceived decline is linked to the regression of a social hierar-chy structured around the embodiment of a moral code of respectability, monitored through ideological conceptions of space, bodily practices, and social interactions. These transformations do not result in an outright rejection of a morality system, nor can these changes be considered a mere generational shift. Discussions with Lamu's youth showed that *heshima* has not lost its value to the younger generation. Aware of its relation to religion and its ideological and political significance as formative of a "Lamu identity," young people do not deny the importance of *heshima*; rather, they endeavor to renegotiate how this respectability can be mediated within everyday practices, and they especially try to demonstrate that a careful and critical engagement with development and change in itself can imbue someone with *heshima*.

The discussions on which this book thus far has focused—the disentanglement of complex and multiple ideological evaluations and value judgments differently linked to age, social class, gender, and individual disposition—illustrate a discursive creation of (a particular) social imaginary, of a social world in which different groups are identified and compartmentalized based on observed semiotic practice. As a consequence of macro-sociological shifts, however, the social world against which acts are evaluated is no longer agreed upon, and the iconic links that tie practices to social personas are questioned and challenged. "Those people" are no longer necessarily high class, while speaking "like that" is no longer evidently disrespectful. As the authority of elders, *baraza*, and other local institutions is being renegotiated, so are the ideological connections they make. While unemployment, a dip in the tourism industry, or random arrests are very real and impactful consequences of Lamu's altered geopolitical position, the effects of economic and political transformations are also noticeable in the everyday lives of Lamu residents in much more nuanced and seemingly insignificant ways. Indeed, semiotic confusion—the uncertainty about how to evaluate individuals and their intentions but also about how to be a "good Lamu resident"—permeates everyday interactions, redefines social relations, and informs whether and how young people can claim new subject positions in Lamu society.

The destabilization of indexical reference and the moral apprehension that accompanies it are, in a way, the most tangible local articulations of broader changes, not much under Lamu residents' control. The anxiety surrounding changing signification, around the inability to assess someone's true intentions and moral uprightness, is then informed by an acute awareness of Lamu's contemporary marginal position in a national and global context, and by a mindfulness that one's own practices can be read and evaluated in ways not much under one's control—as archaic, as backward, as conservative, as extremist. For Lamu youth, what it means to be a "good Muslim" or a "good Lamu resident" while negotiated within shifting local ideological frameworks of respectability is then also always already informed by other discourses—on development, modernity, cosmopolitanism, political resistance, and Muslim piety understood in relation to global Islam. Moral uprightness is not viewed solely in terms of embodying particular kinds of piety and a striving toward devoutness; it also entails important considerations in relation to how youth ought to participate in change and respond to political marginalization.

Young people's own opinions on social and economic change already hinted at how others' discourses and the ideologies that inform them become part of young people's self-evaluating frame; they become part of the discursive regimes through which Lamu youth navigate and upon which they draw to position themselves as particular kinds of individuals. Precisely this metapragmatic awareness is central to young people's everyday practices and their negotiation of new social positions, as we will see in the next two chapters.

CHAPTER 4

Reframing Morality through Youthful Voices

Although it was only ten in the morning, it was already blazing hot when I made my way through Lamu's alleys. The gentle ocean breeze that reached me as I turned corners offered only temporary respite from the heat that hung heavily in the air. It was one of those last, unbearably humid days before the coming of the monsoon rains, and it felt like the air might turn into water. Already sweating profusely, I was rushing to the office of the aid organization where Maryam worked. I was to attend the weekly meeting of a group of young volunteers and did not want to be late.

Volunteers formed a core part of this aid organization's activities in Lamu. Young men and women participated in awareness-raising campaigns on HIV/AIDS or drug and substance abuse by organizing educational drama performances or by providing information sessions in local schools. They also offered assistance in times of emergency (for example, during floods, fires, or health crises) and helped out during major community events (like Lamu's annual cultural festival). In return, these youth received training in first aid, community development, and team-building strategies.

Most of the young people participating in these activities were between the ages of eighteen and twenty-six and were awaiting admission to college, searching for employment, or looking for an excuse to escape household chores. While the organization targeted all Lamu youth and while it did not set any criteria for participating, volunteers predominantly derived from the same social background. Many lived in Langoni and identified as Bajuni or as coming from Siyu or Pate Island. With only a few exceptions, all volunteers were unmarried. A couple were immigrants from the mainland and belonged to the Kikuyu ethnicity, whereas only a few volunteers came from the Mkomani side of town. None of the (male) youth worked in the tourism industry or would identify as beach boy or tour guide. Thus, the volunteers appeared to comprise a particular section of the Lamu community: medium-level-educated, middle- to lower-class youth from Lamu's Langoni neighborhood.

That is not to say that volunteering did not appeal to other young Lamu residents. The organization's reliance on a mixed-gender group of youth, however, was much debated in Lamu. Male and female volunteers interacted openly during workshops, meetings, and activities in an environment where interactions with the opposite gender were otherwise restricted outside of the family home. While young people often encountered one another on the streets and in the shops of Lamu and while (gender-segregated) schools sometimes organized joint activities, such interactions were limited and highly policed. Family discussions about the possibility of joining the organization therefore often centered on the respectability of the youth involved, and especially of the female volunteers. Volunteering, many suggested, was merely an excuse to socialize with members of the opposite gender and evidently lacked *heshima*. In other words, young people like the volunteers were faced with the challenge of maintaining ethical subjecthood under significantly changed contextual conditions.

The organization's emphasis on "youth empowerment" intended to overcome some of these challenges and motivate young people to join as volunteers. Employees underlined the central role young men *and* women played in the future well-being of Lamu and thereby drew upon discourses on modernity, development, and emancipation, including an emphasis on young people's capacity to actively contribute to community development. Staff like Maryam underlined that female volunteers in particular fulfilled a role-model function, showing other girls that early marriage did not need to be their only focus; they could also study, work, and contribute to the welfare of the community. In present-day Lamu, Maryam suggested, a young woman's respectability no longer derived from staying at home; rather, she could command respect by making active contributions to development.

Aid organizations, most of them international, therefore not only offered a new context for mixed-gender interactions; they also invoked "youth" as a social category that played a central role in the advancement of the community. What this social category entailed within the local context—who felt addressed by discourses on youth empowerment, what young people's new roles as community leaders involved, and on what grounds respectability could be assigned—was not evident or straightforward, however. These new respectable subject positions were not readily available for youth to step into; rather, the position of "youth" as socially responsible, development-focused, knowledgeable, modern, and upright needed to be fashioned and carefully negotiated by the young people involved. This included young people's claiming a voice within community debates and their creating a space where they could be recognized as both authoritative *and* respectable.

Volunteering for a reputable aid organization offered a framework through which such new understandings of *heshima*, based on community involvement and development work, could be enforced. In claiming a new voice for "youth," however, these young volunteers positioned themselves in relation to, not only elders (including parents and other authority figures) but also other Lamu youth—young people who were not actively involved in the organization. By proposing that development work was a moral responsibility, Maryam, for example, expressed an opinion on the respectability of those young women who opted to stay at home. Similarly, volunteers explained the absence of beach boys—who equally claimed a progressive attitude and challenged previously hegemonic notions of respectability—by arguing that these young men only focused on the material benefits of westernization; they wanted to leave the community rather than invest in it. Volunteering therefore also entailed a moral stance; it comprised a claim to certain moral possibilities of respectable personhood (Keane 2010).

Young Lamu residents fashion these new subject positions and redefine associated morality models through everyday interactional practices. Volunteers' language use, for example, demonstrates how linguistic choices allow them to tactically exemplify some aspects of *heshima* while challenging others. In so doing, they endeavor to redefine notions of moral personhood, including understandings of virtuous femininity and masculinity. Lamu youth are then not just flouting behavioral norms or rejecting notions of morality upheld by their parents and elders; rather, they are actively negotiating what *heshima* entails in contemporary Lamu and are deliberating (even among themselves) the role youth can play in the well-being of the town. In other words, while interactionally situated, the choices young people make within everyday exchanges—when they speak, in which language, directed at whom—is importantly informed by their perceptions of broader societal shifts, including changing views on social class, gender, age, and genealogy.

Such quotidian negotiations of new subject positions involve an important form of reflexivity—the ability to critically evaluate ongoing activities, the ideologies that shape them, and one's position within them (Dick 2017). Goffman (1956) has long argued that individuals can knowingly adhere to, transgress, or challenge the behavioral rules that govern a particular exchange and in so doing reaffirm or challenge the moral values of their community. A speaker's selection of a language variety from their linguistic repertoire can thus also often be considered a *moral* choice, since it is a choice among options that calls upon the social figures to which a particular variety is tied (Hill 1995, 97; Keane 2011, 171). The ideologies and discourses analyzed in earlier chapters of this book—discourses on (moral) transformation and its transposition in verbal and nonverbal practices— therefore form the background against which to understand the subsequent analyses of young people's language use. These previous discussions help to comprehend why youth might opt to speak one language over another, or why young women are particularly conscious of their language use when they address an audience of (male) elders, for example.

As young Lamu residents are watched and evaluated because of their perceived crossing of a range of ideological and physical boundaries, language offers them a tool to navigate this contested social field. A consciousness of audiences' potential evaluations allows for a strategic presentation of self, while simultaneously enabling young people to subtly voice opinions on what it means to be young and Muslim in contemporary Lamu. In so doing, they not only claim new respectable positions but also express a moral and political stance, expressing views on social stratification, lasting inequality, increasing economic degradation, and political sidelining (Hill 1995; Jaffe 2009; Keane 2011).

What Is a Meeting Anyway?

When I arrived at the organization's office, I plopped onto the chair in front of Maryam's desk, wiped the sweat of my forehead, and thanked Maryam for pouring me a steaming cup of chai. As I sipped my tea, I sighed that I still had not adjusted to Lamu timing. While it was almost ten past ten, I was clearly still too early for the ten o'clock meeting—I had not seen any of the volunteers. Maryam laughed and said that I had adapted to Lamu timing much better than I had to the heat, as she watched me break more sweat while I drank my tea. She suggested that I drink quickly and hurry upstairs because the meeting had started at ten sharp. I reacted with surprise, because meetings in Lamu generally started at least half an hour late—if things went well. Upon noticing my amazement, Maryam reminded me that these meetings differed from other community gatherings; punctuality and efficiency were important to this organization, so I better hurry and join the volunteers. After all, it would be rather funny if the *mzungu* could not keep *mzungu* time, she remarked jokingly. In other words, the youth of the organization insisted on adhering to Western notions of punctuality and efficiency, something they easily associated with development and a "modern" way of doing things.

Although *mikutano* (meetings) and *baraza* (councils) have always been part of life in Lamu—the town was after all ruled as a republic through-out its history—such assemblies were historically restricted to upper-class men. In these councils, seniority and social status determined authority. Youth and women historically did not join these meetings. More recently, aid organizations, together with a more general spread of discourses on democratization, introduced a new kind of *mikutano*: community gather-ings in which both men and women from different social backgrounds could participate. Young people's participation in these meetings, however, remained limited and was subordinate to elders' authority. The volunteers' weekly meetings therefore offered a unique forum for young people to voice their views on issues impacting their community, and particularly on how they—as youth actively involved in community development—ought to address these social ills. Just as the mixed-gender volunteer group was framed in terms of progress, so did the organization present these meetings as integral to a progressive, modern approach to commu-nity development. The practices that regulated these meetings—including the emphasis on punctuality rather than "African" timing—were very much part of this new framing. "Proper" meetings started on time and had a particular, almost bureaucratic structure.

When I entered the upstairs room where the meeting was held, a lively discussion was underway. I mumbled a quick *assalaam aleykum*, found my-self a spot on the floor, and looked around the room. As many times be-fore, I was fascinated by the dynamics of the meeting and especially by how it differed from community gatherings not just in terms of punctuality but also in matters of seating arrangements and overall interaction. Whereas community meetings kept a strict separation between the seating areas for men and women, no such division was to be noticed in this room. Although some of the young women had gathered in a corner to separate themselves from the male attendees, the majority of young men and women comfortably sat next to each other. Young women who usually wore a *ninja* had removed the facial veil when entering the room, complaining about the unbearable heat. Others had pulled up their *buibui* slightly as they sat on the floor, revealing jeans and fashionable shoes otherwise hidden underneath the black cloak. Whereas a nod of the head or a quick glance generally sufficed as a greeting when these young men and women encountered each other on Lamu's streets, latecomers now greeted everyone present, shook hands, and sometimes even exchanged hugs.

As I observed these interactions unfold, I wondered how elders—particularly the former *waungwana* elites—would respond to this mixed-gender environment, assuming they would view it as disreputable and lacking *heshima*. At the same time, however, I noted how well attended these meetings were. That particular day at least thirty members had already gathered, and young people kept trickling in as agenda points were announced: Participants for a peer education workshop had to be selected and the upcoming board elections needed to be discussed. The selected note-taker for the day (who had been given the only chair in the room) diligently noted down what was announced and a sheet of paper was passed around to register attendance.

When I first joined these gatherings, I was not sure what to make of the volunteers' insistence on these different administrative practices. The gathering had to open with prayer, someone needed to take minutes, and attendance had to be recorded, after which a specific list of agenda points needed to be announced. Although considered essential to the meeting, these practices' purpose was not always clear to me. Attendance lists were often thrown out at the end of the meeting and the minutes, written on loose-leaf paper, tended to disappear before they could be filed. Nevertheless, the meeting could not take place without them. In contrast, the gatherings were often rather chaotic: While some young people actively engaged in the discussions, others socialized with their peers and appeared uninterested in the topics covered in the meeting. The attendees who were involved in the discussions often interrupted one another, went off on tangents, or made fun of what others said. At the end of three-hour meetings, it often happened that none of the agenda points had been resolved satisfactorily.

I was initially confused by this seeming contradiction between, on the one hand, a display of efficiency and organization through the emphasis on bureaucratic practices, and, on the other hand, the disorganized nature of the meetings themselves. I soon realized, however, that the official practices were more than mere administrative protocol; for young volunteers who endeavored to carve out new respectable positions in Lamu such formalities framed the meeting as proper, reputable, and potentially authoritative. Informed by translocal discourses on how effective, "Western" meetings ought to be conducted, these habits distinguished volunteer meetings from community gatherings and established a particular modern interaction frame that endorsed youth as playing an authoritative role in community-development. The volunteer meetings thus offered an environment through which a new kind of moral presence—a responsible and respectable engagement with development—could be, quite explicitly, discussed and negotiated among young people, including how they ought to present "youth" to the wider community.

But while volunteers' bureaucratic practices enabled the shared recognition of this specific interaction as a youth meeting, the behavioral norms that ought to structure this new frame were much less obvious. Both the conduct expected from participants and how they were to relate to one another appeared to not yet be determined. The two participants who were vigilantly debating the agenda topics, for example, seemed to have a different conception of participation in Western-style meetings from the young men and women who were talking among themselves. In other words, what constituted respectable behavior in this newly established context—which aspects of social identity imbued a participant with *heshima* and associated authority—was not evident or agreed upon.

Precisely this ambiguity of behavioral norms, however, enabled young volunteers to negotiate both social relations among themselves and their emerging position within the Lamu community; it permitted participants to claim authority and respectability on grounds different from established social category belonging, including gender and age. Attendees' contributions to ongoing discussions therefore performed important identity work (Antaki and Widdicombe 1998): Young people's linguistic practices provided their peers with information on how they positioned themselves within the ongoing exchange and toward the broader community.

While framed by a new interactional context and the organization to which it was linked, such self-presentations and their evaluations nonetheless remained locally situated; they continued to be informed by ideologies of ideal behavior and *heshima* (Chapter 1), notions of appropriate language use (Chapter 2), and an awareness of others' evaluations of Lamu youth (Chapter 3). By drawing upon or speaking back to such ideological discourses, the young volunteers who participated in the meeting took a moral stance—toward each other as well as the broader societal context; they expressed opinions on what kind of development Lamu needed, the role youth played therein, and thus also what moral presence entailed in contemporary Lamu. Strategic language use enabled precisely this careful navigating of both adhering to notions of respectable conduct and transgressing expectations of social category belonging.

"We Youth, We Have Our Rights"

Spirits ran high in the cramped meeting room on that hot, humid morning. One of the agenda topics for the day's meeting was the selection of twenty volunteers to partake in one of the organization's upcoming education workshops. The discussion had been much anticipated, and volunteers were keen to know how these twenty participants would be selected from among the more than forty members. Young volunteers who had not finished high school suggested they should have priority, because they needed the training more than their peers who now attended college. Others suggested that educated volunteers would participate in the workshop and subsequently leave for Mombasa or Nairobi, therefore not using the acquired knowledge to contribute to community development. Others still argued that noneducated volunteers would not be able to fully participate and benefit from the workshop, thereby defeating its purpose. Some other voices hinted that volunteers who were related to the organization's management would be selected to participate in the workshop, so there really was no point in debating the issue.

While nobody had appointed them as monitors, two participants— Khadija (K) and Sadiq (S)—stepped in to ease the tension and soon dominated the discussion. After having interrupted her peers, Khadija stood up and addressed the volunteers gathered. Referring to the senior coordinator of volunteer activities who tended to impose decisions on these youth, Khadija argued that they ought to quickly come to a mutual agreement before the coordinator joined the meeting.

Regular script: Standard Swahili
Underlined: kiAmu
Bold: English

к: Sisi ambao tuliko hapa, tu**decide** kama ni sawa sawa ili ye akija iwe yani haina kazi ya kuanza mpya. Itakuwa sisi tume**decide** kitu fulani na hicho tunachotaka kumwambia.

к: We, the ones who are here, we **decide** if it is good such that, when she returns, we don't have to start anew. It will be us, we **decided** a certain thing and that is what we want to tell her.

s: Nataka kuwafahamisha jambo moja. Sisi **youth**, tusijipeke nyuma. Sisi ndo tumewaandika watu ofisini kazi. Sisi ndo tumemweka kila ntu hapa. Sisi leo tukiamua hatuendi skuli, hatuendi popote, nafikiri hakuna karatasi itaandikwa hata moya.

s: I want to make you understand one thing. We **youth**, we should not put ourselves back. We are the ones who gave people in the office work. We placed every person here. We, today, if we agree that we are not going to the school, we are not going anywhere, I don't think there will be even one paper written.

x: (Unknown volunteer). [Kama hakuna karatasi na senti haziyi [laughs]

x: If there is no paper, then money won't come in. [laughs]

s: Skiza! Nitawaelezea. Hakuna yoyote itakayofanywa. Kwa hivyo, hiyo **training**, hiyo **training** ambayo itakuja kufanywa ni sisi. Sisi pia tumefundishwa tuna **right**, vile tunavotaka sisi. Ni sisi tupange, tumweleze sisi twataka hivi. Waweza? Sawa. Huwezi? **Cancel**. Umefahamu?

s: Listen! I will explain it to you. Nothing will be done. Therefore, this **training**, this **training** that will be done, it is us. We also, we were taught that we have **rights**, [to claim] what we would like to have. It is up to us to plan, we explain we want this. Can you do it? Ok. You can't? **Cancel**. Do you understand?

Khadija and Sadiq proposed a rather drastic solution to the issue at hand: none of the volunteers were to participate in the workshop unless the management could accommodate all forty of them. Because the aid organization depended on the volunteers for the majority of its activities, Sadiq suggested they had a right to ask for what they wanted, which was for all members to participate in the training. If the coordinator could not understand or accommodate this, Sadiq argued, the volunteers were to propose the cancelation of the workshop and refuse participation in any of the organization's upcoming activities. He further elaborated that the organization itself had taught them that youth have rights, and that they therefore should now claim those rights, knowing that the organization could not operate without them.

Through this proposal, Khadija and Sadiq not only invoked attendees as a particular group of youth, but they also established themselves as individuals with authority in this group. The differences in how Khadija and Sadiq achieved this, however, revealed their differing understandings of the behavioral norms associated with this new interactional frame and what constituted respectable conduct in this context—who could speak before whom, who was better positioned to monitor the meeting, and on what grounds such roles could be assigned.

Khadija, whom we previously encountered in Chapter 3, was a nineteen-year-old woman from an affluent Bajuni family and was about to begin university studies in Nairobi. Contrary to the majority of her peers, she had also attended secondary school in Mombasa and was not shy to talk about her exposure to and experiences in both cities. She was known to be bright, passionate, and popular among her friends. Her peers, however, did not always appreciate Khadija's emphasis on her urban and educational experiences. Sadiq, on the other hand, was a young man of twenty-six with little educational background. His inability to obtain stable employment provided him with ample time to engage with aid organizations in Lamu, an involvement that allowed him to partake in many educational workshops. Sadiq was overtly proud of his active presence in this particular organization and often underlined his extensive experience within the group. In a way, he perceived his volunteering to compensate for his lack of employment, since his participation could be framed as a moral good, contributing to the betterment of the community.

When they discussed Lamu's social transformation in Chapter 3, Khadija and Sadiq had both expressed concern for the changes impacting the community and particularly for the moral deterioration of its residents. At the same time, both these young people had underlined the importance of community development, including an appropriation of Western notions of progress, as a response to this moral decline. This dual orientation toward conservation and change can be considered as a position of inbetweenness, an enduring ambivalence that Lamu youth were trying to negotiate in day-to-day life. The deliberation of this new ambiguous position was evident during this meeting, and particularly in how these two young people positioned themselves toward each other and their peers.

Khadija and Sadiq's active involvement as volunteers testified to their shared view of youth as playing a central role in the future well-being of Lamu Town. Indeed, young people's moral responsibility to contribute to development emerged strongly from their contributions to the ongoing discussions that morning. Through explicit statements and implicit discursive strategies, Khadija and Sadiq both invoked the young volunteers as a particular category of youth—as locally situated but importantly informed by translocal discourses on development and empowerment. They not only explicitly and repeatedly referred to the volunteers as "we as a group" or "we youth," they also outlined the characteristics of this category and how it ought to be perceived from the outside—knowledgeable, responsible, educated, unified, and striving for development.

This discursive reference to and invocation of youth as a clearly delineated entity was strengthened by Khadija and Sadiq's emphatic use of deictics, and particularly of the personal pronoun "we" (Wortham 1996). In kiSwahili, the independent pronoun *sisi* serves as an emphatic marker because person is automatically indicated within the conjugated verb through the verbal prefix "*tu–*." The repetitive use of this deictic reference together with the verbal prefix therefore worked to amplify the discursive construction and recognition of "us" as a distinct group (for example, *sisi tumedecide*, *sisi tupange*, *sisi tumefundishwa*). This emphatic appeal to "we" as a unified group was supported by the use of jargon associated with humanitarian aid organizations (Higgins 2007). Both Sadiq and Khadija repetitively used words such as "meeting," "training," "workshop," "rights," and, most important, "youth." While all of these lexemes have rather evident translations in kiSwahili, the use of the English words distinguished the volunteers as a group of young people, familiar with humanitarian aid organizations' development discourses and their core concepts. This was particularly striking for the term "youth." Rather than the kiSwahili lexeme *vijana*, volunteers generally used the English "youth," even when speaking kiSwahili (much like Khadija and Sadiq did in the excerpt above). "Youth" more so than *vijana* captured a particular section of young Lamu residents; it referenced a specific understanding of what it means to be young in contemporary Lamu. Phrased differently, the frequent use of terms like "youth" by these volunteers created "register effects": They became identifiable to outsiders as a distinct group of young people who spoke "like that" (Agha 2005, 2007, 2011; Irvine 2005).

While Khadija and Sadiq discursively constructed and appealed to a unified category of youth, the unfolding of the interaction further revealed differing opinions as to who understood what the (social and moral) responsibility of youth entailed. And just like linguistic and discursive practices enabled them to invoke a new social category, so did these participants rely on language use to negotiate their authoritative voice within this newly fashioned group. Through Sadiq and Khadija's linguistic self-fashionings and the response they each received from audience members—the participant roles they were able to occupy during the meeting—different views of social category belonging, social status, and *heshima* emerged, informed both by local behavioral expectations and translocal discourses on emancipation and development.

Although she was fluent in English, Khadija did initially not rely on this linguistic competence to claim authority. On the contrary, she kept her use of English to a minimum and mainly spoke Standard Swahili. The few lexemes she did used were easily understood by the audience of volunteers and appeared to function as mere reminders or signs of her educational background and urban experiences.[1] Khadija balanced this limited use of English by explicitly aligning herself with her audience through the use of the first-person plural "we." Finally, she merely proposed a group decision instead of dictating what the best resolution would be. While she did not explicitly claim authority, the reference to a shared group identity together with her strategic insertion of English subtly signaled her leadership capacities.

Sadiq used a different strategy. He interrupted Khadija quite abruptly and announced that he would clarify for his peers the issue at hand. In so doing, Sadiq not only challenged Khadija's position (and her right to lead the discussion), he also immediately claimed an authoritative stance: I (as the elder, experienced, male member of the group) can make you (the unified group of peers) understand. While he adopted Khadija's reference to a shared group identity, his assertions were much more explicit, repetitive, and seemingly exaggerated. His argument that the volunteers provided work for the employees of the organization—all of whom were the volunteers' seniors—caused some of the members to chuckle in disbelief. One of the younger, female participants even objected to Sadiq's suggestion. In responding to this contestation, Sadiq made two adjustments. Although he maintained his footing—separating himself from his peers when suggesting that he "will explain to them" and asking whether "they understand"—his appeals to joint group membership became more explicit: he used *sisi* no less than five times in this short statement. There were also some subtle shifts in Sadiq's language use. In his first statement, he relied mainly on kiAmu, with parts of his statement being in the local dialect. After the younger female volunteer challenged his authority, Sadiq switched to Standard Swahili and incorporated some of the register effects I mentioned earlier. While having a limited knowledge of English, the use of words like "training" and "rights" signaled Sadiq's experience within the aid organization and his familiarity with its development discourses. Following these changes, the female audience member did not challenge Sadiq's suggestion again.

But Sadiq appeared to have miscalculated, as we will see. In the more established context of a community gathering in Lamu, the authority of participants would have been assigned based on their age (the older, the more authority) and gender (male speaks before female), and based on these participant roles Sadiq would have occupied a commanding position in this gathering. But this meeting—with its mixed-gender attendance, lack of elder supervision, and its association with an organization focused on development—already defied established norms and created a context for young people to claim authority on different grounds, including education. Sadiq seemed to have assumed that the behavioral expectations and participant roles associated with *mikutano* (meetings) still applied and that his authority as the eldest, male participant would remain uncontested. Yet, in this relatively new context, Sadiq's seniority and gender had little influence. On the contrary, Khadija's alignment with her audience as well as her use of Standard Swahili and limited English were valued within this particular interaction frame; these discursive strategies underlined simultaneously her educational and translocal experiences and her familiarity with, and concern for the local context. Khadija's position, as reflected in her linguistic practices, contrasted with Sadiq's lack of education, his unemployment, and his firm situatedness within the context of Lamu, equally evident in the way he spoke. Their different contributions therefore enabled other participants to make judgments about their peers' ability to speak authoritatively about the kinds of development Lamu, and Lamu youth, needed. As the discussion further unfolded, it became increasingly evident how Khadija's strategic language use allowed her to display concurrently a cosmopolitan stance and a local rootedness, thereby crafting a kind of ethical subjectivity that resonated with young people.

Shifting Languages, Shifting Alignments

Khadija and Sadiq's initial suggestion to refuse participation in the organization's upcoming workshop resulted in a lengthy debate over the benefits and risks of such a decision, yet nobody overtly objected to their reasoning. The tension in the room increased, however, when Sadiq (S) continued to interrupt Khadija (K), claiming to either elaborate on or correct her statements. Khadija eventually remained silent for a while, but as the group was about to move on to the next agenda item, she insisted on making one last statement.

Regular script: Standard Swahili
<u>Underlined</u>: kiAmu
Bold: English

κ: Nataka ku**emphasize** kitu kimoja. **Just a minute.** Nataka ku**emphasize** kitu kimoja. Wajua hapa, sisi **we are a group**, siyo? Tume**decide** kitu (xxx)

s: Aeleza kitu kimoja. Ngoja, ngoja. **Meeting**i lazima tuwe na mikakati ili tuelewane. Mtu akizungumza, inua mkono. Mtu akitaka kuzungmza, inua mkono na mwenzako atoe maoni. <u>Amwate. Sikiliza.</u> Kisha anaweza kujibu.

κ: **Okay**. Sasa, sisi hapa tuko **as a group**. Sisi, tuseme wao waliyoko hapa, ndio **youth** ya **the branch of Lamu**, siyo? Sasa sisi tuki**decide** kitu, **we are supposed to move as one. Among the principles of the organization** najua kuna **unity**, siyo? **We don't exercise that.** Kwa sababu, sisi tuki**decide** kitu hapa, tuseme kama haiwezekani kwenda sote tubakie nyuma, **I am sure** katika sisi tulioko hapa kuna wale ambao watakwenda wao **not thinking about** wale wengine.

κ: I want to **emphasize** one thing. **Just a minute.** I want to **emphasize** one thing. You know here, we **we are a group**, right? We have **decided** something (xxx)

s: Let her explain something. Wait, wait. In a **meeting**, we need rules such that we understand each other. When a person is speaking, put your hand up. If someone wants to speak, raise your hand and [let] your peer express his/her opinion. <u>Let him/her speak. Listen.</u> Then he/she can respond.

κ: **Okay**. Now, we, we are here **as a group**. We, let's say those who are here, this is the **youth** of **the Lamu branch**, right? Now, when we **decide** something, **we are supposed to move as one. Among the principles of the organization,** I know there is **unity**, right? **We don't exercise that.** Because, we when we **decide** something, let's say if it's not possible for us all to go, we all remain behind, I **am sure** some among us will go, **not thinking**

Kwa hivo naomba, tafadhalini, tuwe kitu kimoja kwa sababu **that's the only way** ambao sisi tutafanya mambo yaelekea sawasawa. Kwa sababu **so far we have decided on doing so many things** lakini hatufanyi hata kitu kimoja kwa sababu hatuna umoja. **We should like**, tushaamua **this is our goal. We should all be going forward for that.**

about the others. Thus, I beg you, please, let's be as one because **that's the only way** things will go right. Because **so far, we have decided on doing many things** but we don't even do one thing because we have no unity. **We should like**, we have agreed, **this is our goal. We should all be going forward for that.**

The tone of the discussion, or at least Khadija's alignment with the other volunteers, appeared to shift at this moment in the meeting. Wanting to make one last remark on the topic of the upcoming workshop, Khadija called for the volunteers' attention. When not everyone settled down, Sadiq stepped in to explicitly instruct participants on what constitutes appropriate conduct during this kind of meeting and how they ought to behave themselves when one of their peers—in this case, Khadija—wanted to speak. Rather than acknowledge Sadiq's interference, Khadija brushed off his instructions with a simple "okay" to subsequently make her point. She reminded the volunteers that, while they often planned activities and agreed on a certain course of action, these decisions frequently did not materialize and were forgotten on the way out. She therefore warned her peers that the choice to not partake in the workshop could be taken advantage of by less sympathetic members who might agree to participate after all. Reminding volunteers of a core principle of the aid organization—unity—she urged them to stick together in order to work toward development.

Through her contribution, Khadija took a critical stance toward her peers and the volunteer group of which she formed part. Subtle shifts in her linguistic and discursive practices allowed her to do so without much contestation. First, she changed alignments. Rather than use the inclusive "we," she opened her statement by separating herself from the group: "*I* want to emphasize something." While she retained an emphatic reference to joint group membership, she situated herself in a position of expertise in relation to that group and ratified this through a distinct increase in her use of English (Higgins 2007). Second, rather than merely insert a few lexemes frequently associated with development discourses (as she had previously done), Khadija now extensively code-mixed kiSwahili and English, using large chunks of English in her sentences. Giving the ideological value of English within the Lamu community—as a language frequently associated with education, development, and globalization—the shift attributed weight to Khadija's critical stance. Combined with a reference to her familiarity with the principles by which the aid organization operated, the language shift signaled a kind of reframing of the ongoing interaction and a change in Khadija's alignment with her peers.

When announcing her statement, Khadija initially switched to English only to call the attention of the group—"just a minute!" Sadiq subsequently interrupted to "help" her obtain the floor. He did so exclusively in kiSwahili, except for the term "meeting" (the English term often being used to distinguish these gatherings from other kinds of community meetings or *mikutano*). Sadiq not only urged his peers to "let her [Khadija] speak," but he also endeavored to retain his footing within the interaction—his authoritative position in relation to his peers, and particularly Khadija. We need to view Khadija's shift to English in relation to this interference. Precisely because Sadiq did not speak English very well, Khadija's move distanced him from the interaction and allowed her to claim expertise.

Khadija's authority and her ability to evaluate her peers were indicative, not only of shifting alignments within this situated interaction, but also of ideological changes on a macro-sociological level. Lamu youth, and these volunteers in particular, increasingly oriented to translocal discourses (on, for example, development and modernity) and redefined local values (of respectability, authority, virtue) in relation to them. Khadija's ability to display familiarity with and concern for the local context, while simultaneously exhibiting an embodied experience with urban contexts, enforced respect and answered these young volunteers' longing for change and development. In other words, Khadija's linguistic self-fashioning appeared to capture the balance between development and conservation that youth strove for. Sadiq, despite being the eldest male volunteer, was often discounted precisely because his use of kiAmu placed him firmly in the local context, but also because he assumed authority on grounds undermined by the development discourses to which these young people adhered.

Whereas gender and age continued to influence notions of authority in the broader Lamu community, these alignments were continuously negotiated among youth and especially among those actively involved with aid organizations. Level of education and translocal experiences, as expressed in linguistic and material practices, increasingly became factors in young people's conceptualizations of social relations and category belonging. But because such negotiations were ongoing rather than stable, newly acquired positions were easily contested if not carefully monitored. An overreliance on claims to translocal expertise, for example, could eventually undermine the speaker's newly acquired authority, signaling a removal from the local context. While languages like English generally signal education, an exaggerated use of this linguistic resource could also result in a negative assessment of the speaker as arrogant rather than respectable. In Khadija's case, the ambiguity of the meeting's interactional frame and the instability of its participant roles required her to carefully monitor her language use as the audience's evaluation of her self-presentation was neither guaranteed nor predictable. This became evident when Khadija continued her criticism of the local context. This time she did not evaluate her peers, but rather expressed her opinions on the management of the aid organization.

Translocal Experiences, Local Criticisms

Shortly before the gathering, the volunteers had been informed about the upcoming reelection of the organization's management committee. They were told that volunteers, as active members, had the right to cast a vote and thus help determine the management structure of the organization. This caused much excitement. The majority, if not all, of the youth had never voted—in the national elections or on any other matter. Moreover, the existing management consisted of rather prominent members of the Lamu community: middle-aged and older men from patrician families. Volunteers' right to help determine the executive structure of the aid organization, and thus indirectly to evaluate their elders' performance, made these young people acutely aware of the voice they as youth had acquired through their participation in the organization. The upcoming elections were therefore taken seriously, but also required much explanation. Many attendees expressed ignorance about the organization's administrative structure, the voting process, and the requirements they had to fulfill in order to vote. It was Khadija who took it upon herself to address the many queries this particular agenda topic raised.

She started by explaining the structure of the committee, outlining what positions were up for election and who occupied them at the time. She did so using English terminology exclusively, referring to positions like "chairman," "vice chairman," and "secretary" without providing kiSwahili translations or elaborating on what each of these positions entailed. When she failed to identify one of the committee members, some of the other volunteers remarked that maybe Khadija did not know what she was talking about. This overt challenge to her expertise did not go unnoticed, and Khadija, while ignoring the comment, subsequently endeavored to reclaim her authority by voicing criticism of the organization's management.

Regular script: Standard Swahili
Underlined: kiAmu
Bold: English
[: Overlap/Interruption

к: **I mean, the whole idea** kuwa na **elections** ni kuwa si tuangalie **what they have done** ile miaka iliyopita. Sasa tuangalie sisi **whether we want to change it or not.** Kwa sababu **so far** . . . Mimi **I know the branch management is there,** lakini **honestly speaking,** si kwa ubaya, lakini **I've seen nothing going on.**

x: (Unknown young woman 1). WOW

к: Kwa hivyo, yani **that's my opinion.** Sawa? kwa hivyo sisi ndo twafaa tu **decide whether we change them** au tuwaweke pale

s: [Khadija.

pale **If we still want to become dormant** . . . Kwa sababu sisi **we are a branch of the organization.** Kwa hivyo twataka na sisi pia tuwe kama zile **branch** nyingine. **There is no,** kule piya kuna **youth.** Kuna people **working in the office,** kuna **management I think.** Lakini sasa ukiangalia **branch** nyingine ziko **more advanced compared to** sisi.

к: **I mean, the whole idea** to have **elections** is that we look at **what they have done** these past years. Now, let us look **whether we want to change it or not.** Because **so far** . . . me, **I know the branch management is there,** but **honestly speaking,** I don't mean it badly, but **I have seen nothing going on.**

x: WOW

к: So, I mean, **that is my opinion.** Ok? Thus we have the right **to decide whether we change them** or we place them right there.

s: [Khadija.

If we still want to become dormant . . . Because we **we are a branch of the organization.** Therefore we also want to be like those other **branches. There is no,** there they also have **youth.** There are people **working in the office.** There is **management I think.** But now if you look at other **branches** they are **more advanced compared to us.** Do you see? Now we also

Ushaona? Sasa sisi pia twataka kufika hapo. Na kufika hapo **we have to change those on top.**

want to arrive there. And to arrive there **we have to change those on top**.

Y: (Unknown young woman 2). [claps]

Y: [claps]

The room got rather quiet after Khadija's statement. With the exception of a few volunteers who were socializing among themselves and had not really been following the discussion, all attendees remained silent for a minute. No one seemed to know how to respond to Khadija's claim that the current management was responsible for the organization's lack of progress. Her suggestion that the volunteers would need to vote out senior community members in order to see the changes young people were longing for was a harsh one. The one young woman who had clapped in response to Khadija's statement quickly stopped when nobody joined in. The hesitant clapping was, in a way, reflective of these young volunteers' ambiguous position and the new roles they tried to claim for themselves within contemporary Lamu. While wanting to challenge the authority of elders and draw attention to the role young people can play in the advancement of life in Lamu, it wasn't evident what such critical voices should look like. The paused applause to Khadija's explicit critique signaled hesitant support, recognizing the partial truth of her statement but also the inappropriate way in which it was delivered, lacking *heshima*.

Right at the onset, one of the volunteers had expressed her surprise at the frankness of Khadija's commentary. Sadiq subsequently called out to Khadija, but unlike earlier in the meeting, he did not further interrupt. These minor expressions of surprise or disagreement, however, did not deter Khadija. Rather, she emphasized that this was *her* opinion and thereby distanced herself from the group she had previously aligned with. She then substantiated her comments with her exposure to aid organizations on the Kenyan mainland, arguing that Lamu lagged behind when it came to matters of development and laid the blame, partially, with the organization's management. In so doing, Khadija not only reminded her peers of her translocal experiences but also called upon their longing for development and progress. By suggesting that she only had the interest of Lamu youth in mind, she reincorporated herself in the discursively created category of young volunteers who strove toward progress and development.

These claims to authoritative judgment were substantiated, once again, by Khadija's language use. Whereas at the onset of the meeting, Khadija had spoken Standard Swahili, with the insertion of a few English words, she now predominantly spoke English. When she tried to switch back to Standard Swahili, she seemingly struggled to express her thoughts in this language, often hesitating, to then eventually end the sentence with a switch back to English. Knowing that the majority of volunteers had limited knowledge of the language, Khadija's insistence on English and her supposed struggle to speak kiSwahili was marked.

The content of the statement together with language choice and an altered alignment shows that Khadija no longer sought to claim authority only within the immediate context of the meeting; rather, she also cultivated a position from which she could criticize the wider community. In other words, Khadija did not just renegotiate her relation with her peers, but also took a moral stance toward the broader social context and did so by selecting a particular "voice" (Bakhtin 1981) with which to speak.

Khadija expressed her stance—her ethical self-positioning in relation to her peers, her elders, and the topic under discussion—mainly in English, a language she presented as her naturalized way of speaking. While she did not have difficulty speaking kiSwahili at the onset of the meeting (and while she did not appear to have any problems with the language in her interviews with me; see Chapter 3), Khadija's overreliance on English toward the end of the meeting presented the language as part of her linguistic habitus (Bourdieu 1992). Rather than a resource she tactically drew upon, she performed this as her established, embodied way of speaking. I suggest this was a strategic choice in order to claim authority and challenge Sadiq's continuing interferences. This claim to embodied linguistic practices, however, also distanced Khadija from her peers and the local context.

When I later asked other volunteers about Khadija's contributions to the debate, many admitted to their ignorance about the topics discussed and reminded me that Khadija was very knowledgeable. When pressed, however, they added that, while they appreciated Khadija's insights, her statements made them feel rather incompetent and ignorant. Some of the female volunteers admitted that while they liked Khadija as a friend, they found her attitude in meetings to be somewhat arrogant. The young women underlined that it was good to have Khadija be part of the group, but they wished she could be more considerate of her peers, who did not all have the same opportunities as her.

During a meeting a few weeks later, Khadija's language use was overtly challenged. As she made a statement predominantly in English, one of the volunteers stood up and reminded her that not everyone present spoke or understood this language. The young man therefore requested that the rest of the meeting be conducted exclusively in kiSwahili, and preferably ki-Amu as they were, after all, in Lamu. Khadija's response to this appeal was fascinating. She apologized and promised she would try to "translate" her argument into kiSwahili. The remainder of her contribution was stilted as she appeared to struggle to express her thoughts solely in kiSwahili. She frequently paused as she perhaps inadvertently switched to English and could not find the right kiSwahili words. At the end of her contribution, Khadija sighed that it was "so hard" to speak only kiSwahili and not use English. Precisely this claim to an embodied practice and thus an inability to use kiSwahili—and particularly kiAmu—distanced Khadija from her peers and, most important, seemed to signal an altered moral condition. Instead of reflecting a desired balance between change and conservation, her language use appeared to index an orientation away from the local context, motivating, not a mere redefining of respectable behavior, but rather a discounting of *heshima* altogether. The strategic nature of Khadija's verbal performance among volunteers became even more evident when I observed her presentation of self in front of an entirely different audience a while later.

Taking a Stance toward Elders: Negotiating Positions by Respecting Expectations

A few months after the volunteer meeting, I was present at a community gathering at which Khadija addressed an audience of elders and local authority figures. At this particular occasion, she did not seem to struggle to only use kiSwahili and kiAmu. The community meeting, however, differed significantly from volunteer gatherings, not just in terms of the audience, but also in seating arrangements and the order of contributions made. Although women and youth were welcome to join, the attendees were predominantly male, and former authority structures continued to inform behavioral norms in these meetings.

Community gatherings were generally held in the old fort located at Lamu's main square. The breezy hallways of the monument, where the meetings took place, differed from the small, damp room where youth gatherings were held. Attendees sat on neatly arranged chairs, facing a centrally placed table where community leaders sat, and seating areas in different hallways clearly parted the men from the women. Separate entranceways assured attendees could take their seats without having to draw attention from, or interact with the opposite gender. A master of ceremonies generally monitored community gatherings, and the use of a sound system assured that everyone could hear contributions made. The meetings followed a clear order of address: Those at the high table spoke first, then questions and comments were solicited from the male side of the audience, after which the women were asked for their contributions. Women could either request the microphone or write down their remark on a piece of paper that would be passed on to the emcee, who would read the contribution out loud.

While these gatherings were organized in terms of their structure, they were far from punctual. Meetings frequently started an hour late, and people more or less arrived as they pleased. A meeting scheduled to start at 9:00 in the morning sometimes would not commence until two hours later. When the *muaddhin* called for prayer an hour into the meeting, however, male attendees would promptly stand up and make their way to the mosque. The meeting would subsequently be adjourned until after lunch, when the same scenario unfolded.

The gathering discussed here resembled the picture I just painted, although attendance was higher than usual. The meeting took place in December 2008, shortly after Lamu had experienced a case of land grabbing on Manda, opposite Lamu Island, where many Lamu residents owned pieces of land. After a plot had been sold to a Western tourist, local police had forcefully removed people living on the land, who were accused of squatting. The displaced residents subsequently came to Lamu and camped in front of the District Commissioner's office. Since this was not the first incident of suspected land grabbing, the event had stirred up emotions in Lamu: Residents participated in rowdy demonstrations, and the District Commissioner called upon government security forces to control the situation. Such violent incidents were unusual in this otherwise quiet town, where things had remained peaceful even after the contested 2007 elections when violence erupted elsewhere in Kenya. The issue of land grabbing, however, was a sensitive one for Lamu residents, since it recalled other moments in history when land had been allocated to nonlocals. At the same time, events like these underlined Lamu's marginalized position in Kenya and drove home the perceived intentional sidelining of the archipelago's residents at the hands of the government.

A couple of weeks after these demonstrations, prominent Lamu elders organized a community meeting to address land grabbing in Lamu County and the broader processes of political and economic disenfranchisement that appeared to underlie these incidents. While not attended by government representatives, the meeting was one of the few forums through which Lamu residents could express their grievances and, indeed, hope for their objections to be recognized or at least heard in Nairobi. The town crier, who went around town announcing the meeting using a megaphone, broadcast the focus of the meeting as a question: How could Lamu residents improve the local economy and strengthen their political position within Kenya? In his announcement, the crier added that prominent elders from Mombasa would be present and that all Lamu residents were encouraged to attend. The attendance of well-known elders highlighted the importance of this council, calling upon the historical role of *baraza* to weigh in on the governing of the town. Through his announcement, the crier obviated that this was not just any other meeting, but rather a significant moment for Lamu residents to express opinions on both Lamu's future and the archipelago's position within Kenya.

Khadija's contribution to this community meeting was a successful critique of the local community, and particularly of the enduring influence of social hierarchy structures. She managed her controversial contribution by carefully monitoring her language use and displaying an awareness of the behavioral expectations tied to both the particular frame she was participating in and the social category audience members ascribed to her. In so doing, she defied popular views of Lamu's younger generation as lacking *heshima* while also successfully claiming a uniquely authoritative voice. In other words, by strategically displaying an adherence to certain societal norms and behavioral expectations, she was able to challenge others.

Khadija's Opinion on Contemporary Lamu

The meeting was well attended, and there was a buzz of excitement as attendees waited for the chairman of the Council of Elders to open the assembly with a word of prayer. At the high table, several prominent community members had taken their place: the chairman of Lamu's Council of Imams, representatives of the Councils of Elders, and several prominent elders from Mombasa. The woman sitting next to me excitedly whispered that a few university professors—former residents of Lamu who had moved to Mombasa and Nairobi—had flown in to attend the meeting, but she was not sure who they were. While often less crowded, there was not one chair left empty on the women's side of the hall. Many female attendees carefully covered their faces as they glanced at the high table to identify who the prominent visitors were. Once the meeting started, the women halted their excited whispers but at times expressed their agreement by shouting words of approval (such as *ndiyo!* "yes" or *kweli!* "true") or by ululating.

The gathering followed the usual structure: the emcee announced the different agenda topics, each of which was subsequently addressed by one of the people sitting at the high table. Following these speeches, the male attendees elaborated at length on the different themes and provided suggestions as to how Lamu's political and economic position could be improved. The emcee subsequently directed his attention to the female side of the audience for questions and responses. After a couple of older women had voiced their opinions, Khadija (as one of the few young women present) raised her hand, and the microphone was passed on to her.

Until then, the meeting had focused on the many injustices that Lamu residents are believed to have suffered under the Kenyan government, starting at independence until the present day. Discussions had highlighted the unjustified assigning of employment opportunities to nonlocals and practices of tribalism on the part of the government. Other speakers focused on Lamu residents' lack of political representation at the national level and its associated problems. Several participants proposed that Lamu residents ought to form an alliance with people from Mombasa and other coastal towns, like Malindi, in order to fend for the political and economic rights of Muslim coastal residents. The overall tone of the meeting had been one of resentment, of bitterness toward the Kenyan government and mainland immigrants who were seen as increasingly taking control of Lamu's economy and politics. Khadija's contribution, formulated toward the end of the meeting, differed significantly from this overall consensus and verbalized a sharp critique toward the Lamu community itself.

Regular script: Standard Swahili
Underlined: kiAmu
Bold: English

к: Khadija
х: Audience response

к: Assalaam aleykum	к: Assalaam aleykum
х: Waleykum salaam	х: Waleykum salaam
к: Tumezungumza, kila mtu. Kwa sababu karibu kila mtu amekuja hapa kuchangia. Amezungumza kuwa watu wengine wapewe nafasi zetu, watu wa nje ama tuseme watu wa	к: Every person has spoken. Because almost everyone came here to contribute. He said that other people were given our opportunities, people from outside or let's say

bara. . . . Lakini tufikirie kiIslamu peke yake, kwa sababu tuangalie katika Uislamu peke yake. Ikiwa waIslamu, sisi wenyewe, tumegawanyika. . . . Na mi nitatoa mfano wangu mimi mwenyewe. Mimi nimekwenda kufanya **interview** mahali. <u>Swali la kwanda mimi nililoulizwa, babako wewe nshariffu gani? Mimi kabla siyafanya chochote, hapo imekuwa nishayua mimi sipati.</u>

people from the mainland. . . . But let's think Islamically alone, because we need to look in Islam only. If we ourselves are divided as Muslims. . . . And I will give you an example of myself. I went to do an **interview** somewhere. <u>The first question I was asked, you your father which shariff is he? Before I had done anything I already knew that I was not getting that job.</u>

Khadija recognized the validity of previously expressed grievances, but she reminded the audience that outside imposition should not come as a surprise if Lamu residents could not overcome local social divisions. To substantiate her claim, she recounted her personal experience with discrimination when applying for a job in Lamu, an exclusion supposedly based on her Bajuni background. The statement caused much uproar during the otherwise reasonably ordered meeting. Several people expressed their agreement with Khadija, while others started to discuss the matter among themselves. The emcee intervened, requesting order in the meeting, and Khadija continued. She provided another example, describing how a local chief had not publicized employment opportunities in order to propose his own family members as candidates for the jobs. Audience members once again loudly responded, and after having waited for people to settle down, Khadija concluded her contribution by expressing her opinion on what was required from Lamu residents in order to advance and stand up to government injustices.

Regular script: Standard Swahili
<u>Underlined</u>: kiAmu
Bold: English

к: Khadija
x: Unknown male
y: Audience response

<u>Kila alilonena ni shida alitaya ya binafsi yake mwenyewe. Na ikiwa</u>

<u>Everyone who spoke mentioned his/her own personal problems.</u>

sisi, mimi sitaki jirani yangu aendelee. . . . Hatutaendelea. Kwa sababu nikikumbuka mimi ule mwana jirani yangu akiharibikiwa yeo, akiwa mwizi atajepa kwangu kwanda. Hajepi kwa mwengine. Sasa mimi, maombi yangu, ni kuwa, hata kama iko **discrimination** kule yuu. Siku zote sisi hu**discriminatiwa**.

And if we, me I do not want my neighbor to progress. . . . We all won't progress. Because if I remember that when the child from my neighbor gets ruined today, if he becomes a thief, he will steal from my home first. He will not steal somewhere else. Now me, my request is that even if there is **discrimination** up there, we are being **discriminated** against every day [here].

[applause]

[applause]

K: Sasa mimi ningeomba kama waIslamu Tuongane. Kwa sababu ikiwa tutaongana kwa sisi hapa hapa na huko mbe tutaendekewa. Ahsante.

K: Now me, I would beg that, as Muslims, we stick together. Because if we work together here then we will make progress up there. Thank you.

[applause]

[applause]

x: Takbeer!

x: Takbeer![2]

y: Allahu Akbar!

y: Allahu Akbar!

Khadija highlighted that Lamu residents tended to focus on their own personal issues rather than be concerned with the overall well-being of the community. Such selfishness, she argued, explained why people preferred to take bribes rather than assure that the right person was assigned to a certain job or elected to a particular political position. Khadija reminded the older audience members that Lamu residents' Muslim identity ought to supersede such local divisions, allowing them to strive jointly for development.

The statement, once again, stirred up the meeting. Several elders were disturbed and vigorously responded to Khadija's account. The women, who had enthusiastically responded to the *takbeer*, were unreservedly talking among themselves. Unable to call the meeting to order, the master of ceremonies announced a short break before the gathering could continue.

Khadija—as a young, female participant of Bajuni background—was able to make a significant impact in a community gathering consisting mainly of elder, male residents, many of whom derived from the former merchant elites. Her rejection of the proposed collaboration with other coastal communities, and her objections to the accusations of tribalism on the side of the government, in a way, resembled her critique of her peers in the volunteer meeting. In both contexts, she argued that internal social divisions caused Lamu's underdevelopment. How she presented this argument, however, differed significantly in both contexts and contributed importantly to the authority she was able to claim. Among her peers, Khadija had taken a leadership role from the onset. And she drew on her education, her urban experiences, and her familiarity with translocal discourses to substantiate her expertise. She signaled all of this through her language use, including an overreliance on English. At the community meeting, however, Khadija did not claim a position of authority from the start, nor did she rely on English to make her statement.

Having waited until the very end of the meeting (and thus acknowledging the behavioral expectations associated with her being a young, female member of the audience), Khadija greeted the audience of elders and officials with the Islamic *assalaam aleykum*. She thereby presented herself as a religious young woman, countering conceptions of youth as lacking an awareness of norms of appropriate conduct (particularly within this interaction frame) and thus *heshima*. She subsequently used Standard Swahili to introduce her initial argument: the audience's unified identity as Muslim (which was equally called upon by her initial greeting). As Kenya's national language and the language of instruction in primary school, Standard Swahili signaled Khadija's educational background without coming across as arrogant (something the use of English would have done). She countered possible objections to this use of Standard Swahili (and its ideological associations with the Kenyan state) by narrating the subsequent personal account entirely in kiAmu.

Both the narrative and the language shift situated Khadija firmly within the local context. Her continued use of kiAmu when underlining Lamu residents' shared responsibility to insure community safety mimicked elders' nostalgic discourses about Lamu's past, analyzed in Chapter 1; it appeared to invoke the town's glorious history and a time without crime. However, Khadija reminded her elders that, in the current context, this safe community could only be achieved if residents overcame the social divisions that historically structured life in Lamu and that continued to divide the town. Khadija switched back to Standard Swahili when alluding again to the audience's shared identity as Muslim, while her subsequent use of kiAmu spoke to Lamu's future and its possible development. Whereas among her peers, Khadija struggled to finish one sentence in kiSwahili, she now did not stutter once when speaking the local vernacular and throughout her statement did not insert English, except when referring to the job "interview" and to experiences of "discrimination."

Khadija's success during the community gathering shows her careful and strategic consideration of context, audience, and self-positioning. Precisely her appeal to local norms of interaction allowed her to criticize the present in function of the future. By strategically using kiAmu and Standard Swahili, Khadija did not distance herself from the different social figures to which the languages were tied; rather, she took a moral stance toward the contemporary context through a combination of "voices" (Bakhtin 1981)—a position that joined, rather than opposed, the social figures of the respectful local and the educated youngster respectively. Khadija was able to take this moral stance because of her awareness of the ideological interpretations of language use and the behavioral expectations tied to the immediate context of interaction and the broader social categories to which she belonged. In strategically using this awareness, Khadija could express a judgment of both her audience and the macro-sociological context in which the interactions took place. In so doing, she simultaneously adhered to and successfully challenged behavioral expectations tied to social categories such as "youth" and "women."

Khadija's linguistic practices displayed a moral consciousness of the ideological boundaries she could or could not cross in order to achieve her immediate interactional goal and to make claims on a broader societal level. Mobilizing different voices is then a process of moral self-discovery (Keane 2011): an attempt to balance the different expectations of a changing society and redefine one's position therein. Khadija's linguistic practices illustrate young people's position within Lamu; within different interactions, and in different ways, she voiced her desire for change and development by being critical of her own community. Yet she simultaneously expressed her respect for the moral norms and values that structured life in this society. Young Lamu residents' participation in ambiguous interactional frames enabled these situated negotiations of roles and responsibilities. In this creative act, however, individuals also partly reestablished the ideological framework in which they were operating. During the community meeting, Khadija's self-positioning—her deference to elders and her use of kiAmu—in many ways confirmed young women's position in the local context. And Khadija's use of English among her peers reasserted its status as a prestige variety, tied to translocal discourses and desirable to noneducated youth.

While illustrating how attention to details of linguistic practice can help us understand how local roles and subject positions are renegotiated in relation and in response to macro-sociological changes, Khadija's statement at the community meeting also speaks to the focus of this book in other ways. From the onset of her contribution, Khadija underlined Lamu residents' Muslim identity—from the greeting she used to the explicit appeal to audience members' shared religious identity. More important, she called upon Lamu residents to unite in opposition to the Kenyan government and the injustices it had inflicted upon Lamu residents. Through her language, and her strategic use of kiAmu in particular, she excluded other audience members who did not derive from the coast, and thus underlined the link between being Muslim and being from Lamu. In addition to a critique toward Lamu residents and the social tensions that divided the community, Khadija thus also took an important political stance. In her own way, she formulated an opinion of what it means to be from Lamu in contemporary Kenya, placing a Muslim identity right at the center. While government officials might not have been present, reports about this council would be sent back to the District Commissioner and, undoubtedly, to other government offices in Nairobi. Khadija's statement can thus not be separated from other translocal discourses—from the Mombasa Republican Council's rejection of the coastal integration into Kenya, and from the Kenyan government's investigations into Islamic radicalization along the coast. While calling upon Lamu residents to unite, Khadija equally distanced herself (and Lamu) from the Kenyan nation to which the island belongs.

Young people, like Khadija, who study in Nairobi and appropriate urban habits as well as languages like English in the process, are often perceived as succumbing to the appeals of urban or mainland lifestyles. By taking explicit interactional stances, like Khadija did at the community meeting, these youth overtly challenge such views and demonstrate how their education can aid the Lamu community in defining itself in relation to Kenya. The *takbeer* Khadija received at the end of her contribution illustrates the audience's recognition of this effort.

Local Voices, Global Claims: Speaking like a Traveler

A broadened linguistic repertoire forms an important resource for Lamu youth in calculated self-presentations, the negotiation of new subject positions, and taking a political stance. At the same time, however, youth struggle with the multiple possible ideological understandings of the language varieties on which they rely as well as the interaction frame in which they partake. Both Khadija and Sadiq miscalculated as they over- or underestimated the situated value of particular language varieties. Presumably calculated presentations of self are therefore not evident: Multiple ideologies circulate, behavioral expectations can differ, boundaries can be misrecognized, and audiences can assess the speaker's language use differently from what was intended. In other words, though set on presenting a particular kind of (respectful) self, strategic self-fashionings do not always succeed, especially because they happen in relation to other people; they are always intersubjective. More important, even, audiences not only assess language use but also evaluate the person speaking based on connections between details of talk and other nonverbal semiotic forms, such as details of appearance. Whereas Khadija, for example, could selectively use English to present to her peers simultaneously a cosmopolitan stance and a local rootedness, their recognition of that position was strengthened by the latest-fashion *buibui* Khadija wore, as well as other material practices (like her handbag or fancy eyeglasses) that validated her use of English as truly "cosmopolitan." This also means, however, that strategic negotiations of new subject positions are not equally available to all, but are meaningfully influenced by social class and wealth as well.

Other youth who were set on negotiating new (cosmopolitan) subject positions and who equally used linguistic tactics in doing so were not always equally successful as Khadija. Lamu's beach boys, for example, frequently used linguistic details or accents to display their familiarity with a world beyond Lamu, and Europe or North America in particular. One of these young men working in Lamu's tourism industry and spending his time along the seafront was Jamal; he was about twenty-seven years old and had worked with tourists since the age of fourteen. As had many of Lamu's beach boys, he had found himself a Western girlfriend, married her, and moved to her home, in this case in France, for several years. After the marriage failed, Jamal had returned to Lamu, where he resumed his job as beach boy.

I had asked Jamal to carry around my recorder for a couple of days to document his language use when interacting with peers, tourists, and elders. Once Jamal returned the voice recorder, I listened to his interactions with my research assistant, Omari. When we came to an exchange where Jamal switched from kiSwahili to English to address two female tourists Omari laughed loudly. "*Umesikia?* Did you hear that?" he asked. We played the same extract several times again, and when I failed to hear what was so amusing, Omari pointed out that Jamal infused his English with what he referred to as a "French" accent. When I asked why Jamal would do so, Omari clarified that "they"—the beach boys—strategically used different accents in English (for example, French, British, American, Australian, or German) in an attempt to convince tourists to join them on boat trips. Through this strategic use of accents, he suggested, the beach boys intended to signal their experience in the tourists' country of origin and thus to present a particular cosmopolitan persona, one that was hoped to instill a sense of familiarity and trust in the anticipated customers. Such verbal performances were often accompanied by other material forms that were to provide evidence to this embodied cosmopolitanism; the beach boys' dhows were decorated with painted English (or other language) proverbs and different country flags, and the T-shirts these young men wore similarly derived from different places in Europe or North America. In other words, through these strategic self-fashionings, beach boys intended to present themselves as respectable and trustworthy in the eyes of tourists.

Jamal's claim to a French accent fascinated me, particularly because I knew that his knowledge of French was limited (and definitely not enough to leave traces in his already limited use of English). While Jamal often greeted me using French, knowing that I am Belgian and thus speak the language, his knowledge did not extend much beyond these casual greetings, and he generally switched back to a mix of kiSwahili and English to continue our conversations. Yet other young men working along the seafront equally performed, for example, Australian or British accents as a testament to their extensive interactions with international tourists, their relationships with these foreigners and, sometimes, their travels to their girlfriend's home country. Moreover, beach boys weren't the only ones who used seemingly minute details of language in strategic self-presentations. In fact, I noted something similar when a few of the previously discussed volunteers, including Khadija, had the opportunity to travel to the UK on a short-term exchange program through the organization they volunteered for. Upon their return from their one-month stay in England, Khadija spoke English with a remarkably British inflection. This strategic use of "foreign" accents did then not merely function to appeal to tourists; it also served to instill respect and awe among local peers. In other words, these nuances in young people's language use functioned as signs of cosmopolitanism, as remnants of their personal familiarity with the global (without necessarily needing to prove their actual fluency in the language). In

Jamal's case, his French accent—a part of his linguistic repertoire as a former resident of France—formed a testimony to his extensive travels abroad and thus his personal experience with French culture.

There were some interesting caveats, however, to this use of accents in acts of self-presentation and negotiations of new grounds for respectability. When listening to Jamal's recordings, for example, I had not identified the accent as French, even though French is my second language. I merely considered Jamal's use of English, including his pronunciation, to be somewhat limited. If I recognized an accent, it was a Kenyan one. Jamal later informed me that his language use also had not appealed to the French tourists, since they had not joined him on the boat trip, nor had they inquired about his connections to France. From my discussion with Jamal, it wasn't clear whether the women had recognized the accent as French.[3]

Although Omari, the French tourists, and I might have all recognized Jamal as having some kind of accent, we each interpreted it differently. Not only did his manner of speaking not convince the tourists to join a boat trip, I only recognized the distinguishing details of his speech as part of his restricted fluency in English. Omari did identify the accent as "French" but laughed because he recognized Jamal's tactic, not because he heard his experience in France. Audience evaluations of strategic language use and of calculated self-fashionings are therefore not guaranteed, nor are they the same across the board.

One could argue, however, that Jamal did not entirely fail, since Omari did acknowledge his accent. And for the negotiation of newly emerging subject positions—such as the cosmopolitan beach boy—to succeed, it was the accent's valuation within local "regimes of value" (Appadurai 1986) rather than foreigners' recognition of the pronunciation that was important. For it to signal a cosmopolitan persona, it was not necessarily important *what* Jamal spoke—whether his accent was phonetically identifiable as French—but rather how he sounded to local audiences and whether these locals perceived the quality of his accent as "French." But while Omari might have "correctly" identified the inflection, he found it humorous rather than laudable or truly cosmopolitan. This contrasted with evaluations by Khadija's peers, who recognized her British accent and acknowledged it as signaling a worldly attitude, although they found it somewhat arrogant.

Phrased differently, there was nothing inherent to Jamal's manner of speaking that characterized him as cosmopolitan. His accent retained its French flair for locals, but did not depict this particular speaker as sophisticated or respectable to them. Linked to his raggedy clothes, hoarse voice, and drugged eyes, his manner of speaking rather turned Jamal into a symbol of young people's moral decay, to both local elders and his peers. Rather than imbue audiences with respect for Jamal's translocal experiences, it became a source of contempt. Khadija's use of a British accent upon her return from the UK was accompanied with dress styles and vocabularies considered fashionable, thus framing her language use and encouraging the evaluation of a British accent as "cosmopolitan" rather than as a disreputable desire for the West.

The success of tactical self-presentations thus does not solely depend on a shared identification of linguistic details as being representative of a certain language—as French or British, for example. Rather the value of such linguistic tactics is only derived in relation to the speaker's other material and bodily practices. In other words, language use as a "sign" doesn't stand on its own, but only signifies together with other material aspects of self-presentation and the context in which it occurs. Khadija's material practices assured that her claims to a "respectable cosmopolitan" subject position remained rather uncontested, but then she also possessed one element that has historically contributed to notions of respectability and social status within Swahili societies: financial wealth. In a way, her innovative practices entailed a reproduction of wealth and class that has always been part of Swahili culture. Lamu's altered socioeconomic status, however, has made such strategic presentations of virtuous selves much more difficult for young people who do not possess extensive wealth, and one rightly wonders if it would even be possible to become a "respectable beach boy."

Conclusion

Young people's strategic language use underlines the complexity of calculated presentations of self and of the everyday negotiations of new subject positions. Lamu youth tactically use their extensive linguistic repertoire to express changing understandings of social category belonging (such as "youth" or "women") and altering views of the grounds on which authority and respectability can be granted (for example, education or translocal travels); yet such self-fashionings are not always effective. The example of Khadija showed that negotiations in clearly defined settings are possible, but equally demonstrated that successful evaluations are neither stable nor guaranteed. Moreover, the contrasting example of Jamal illustrated that self-fashionings are not equally available to everybody: Not everyone has the same rights, privileges, or power to have their presentations accepted.

The assessments of Khadija's language use differed from Jamal's use of a French accent partly because of the location where statements were made: There is a particular value attached to making statements in a meeting rather than along the seafront; it is in itself a value-creating act. This partly explains why Khadija can be viewed as cosmopolitan, whereas Jamal is socially undesirable. The analysis, however, also underscored the important connections between language use and material practice. While features of speech might be recognizable as French or English, their full meaning only becomes evident in relation to other aspects of semiotic behavior and thus in the particular realization in which they appear.

The recognition of details of speech as signs of new respectable subject positions thus depends on their link to other aspects of behavior; it is but part of a larger set of semiotic processes through which new social categories can emerge. While Jamal and Khadija each endeavored to establish new positions from which to speak, not one new category of "youth" emerged, and the respectability of their positions was evaluated quite differently. Phrased differently, the materialization of new youthful voices is also a sociohistorical emergence in relation to, for example, *baraza*, new aid organizations, and tourism. While highlighting the agency of youth to alter their position within a transforming society, these ethnographic examples thus also underlined the limits to agency imposed by the spatiotemporal embeddedness of semiotic forms and the intersubjective nature of negotiation.

Throughout this book, I have drawn attention to the significance of details of nonverbal material practices as these relate to understandings of *heshima* and social status. I have underlined the importance of nuances in language use and norms of social interaction, but I have also made clear how attributions of respectability were based on aspects of bodily comportment and material appearances as well, which could be linked to or contrasted with an interlocutor's language use. I previously considered the layout of Lamu, the structure of stone houses, the importance of scent, and even movement through town as core elements of *heshima*, the obliviousness to which was grounds for moral condemnation. These seemingly minute details of everyday comportment help us to understand how social relations and new subject positions are negotiated in ways other than strategic language use. Precisely because communication happens in ways beyond what is verbalized and how it is said, I now turn to explore how young people, within their everyday nonverbal practices, negotiate and challenge how social distinctions can be semiotically mediated.

Tupijeni Makamama
(Let's Embrace)

MAHMOUD AHMED ABDULKADIR

Composed in March 2010, this poem was written for a workshop organized by the Research Institute of Swahili Studies in Eastern Africa (RISSEA). Focused on the preservation of Swahili culture in changing times, the workshop asked whether development necessarily entailed leaving one's traditions. In this poem, Mahmoud Abdulkadir reminds the reader that waSwahili were historically more advanced than other population groups in Kenya, and he suggests that Swahili people can again attain that status. According to the poet, development does not require abandoning cultural practices. Rather, waSwahili ought to be selective and appropriate only those developments that do not contradict or violate Swahili traditions.

Muliyopo hadhirani
Those who are present

Waume na wanawake
Men and women

Masikizi funguwani
Open your ears

Maozi musiyawike
Eyes lower them not

Nina machache moyoni
I have some things in my heart

Napenda niyatapike
That I would like to share

Naomba munipulike
I urge you to listen to me attentively

Sitoyafanya marefu
I won't make it long

Nitakayo waeleza
That which I want to explain

Machache tawaarifu
Just a few things

Kusudi kutowembeza
Deliberately, not to engulf you

Tusiiyone nidufu
Let's not feel worthless

Mila yetu tukapuza
And ignore our culture

Chombo chetu kitasoza
Our vessel will drown

Tupijeni makamama
Let's embrace

Mila yetu ya aswili
The traditions from our home

Kwani hatukuwa nyuma
We were never behind

Twali mbee waSwahili
The Swahili were leaders

Mila tukiisukuma
If we push our traditions away

Hatutoshika mahali
We won't achieve anything

Tutasaliya zivuli
Only shadow will remain

Mila yetu si kikwazo
Our traditions are not a burden

Kwenda mbee haipingi
They don't hinder development

Tusome tuhitajizo
Let's learn what we need

Na ilimu nyingi nyingi
Acquire much knowledge

Tuepuke yamuwozo
Let's avoid bad things

Yasokuwa na misingi
That have no value

Tamu ya chai si rangi
The sweetness of tea isn't its color

Zama za utandawazi
The era of globalization

Mipaka imeondoka
Is boundless

Aswilani hatuwezi
We cannot completely

Pweke yetu kutengeka
Stay by ourselves, separated

Zilizopita zizazi
The past generations

Mno zali hifadhika
Were shielded fully

Mambo sasa megeuka
Now things have changed

Natuweni na hadhari
Let's be cautious

Twangaliye kwa makini
And look carefully

Tutenge yasomazuri
Let's keep aside what is not good

Hayo tusipokeeni
That which we cannot accept

Na tufanyeni shauri
Let's make an effort

Kuzama tusingojeni
Let's not wait until we drown

Tutangia lawamani
We will be blamed

Kutumiya si makosa
It's not a mistake use

Zasasa ala na zombo
Modern technology

Walakini yatupasa
Rather, it is our obligation

Tuifunde na mitambo
To learn about new machinery

Tusibaki kubebesa
We should not remain stammering

Likitokeya la kombo
Nor should we stay dumb

Si mambo hayo si mambo
Things should not be like that

Tuifunde kwa undani
Let's learn fully

Na mambo tuyafahamu
With much understanding

Twangaliye majapani
Look at the Japanese

Hawayundi mabomu
They don't build bombs

Lakini ulimwenguni
But in the world

Japani ni maimamu
The Japanese are leaders

Waendemwe na kaumu
Many people follow them

Ulimwengu haukiri
The world doesn't acknowledge

Umma uliyodhaifu
A weak community

Natufanyeni shauri
Let's decide

Tukitaka utukufu
If we want fame

Zilizopita fakhari
Pride of the past

Sasa hazifui dafu
Doesn't serve us now

Yatakiwa ubunifu
There is a need for creativity

Natubuni yetu sasa
Let's invent new things

Kwa misinji ya zamani
Based on old foundations

Maadili kutotusa
But let's not overlook morality

Mipaka tusiukeni
Nor jump boundaries

Tuyapijeni msasa
Let's clean up old practices

Yakae tufufuweni
And revive them

Na usasa tutakeni
And let's pursue modernity

Usasa twauhitaji
Modernity we desire

Katika yetu maisha
In our lives

Kutuwama kama maji
To be stagnant like water

Mwiso kutatunukisha
Will produce a bad smell

Kwa ndoto mambo hayaji
Things don't happen in dreams

Mwenye kulinda hukesha
He who guards stays awake

Havuni asiyonosha
He who doesn't sow will not reap

Tamati sitoongeza
This is the end, I won't add more

Narudisha shukurani
I just give thanks

Nashukuru manahuza
I thank the only captain

Wapeka mashua hini
Who sails this vessel

InshaAllah hatutosoza
God willing we will not capsize

Tutapata bandarini
We will reach the harbor

Kipenda Mola mannani
If He so wishes, God the most benevolent

CHAPTER 5

Senses of Morality and Morality of the Senses

Sisi wanawake wa kutoka kwa jamii yetu ya kiAmu, tuko na unique culture. Na kitu ambacho hapa kwetu kiko sensitive hakuna kitu kingine kuliko ni culture. Ukiharibu umetengeza kazi yako, umetengeza tabia yako, na umetengeza na dini yako piya. Na ukiharibu, umeharibu na kazi yako, na wale wanaofanya kazi na wewe, na majirani yako, na yoyote ambaye atakuwa amefuatana na wewe. Ni kweli ni urongo?

We women from our Lamu community, we have a unique culture. And there is nothing more sensitive here than culture. If you spoil it, you impact your work, you impact your *tabia* (habits) and you impact your *dini* (religion) as well. And if you spoil it, you spoil your work, and those who work with you, and your neighbors, and all those who are your friends. Is this true or false?

Maryam spoke vehemently as she addressed the group of young women gathered before her. As one of the few female employees of an international aid organization in Lamu, she had called a meeting with the organization's female volunteers after allegations of improper interactions with male volunteers had circulated through town. During a recent outreach activity, the youth had been seen intermingling openly and conversations had apparently included the exchange of hugs. Reprimanding the young women for their behavior, Maryam emphasized that they needed to be conscious of audiences' possible evaluations of their conduct and of the wider impacts their behavior could have. While the girls might see exchanging hugs with their male peers as a harmless display of Western-style modernity, Maryam argued, observers—other Lamu residents who watched these youth— evaluated such greetings differently. Read as a sign of impropriety, the young women's greeting styles had been assessed as a moral transgression that undermined their own respectability and that of their extended families. Although they were held personally responsible for monitoring their behavior, Maryam emphasized that the effects of the young women's conduct reached far beyond their individual persons.

The girls sitting in front of Maryam were between the ages of eighteen and twenty-two, many of them having joined the organization as volunteers after their high school graduation. These young women often explained their volunteering to me in terms of the educational opportunities the organization offered and the contributions they could make to the betterment of the Lamu community. They confessed, however, to also enjoying the mixed-gender environment the organization provided, suggesting that this was the "modern way" (*mambo ya kisasa*). While the young women admitted that socializing with male peers on Lamu's streets would be inappropriate and disrespectful, they suggested that the organization offered a rare opportunity to mingle in a respectable environment.

The broader community, however, did not always share this opinion and the respectability of this new, mixed-gender space was often contested. One of my interlocutors—a forty-five-year-old woman living in Lamu's Mkomani neighborhood—explained her refusal to let her daughter volunteer by emphasizing that this activity was just an excuse to socialize with young men and evidently lacked *heshima*. "Why would a respectable young woman feel the need to socialize with men? Nothing good can come of that," she would tell me smilingly. Negative moral judgments of young women's volunteering and a questioning of their underlying intentions therefore easily trumped their own insistence on the moral value of participating in community development.

To many Lamu residents, the incident for which Maryam reprimanded the volunteers only confirmed their assumptions about these young people's true intentions. The event had negatively affected the organization as well and had challenged the discourse of development in which it framed its activities. Maryam, however, did not hold the male volunteers accountable for the negative criticisms the organization had to endure. Rather, she reminded the young women that *they* were answerable for their comportment and depicted their conduct—their greeting styles, clothing, gaze, and stride—as conscious decisions in a presentation of self:

> Ukipita huyu atakuita. We utafanya nini? Yule mtu hukuangalia ile reaction yako, haswa huku barabarani. Ikiwa utago in, ile siku ya pili atakuvuta. . . . Siku ya kwanda, atakuita Swabra! Utazunguka. Ukimtekea, siku ya pili atakwambia "vipi"? Ya tatu, atakushika mkono. Ya nne, atakuweka mkono.

> When you're passing by, he will call you. What will you do? That person watches your reaction, especially on the street. If you will go in [respond], the second day he will pull you in . . . The first day he will call you: Swabra! You will turn around. If you smile at him, the second day he will tell you "what's up?" The third day, he will take your hand. The fourth, he will place his hand on you.

She did not condemn the man calling Swabra, but rather focused on the fictional girl's response to such hailing. Maryam suggested that the girl's reaction to the (nonetheless inappropriate) call had allowed observers—the man calling as well as other onlookers—to assign flirtatious intentions to her response and subsequently act upon that evaluation, approaching Swabra in ways she might not have anticipated.

Altered socioeconomic circumstances, as we have seen, including educational and employment opportunities, have significantly changed Lamu women's participation in public life. These relatively new engagements, however, muddled previously more or less straightforward readings of women's public presence as improper or low-class. Maryam's exposition underlines how someone observing young Lamu women relies on seemingly banal details of their behaviors—like a smile or stride—to assess the "real" intentions behind their public activities. Linked to her presence at a particular physical location at a certain time of day, the response of a female volunteer to a man's greeting could be viewed as an invitation to flirtation rather than a social obligation to respond to the salutation she was offered. Similarly, a slight smile or a turn of her head could open the door to advances, depending on who is doing the observing. In contemporary Lamu, the details of young women's everyday conduct are therefore read against different possible evaluations and the moral dispositions to which these are believed to be linked. By lecturing the female volunteers, Maryam reminded them of this hypersensitivity to indexical possibilities in everyday interactions and cautioned the young women to carefully monitor their conduct, because all aspects of behavior were considered possibly meaningful, even the slightest smile.

Reminders like these once again illustrate the challenges young women face when trying to negotiate new subject positions in contemporary Lamu; indeed, a morally responsible engagement with development seems at times out of reach for these girls, as observers can easily critique young women's presence on Lamu's streets and question the propriety of their intentions. In the Introduction to this book, Ustadh Taha called for "presence"; he urged Lamu residents to reconsider what *heshima* might entail in a community faced with political and economic marginalization. The respectable and religiously responsible, he argued, was not to sit and debate political or economic injustices, but rather to actively and selectively engage with those aspects of change that would aid Lamu's development. However, this kind of morally responsible engagement with change is not equally available to all. And while Lamu residents in different ways and to different extents question the contemporary respectability and authority of the *baraza*-sitting elders, an alternative morality model is not immediately available either. On the contrary, foregoing discussions have shown how different opinions on *heshima*, its appropriate mediation, and its contemporary relevance circulate widely and impact the assessment of young people's everyday practices as morally upright or disreputable.

Young people are mindful of the multiple interpretations that can be assigned to their everyday behaviors. This awareness of the signifying sensitivity of their seemingly mundane behaviors, however, also enables youth to negotiate newly emerging subject positions. They do so not by openly resisting local notions of modesty, piety, or femininity, but rather by strategically inhabiting certain social norms while renegotiating the proper mediation of others. Yet, such everyday negotiations of a new moral presence are not immediate or unrestricted; rather, they are troubled both by indexical ambiguity—doubt whether the meaning of certain practices is shared with observers—and by the scalar, intersubjective nature of such negotiations—uncertainty about who will be evaluating behaviors, at different levels of society.

While young women, for example, are conscious that *baraza*-sitting elders might view them as a particularly ambivalent sign of social transformation (Chapter 1 and 3), they are also increasingly aware of how different "others" read them—the Euro-American tourists, the mainland immigrants, but also governmental officials, police, or international aid organizations. While refusing to shake hands with men can be central to upholding respectability within the local context, young women also realize that visitors from mainland Kenya or the United States might see such refusal as a sign of oppression rather than *heshima*. Young women thus are not only adjusting their behavior to the male gaze, nor are their everyday choices only concerned with a striving for (or rejection of) religious piety. Rather, the choices they make are informed simultaneously by local social norms, religious values, translocal discourses, economic necessities, and political stances (among others).

The burden of negotiating new subject positions and appropriate conduct in an altered social context, though, is not on women alone. Observers' moralizing gazes target young men as well, albeit in different ways and to different extents. I have already argued that economic shifts place a burden on young men to make choices with regard to how they want to provide for their family, thereby sometimes transgressing local norms of respectable conduct (Chapter 3). But young men are also increasingly adjusting their behaviors in relation (and in response) to a range of other discourses, at different societal scales. They are, for example, increasingly conscious that their beards, while a sign of Islamic piety in Lamu, can be read as a sign of religious extremism outside of the local context and can have undesired repercussions as well.

Young women and men *both* struggle to get their self-presentations accepted. More important, much of these negotiations happen in relation to one another as youth cooperatively negotiate new forms of respectability. While young women might form an evident focus of moralizing gazes, the deliberation of new subject positions for "youth" is a joint endeavor. This happens in evidently visible ways when young volunteers greet each other using handshakes and hugs, for example, but also occurs in more subtle manners, when young women adjust their behaviors in response to previous encounters with young men, and the (un)desirable interaction their behavior evoked. In short, this final chapter offers ethnographic depth to the claim that projects of ethical self-fashioning, rather than directed inward, are inherently intersubjective as they are always directed at others with whom a shared perspective is assumed or negotiated. And they are intrinsically dialogic as they continually respond to views or information previously received.

As they plan everyday actions, young people consider how different practices might entail possible viewings, comments, and interpretations. These projected evaluations, differently associated with physical spaces and social persona, become part of a young person's self-evaluating frame and desired new social positions—such as the pious professional—are derived in relation to interactions with these imagined viewers. It is precisely through this integration of others' evaluations in the calculation of everyday habits that the seemingly mundane can become a meaningful political tool as well (Bourdieu 1977).

Monitoring Bodies, Negotiating Spaces

As a young professional focused on her career and committed to her religious and cultural background, Maryam was well aware of the challenges young Lamu women faced as they tried to occupy new social positions that accommodated simultaneously modern aspirations and local emphases on *heshima*. Much more than a mere condemnation of their behavior, Maryam's lecture warned the female volunteers of the everyday evaluations they were exposed to and contained instructions on how one ought to comport oneself in Lamu. In its explicit reflexivity and concerns about possible onlookers' moral judgments, her reprimand spoke to what it means to be a "good Muslim woman" in contemporary Lamu and, in a way, offered a response to the discourses of elders and young men analyzed previously in this book. Not only did Maryam remind her audience that they were "observables"—that, in Harvey Sacks's phrase, they ought to be "aware of having an appearance that permits warrantable inferences about one's moral character" (Keane 2016, 79), but she also underlined that observers relied on the smallest details of young women's material practices to make those moral inferences; seemingly minute aspects of everyday comportment had become "ethical affordances" (Keane 2016, 27).[1]

The ethical of the everyday, Keane suggests, lies precisely in this kind of reflexivity—this hyperawareness to the signifying potential of mundane material practices. More important still, it lies in the fact that such mindfulness provides individuals, like young women in Lamu, with the freedom to make choices as to how they present themselves and how they respond to others in everyday interactions. As Maryam's statement revealed, however, this freedom simultaneously contains a limiting responsibility. Exactly because material practices are viewed as choices in presentations of self, addressees and observers can evaluate movements or appearances as signs of individual intention (Keane 2016, 84); they afford judgments of actors' moral personhood and, in the case of Lamu, their *heshima*. In presentations of self, the individual therefore ought to be conscious of the possible intentions observers could ascribe to their conduct.[2] At the same time, the ideological discourses analyzed in the first three chapters of the book obviated that these assessments are not entirely under the individual's control either, since valuations can divert significantly from the intended signification. After all, audiences are sign readers rather than mind readers (Keane 2016, 83). In the ethnographic vignette with which I started this chapter, the young volunteers might have meant for their greetings to portray them as modern or urban, observers had read these practices as signs of indecent intentions. And as Maryam explicated, such negative moral evaluations could quickly take on a life of their own, circulating far beyond the momentary exchange. According to Maryam, the young women's responsibility lay in being conscious of all of this: of who might be observing them, of the different possible readings audiences could assign to their practices, and of the consequences such moral judgments could have for both their social status and that of their extended social networks.

Maryam's appeal to her female volunteers' senses of morality—to their awareness of the importance of respectability and modesty in everyday life in Lamu as well as these values' proper mediation within practice—speaks to recent attention for the ways in which (Muslim) women's bodies frequently become the arenas for contestations about modernity, authenticity, and morality.[3] Across different ethnographic contexts, altered political and socioeconomic conditions have expanded the visible range of movement for women, in different ways, and inspired an examination of how (Muslim) women view and negotiate their presence in different, previously "male" spaces (Newcomb 2006). Many of these studies focus precisely on how Muslim women endeavor to "create their own blend of professionalism and public lifestyles, and religiously inspired definitions of virtuous femininity, amidst a constant wondering about, and anxious discussions of, man's preferences" (De Koning 2009, 504). While a marker of modernity and an indicator of elite class membership, women in Cairo and Mumbai for example, are acutely aware that their highly mobile and public lifestyles could also be associated with moral and sexual looseness if not carefully managed (De Koning 2009; Phadke 2007). These possibilities for misconstrued identifications inform women's movements through the city and motivate the construction of and claims to "safe" spaces, such as upscale coffee shops or shielded fitness studios (De Koning 2009; Newcomb 2006). These distinctly respectable locales are meant to frame a woman's practices and regiment interpretations of her public appearance as evidently modern and cosmopolitan rather than improper.

These studies of women's careful movements through, creation of, and claims to specific physical spaces resemble this book's earlier descriptions of Lamu's geographical layout and the different moral values inscribed in the town's public space (Chapter 1). Specifically, I argued that Lamu women carefully monitor their movement and strategically make use of different physical divisions in town to manage the respectability of their public presence. Relying on an assumed shared ideological valuation of the divisions between the neighborhoods of Mkomani and Langoni, for example, or of the separations between the seafront, the main street, and the quiet labyrinth of backstreets, women deliberately choose which route to walk. Their physical location therefore becomes a sign of their embodied *heshima* or of their rejection of previously hegemonic notions thereof.

Such micropolitics of public space, however, cannot be separated from other aspects of observable behavior, including dress styles (Secor 2002, 2004). Associated with different kinds of femininity, the meaning (and interpretation) of clothing styles needs to be negotiated and evaluated across, and in relation to diverse spaces: a particular neckline can be considered cosmopolitan in an upper-class coffee shop, whereas it can be viewed as slutty and flirtatious on public transportation (Secor 2002; De Koning 2009).

Lamu is not an international city like Istanbul or Cairo, and while women are not trying to navigate distinctly different spaces—there are no popular upscale coffee shops,[4] different forms of public transportation, or fitness studios—their clothing styles play an important role, both in self-fashionings and in observers' assessments of such self-presentations. In fact, precisely because there are no evidently "modern but respectful" spaces, Lamu women rely on the details of their appearance to navigate this contested social field. Nuances in dress style and bodily comportment become central to communicating intentions behind a presence at the seafront, main street, or backstreets, as movement through these different spaces might be necessitated by employment or family obligations, or deliberate for personal enjoyment. Nuances contained in the black cloak women habitually wear, for example, play an important role in signaling pious or urban dispositions.

Although most Lamu women wear the *buibui* while out in public, the garment signals different values and social categories to Lamu residents, ranging from the religiously conservative and culturally traditional to the urban and even flirtatious. While nonlocal observers might view the *buibui* merely as a black cloth effectively shielding women's bodies from the public eye, the garment's different designs and shapes have become sophisticated means to signal the wearer's combined orientations to piety, conservatism, modesty, modernity, or even promiscuity (Fair 2013; Lewis 2015a; Meneley 2007; Renne 2013; Tarlo 2010). The decision to wear a traditional Swahili *buibui* instead of a Middle Eastern-style *abaya*, for example, portrays a young woman, respectively, as traditional and conservative or as sophisticated and pious (see also Meneley 2007).

Figure 13. Woman wearing traditional Swahili *buibui*. Photograph by Eric Lafforgue.

The traditional Swahili *buibui* (Figure 13) is a tubelike piece of cloth that one has to step into and then hold up the material by hand to fully cover the body. If held properly, it can effectively conceal the body and its shape, but due to its clumsiness (having to use both hands to keep the material in place), women frequently let go of the material, thereby revealing the upper body (and generally bare forearms). Young women often refuse to wear this *buibui*, suggesting its clumsiness prevents "proper" covering, thereby drawing upon reformist Islamic discourses, present at the Kenyan coast since the 1980s (Kresse 2003, 2009).[5] At the same time, they suggest that the traditional *buibui* is unsuited for professional women, who need their hands available to carry purses, work on computers, or deal with customers. The introduction of the *abaya* from the UAE and Saudi Arabia (locally still referred to as *buibui*)—more a long-sleeved coatlike garment than a tube—caused the Swahili *buibui* to be relegated to the realm of the traditional. Covering the body completely at all times, the new-style *buibui* is then at once a claim to "proper" Islamic practice and a sign of a modern and youthful disposition; it "signifies both piety and sophistication" (Meneley 2007, 222). While many Lamu brides are given a Swahili *buibui* at their wedding, wearing it signals traditional demeanor and old age. By wearing the newest *buibui* designs imported from Dubai, however, a young woman can display her global orientation and high social status as well as her devoutness. Moreover, choosing an open-design, coatlike *buibui* (which partially reveals the clothing worn underneath), opting to tailor the garment to her bodily shape, or leaving it unaltered can signal a woman's progressive or pious attitude.

During my time in Lamu, young women increasingly brought their new *buibui* to a tailor before showing it to their parents. The tailor would then take the *buibui* in on the sides, fitting it to the young woman's bodily shape. Elders strongly disapproved of such practices, because altering the garment's loose-fitting form was said to defeat its purpose; it became a dress rather than a pious cover-up. A young woman who did not adjust the garment was therefore praised. This same woman, however, could grab the material of the *buibui* and pull it to the side thereby equally showing her (slender) shape. Selecting the areas where to do so, she could, nevertheless, monitor unintended negative evaluations.

In recent years, some young women started to move away from the standard black material of the *buibui* and began to wear outer garments in different colors (for example, gray, brown or white-colored outfits). While these colored *buibui* were initially viewed as daring and bold (thus challenging local ideals of virtuous femininity), I was struck by the range of colors available in local stores when I visited Lamu in 2018 (only about a year after I first noticed colors other than black on Lamu's streets). Storeowners explained they were merely answering a local demand rather than supporting this new fashion trend. Some of my female interlocutors living on the Mkomani side of town underlined that I would be hard-pressed to find a mwAmu woman wearing a colored *buibui* and emphasized this was a practice of "other" Lamu residents and waBajuni in particular, whose notions of *heshima* differed from those of the former elites. While they admitted that the colored *buibui* was still modest as it appropriately covered the woman wearing it, they underlined the practice was not respectful of local custom. "They must think they are in Dubai or something," Maryam laughingly remarked when I asked her about the new trend.

While the commodification of the *buibui* as fashion provides information about status, its indexical function thus extends beyond a signaling of class membership. A young woman's choice of a colored or open design, opting to get it fitted, or leaving it unaltered also provides observers with information about her piety and progressiveness (which can nonetheless remain associated with social status) and the garment thus permits the simultaneous mediation of urban, global, and religious discourses. The moral values of these stylistic practices are, however, not agreed upon as Lamu

Figure 14. Young women wearing *ninja* and *abaya*. Photograph by Eric Lafforgue.

residents differ in opinion as to whether an open-style or colored *buibui* still signals piety or merely the wearers' orientation to global fashions.

The facial veil fulfills a similar role. Shielding her face from the public eye, the *ninja* is intended to signal the pious and conservative demeanor of the woman wearing it, notifying observers she is not to be interacted with (see Figure 14). Because the *ninja* guards the wearer's anonymity, however, women have used it for reasons other than signaling and preserving their piety (see also Fair 1998). Women on their way to meet boyfriends or lovers are known to wear a *ninja* to avoid being identified when entering a particular house, for example. The facial veil's double meaning as potentially signaling conservative piety or its opposite therefore poses a challenge for pious women as well as for observers, as the veil's indexical meaning is not straightforward.[6] It is here that *buibui* design, route, bodily posture, gaze, and greeting styles become significant—within the local context, the *ninja* as an indexical sign does not stand on its own but is linked and signifies in relation to other aspects of observable behavior.

Details comprised in veiling practices thus provide crucial information to interlocutors and observers about how to estimate and interact (or refrain from engaging) with women they encounter on Lamu's streets. At the same time, the meanings ascribed to different styles provide these young women with tools to present themselves in particular ways. These same women, however, are increasingly conscious of the fact that those signifiers can be erased or ignored by a range of actors both within local and translocal contexts. To the Euro-American tourist visiting Lamu, the black cloaks and facial veils, while sometimes embroidered or studded with decorative pearls, all look the same and signal only Lamu residents' conservative adherence to Islam. There is little recognition of a veiled woman's potential sophistication, urban demeanors, or traditional orientations. For the Kenyan government, the *ninja* and *buibui* are linked to the potential presence of Al-Shabaab and the ability of the facial veil to hide the wearer's identity, including whether the person underneath is female or male. Rather than a sign of piety or conservatism, the *ninja* and *buibui* can then be constructed as a potential threat (as is equally evident in the panics surrounding the burqa in the European context). This inability (or unwillingness) to distinguish and recognize signifying nuances in these material practices enables a unified reading of veiling as signaling a (particular kind of) conservative Islam. While young women take into account the elders or peers who might be observing them, they are also partially responding to these other observers and the discourses through which the latter evaluate their practices.

In many ways, young Lamu women's everyday negotiations of their public presence thus resemble the deliberations of young women in Istanbul, Cairo, or Mumbai. In these distinct ethnographic contexts, young women's modern and cosmopolitan aspirations together with their claims to respectability, piety, and—in many cases—class status demand a carefully monitored behavior that is informed by an awareness of imagined viewers and their possible evaluations. These studies' emphasis on how so-called macropolitical and economic shifts inform and impact the perceived micropolitics of space and everyday interactions speaks to some of the main concerns of this ethnography. And while the everyday material practices of young Lamu women illustrate this point clearly, I am not just interested in the fact that this happens—that women, in particular sociohistorical contexts following specific sociopolitical and economic changes, have become "observables." Rather, the case of Lamu also shows that young women are not just attuned to the male, public gaze; they equally adjust their behavior in relation to the female gaze, as women frequently are each other's own worst judges. Moreover, young men in Lamu have also become subjected to moralizing gazes that demand them to carefully monitor their conduct, be it in different ways and to different extents. Indeed, young men and women negotiate new youthful positions in relation and response to one another. The subsequent discussion of hand greetings illustrates precisely these dynamics of ethical self-fashioning. The negotiation of social positions through the touch comprised in hand greeting draws attention to the significance of embodied signs more subtle than linguistic accents or nuances in material practice.

The Tactics of Hand Greetings

Throughout this book, I have underlined the importance of *heshima* as a moral code that informs social stratification, status attribution, and everyday comportment in Lamu. Because these norms of respectability include conceptions of appropriate social interaction (McMahon 2006), they also meaningfully inform bodily comportment, including greetings, as Maryam's scolding of her volunteers already indicated.

Respectful greetings require a careful balancing act of recognizing and negotiating status through the use of salutations that demonstrate respect to the other while simultaneously demand respect for the self (Caton 1986, 305). At the same time, intended and unintended audiences might be observing the exchange of greetings. Improper extensions of courtesy can thus not only undermine interpersonal relationships but can also threaten one's respectability and social status within the wider community, something Maryam explicitly warned her volunteers of. This awareness of being observed encourages Lamu residents—from tourist-baiting young men to self-protective professional women—to use hand greetings strategically in the negotiation of interpersonal relations, social status, and moral values. The nuances of touch comprised in these hand greetings, however, also allow for subtle communications between the individuals shaking or kissing hands, often invisible to those observing the exchange.

The significance of hand greetings to the presentation and negotiation of respectability was brought to my attention during my initial weeks in Lamu. When I first arrived on the island, a group of beach boys warmly greeted me, as they did all tourists. Their familiar yet "exotic" greetings— *jambo my friend, hakuna matata*—welcomed visitors, including myself, to the island and were followed with offers for cheap hotels, town tours, or sailing trips through the lagoon. Upon clarifying my reasons for visiting Lamu—and thus attempting to establish my position as researcher rather than tourist—these young men's comportment changed considerably. *Jambo*—a Swahili greeting popular among tourists—was replaced with the more grammatically correct *hujambo* or *habari gani*, which can be roughly translated as "How are you?" and the occasional *assalaam aleykum*. Some of these young men even reached for my hand when greeting me, but rather than merely shake it, they lifted it up to place a kiss on the back of my hand. When I objected by pushing their hand down, they lifted it more forcefully, while reassuring me that they were paying me respect in the locally appropriate way. While pleased that they had not put me into the "white female backpack tourist" category, I was confused about the meaning of this practice: Did these young men really express respect for me as a scholar, as they claimed? Or were they exploring ways of flirting with me?

I questioned the deferential nature and overall appropriateness of the hand kiss and consulted a local Swahili scholar. "*How* do they kiss your hand?" he asked me, upon hearing the reasons for my concern. "Do they grab your fingers and bring the back of your hand up to their lips? Or do they grasp your full hand and bring their head down to kiss it? Do they fully kiss your hand or is it a mere swift touch of the lips? The former—where they grab your fingers, bring your hand up, and kiss it—is adopted from Bollywood movies and is flirtatious," he explained. "The latter—comprised of slightly bowing down from the waist and a quick raising of the full hand with an equally swift touching of the lips—is respectful."

Shortly after this exchange, my female interlocutors warned me that neither of these greeting practices entailed respect and that the beach boys' hand kiss—whether they merely brazed my hand or fully kissed it, whether they pulled the hand up when I exerted resistance or yielded when feeling opposition—was, in fact, extremely inappropriate. Because physical touch between genders was considered unfitting for anyone with *heshima*, the beach boys' use of the hand kiss when greeting me nearly made a mockery of my attempt to establish myself within the community and of my claims to a status different from the average tourist. While I exerted resistance to their lifting of my hand, observers only noticed the visible, and to them straightforwardly flirtatious, act of the kiss and not the sensory details of my opposition to the gesture.

This first encounter with the intricacies of greeting practices in Lamu, and the social consequences their assessments can have, taught me the signifying nuances comprised within hand greetings. The explicitness with which my female interlocuters discussed the different tactile details of greetings and how these can be exploited, however, also revealed a strong meta-awareness of the semiosis comprised in touch. More important, over the course of my residency in Lamu, people's changing views of what constituted an appropriate manner of greeting me provided insight into the systematics of this practice, and its ties to individuals' life course as well as to sociocultural, political, or economic evolutions.

While other studies of African greetings have considered bodily movement in greetings (for example, Schottman 1995), few have looked at the role hand gestures play in these ritualized exchanges. In Eastern Africa, and Kenya in particular, handshakes often accompany verbal greetings and interlocutors tend to hold hands for the entire exchange. In Lamu, hand greetings are an essential part of proper courtesy, not as handshakes but in the form of the hand kiss (although interlocutors of the same gender can continue to hold hands following this initial greeting, while inquiring about the well-being of the extended family). More than the initiation of a greeting, offering to kiss someone's hand affords an explicit and nuanced display of *heshima*. Kissing the right hand of one's senior is considered a manifestation of esteem—an acknowledgment of the other's social rank, age, and life experience as well as a display of one's own proper upbringing and respectability. Parents, siblings, and family members socialize children into this practice from an early age by taking the child's right palm, placing their right hand on top, and subsequently forcing both to the child's lips, while admonishing them to *shumu* or kiss. As they grow older, children are expected to greet elders by extending both their hands palm-up, right on top of left, offering to kiss the senior's right hand (see Figures 15 and 16). Upon reaching puberty these habits are redefined: Young people gradually refrain from kissing the hand of members of the opposite gender, with the exception of those elders to whom they are related. Girls in particular will only kiss the hand of those men who are their senior and their *mahram* (that is, anyone who they cannot marry according to Islamic jurisprudence).

Men uphold the hand kissing practice throughout their lifetime, but use the greeting more sparingly, only kissing the hand of elders who have a socially recognized higher status, such as descendants of the Prophet Muhammad. Among women, hand kissing occurs in the majority of interactions and a repertoire of greeting styles allows for nuances in the expression of respect and thus the articulation of a range of social relations.

An individual's observable use of proper greetings is therefore socially significant because audiences view it as an embodied sign of *heshima* and, by extension, as indicative of the respectability of her family. When arriving at social gatherings, for example, young women need to make considerations in relation to their own social status and the respectability of those they encounter. Upon entering a get-together, a young woman should locate the eldest women present and, if possible, greet them first. With these seniors, she will use a full hand kiss, including a bow from the waist down (see Figures 17 and 18). With women closer to her in age—anywhere between approximately five and ten years older than

Figure 15. Child greeting parent (1). Image by Sarah Hillewaert.

her—she needs to contemplate the appropriateness of the gesture: Will the addressee evaluate the offering of a hand kiss as respectful, flattering, or offensive? Offering the full hand kiss to someone who is not much older could be evaluated negatively, as it signals the attribution of an age greater than is the case. Conversely, not offering the respectful hand kiss to someone who is sufficiently older could be seen as preten-

Figure 16. Child greeting parent (2). Image by Sarah Hillewaert.

tious and disrespectful. One caveat is that the difference determining the greeting is not merely a function of the addressee's factual age but is also shaped by sociocultural attitudes toward (religious) education, community involvement, and family lineage. These relative factors become increasingly important in contemporary Lamu, as understandings of who ought to extend deference are gradually changing. With secular education and employment becoming progressively valued, they increasingly factor into the attribution of *heshima*.

Figure 17. Younger woman greeting older woman (1). Image by Sarah Hillewaert.

The successful completion of the hand kiss, of course, also depends on the addressee's response to the hand offering: Does she willfully allow her hand to be kissed, thus signaling that, indeed, the young woman ought to pay her respect? Or does she swiftly and gently resist by pushing back as the young woman tries to bring the hand to her lips, eventually allowing a hand kiss? The subtle opposition signals the addressee's reluctance to recognize the need for deference, while simultaneously accepting (and maintaining) their unequal relation. While this sensory resistance to the hand kiss can result in the eventual refusal of the gesture, the tactile negotiation that precedes this decline is of central importance. A young woman's immediate acceptance of the addressee's subtle opposition, and thus failing to attempt to lift the hand again, could be evaluated as disrespectful (as an almost taken-for-granted acknowledgment of near-equal status). Resis-

Figure 18. Younger woman greeting older woman (2). Image by Sarah Hillewaert.

tance ought to be responded to with a second, more forceful attempt to bring the hand up to the lips. The addressee might allow this, or might respond by pushing back again and removing her hand, to kiss it herself; the act of kissing one's own hand being a symbolic gesture reflecting the reciprocal nature of the hand kiss—if you had kissed my hand, I would have kissed yours (see Figure 19). Women often exploit the sensory nuances of this tactile interaction to take a stance toward each other. Immediately accepting resistance (and thus defying the status of the addressee) or not offering resistance when socially expected (and thus challenging the

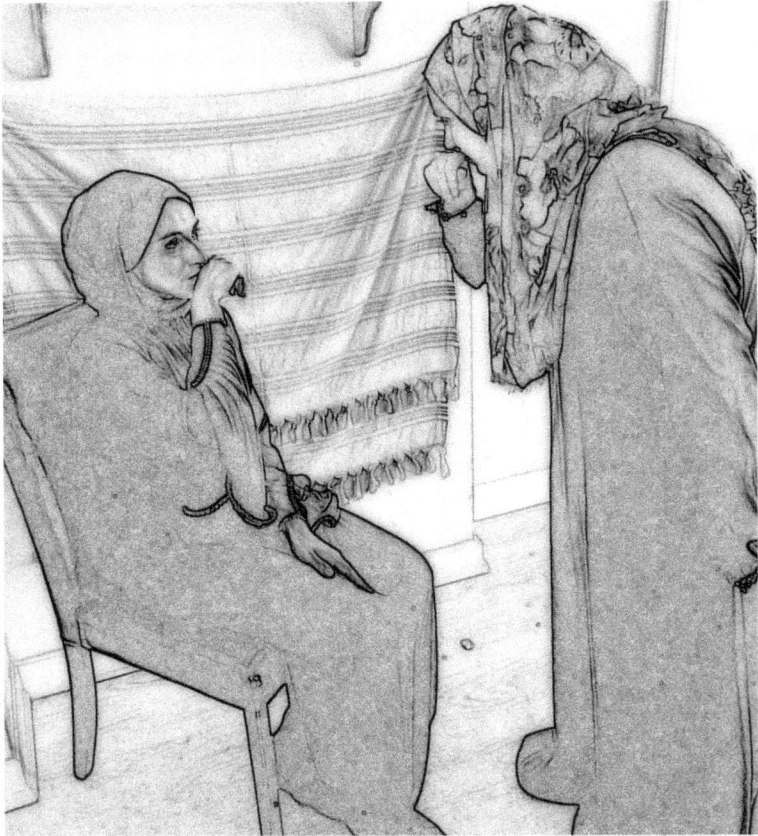

Figure 19. Greeting among women. Image by Sarah Hillewaert.

status of the addresser) are effective tactile tactics in the negotiation of interpersonal relations.

Another version of the hand kiss consists of the addressee simply tapping the actor's outstretched palm with her right hand and subsequently kissing it (i.e., her own hand). This gesture acknowledges the young woman's offering of respect, but signals that they are too close in age or social status for the initiator to physically kiss the addressee's hand or to even negotiate a closer relation through the aforementioned push-and-pull motion. Through this mutual recognition of respectability, the women publicly exhibit their embodied *heshima*: The initiator's willful offering of the hand kiss and the addressee's swift decline demonstrate their awareness and upholding of social norms of respectability and simultaneously imbues both with *heshima*.

A more explicit acknowledgment of shared status and a sign of close so-cial bond among peers consists of what I refer to as a "hand flip," for lack of a better word. In this case, a woman would offer her right hand, palm-up, signaling her willingness to greet her friend with a hand kiss. As a re-sponse, however, the interlocutor at whom the greeting is directed fully grabs the hand of the initiator, flips it around and (rather forcefully) brings the back of her friend's hand up to her lips to kiss it. The initiator (whose hand was just kissed) will then quickly flip the clasped hands again and kiss the back of her friend's hand as well. This movement is not only difficult to break down in writing, it also happens incredibly fast. Through the mutual hand kiss young women express shared admiration and social closeness, for everyone to see. However, the speed of the gesture is not without significance as it demonstrates that there is absolutely no hesita-tion as to how the interlocutors esteem one another.

Nowadays, young women are gradually moving away from hand kissing, with kisses on the cheek increasingly replacing these deferential practices. This newly introduced and not yet very established habit is appropriated through travels abroad and by watching movies and is meant to signal a distinctly "modern" attitude. Some young women, however, combine the two. Upon greeting one another, they will first kiss on the cheek, while holding hands, to subsequently perform the "hand flip." Such combination signals both a modern attitude and embodied respectability, to the other participant to the exchange as well as to observers of the interaction.

These tactile tactics mirror the negotiation of women's respectability: to different degrees, the sensory details of the hand greeting signal the ad-dressee's recognition of her interlocutor's social rank, while simultaneously indicating the status differential between them (or precisely the denial thereof). These gestures are then socially conditioned, embodied practices that concurrently allow for signifying deviations through the sensory details comprised in touch. The way in which the hand is offered and how the hand kiss is executed creates gradations in the polite/impolite opposition that ap-pears to have shaped discussions on greeting practices in Swahili contexts (Yahya-Othman 1995). Rather than a dichotomous distinction between the visible act of offering and its refusal (Goffman 1956; Schiffrin 1974), women strategically use the sensory details enabled by touch to negotiate their in-terpersonal relation and their position within the community.

These tactile tactics are meaningful tools for young women who need to navigate a complex set of social expectations in contemporary Lamu, where understandings of respectability and the grounds on which *heshima* is attributed are being redefined. In present-day Lamu, for example, young women are not only highly invested in education, but also progressively occupy respected positions in professional contexts, as administrators, doctors, or politicians. However, not everyone agrees on the propriety and respectability of women's higher education and thus on the kind of greetings educated young women ought to extend (or receive). The sensory details comprised in the hand kiss facilitate the expression of a gradation of positions between the completely respectful and the impolite and thus allow for a subtle negotiation of changing understandings of social status and respectability, on the part of the young women as well as the people they are interacting with.

Greeting practices enable young women to explicitly (and visibly) demonstrate a lasting respect for local norms of piety, while also allowing a more nuanced, selective, situated, and often invisible attribution of respectability between the two women greeting each other. For example, professional young women often initiate greetings and offer a full hand kiss to older community members, thereby visibly displaying deferential behavior and defying accusations of a loss of piety that supposedly accompanies employment. Some senior women, however, recognize the new social positions these young women occupy and demonstrate this altered valuation through their responses to the deferential hand kiss. Elder women can refuse young women's hand kissing gestures either partially by subtly resisting the upward lifting of the hand, or completely by retracting their hand. Such responses are increasingly used with young women who traditionally would have fully kissed their seniors' hand, but who are now recognized as occupying valued positions in society, albeit on grounds different from those used to assess social status in the past. The elders' subtle refusal to have their hand kissed thus imbues these young professional women with respect. The opposite is also true. Women who do not approve of the shifting social status (or who just do not like a particular young woman) might not exert resistance when they are socially expected to. For example, when a young woman greets someone close to her in age by offering a hand kiss, she would expect the addressee to either retract her hand or oppose the kiss by pushing back. The addressee, however, might not resist the hand kiss and thus "force" the addresser to kiss her hand.

The gradual recognition of changing norms of status attribution lies then, not in a reversal of interaction roles, but in subtle shifts within hand greetings' tactile details. The greeting's performative potential lies in this simultaneously intimate and public nature: It enables the visible display of esteem and respectability and the covert, sensory negotiation of interpersonal relations that will impact social life beyond the here and now.

Elders' hesitations surrounding employment and its respectability are, however, partially justified. These professional contexts form ambiguous spaces where norms of interaction are redefined and where young women are most clearly confronted with having to navigate the expectations of different social realms. I came to understand these challenges as I participated in Lamu women's social life and in the professional contexts in which many young women were employed. While I had grown accustomed to local greeting practices (and thus had long understood the inappropriateness of the beach boys' initial greetings), situations locally viewed as "professional"—meetings at local government offices or development agencies—remained problematic. Contrary to the beach boys, the "professionals" I met in these environments did not kiss my hand. Rather, they offered a Western-style handshake, reaching out horizontally in order to grab and shake my hand. Once again uncertain as to its appropriateness and anxious not to insult anyone, I accepted the outstretched hand. I understood the greeting to be part of the professional context in which I found myself and believed a refusal to shake hands would reflect negatively upon me, as unprofessional, as well as upon the organization for which I volunteered.

In subsequent encounters with these officials, this professional handshake frequently began to extend beyond the comfortable (or familiar) four- to six-second range. Some of my male acquaintances continued to slightly shake my hand as they extensively inquired about my well-being, while others would leave the shaking behind and simply held on to my hand and gently squeezed it as they engaged in small talk. Sometimes, though not often, my interlocutor would use his finger to stroke my palm as we shook hands. The invisible touch was sexual and transgressive, yet due to the discrepancy between the visually normative (shaking of hands) and the invisible sensory transgressive (stroking of palm), onlookers could evaluate the handshake as an acceptable way of greeting a Western researcher.

My subtle—or not so subtle—endeavors to "free" myself from those handgrips were often responded to with teasing remarks about my fear of men, loss of my Western background, or insinuations of disrespect. Attempting to avoid such interactions, my subsequent refusals to shake hands resulted in my interlocutors overtly questioning my professional attitude: As a Western woman, ought I not recognize our interaction as a professional one? Was I attributing improper intentions to my interlocutor? Or had I acquired the habits of Lamu women who thought they were "too good" to shake hands?

Feeling increasingly uncomfortable, I raised the issue with Maryam. A young professional herself, I hoped she would be able to tell me whether I was misinterpreting the greeting and thus whether I wrongly assumed my male interlocutors were flirting with me rather than recognizing my professional status through their handshake. As I recounted one incident, she interrupted me to complete the story for me and described the behavior she assumed my interlocutor to have displayed. She explained that she had experienced similarly awkward, and borderline offensive, interactions. Assuming that professional exchanges required the use of Western-style greetings, she had likewise shaken hands in official contexts. Her willing response to her male interlocutors' outstretched hand and the tactile interaction that followed, however, were often read as openness to flirtation (by her interlocutors and observers of the exchange), despite her interlocutors' own explicit emphasis on their professional nature. Phrased differently, male interlocutors read young women's reciprocation of the handshake as an implicit agreement to flirtation, allowing them to further "test the waters." Overt objections to lengthy handholds, however, were often interpreted as an aspect of (obligatory) shyness or as part of the game.

Amused by my confused facial expression as I listened to her interpretation of my encounters, Maryam suggested I "phase out" of handshakes, just as she had done. An immediate, complete refusal to shake hands, she explained, would result in dismissive remarks about an unprofessional attitude or arrogant demeanor. A gradual rejection would convey my pure intentions without insulting my male interlocutor. "Start by never initiating the handshake," she suggested, "but also be on guard because some men might simply reach out and grab your hand rather than just offering theirs." She elaborated: "When entering offices, keep your hands low and assure the sleeves of your *buibui* cover them. This will prevent men from grabbing your hand, or at least make it less accessible." If my male interlocutor did offer a hand upon greeting me, she suggested I offer my wrist, covered with the sleeve of my *buibui*. "That way you acknowledge his greeting, but you do not have to hold his hand." This offering of the wrist is generally responded to with a slight tap on the wrist, replacing the actual handshake.

Maryam cautioned me that men might initially still grab my wrist, but eventually they would (hopefully) reduce the contact to a gentle "tap." "Your refusal to have your skin touched shows your religious motivation for the avoidance of the handshake and won't be taken personally," she argued. She also recommended I simultaneously start to emphasize the use of the verbal Islamic greeting, *assalaam aleykum*, upon encountering men. This would remind them of the religious norms, even if they did offer their hand. Only after having done all of this, she argued, should I start refusing any form of touch altogether. This "phasing out" would eventually allow me to greet men, even in professional settings, by just placing my hand on my chest and giving them a polite *assalaam aleykum*—even in response to a stretched-out hand.

My description of Lamu women's use of hand greetings in different contexts challenges popular views of the handshake as a mundane and socially normative act and underlines the communicative and, indeed, transformative potential of which this fleeting physical touch is comprised. Young women's deliberate use of this practice when greeting their seniors shows that the execution of conditioned practices can be a (deliberate) performance of social conformism—a display of embodied social norms intended to be observed by an audience. The sensory details of touch comprised in the hand kiss, however, simultaneously permit the subtle, novel, or unconventional attribution of respectability, specifically to those young women whose piety might appear in jeopardy because of their educational and professional activities.

The depiction of women's awareness of the possible social interpretations of their bodily comportment, by (male) interlocutors as well as other observers, and their use of a ritualized practice to establish new social positions like the "pious professional" show that hand greetings can be semiotic tools, strategically used in the negotiation of shifting norms of conduct. A view of hand greetings as a tactile tactic, as a tool that is embodied and culturally scripted as well as consciously manipulated, demonstrates that changing understandings of piety, respect, and professionalism are negotiated, not only through sequential (oral) exchanges (as analyzed in Chapter 4) or through the mere refusal of a hand greeting, but rather in the midst of the handshake, through subtle details of touch and thus, together *with* someone else. At the same time, however, evaluations of handshakes—who to use what kind of handshake with but also others' evaluations of the observed greeting style—do not stand on their own, but are rather made in relation to interlocutors' other observed practices, including language use and material details of appearance and movement.

The following ethnographic example documents precisely these intersections by recounting the story of Asya and her strategic anticipations of potential sign readings, which were linked to different locales and audiences. In recounting some challenges Asya faced when trying to negotiate a newly emerging subject position as a professional, pious woman, I illustrate the intersubjective nature of self-fashionings and the potential risks of relying on ambiguous semiotic forms. While Asya's reflexivity had motivated the strategic use of material and bodily practices as well as physical space, her attempts at renegotiating their moral values caused her trouble, as she did not expect her signs to be read the way they were. Asya's case shows that moral reflexivity in itself—the endeavored prediction of possible audiences and their evaluations (Goffman 1955, 1956)—does not suffice to manage moral judgment. While her behavior might have been calculated and set on portraying a respectful yet urban self, the material practices on which she relied carried other significations for some of her locally situated audiences.

Asya's Ascribed Impropriety

Asya was a professional woman of twenty-five who worked in a local government office. Coming from a respected Mkomani family, Asya was religious, proud of her cultural background, and focused on her career. Having finished secondary education, she was completing a college degree and combined studies with employment in order to provide for her extended family. Asya did not see a conflict between her respect for local norms of propriety and religious piety and her desire to be an educated, successful professional. The broader community, however, did not always recognize this position.

When I met Asya at the onset of my fieldwork, she would leave for the office wearing a colored headscarf and a black *buibui*, the sides of which a tailor had slightly adjusted to better fit her bodily shape. She walked via the backstreets of Lamu, only crossing to the main street as close to her office as possible. Upon reaching the main street, she put on her *ninja* until she reached the office. There, she removed the facial veil, greeted everybody, and interacted freely with men entering the office. When (male) officials or visitors from the capital Nairobi entered she would shake their hand and engage in professional discussions.

Asya's behavior was the topic of gossip around town. I was stunned to hear people say she was immodest, had boyfriends, and had loose morals. Not her colleagues, but Asya's female cousins (young women who did not go to school and hardly left the house) and a few community elders were among those spreading the rumors. Talking to my female friends, they explained that Asya's position in a public office, where interactions with men were common, had inevitably caused people to start gossiping. *She should have known better.* While Asya knew about the gossip and was affected by it, she shrugged and told me that these were the habits of *wanawake wa ndani* or women from inside, who do not leave the house: They had nothing better to do, did not understand what a working life was like, and clearly did not have religious knowledge, as gossiping was prohibited in Islam.

The negative evaluations nevertheless concerned Asya. She was well aware that local norms of piety and propriety expected her to limit her interactions with men, especially physical greetings. She argued, however, that not shaking hands with officials from Kenya's mainland or visitors from abroad would cause her to appear unprofessional and conservative, since many lacked an understanding of the reasons why handshakes between genders is prohibited in Islam. Aware of potential valuations of a refusal to shake hands, she told me she was set on showing visitors that Lamu was not a backward place where people had no awareness of how interactions unfolded elsewhere nor did she want to reproduce the image of the seemingly oppressed Muslim woman. Young, professional, and ambitious, she wanted visitors (including government officials) to see the central role young Muslim women play in Lamu's development. Through our conversations, it became evident that Asya was not merely trying to negotiate a moral presence within Lamu, but also in relation to those (international and government) actors on who Lamu depended for development initiatives. Contrary to what other Lamu residents thought (Chapters 1 and 3), however, such moral self-positioning did not entail a blind hailing to those outside others' norms and values, but rather a strategic uptake (and rejection) of certain practices within particular contexts.

Asya defended her behaviors through a reliance on translocal discourses on development as well as global Islam. As an educated, working woman she was obliged to engage in "professional" interactions, a context within which handshakes were "proper" greetings (particularly with those unfamiliar with Islam), rather than inappropriate physical contact. Her familiarity with global Islam (discourses introduced through satellite TV channels such as Peace TV) permitted judgments on the validity of others' (moral) critique, refuting them as mere gossip. Through their criticism, Asya argued, those gossiping women displayed their old-fashioned mentality as well as their ignorance of Islamic jurisprudence. She appeared to believe that, as a working woman, she had acquired liberties that were not subjected to local moral evaluations; or rather, she believed they would be evaluated in a framework of professionalism and urbanity.

Asya often explicated that she did not see a conflict in being both pious and professional, and she frequently argued that her professional development had not caused her to disregard local expectations toward respectability and piety. During those discussions, her language use reflected this ideological orientation to both local and translocal discourses. During a focus group discussion with other young Lamu women, for example, Asya reminded her peers of the need to uphold local norms of piety and propriety, even when pursuing professional development. When traveling to cities like Mombasa or Nairobi, she argued, one might encounter Muslim women who dress or interact differently, yet those are not habits that Lamu women ought to emulate. Asya emphasized that, despite her professional experiences and her travels abroad, she always retained behaviors that were proper to her Lamu (rather than just Muslim) identity. Switching between English and kiAmu while making this statement, Asya's language use mirrored this balance between professional goals and respect for local norms.

Bold: English
Regular: kiAmu

> **I have been there** . . . kila pahala ambapo mmekwendra, **I have gone to all of them.** Siyisifu, lakini **experience** yangu, **it is more than anybody from here**. Na siyo kwamba hayo mambo hayatendreki, **It happened** lakini **it doesn't happen to our society**. Hapa kwetu **it doesn't happen and it doesn't apply.**

> **I have been there** . . . every place where you have gone, **I have gone to all of them**. I don't want to brag but my **experience, it is more than anybody from here**. And it is not that those things did not happen. **It happened** but **it doesn't happen to our society**. Here with us **it doesn't happen and it doesn't apply.**

This moral stance became even more evident when, later in the discussion, Asya contributed to a debate on Lamu women's declining respect for local norms of piety, particularly in their public appearances. Speaking only kiAmu, Asya referred to the rumors about the inappropriate interactions between young men and women who worked as volunteers for aid organizations. Whereas young women had recently reappropriated the more pious, closed-style *buibui* rather than the open style that revealed tight clothing underneath, Asya objected to the introduction of hugs between young men and women and argued that those practices did not have a place in Lamu. By speaking exclusively kiAmu, she subtly linked her own comportment to her embodied respect for local norms of appropriate conduct.

> Ya kwanda ilikuwa kuvaa buibui ya wazi na kuvaa masuruali ya kutubana. Tulikuwa namna hiyau na tumekuwa yamefunguka, Alhamdulillah. Siku hizi kunena ukweli, imepunguwa na siyamwona mtu kwendra ile wazi wazi. Tumeieka heshma. Lakini sasa tumetoka

kwenye mavazi tumeingia kwenye kufanya vitendro ambavyo **they are not acceptable.**

First it was wearing open abaya and tight pants. We were like that and that has now been closed, Alhamdulillah. These days to say the truth, it has reduced and I haven't seen someone walking around open like that. We placed *heshima* (respect) in it [our clothing]. But now we have left clothing and we entered into habits **[that] are not acceptable**.

When she subsequently spoke from her professional position, indirectly addressing young women who worked for her, she switched to English to underline that she would never tolerate such behaviors in her workplace.

Nikizungumzia **on behalf of the administration, whatever happens, action will be taken. My friend, action will be taken. Nonsense, I can tell you, will never be tolerated.**

When I speak **on behalf of the administration, whatever happens, action will be taken. My friend, action will be taken. Nonsense, I can tell you, will never be tolerated.**

Through the content and language of her statement, Asya took a moral stance and thereby displayed an embodiment of professionalism as well as piety, modesty, and respectability. For Asya, there was no conflict in being pious *and* professional; she oriented to, and embodied both (see also Deeb 2009). But while Asya's stance might have been clear and uncontested during the focus group discussion, the presentation of such social position within daily encounters, where audiences and their evaluations are not much under one's control, was much less straightforward.

Discussing with me the gossips about her supposed inappropriate conduct, Asya maintained that her shaking hands with men in the office differed meaningfully from volunteers exchanging hugs during their activities. Her refusal to shake hands with male officials, she claimed, would result in those (international) guests evaluating her as unprofessional, impolite, and even backward—like those girls who never leave the house. Her otherwise pious composure and her rank in the office framed the handshakes as a professional practice rather than as flirtation, so Asya claimed. Locals' negative evaluations, however, resulted from what they perceived as a contrast between Asya's supposed inappropriate behavior in the new and still ambiguous space of the office and her displays of piety on her way to work.

Observers evaluated Asya's behavior on the streets as secretive rather than pious. Her cousins, for example, tied her interactions with men in the office to her wearing of the *ninja* while walking down the main street, viewing the facial veil as an attempt to remain anonymous and conceal inappropriate conduct. Similarly, they considered Asya's preference of the shadowy backstreets over the busy main street as an effort to hide from the public eye rather than her trying to uphold a respectful and pious demeanor. Unlike Asya, these observers did not make a distinction between the "professional" office and "public" streets, each with their own behavioral norms; rather, they evaluated all of Asya's behavior in a framework of the visible and observable.

So Asya miscalculated. Her "mistake" was with her assumption that her profession, her education, and her authoritative position in the office had exempted her from or redefined local norms of *heshima*—that they were sufficient to establish a new frame, an alternative context that would stabilize indexical reference and allow for the crystallization of a new social type of the "pious professional." She assumed these contexts would validate her behavior rather than make it the subject of gossip.

Three years later, at the end of my fieldwork, Asya appeared to have found somewhat of a balance; something she achieved through subtle shifts in her behavior, having taken note of the evaluations of her conduct. She no longer wore the *ninja*, generally used the main street to reach her office, and avoided the seafront. In the office, she no longer shook hands with men, and a centrally displayed sign announced: *"According to Islamic law, shaking hands between men and women is prohibited."* Written in English rather than kiSwahili, the sign evidently addressed a nonlocal or international audience. Signed by *The Management*, the responsibility for its implementation did not lie with Asya, but rather with an official, professional institution. While still interacting with men, the sign allowed Asya to refuse handshakes while retaining her professional attitude. The authoritative announcement regimented possible evaluations and left no doubt as to how one ought to read Asya's behavior. Her refusal to shake hands was not "outdated," "conservative," or "unprofessional"; it was office policy. When I questioned Asya about her previous fears of reproducing stereotypical images of Muslim women through her refusal of handshakes, she smiled and explained that she had learned that precisely a refusal to shake hands while actively participating in development work would challenge those images. Echoing her previous arguments, she suggested that practices like the refusal of handshakes showed others how Lamu women can stay true to their values while importantly contributing to the betterment of their community. Precisely this insistence on moral uprightness, especially in relation to the encroachment of nonlocal practices, would enforce respect, she stated firmly.

One might suggest that Asya's case illustrates how young people's strategic self-fashionings can stabilize indexical reference, resulting in the crystallization of a new and recognizable social type in contexts of social change (Agha 2007). This particular regimentation of diverse evaluations, however, needed a rather explicit, authoritative intervention. We can then ask how successful young women's renegotiations of material forms' meanings are and what this implies for acts of self-fashioning. The aforementioned sign might have regimented evaluations for Asya; it did not guarantee positive evaluations of other handshakes (or refusals thereof) in other contexts and an established recognition of a social position such as the "pious, progressive, professional woman" was not certain.

While I do not mean to suggest that semiotic stability is an ideal end goal, the identification and ascription of certain observed practices to particular roles and social types—enregisterment—facilitates social interaction (Agha 2007) and, indeed, self-presentations. Individuals, like Asya, intend their practices to be read in a particular way, hoping to validate new subject positions in an altering social context. The examples discussed do then not merely question the implications of semiotic stability or indeterminacy, but also the relation between semiosis and changing moral values in projects of self-fashioning.

In contemporary Lamu, young women cultivate high levels of awareness of how their behavior could be interpreted in different settings, especially because of the sometimes-contradictory implications an act can have. Young women like Asya may become acutely aware that interpretations of their behavior are quite open-ended and not, in fact, much under their control, even though they will be judged based on a strongly personalist theory of intention, grounded in notions of sincerity. Does the *ninja* a woman wears represent her sincere piety or her insincere attempts to avoid censure for immodest intentions? Who can know her intentions for sure? And so, each action is judged in context, including what other behaviors have been observed, and where. From the perspective of young women, seeking to manage their reputations, the locations they move through become semiotically meaningful, as if they were the most tangible experiences of the dangers of semiotic misconstrual. It is this sensitivity—this charged moral reflexivity—that creates affordances; it permits women to exploit material forms and negotiate the mediation of moral value, but it equally avails details of material practice for moral judgment by observers.

Dreadlocks or Kanzus—Does It Really Matter?

While arguably most observable, young Lamu women are not the only ones tactically using everyday material and embodied practices in an attempt to negotiate their orientations to seemingly contrasting ideological discourses. In previous chapters, young men like Sadiq and Jamal strategically used their linguistic repertoires to present authoritative and cosmopolitan selves, but struggled to have these self-presentations accepted by intended and unintended audiences.

While young men in Lamu did not need to actively negotiate their presence in public space, attempts at conveying differing or new understandings of and orientations toward development, westernization, religious piety, or cultural conservation did require careful considerations of everyday comportment in relation to local notions of respectability and piety. But just as the moral value of women's outward appearances had become muddled by their mediation of different (trans)local discourses, so were men's material practices not necessarily straightforward signs of their inner moral conditions. For observers, assessing young men's intentions based on their appearances wasn't any easier than evaluating young women's everyday practices and their motivations. Maryam referred to this ambiguity of men's appearances when advising her female volunteers to carefully monitor their behaviors when being approached by a pious-looking man. She argued that young women should not rely solely on the apparent virtue of men's attire (like the *kanzu* and *kofia*), but rather ought to evaluate those material practices in relation to their language use, bodily comportment, and physical location.

> Kwa sababu gani? Wamekuliya kwenye same environment. Yule rasta na yule non rasta, wote wamekuliya kwenye environment moya. The difference? Yule ameweka rasta aende zake pwani, na yule hakuweka rasta na yuko kwake mtaani. Lakini twabia ni hizo hizo. Atakuita, akutezee.

> Why? They grew up in the same environment. The one with dreadlocks and the one without dreadlocks, they all grew up in one environment. The difference? That one put dreadlocks and went to the seafront, and that one did not put dreadlocks and he is in his neighborhood. But their habits are the same. He will call you, he will play you.

Just as the *ninja* was not a candid sign of a young woman's piety, so was a white robe or dreadlocks not immediately indicative of a person's devoutness or corruption respectively. Rather, these seemingly evident signs acquired their full significance only when estimated in relation to other aspects of a man's behavior as well as previous encounters with this individual. Young men in Lamu were therefore also subjected to moralizing gazes, although some of them appeared to be targeted more than others.

PROBLEMATIC INBETWEENNESS?

Salim's story is one that unfolded over the span of about three years. When I first met him, Salim was a young man of twenty-five. Born in Rasini on Pate Island, he came to Lamu at a young age and only seldom returned to his hometown. Having lived in Langoni for the majority of his life, Salim viewed himself as belonging to Lamu, but was equally proud of his Bajuni heritage. While he had gone to secondary school until the age of sixteen, he had traded his studies for a life at the seafront and never obtained his diploma of secondary education.

As for many young Lamu men from less wealthy backgrounds, working with tourists had appealed to Salim. Coming from fishermen families, many Bajuni youth are familiar with the ocean and operate the local, wooden dhows with ease. Taking tourists on sailing trips through the lagoon is therefore an evident occupation that can be quite lucrative during the tourism high season. Salim often told me that these sailing trips, while physically demanding, were enjoyable for and appealing to young men because they could spend their time at sea in the company of people from across the globe, rather than on school benches studying for jobs that were not available in Lamu in the first place.

A few years before we met, Salim neatly fit the image of the local beach boy. He had long dreadlocks, wore chain necklaces and rings, and spent his days luring tourists along the seafront. When I got to know him, however, Salim claimed to have altered his lifestyle. I clearly remember our first encounter. I was looking for an interlocutor of mine and had been told I could find him along the seafront. Walking past the *baraza* to which I had been directed, I noticed a young man sitting with a group of somewhat older men. Being more comfortable addressing someone my own age, I hesitantly asked Salim whether he had seen my research participant. Our subsequent fruitless search for the latter ended with a fresh fruit juice at a local juice bar, a popular joint overlooking the ocean. Sipping his avocado juice, Salim stared at his former friends, who were catcalling the young female tourists strolling along the seafront, and he subsequently told me how he intended to change his life. Not only had he recently cut his dread-locks, but he had also started to attend the five daily prayers in the mosque and was refraining from using any kind of drugs, including alcohol, after having attended a rehabilitation program on Kenya's mainland.

While Salim still spent time at the seafront, he took his distance from the beach boys. Anxious that his peers would reintroduce him to the be-haviors he tried to leave, Salim now sought the company of elders on the *baraza*. This attitude, however, did not make him very popular along the seafront, with his former friends accusing him of arrogance, suggesting he thought he was now better than them. When seeing him at the *baraza*, they would inquire how the *sheikh* was doing. The exaggerated reference to Salim as a Muslim scholar based on his altered behaviors hinted at young men's challenges in negotiating altered subject positions and, indeed, at finding a middle ground between the religiously devout and the globally or Western-oriented. When Salim observed one of his former friends en-ter a bar during our first conversation, he noted, "You cannot belong to both worlds simultaneously. Either you are at the seafront or you are at the *baraza*. Belonging to both just doesn't work."[7]

A couple of months after this first encounter, Salim was back with his friends at the seafront. When I saw him, he strongly emphasized that he was not using anything, except for occasionally chewing stimulant *miraa* leaves. When asked about his prayer habits, he smiled, shrugged, and mum-bled: "you know how it goes."

NEW FRAMES, NEW INTERPRETATIONS

In November 2010, Salim was elected as city councilor and became the youngest member ever of the Lamu county council. In a little over two years, his position and social standing in the Lamu community had changed significantly. In addition to being a city councilor, Salim was the chair-man of Vijana, a youth organization that united the beach boys working at the seafront, and he intended to run for Parliament in Kenya's 2013 elec-tions. One could rightly wonder what happened during those two years, and how Salim was able to appease his seafront "brothers" while simulta-neously appealing to the broader Lamu community, who had been so skep-tical of the group of youth with which Salim was still associated.

During my second year of fieldwork, the young men working along the seafront organized themselves in a manner many Lamu residents had guaranteed me would not work. One of the aid organizations where I conducted participant observation was implementing awareness-raising campaigns focused on drugs and substance abuse. Discussing the progress of the program with one of the organization's employees, however, I noticed none of their events had included or targeted Lamu's beach boys. Aware of this social group's exposure to drugs and alcohol, I inquired why the organization had not focused on these young men. The employee shrugged and told me that these youth would not attend a workshop, nor would they pay attention to what the organization had to tell them. What if I tried to gather them? I asked. Through my research, I had interacted frequently with these young men and figured that maybe they would be willing to sit down with me. If anything, the gathering would provide an interesting discussion on topics relevant to my project.

Approximately twenty young men showed up for that initial meeting, undoubtedly motivated more by the soda and snacks we provided than by the topic of substance abuse. But the discussion that unfolded around the central question I raised—what were the challenges they faced in contemporary Lamu?—provided meaningful insights into these young men's own perceptions of their position within the community and how they associated these views with the rising substance abuse among their peers. The attendees complained about the failing tourism industry, the competition among dhow operators, and the negative image they had within the Lamu community. After some intense debates, a few participants proposed that these issues might be resolved if there was more unity among them. If the beach boys were more organized, they could legitimately ask higher compensations for tourist excursions, they could possibly educate themselves on the tourism industry, and eventually they could show the community that they were professional dhow operators rather than just beach boys who were out to charm Western tourists.

Vijana was the organization that resulted from that initial meeting. While many of the young men working along the seafront initially objected to the idea of an organization, the attendance at group meetings grew larger every week. During those initial gatherings, the young men proposed concrete steps as to how they could change their image in the community: they exchanged the name "beach boys" for "dhow operators" and composed a code of conduct that each member had to sign upon joining the group. The weekly meetings opened and ended with prayer, charity was donated to local mosques, and town cleanup activities were organized.

During one of the organization's first meetings, Salim had given an impromptu speech in response to quarrels that had unfolded between young men who supported and opposed this new youth group. Salim's spirited reaction, calling upon the young men to take up responsibility and actively work toward a positive future for themselves and their families, had been welcomed with agreement by all present and the attendees subsequently unanimously voted Salim to be the chairman of the newly created group. Under Salim's leadership, Vijana made history and became Lamu's biggest, most successful youth organization. With financial aid they received (through grant applications written with the help of the aid organization that wanted to address drugs and substance abuse), the young men acquired an office, printed flyers and price lists, provided all members with a uniform and a badge, and rightly claimed to be a professional "dhow operator organization."

The impact of the group became evident during the official launch of Vijana. After many months of hard work, the young men set up a community meeting at the town's main square to officially introduce the organization to the Lamu community and to present the uniforms, badges, and price lists that distinguished members of the group. As with all community events, the young men had insisted on inviting several notables to be present at the launch—the heads of the Council of Elders, representatives of WWF, Kenya Wildlife Service, and the National Museums of Kenya, and some local politicians. Few of the organization's members, however, believed these speakers would attend, suggesting these well-known individuals "would not speak during an event of ours." Against all odds, all of the invited speakers were present and openly expressed their support for the young men during their respective speeches. The atmosphere among the members of Vijana following this launch was one of excitement and disbelief: Did these prominent community members really just validate the organization?

Being involved with these young men's attempts at setting up this group, I was struck by their continuous emphasis on the need for visible signs. From the initial meetings, the beach boys underlined the need for uniforms—for badges and T-shirts that would make them recognizable as "real" dhow operators. They argued that uniforms, more than receiving training in first aid, professionalization, or management, would improve their chances at securing dhow excursions, since it would give them credibility with tourists. Soon after the launch, however, I noted that the majority of the organization's members wore their uniforms and badges not while working, but when walking through town, visiting family, or attending community gatherings. These material practices, as visible signs of (newly legitimate) employment, were then just as, if not more, important to manage moral evaluations within the local community as they were to appeal to tourists. Instead of being "beach boys," these young men could now claim to have an occupation as "dhow operators" and could attribute their comportment and appearances to a profession rather than a mere admiration and longing for Western culture.

While not fully alleviating negative moral evaluations, the organization did meaningfully (though temporarily) alter beach boys' position in the community. As a proclaimed professional organization working toward youth empowerment, Vijana provided a framework within which these young men could justify their everyday material practices and argue that these were strategically manipulated symbols rather than outward signs of changed inward moral conditions. Dreadlocks now did not signal laziness, addiction, and disrespect, but were tactics used as part of a professional toolkit. In a way, the organization enabled these young men to negotiate a morally responsible engagement with change, answering Taha's call for "presence" (as discussed in the Introduction). Vijana demonstrated that, given the current economic context, a selective and calculated appropriation of translocal practices was necessary in order to provide for (extended) family.

The success of Vijana, however, also hints at the gendered nature of these negotiations and the complex historical and ideological embeddedness of moral values. One could argue that these young men were more successful than, for example, Asya in getting their signs accepted both because women's public presence as such was viewed as a sign of transgression, and because men's (historical) presence at the seafront (and the interactions with translocal and transoceanic others) had always entailed more frequent renegotiations of signs and their values. At the same time, however, the young men were not able to uphold this newly acquired position, for the further decline of the tourism industry undermined the survival of Vijana. On return visits to Lamu, the young men continuously urge me to try and revive the organization, the remnants of which are now only a few faded T-shirts worn by unemployed youth.

But what about Salim? While the success of Vijana under his leadership had put him on the community radar, his election as councilor did not result organically from this position. Only through a careful balancing of his material and linguistic practices was Salim able to successfully present himself as a potential councilor. Just like Asya, Salim subtly shifted some aspects of his behavior, permitting him to portray a balanced orientation toward different ideological discourses, including the preservation of religious and cultural values as well as the need for development and change.

While Salim had been married for a while, this had been a public secret since beach boys presumed that being married would make them less popular among female tourists. Following the success of Vijana, however,

Salim often took his young daughter for walks through town—not just along the seafront but also through the backstreets of Lamu. In addition, the *kofia* and *bakora* (walking stick) became part of his regular attire. He often attended the five daily prayers in the mosque and always wore a *kanzu* on Fridays. Whereas these practices would previously have easily resulted in his fellow beach boys referring to Salim as *sheikh*, these young men now addressed him as "chairman" or "councilor" (even before his election to the city council). One could shrug and suggest that these few behavioral changes are examples of local political strategies—presenting oneself as a family man rather than someone focused on partying. The event of Salim's election was unique, however, because he was able to appeal to a community that was previously opposed to young men from the seafront while simultaneously retaining his popularity among peers.

His explicit discourse of professionalization, leadership, and development had allowed for a perception of his material practices as strategically manipulated signs, for the community as well as the beach boys. Salim's sudden use of the *bakora*, for example, was meaningful in that sense. In Swahili culture, older, upper-class men generally use this kind of walking stick to signal authority as well as social standing. Salim's deliberate use of the *bakora* indicated his claim to authority, not based on age, but rather on his experience as the chairman of the successful youth organization. In so doing, Salim negotiated alternative grounds on which authority could be claimed and strategically mobilized the local value of a material practice like the *bakora* in the process. Salim's dhow operator friends viewed his use of the *bakora* as a symbol of his leadership and a possible future councillorship that would defend the rights of youth in Lamu, while the local community read it as an adherence to and respect for cultural traditions. Similarly, his presence at the seafront was no longer viewed as exclusively signaling improper conduct but instead was interpreted within the framework of professional leadership. For Salim's friends, it signified that he was still part of their group of youth. Professionalism and leadership therefore provided an ideological framework for Salim as well as the local community who could justify their shift in moral judgment by phrasing it in terms of much-needed development and youth empowerment—a framework Vijana provided.

Successful Negotiation: A Gendered Question?

Comparing this ethnographic account to the story of Asya, it is tempting to explain Salim's success in gender terms, arguing that young women are structurally more limited in negotiating newly emerging social positions. In other words, we could suggest this is a matter of gendered agency. Although women's conduct is often more observable and sensitive, I argue against a complete reliance on a gendered explanation of Salim's unexpected political career. After all, Asya's attempt at negotiating a new position was not entirely unsuccessful. She worked herself up the office ranks and currently fulfills a role model function for young Lamu women, often traveling to the mainland and abroad for work purposes. Individuals' ability to successfully negotiate changing subject positions and altered mediations of moral values is meaningfully shaped not just by social category belonging but also by the historical and ideological embeddedness of the material forms on which they rely. To fully understand the everyday transformation of moral values and ethical self-fashioning we therefore need to consider not just who is subjected to and limited by moral judgments, but also who is doing the evaluating together with the different kinds of judgments they express, and on what grounds.

Looking back at the data discussed, not one moral evaluation was voiced. Rather the range of evaluative responses is striking for how various subject positions seem to be constituted or reinforced through participation in particular genres of evaluation. For example, Maryam's admonitions to other young women, quoted at the onset of this chapter, refer to men watching women on the street and their tests of a passing woman's openness to flirtation. A more coercive evaluative genre is that of gossip to which Asya became subject. These differences in moral evaluations—participating in calling to women on the street versus gossiping about them—constitute very different subject positions, especially with regard to gender and respectability. Through these different genres of moral assessment, these observers not only situate the people whom they are evaluating, but they also position themselves as a particular kind of subject.

These verbalizations of evaluations—the reprimanding, gossiping, catcalling, or advising—are different appraisals of Lamu's moral transformation; they are signs of moral self-positioning that themselves will be subjected to evaluation. By gossiping about Asya's behavior, young women express a stance on what women's behavior ought to be like and thus evaluate discourses on emancipation. By insisting on shaking my hand, the beach boys or other acquaintances not only positioned me as an openminded, nonconservative young woman; they also situated themselves as someone who adheres to changing conceptions of appropriate interactions. By publicly supporting Vijana, local dignitaries positioned themselves as being progressive while simultaneously demanding respect for local norms.

Exactly these circuits of semiotic interpretation and the different conditions under which they develop highlight the emergence of different social groups, distinct from the former social hierarchy. The developing differentiation among young women according to whether they are *wanawake wa ndani* (women from inside) or educated, working women, each commenting on the limits of the other is constituted on differing interpretations of local norms and values and their "correct" mediation in practice. Similarly, volunteers' remarks on beach boys' language use and the possibilities for a future failure of their organization are reflective of their interpretation of a moral narrative of modernity—what it entails and how it should be mediated within verbal and nonverbal semiotic practices. These responses to observed signs are relevant because they engender reactions in return, informing future self-fashionings by young people like Asya or Salim, who altered their behaviors to accommodate the different evaluative discourses to which they were exposed. At the same time, however, not reacting to evaluations equally entails a stance. In other words, maintaining behavior in the face of potential critique or faulty interpretations conveys important social or political meanings (as Asya alluded to in her eventual refusal to shake hands).

The management of moral evaluations in projects of self-fashioning is inherently linked to the embeddedness of material forms in intricate webs of signification. The examples here show that individuals' balancing acts are not straightforward precisely because the social dynamics at play are not reducible to the individual (Goffman 1955, 1956; Keane 2016; Irvine 1996). Material practices become meaningful in relation to each other, to the individual mobilizing them, *and* to the differently situated audiences evaluating their usage. In other words, observers' judgments can become signs to be evaluated and acted upon by individuals looking to negotiate moral value and social positions, making projects of self-fashioning intensely intersubjective and dialogic.

Yet beyond this linguistic anthropological contribution to understanding the intricacies of ethical self-fashioning, this chapter also showed the many considerations Lamu youth need to make as they navigate a range of social, economic, and political expectations. Young people's everyday practices are not just about appeasing elders or peers who are watching and judging them. Throughout this chapter, it has become evident that seemingly mundane practices, like hand greetings, are appropriated, challenged, or redefined in relation to local norms but also to translocal views of who Lamu people are. Supposed micro-interactional practices, while locally situated, are thus meaningfully framed by and responsive to larger scale discourses as well—whether it was Asya speaking back to nonlocals' perception of veiled Lamu women or it concerned beach boys who anticipated tourists' trouble with the lack of alcohol. At the same time, however, many of the signifying distinctions outlined throughout this chapter, while central to young people's subtle negotiations of new subject positions in the local context, are erased when traveling outside of Lamu or when nonlocal audiences observe these youth.

Awareness of such translocal perceptions, though not always explicitly acknowledged, forms the backdrop against which young Lamu residents' everyday interactions unfold. This mindfulness of different kinds of valuations, at different scales of society, instills daily interactions with not only religious or moral value but also political significance. Being a "good Muslim" in Lamu today therefore does not merely concern questions of piety or lack thereof, nor are anxieties about *heshima* only about the preservation of particular cultural norms. Rather, for Lamu residents, negotiations about properly embodied respectability also entail important political stances. It is precisely through the seemingly mundane, therefore, that views on what it means to be "from Lamu" in contemporary Kenya are communicated and negotiated.

Epilogue

As I was completing this book in June 2018, a video clip regularly appeared on my Facebook newsfeed. Kenyan news agencies, government watch groups, and (mostly male) Lamu youth shared a two-minute amateur video in which a young Lamu resident, growing a full beard, voiced his frustrations over having been arrested several times on suspicion of terrorism. Speaking kiSwahili with a distinctly coastal accent (but not evidently ki-Amu or kiBajuni), he explained how security forces time and time again assumed his beard to be a sign of an affiliation with Al-Shabaab, the Somali-based terrorist group. He objected that his beard was part of his religious practice and adherence to the Sunnah—to following the lifestyle of the Prophet Muhammad, who had advised men to grow a beard. While Lamu residents recognize and value this practice, the young man suggested, the meaning of a beard as a sign of piety and moral uprightness was erased outside of Lamu.

The young man recounted when and where he had been detained, and he described how soldiers at checkpoints along Kenya's roads responded to his appearance. "That gun they carry on their back immediately gets shifted to the front (as if ready to shoot)." He elaborated: "Even when I need help when I am on the Kenyan mainland, I am unable to get assistance due to my beard." The young man lamented the misreading of his beard as a sign of terrorist affiliation rather than of virtue, and he argued that such judgments prevented him from effectively doing his work as a children's rights activist, for which he traveled within and outside of Kenya. He urged the Kenyan government and its security forces to be careful and contemplative in their fight against religious extremism and learn to distinguish between terrorists and mere civilians.

On Facebook, the video was shared numerous times and received a range of comments. Male residents from Lamu acknowledged and sympathized with the young man's experiences. Commentators disagreed, however, on the solution to this problem. Some suggested that men should shave their beards to distinguish themselves from Al-Shabaab affiliates, while others encouraged young men to remain steadfast and adhere to the Sunnah of the Prophet. "It is your right as a Kenyan citizen," several proclaimed. Accompanying their remarks with a cartoon of "bropunzel" (Figure 20), these contributors jokingly proposed Lamu men grow their beards as long as possible, as a sign of religious devoutness but also as a form of resistance to the government's targeting of coastal Muslims, and Lamu residents in particular. Some commentators cynically noted that all terrorists apparently have beards and are mysteriously incapable of shaving. To underline the sarcasm in their remark, they supplemented their observation with an image of "Alshabab razor blades" (Figure 21). Arabic for "youth," the Alsha-

Figure 20. "Bropunzel."

bab brand merely promotes razor blades for young men. Yet because it shares its name with the Somali-based terrorist organization, the razor blade brand effectively illustrated commentators' sarcastic objections to the profiling to which young (Lamu) Muslim men fall victim.

Lamu residents' uncertainty surrounding how nonlocal others—police, security, government officials, mainland immigrants, or even tourists—evaluate their everyday practices is, however, not limited to travels to mainland Kenya. When speaking on the phone to a friend in Lamu during the holy month of Ramadan in 2018, he told me that hotels and government offices on the island had increased their security, with a remarkably higher number of soldiers and watchmen being visibly present on Lamu's streets. "Isn't it ironic," he remarked, "that this is a month of devotion and prayer, yet they somehow assume that we become dangerous?" Having grown his beard for the month of Ramadan, as a sign of devoutness, he jokingly noted he ought to be careful walking around at night, since he might be arrested. Asking him why this would be the case, my friend responded that mainland soldiers could not distinguish between someone who grows a beard because it is Sunnah, because he is an Al-Shabaab affiliate, or because he is addicted to drugs and simply is too lazy to shave. I proposed that he shave his beard to avoid being arrested, allowing him to walk around more freely at night. Somewhat agitated, my friend objected that the Prophet had suffered much more than being arrested for a few hours, so why would he give up a Sunnah just because "they" could not recognize, or rather misrecognized, the pious intentions behind his appearance? On the contrary, he should grow his beard longer.

What does it mean to be a "good Muslim" in Lamu today? And what does it mean to be a "good Lamu resident" in contemporary Kenya? This book has shown that, for Lamu residents, these questions are ineluctably, but very complexly, intertwined. For scholars of the Swahili coast, the inseparability of Islam and Swahili identities is self-evident; it has long been acknowledged that, in the past, to belong to a Swahili community—to be recognized as mSwahili or mwAmu—one first and foremost had to be Muslim (Introduction and Chapter 1). *Heshima*, as one of the core concepts of this book, was and continuous to be an organizing principle in Lamu society and has Islam at its core. To be a good or respectable member of the Lamu community, one was expected to be a virtuous Muslim. One might suggest, however, that what it means to be a "good Muslim" is a different question altogether, since it concerns an individual's ability to adhere to religious prescriptions and strive for religious devoutness (e.g., Mahmood 2005; Hirschkind 2006): five daily prayers, charity, veiling, and growing a

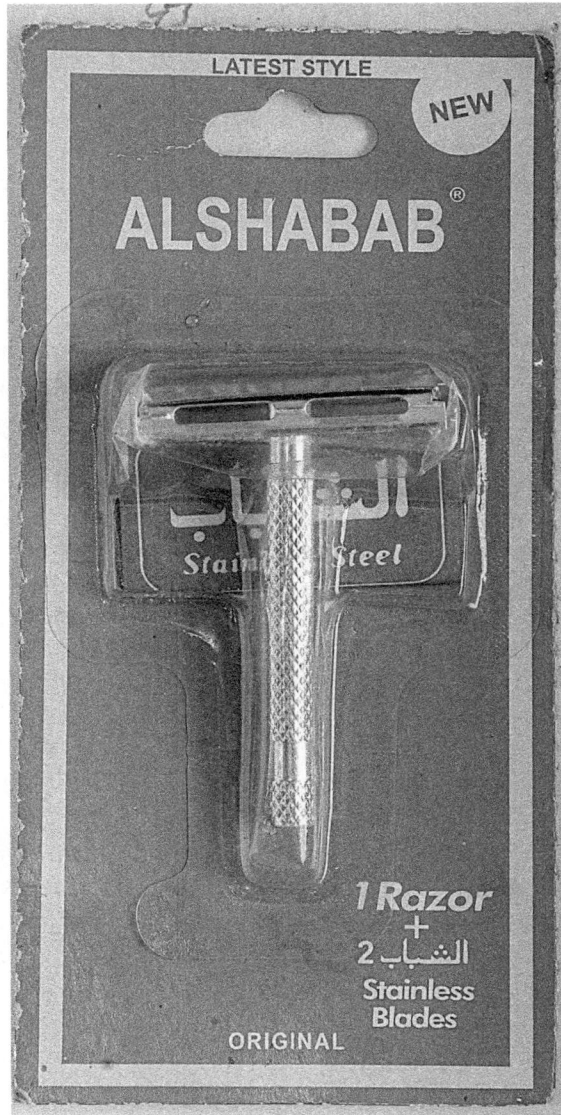

Figure 21. Alshabab razor blades. Photograph by Abdalla Bargash.

beard (among other things). By examining everyday life in contemporary Lamu, this book endeavored to complicate the answers to both these questions, illustrating that being a "good Lamu resident" is about much more than being a "good Muslim" and that being a "good Muslim" in Lamu extends far beyond questions of religious piety. The anecdotes highlight that being a "good Muslim" in Lamu today does not just concern appropriating material practices as (outward) signs of (inner) religious devoutness. While growing a beard should first and foremost be a sincere emulation of the Prophet, upholding such pious practices when confronted with profiling and perceived persecution makes a good Muslim. Being a "good Lamu resident" still entails being a "good Muslim," but it no longer translates into virtues like hospitality and generosity (Chapter 1). Rather, it encompasses being unapologetically Muslim in the face of adversity, defending the rights of Lamu residents as Muslims in Kenya.

This book also showed, however, that these questions—being a good Lamu resident, being a good Muslim—are more complex than this. WaAmu and waBajuni might agree that being a (good) Lamu resident is first and foremost about being Muslim. But the non-Muslim, Euro-American expatriates who live in Lamu Town or Shela Town and who sponsor local education and orphanages, for example, would undoubtedly object that they are "better" Lamu residents than the *baraza*-sitting Muslim elders who complain about social change but do not evidently act upon the needs they identify. Previously an embodiment of *heshima*, there is little manifestly respectable about this idle sitting in contemporary Lamu (Chapter 1 and 3). At the onset of this book, Ustadh Taha identified precisely this inconsistency in the previously hegemonic notion of an ideal Lamu-Muslim identity when he called upon Lamu residents to reconsider their behaviors carefully in the face of contemporary change. A "good Muslim," a truly God-conscious person, does not just sit on a *baraza* to debate disenfranchisement, but neither does he only appropriate Western practices as a display of individual progress; rather, a person with *heshima* and *hudur* (or God-consciousness) actively, though selectively, participates in change to contribute to the well-being of the community. For Taha, however, the goal of this morally responsible engagement with change and development, while religiously inspired, was to protect Lamu residents as Muslims against an impending Christian-majority government and its allies. Social activism, as a religious obligation, then equally entailed taking a political stance. These complex intersections of Islam, politics, and locally embedded notions of respectability, however, made this "moral presence" nearly impossible to achieve, especially for certain groups of Lamu youth. Because such morally responsible engagement with development entails renegotiating the importance and semiotic mediation of previously hegemonic notions of proper conduct, young Lamu residents continuously risk violating social expectations and being condemned for adhering to the values of those encroaching "others" (Chapter 3).

Negotiating a particular new moral presence, then, requires a careful balancing of adhering to certain social boundaries, while crossing others and strategically using semiotic forms in the process. These negotiations, this book showed, happen precisely in the seemingly unremarkable aspects of everyday life. Being a good Muslim at the margins of the state is about pointing out local social divisions that prevent a unified representation at the national level, while using language to mitigate the risk of violating norms of appropriate conduct (Chapter 4). Being a good Muslim at the margins of the (inter)national economy is about searching for employment opportunities and being able to provide for one's family, yet thereby potentially crossing boundaries of what others consider pious behavior (Chapter 3 and 5). Being a good Muslim at the margins of development entails defying certain gender expectations, while embodying other norms of deference, to participate in (inter)national development projects and contribute to the betterment of the community (Chapter 5). Through their everyday interactions, Lamu youth are not only renegotiating what it means to be respectable in contemporary Lamu; they are also making claims about what it means to be young, modern, and Muslim in Kenya today.

A central argument of this book, however, is that such everyday strategic negotiations of new subject positions are neither straightforward nor self-evident. The social embeddedness of material forms' semiotic value and the intersubjective nature of everyday interactions often undermine young people's attempts at strategic self-presentation through the use of (now-ambiguous) semiotic forms. Local perceptions of social and moral transformation linked to the encroaching Kenyan state resulted in a hypersensitivity to indexicality in an attempt to assess (newly arrived) actors' true intentions. Societal transformation also created semiotic confusion; it destabilized indexical reference and enabled a suspicion about the "real" meaning of the verbal and behavioral signs people display, in turn availing diverging interpretations.

Of course, (non)verbal displays of respectability, cosmopolitanism, and other qualities of personhood never were entirely unambiguous. The idea that they once were is itself an ideological or metapragmatic dimension of a historical consciousness. The discursive contrasting of past and present as unambiguous versus ambiguous enables an evaluation of contemporary changes and material practices as indexical of unprecedented and deeper lying moral transformations (Chapter 1–3). The discourses and everyday practices examined in this book therefore not only illustrated the renegotiation of social relations through verbal and nonverbal semiotic practices; they also uncovered epistemologies of certainty and uncertainty in contexts of rapid change.

The example with which I start this epilogue, however, demonstrates that this anxiety derives not just from semiotic confusion at the local level, but also from an uncertainty as to who else will be reading one's signs, how these will be read, and what the consequences might be. Indeed, Lamu residents are increasingly confronted with the fact that this "reading of signs" is not fully under their control. Just as young women within the context of Lamu are much aware that their material practices are the subject of evaluation and misconstrual, so are Lamu residents (and coastal Muslims, for that matter) increasingly confronted with the semiotic miscontruals they can fall victim to. While locally situated and shaped by locally circulating ideological discourses, strategic self-fashionings are also shaped by translocal discourses and occur against a background of political disenfranchisement and economic deterioration. The everyday comportments of Lamu youth are thus informed by a dual-consciousness—an awareness of their (shifting) position within the Lamu community (along the lines of age, gender, social class) and a consciousness of Lamu's position within contemporary Kenya (both at the margins and continuously marginalized).

In examining how these tensions are mitigated, negotiated, and contemplated within everyday interactions, this book showed how often-ignored, seemingly small practices are some of the most important ways in which larger scale transformations materialize in community life, and by which they receive local inflection and resonance. The supposed micro-levels of interaction on which this book focused are therefore meaningfully configured through multiple, (trans)local discourses, each of which encodes a particular approach to notions of identity and social positionality. At the same time, however, young Lamu residents are continuously speaking back to those discourses as well.

The anecdotes at the beginning of this epilogue, for example, illustrates an increasing confrontation with and awareness of the erasure of local meaning-making processes in outsiders' assessments of Lamu residents. Discussions in this book showed how such consciousness can result in a recognition of these translocal discourses and their incorporation within practice, as Asya did when defending her handshaking habits (Chapter 5). Just as translocal discourses (on terrorism, oppression, backwardness, the pristine) define "Lamu residents" to outsiders, so do they increasingly offer locals an understanding of their own condition (in relation to those others). The anecdotes, however, also demonstrate that this confrontation with others' unified reading of (locally distinctive) signs, and its possible consequences, has become increasingly outspoken over the last few years. Indeed, much has changed since I left Lamu in 2010, and those transformations have only exacerbated the processes I outlined in this book.

In the span of nine years, Kenyan military forces have invaded Somalia to engage in a "war on terror," supported by American forces, while Al-Shabaab continues to cause unrest within Kenya. In response to Kenya's invasion of Somalia, these Islamist extremists violently attacked villages in Lamu County. In 2014, the town of Mpeketoni was invaded, and sixty-seven villagers lost their lives. A few weeks later, the town of Witu was assaulted. And about a year later, Al-Shabaab attacked a university in Garissa, and close to one hundred students lost their lives. Because the assaults appeared to target Christian residents rather than Muslims, the government soon suspected coastal Muslims of participating in or facilitating these attacks. In Mombasa, Malindi, and Lamu, many young men (including some of my friends) were arrested and detained, their families often not knowing what the charges were or when they would be released.

As I write this conclusion, the construction of Africa's biggest international port is continuing in the Lamu Archipelago, and discussions about and protests against the commencement of a coal power plant grow increasingly louder. These infrastructural "developments" are accompanied by cumulative cases of land grabbing and dispossession, enabled by corruption among local and national politicians. As the latter are often the biggest beneficiaries of massive projects such as the new port or the proposed power plant, few are left to fend for the rights of Lamu residents. With China as one of the biggest investors in these infrastructural projects, the face of Lamu is changing rapidly. Trying to appease locals, China highlights and celebrates its historical connections to the Lamu Archipelago. Chinese archaeologists are searching for the remains of the ship of Zheng He, an explorer who is believed to have arrived in Lamu in the fifteenth century. Genetic testing is used to demonstrate the historical ties between China and inhabitants of the archipelago, and residents who are proven to be descendants of Zheng He are provided with scholarships to study in China. Yet, whether and how Lamu residents will benefit from the Chinese investments in large-scale projects that will forever change the local eco-environment is left to be seen. Indeed, this epilogue cannot do justice to the rate at which life in Lamu is transforming and neither can it capture the complexities of the (inter)national economic and political interests that inform these shifts.

Assessing the construction of the international port, Lamu residents weigh the prospects of development and modernity against the pitfalls of rapid change, heightened migration, and the imposition of outsiders. Images of what Lamu ought to look like after the port is built, paint—to the project's opponents—a frightening image of a resort-like city with bike paths, fancy cars, and high-rise buildings (see Figure 22). Within the local context, these images are accompanied by politicians' predictions about Lamu's future status as "the Dubai of Africa," a compelling discourse that is welcomed by many (though certainly not all) Lamu residents. Likening Lamu to Dubai, Qatar, or other successful Gulf states speaks to and enables the reimagination of historical ties with the Arab and Islamic world. It revives nostalgic discourses of prosperity, global interconnectivity, and an Islamic lifestyle, discourses that have surfaced throughout this book.

At the same time, the increasingly plausible construction of a coal power plant and the devastating consequences this would have for Lamu's ecosystem as well as the health and livelihood of its population confront Lamu residents with their marginalized position within Kenya and with the fact

Figure 22. Conceptual design for a future convention center in Lamu, "the Dubai of Africa." Kenya Ministry of Transportation.

that these development schemes are hardly focused on the advancement of the community.

The lack of local consultation about the construction of the port and the coal power plant, the land grabbing that accompanies both, the indifference to the environmental and health impacts of a power plant, and the uncertainty about employment opportunities in these billion-dollar projects confront Lamu residents, young and old, with the fact that none of these developments are of their own doing. These transformations are instead the result of outside imposition and reflect or aggravate the ongoing processes of disenfranchisement to which my interlocutors objected (Chapters 1–3). Locals' awareness of these unequal processes of development and, particularly, of their positions at the (economic and political) margins of society comes to the fore when they name neighborhoods "Bosnia" or "Kashmir" or when they refer to Lamu as "the black Palestine." Such sentiments of dispossession and, in a way, occupation are only confirmed and strengthened when young aid workers are arrested for growing a beard, for example. In those moments, the "moral presence" Ustadh Taha called for seems increasingly urgent and simultaneously out of reach.

While they might strive to be recognized as cosmopolitan (like Jamal) or professional (like Asya) or while their actions can be assessed as undesirable within the context of Lamu (like Salim), these locally meaningful distinctions are erased within a translocal context. Within national and international discourses, and thus in debates surrounding economic projects like an international port, little distinction is made between the beach boy and the *madrasa* student, or between someone from the Bajuni Islands and an Omani Arab. Events like the Mpeketoni attacks, the subsequent antiterror campaigns, and the lasting threat of random arrests confront young people from Lamu with the fact that locally distinctive practices are being read and evaluated in a particular way in translocal contexts. Whether one wears a *kofia* and a *kanzu* and the way in which these are worn no longer matter.

Of course, processes of negotiation—of multiple identities, of social hierarchies, of material practices, of qualities of personhood—are not new to the Swahili coast. I do not mean to silence Lamu inhabitants' historical cosmopolitanism, nor do I intend to ignore the significant social transformations that affected Lamu before; rather, I aim to reveal the changing patterns and implications of both contemporary changes and the global connectivity to which Lamu residents' lay claim. As the book showed, Lamu's current geopolitical position invites and even encourages multiple and redefined cross-cultural performances of similarity (Prestholdt 2008);

it avails identifications with Yemen and Oman, but also with Palestine or Kashmir through verbal and material practices. The ways in which such translocal sensibilities are performed, read, and evaluated, however, has shifted significantly, both within the local and the (inter)national context.

International discourses on antiterrorism provide a means through which others can now portray Swahili people, who have always considered themselves civilized and developed, as uncivilized and barbaric; they provide a justification for certain types of acts and define how people ought to be read (Asad 2007). While translocal discourses on "terrorism" and "radical Islam" might not have caused the ambiguity of signs, they offer a possible regimentation of interpretations that provides governments like Kenya's with a discourse to justify particular actions and measurements. In the name of (inter)national security, an American naval base is now situated in the Lamu Archipelago; there have been numerous (unfounded) arrests of inhabitants of Lamu, Malindi, and Mombasa; several Islamic preachers have been killed in unclear circumstances; and Kenyan troops invaded Somalia. This course of events demonstrates how "fear, uncertainty, and the ambiguity of signs are part of the space of violence . . . they are its precondition, for they allow state power to penetrate the density of ordinary life" (Asad 2007, 31). What this book shows, however, is that this penetration of ordinary life equally entails Lamu residents' own everyday negotiations of what it means to be "from Lamu" in contemporary Kenya and, indeed, what it means to be a "good Muslim" in Lamu today. Precisely in this penetration of ordinary life, we see the complex intersections of the supposedly micro and macro. It offers the background against which we need to understand Ustadh Taha's call for moral presence; it is the framework within which we can comprehend "bropunzel"; and it is the context in which we need to evaluate young people's choices when they speak, dress, and greet. Through these seemingly mundane practices, they are positioning themselves within Lamu society and are renegotiating local norms, values, and hierarchy structures. But in so doing, they are also responding and situating themselves in relation to particular readings of "Lamu residents" in Kenya today. Within the context of Lamu, everyday Islam is precisely about this continuous and contentious navigating of the many, often conflicting demands of society; while it concerns making decisions with regard to the embodiment of (particular kinds of) piety, such enactments are informed by economic, social, and political concerns as well.

As I conclude this book, I realize that I started this ethnography with a preface that reflected upon my own position in Lamu and how I learned to distinguish and read signs: signs of social status, origins, piety, flirtation; signs that structure and inform social life in Lamu. I talked about how this ability to identify distinctive features in verbal, material, and bodily practices helped me understand social relations and hierarchies, but also how my own appropriation and embodiment of such significations shaped my time in Lamu. Yet, in this conclusion, I draw attention to Lamu residents' progressive confrontation with the insignificance of those signifying distinctions in a context where official hermeneutics flourish. My friend's remark at the onset of this epilogue—his observation that to security forces there is no difference between a beard as a sign of piety, extremism, or drug addiction—highlights how *wageni* or newcomers are unable to read local semiotic practices, that they are unable to link one aspect of material practice to other signifying details in an individual's appearance. It also demonstrates that Lamu residents are increasingly aware of the translocal insignificance of local social differentiation, as Khadija already vocalized in Chapter 4. Precisely this confrontation with unified readings of locally distinguishing signs encourages a united and more explicit identification as "Muslim"; it informs reformulations of *hiyo ndiyo Amu*, "this is Lamu," and underlies statements like *ina wenyewe*, "it has its rightful owners" (Chapter 1).

I do not know whether and to what extent Lamu residents will be able to resist the coal power plant that threatens their environment and livelihood. Neither do I know what its impacts and those of the international port will be. More significant transformations and uncertainties lie ahead. However, new alliances among local, national, and transnational anti-coal activists, for example, are appealing to a different sense of cosmopolitan engagement and are meaningfully reconfiguring some of the discourses of modernity on which this book focused. Situating themselves in international discussions on environmental conservation and sustainable living, Lamu residents are developing new forms of social (and political) activism. One example of this is Lamu residents' recent construction of a traditional dhow from used plastic slippers—the "flipflopi dhow"—and the international recognition it received as an innovative intervention to plastic's threat to the environment (Figure 23). These new alliances are then equally changing the face of Lamu. Indeed, the name of a locally situated but internationally recognized activist group protesting the coal power plant fully captures these new translocal connections and the position they claim with regard to the Kenyan government: deCOALonize.

Figure 23. The Flipflopi dhow. Photograph by Abdalla Barghash.

Note on Language

Several languages are spoken in Lamu Town and in the wider Lamu Archipelago. These languages include kiSwahili, Arabic, English, and, increasingly, a range of languages introduced by recent national and
international immigrants to the region, such as Kikuyu and Spanish. As
the national and official language of Kenya (next to English) and the language used in primary education, the standardized form of kiSwahili can
be heard frequently in Lamu. However, people from the Archipelago are
mother tongue speakers of a range of dialectal varieties of the Swahili
language, including vernaculars like kiAmu, kiBajuni, kiPate, and kiSiyu.
When I use "kiSwahili" or "the Swahili language," I refer to the language
broadly speaking, incorporating both its standardized and dialectal varieties. When important to the argument, however, I distinguish between
Standard Swahili or kiSwahili Sanifu (as the standardized form is popu-
larly known in Kenya) and vernaculars like kiAmu or kiBajuni.

KiSwahili is a Bantu language, belonging to the Niger-Congo family. It
is an agglutinating language, with an elaborate noun class system. All nouns
therefore belong to a nominal class and have corresponding nominal prefixes (and verbs, adjectives, prepositions, and so forth agree with the noun

through their respective prefixes). For example, the prefix *ki–* refers to a language, thus *ki*Swahili (the Swahili language). A Swahili person is referred to as *m*Swahili, whereas *wa*Swahili signifies several or many Swahili people. Similarly, *ki*Amu refers to the language of Amu (an older referent for Lamu Town, still used today by many Lamu residents), whereas *wa*Amu refers to inhabitants of Amu. In this book, I thus refer to kiSwahili and waSwahili, rather than Kiswahili or Waswahili (a more commonly used orthography) (see also, for example, Caplan 2007). I also use kiSwahili or "the Swahili language" rather than merely "Swahili," since the latter can refer to either the Swahili language, culture, or people or to all of these at once.

Throughout the text, I use "Lamu residents" or "people from Lamu" to refer to all people indigenous to the Lamu Archipelago, now living in Lamu Town. I thus include under this referent people originating from surrounding islands and towns like Shela, Matondoni, Kipungani, Siyu, Pate, and Faza who migrated to Lamu Town. I use the term "waAmu" only to refer to those people who claim to be the original inhabitants of Lamu Town (for example, the former merchant elites) and those who have resided in Lamu for several generations (many of whom migrated from Yemen and Oman in the late nineteenth and early twentieth centuries). The population of Lamu, however, is increasingly diverse and now also includes people from mainland Kenya (such as people from the Kikuyu ethnicity) and Euro-American expatriates who have settled on the island. While all these people are, of course, inhabitants of Lamu, I do not incorporate them under "Lamu residents." When I refer to all current inhabitants of Lamu, I make explicit this inclusion of mainland and international immigrants.

I use kiSwahili lexical items for those words that do not have an exact translation in English. While I provide the English gloss as an approximation, these translations do not always capture the lexical nuances of kiSwahili. The differences between *mila* (traditions), *tabia* (manners, traditions), and *utamaduni* (culture, civilization), for example, are nuanced and do not necessarily correspond with the differences between the English lexemes. *Italics* mark the kiSwahili or kiAmu words that are retained, and their translations appear either between commas as part of the text or between parentheses. When kiSwahili nouns are retained, I preserve the appropriate nominal prefixes in their pluralized form. For example, *mgeni* (one guest) will appear as *wageni* (several guests) in the plural form, rather than an anglicized *mgenis*.

Throughout the monograph, I use transcriptions of interviews and from daily interactions. If the transcript is a quote from an interview, it appears as quoted text in its original kiSwahili form first (for interested experts), followed by its translation into English. If the transcript derives from an interaction with multiple participants, the kiSwahili and English versions appear in columns next to each other to allow the reader to follow the conversation and its turn-taking. All translations of these interactions were done in collaboration with interlocutors in Lamu. The level of detail I include in these transcripts corresponds to the theoretical argument I make using that piece of data. While I sometimes highlight code-switches, I do not provide IPA (International Phonetic Alphabet) transcriptions of kiAmu or kiBajuni, because I want to retain the legibility of the text for a broader audience. I acknowledge that an argument can be made for the use of IPA when dialect shifts are indicated through subtle distinctions like the use of an alveolar /t/, which cannot be represented in Roman script. However, switches are mostly evident through lexical items or other phonological distinctions that can be represented. Moreover, an important aspect of dialectal differences lies in intonation contours, with speakers of kiAmu distinguishing themselves, not just through dialect-specific vocabulary or phonology but also through a particular intonation that cannot be captured in transcripts, even when using IPA.

In transcriptions and quotes I represent the kiSwahili language as used by the speaker; this includes representing dialectical varieties exactly as they are spoken. While not all varieties of the Swahili language are recognized as distinct dialects, and while even established dialects such as kiAmu and kiBajuni do not have a standardized orthography, the distinctions between them and their usage in everyday interactions are important to Lamu residents and carry social and political meanings. I therefore use nonstandard orthography in transcripts when a dialect like kiAmu is used. By "nonstandard," I mean to refer to any transcription that deviates from the standard orthography of Standard Swahili.

My orthographic choices for dialect use were informed both by existing linguistic studies of the different Swahili dialects and, importantly, by local writing conventions as provided to me by interlocutors and research assistants. All transcriptions were conducted by research assistants in Lamu, and were subsequently discussed with them and other interlocutors. These discussions often focused on the notation of a dialect shift within the recorded conversation and on the orthographic choices that indicate that shift. Interlocutors strongly emphasized certain orthographic representations of kiAmu, such as *kuyuwa* (to know) instead of the Standard Swahili *kujua*. As the subsequent section will discuss, the /y/ is a recognized phonological feature of the kiAmu dialect; the /w/ is not. I retained interlocutors' orthographic decisions both to acknowledge their authority over their dialect use and to highlight the arbitrariness of standard orthographies.

In what follows, I substantiate these transcription choices through a more detailed (though, I want to emphasize, not at all comprehensive), linguistic discussion of the Swahili dialects spoken in the Lamu Archipelago. Understanding how these varieties of kiSwahili differ from each other on a phonological, morphological, and lexical level might be of interest to readers with a background in linguistics and will aid their reading of the transcripts and the code-switching highlighted in them.

The Northern Swahili Dialects

The standard variety of kiSwahili, spoken today in Tanzania and Kenya, was introduced only at the beginning of the twentieth century as part of the British colonial (and missionary) project. Before that time, kiSwahili was only found in what are now considered its different dialectal forms. Swahili coastal vernaculars continue to be spoken in Somalia, Kenya, Tanzania, and a few communities in Mozambique and can be divided into three dialect clusters. Those spoken from Somalia to just south of Mombasa (comprising the dialects spoken within the Lamu Archipelago) are referred to as the Northern Dialects (ND). The Central Dialect group includes kiMvita, the dialect spoken on Mombasa Island (also known as kiMombasa). The Southern cluster comprises kiUnguja (the dialect of Zanzibar) and kiVumba (see, for example, Githiora 2002; Nurse 1982; Nurse and Hinnebusch 1993).

Inhabitants of the Lamu Archipelago claim to speak six different dialects: kiAmu, kiMatondoni, kiShela, kiPate, kiSiyu, and kiBajuni. The status of kiAmu and kiBajuni as distinct dialects is not contested. Derek Nurse (1980, 1982, 1985) questions the dialect status only of kiShela (which he considers part of the kiAmu dialect), but he agrees that the phonological, morphological, and lexical differences between the other variants of kiSwahili are quantitatively and qualitatively sufficient to consider them separate dialects. Bakari (1985) recognizes only four dialects, denying the dialect status of kiMatondoni and kiPate, whereas Stigand (1915) identifies five dialects, making no note of kiMatondoni. While the different dialects claimed by Lamu residents might then not necessarily correspond to those identified by linguists, they do represent a dominant "folk dialectology" (Strand 2012, 24) and carry important social meanings.

The island of Lamu is home to three of these dialects: kiAmu, kiShela, and kiMatondoni. KiAmu is the mother tongue of about 8,000 speakers, the majority of whom live in Lamu Town and Kipungani village (Nurse and Hinnebusch 1993). KiShela is spoken in Shela, a town only about a mile and a quarter away from Lamu Town. KiMatondoni can be found in Matondoni village, located on the opposite side of Lamu Island. KiSiyu is spoken by roughly 6,000 speakers in and around Siyu village on eastern Pate Island. KiPate has about 2,500 speakers, living in and around Pate village on southern Pate Island. KiBajuni (or kiTikuu) is spoken by approximately 15,000–20,000 people on the coastal mainland, on the remaining islands of the Archipelago, and across the border with Somalia (Nurse 1982; Nurse and Hinnebusch 1993) (see Figure 3).

In the following detailed discussion of these vernaculars, I greatly draw upon the works of Nurse (1982), Nurse and Hinnebusch (1993), and Stigand (1915), in addition to my own data collection. I use the following abbreviations: Northern Dialects (ND), Standard Swahili (sS), kiAmu (kiA), kiShela (kiSh), kiMatondoni (kiM), kiSiyu (kiS), kiPate (kiP), and kiBajuni (kiB).

Phonological Differences

CONSONANTS

/v/ in Standard Swahili is /z/ or /dh/ in ND

The use of /z/ instead of /v/ is consistent in the Amu and Shela dialects, whereas /dh/ is consistent in kiBajuni, kiPate, and kiSiyu. In the smaller villages of Matondoni there tends to be a mixture of /z/ and /dh/. For example, *vitu* (things) becomes *zitu* (kiAmu) or *dhichu* (kiBajuni).

/z/ in Standard Swahili is /dh/ in kiBajuni, kiPate, and kiSiyu.

For example, the demonstrative *zile* (those) becomes *dhile* in kiBajuni.

/t/ in Standard Swahili is /t̲/ or /ch/ in ND

The /t̲/ in kiAmu, kiMatondoni, and kiShela is alveolar or postalveolar, with some retroflex, making it clearly distinguishable from Standard Swahili. In kiBajuni, kiPate, and kiSiyu /ch/ is used instead of /t/. For example, the Standard Swahili *kupata* (to get) is pronounced *kupat̲a* in kiAmu, kiMatondoni, and kiShela or as *kupacha* in kiBajuni, kiSiyu, and kiPate. It is important to note that most loanwords from Arabic have /t̲/ in all dialects.

Hence, all ND have –*ṯamu* (sweet),—*siṯa* (six), or *haṯari* (dangerous). Recent loanwords of non-Arabic origin retain /t/, such as *gazeti* (newspaper) or *boti* (boat).

/ch/ in Standard Swahili is */t/* in all ND

For example, the Standard Swahili *kucheka* becomes *kuteka* in all ND.

/nd/ in Standard Swahili is */ndr/* in all ND

For example, the Standard Swahili *ndoo* (bucket) becomes *ndroo* in all ND. The degree of rhotacisation, however, varies among the different ND. The strongest rhotacisation is found in kiBajuni, while the least is found in ki-Amu. In this overview *d* is used to represent a slightly retroflexed and postalveoral pronunciation of /d/.

/j/ in Standard Swahili is */y/* or Ø

In all ND, the consonant /j/ is pronounced as /y/ when occurring before the vowels /u/, /o/, and /a/. The Standard Swahili *jua* (sun) is then *yua*, or *moja* (one) becomes *moya*. In all ND, except kiBajuni, /y/ becomes /Ø/ before front vowels. For example, the Standard Swahili *jina* (name) becomes *ina*. In kiBajuni, a class marker *i–* is retained (*y–* in front of a vowel) resulting in *yina*. Another example that derives from this rule is *mui* (city, in kiAmu) and *muyi* (kiBajuni) instead of *mji* (Standard Swahili).

Loss of /l/ before /e/ in all ND

The Standard Swahili *mbele* (in front of) becomes *mbee* in all ND. The imperative *Leta!* (Bring!) becomes *Eta!* In kiAmu this *l*-loss leaves /y/ before /e/ in some cases. For example, *leo* (today) becomes *yeo*, or—*lea* (to raise) becomes—*yea*.

Distinctive Aspiration

Contrary to Standard Swahili, ND have a contrast between aspirated and nonaspirated voiceless stops. For example, *paa* (roof) but *p'aa* (gazelle), *kaa* (sit) but *k'aa* (crab). It is suggested that Standard Swahili used to have distinctive aspiration, but the majority of Swahili speakers have lost this feature, a change possibly attributable to Standard Swahili being a second language for many speakers (whose mother tongue does not have distinctive aspiration) and owing to the difficulty of orthographically representing aspiration using Roman script.

Consonant and Vowel Assimilation

m(u) + consonant

This assimilation occurs most frequently with the nominal prefixes for Classes 1 and 3. Although the basic form of this prefix is [*m*], [*mu*] is heard frequently in the ND. When the vowel does drop, assimilation of [*m*] to the following (stem) consonant occurs automatically.

	ND	*sS*	*Translation*
n before dental:	*n*tanga	mchanga	sand
n before alveolar:	*n*lango	mlango	door
ng before velar:	*ng*eni	mgeni	guest

/*mi* + V/ > *ny*

	ND	*sS*	*Translation*
/*mi-aka*/	nyaka	miaka	years
/*mi-ezi*/	nyezi/nyedhi	miezi	months

n(i) + possessive

When the copular *ni* ("is") is followed by a possessive, it assimilates to the first consonant of the possessive form. The assimilated nasal remains syllabic.

ND	*sS*	*Translation*
Nyumba hii *ndangu*.	Nyumba hii *ni yangu*	*This house is mine.*
Pundra hoo *ndechu*	Punda huyu ni yetu	*This donkey is ours.*

V1 + V2 > V2

Whereas Standard Swahili tends to retain vowels, vowel assimilation or deletion frequently occurs in the Northern Dialects and generally follows the pattern V1 + V2 > V2.

	ND	*sS*	*Translation*
/*si-end-i*/	sendri	siendi	I am not going

Vowel assimilation or deletion, however, does not occur across the board and vowels are retained at various points in the word. Nurse (1982, 2011) does not elaborate extensively on these occurrences. He suggests that

vowels fail to assimilate in at least two occasions, namely when a consonant is lost (in ND) and when the relative suffix occurs in final position.

Verb	ND	sS	Translation
–*leta*	Usiniete	Usinilete	Do not bring me
–*sema*	Wasemao nnyani?	Wasemao nnani?	Who is speaking? (Lit. Those who are speaking, who is it?)

CuCo > CoCo

Vowel assimilation also occurs in the second demonstrative and follows
the pattern CuCo > CoCo.

	ND	sS	Translation
Cl 1	hoyo (kiA)	huyo	that one
	hoo (kiB)		
Cl 17	hoko	huko	over there

Morphology

Verbal Conjugation

Third Person Singular (*y*)*u*–/*w*–

Whereas in Standard Swahili, the verbal prefix for the third-person singular is /*a*–/, the Northern Dialects use (*y*)*u*– in the present indefinite
tense. It is important to note that ND prefer to use the present indefinite
tense (–*a*–) over the present continuous (–*na*–), the former being the exception in Standard Swahili.

	ND	sS	Translation
/*yu-a-m-pend-a*/	ywampenda	anampenda	he loves her
/*yu-end-a-o*/	ywendrao	anaenda	he is going

Interestingly, in the negation of the verb "to be," ND drop the use of
/*yu*–/, whereas Standard Swahili incorporates it (in accordance with the
use of negative verbal prefixes). So, whereas Standard Swahili uses *hayuko*
(he/she is not [here]), one hears *hako* in kiAmu.

Suffixal /–o/ in "to come" and "to go"

In all ND, a suffix –o is used to express a continuing action. This suffix only occurs with two verbs: to come and to go. Recognized as a distinguishing feature of the ND, it is often used in stereotypical depictions of ND speakers.

	ND	*sS*	*Translation*
/ni-a-end-a-o/	nendrao	ninaenda	I am going
/ni-y-a-o/	niyao	naja	I am coming

Use of –*ndo*–

The formative /*ndo*/ (*nda* can be heard in kiB) is used to express an action that took place in the recent past of which the consequences are still relevant to the present. It is particularly used to emphasize an action that recently took place. The form can be used either separately or can be incorporate into the verb.

Saa hii ndo tumefika.	*We have arrived just now.*
Vandokwisa kuingia. (kiBajuni)	*They have already gone inside (just now).*

Lexical Differences

The ND distinguish themselves from Standard Swahili through a range of lexical differences. I merely list a few examples, including some distinctions that occur within the ND.

Gloss	*sS*	*kiAmu*	*kiPate*	*kiSiyu*	*kiBajuni*
Call	–ita	–amkua	–ankua	–ankua	–ankua
Finger	kidole	chanda	chanda/kinwe	kinwe	chanda
Sell	–uza	–zanya	–dhanya	–dhanya	–dhanya
Salt	chumvi	munyu	munyu	munyu	munu
Bird	ndege	nyuni	nuni	nuni	noni

Intonation Contours

None of the linguistic descriptions available elaborate on the importance of intonation contours. Speakers of the ND, however, always identified intonation as one of the most distinctive characteristic of the individual dialects, next to the features listed earlier. These intonation patterns are particularly important, however, to distinguish between closely related dialects such as kiAmu, kiMatondoni, and kiShela. Speakers would describe kiAmu as having a more feminine quality and its speakers as using a more melodious intonation pattern (Chapter 2). People from Matondoni were said to stretch or lengthen their vowels, whereas kiShela was viewed as having a harsher quality and a more distinct use of Arabic pronunciation. While these are folk explanations, they play an important role in local social contexts, for they function as important social indexicals.

Alhamdulillah. I am incredibly grateful to see this work (finally) come to completion. And I am especially thankful to have been surrounded, throughout this multiyear project, by wonderful people who never lost faith in me, even if I did at times. The list of people to thank is long, and I am sorry to those whom I forgot to include. I am grateful to all who helped me along the way.

First, I want to thank the people of Lamu, to whom I am also dedicating this book. Without them, none of this would have been. Their hospitality, generosity, warmth, and patience made this project feasible and added lasting friendship, joy, and beauty to my life. I am forever indebted to them. I have tried my best to represent their voices, and I ask their forgiveness for any remaining flaws in my understanding of life in Lamu today. Many of the people who contributed to this book I cannot thank by name, since I respect their request for anonymity. Those who I can name include Ustadh Mahmoud Ahmed Abdulkadir, Abdallah Abdulkadir (and family), Zahra Aboud, Nidal Babaad, Abdalla Barghash, Omari Hassan, Rahima Hassan, Maryam Hussein, Athman Lali, Azraa Mahmoud, Muneef Mohamed, Mohammed Lali, and Mwalim Hussein Soud. At the National Museums of Kenya, and particularly the Lamu Museums and the Research Institute of Swahili Studies of Eastern Africa (RISSEA), I would like to thank Mubarak Abdulqadir Abdallah, Alawy Abzein, Fatma Bwana Ali, Rukiya Harith, Mohammed Karama, and Mohammed Mwenje. Two people invaluable to this book unfortunately did not see it come to completion. Sheikh Ahmed Nabahany's knowledge of and love for the Swahili language informed much of my understandings of Lamu's linguistic complexity. Mwalim Baddi was a wonderful research assistant, an amazing source of knowledge, and a close friend. Both of them are sorely missed. *Mungu awarehemu.*

I want to thank Judith T. Irvine, Webb Keane, Kelly Askew, Derek Peterson, and Marlyse Baptista for their guidance over the years. Their insights, advice, and support helped make this book what it is. I am especially grateful to Judy for her lasting mentorship and advice. I also thank Janet McIntosh and Susan Hirsch for their generous comments to this book, at its different stages. Their feedback made this a much stronger work. Thank you as well to two anonymous reviewers, for their insightful comments.

I have been blessed to be part of a writing group made up of wonderfully smart and supportive women. They have read chapters of this book, from the roughest to the final versions, and their feedback, encouragement, and deadlines created the perfect writing environment. Susan Frekko, Erika Hoffman-Dilloway, Michelle Koven, Jennifer Reynolds, and Chantal Tetreault, thank you so much for having me. And Chantal, thank you for cranking up your reading during the final stages.

At the University of Toronto, I found an intellectual community that stimulated and motivated me, but that also offered much-needed support and comfort at the most challenging of times. Words cannot express my gratitude to my fellow SWAG-gers Katie Kilroy-Marac, Krista Maxwell, and Alejandro Paz, whose patience, humor, and hugs made all the difference. Alejandro worked through many (rough) chapters and helped fine-tune arguments at the final stages. I am especially thankful to Katie for never tiring of being my sounding board. Andrea Muehlebach's house and office doors were always open, and I am grateful to her for always finding the right words to encourage me. Her generous offer to read the final manuscript was invaluable. I treasure Lindsay Bell's friendship and scholarly feedback, and I thank her for motivating me throughout the years.

I am grateful for inspiring conversations with Rudi Gaudio, Candy and the late Chuck Goodwin, Kai Kresse, Anne Meneley, Shalini Shankar, and Jeremy Prestholdt, whose scholarly work and ideas informed my thinking. Discussions over the years with Anna Babel, Daniel Birchok, David Cohen, Elizabeth Falconi, Gillian Feely-Harnik, Kathryn Graber, Jennifer Hall, Nancy Hunt, Michael Lempert, Bruce Mannheim, and Barbra Meek shaped the arguments of this book. I am grateful to them all.

I thank my colleagues at the University of Toronto, on whose collegial support and scholarly advice I have relied heavily. I am especially grateful to Janice Boddy, Frank Cody, Bianca Dahl, Naisargi Dave, Girish Daswani, Amira Mittermaier, Monica Heller, Michael Lambek, Tania Li, Bonnie McElhinny, Valentina Napolitano, Todd Sanders, Stephen Sharper, and Jack Sidnell. Thank you as well to colleagues and staff at UTM who created a wonderful work environment and helped me succeed. Many thanks especially to Gary Crawford, Tracey Galloway, Kimiko Hill,

Elisabeth Johnson (in linguistics), Heather Miller, Esteban Parra, Lauren Schroeder, Angela Sidoriak, David Smith, Joanna Trochanowski, and Liye Xie.

This book benefited from the insights and feedback from amazing scholars and graduate students at several anthropology departments and workshops, including the Anthropology Department at Northwestern University, UCLA's Center for Language, Interaction, and Culture (CLIC), the Swahili Workshops at Columbia University, the Post-Slavery Societies workshop at Cambridge University, and the Indian Ocean's workshop at Roskilde University. I thank all those who engaged with and provided feedback to my work.

Graduate and undergraduate students at the University of Toronto helped me write this book through feedback on my writing and editorial work and via insightful and motivating conversations about research and teaching. A special thank you goes to Lynda Chubak, Elisabeth Feltaous, Anne Garcia, Leena and Reema Mobeireek, and Anne-Sophie Roussel.

I have been lucky to have a group of friends around the world who provided support in whichever way they could. For bringing a little bit of Kenya to Canada, and for keeping heart (and stomach) full, I thank Zainab Albaity and her family. For making me feel at home in Toronto, I am grateful to Sadaf Ahmed, Golnar Elgammal, Nessa and Shirin Hosseinpour, Nora Khataan, Dina Magdy, Pireen Metwalli, Asmaa Maloul, Afrah Raza and family, Jennifer Taher, and Alaa Yassin. I hope to see much more of you now this book is done.

I also feel incredibly blessed to know amazing women whose friendship is not affected by distance and sometimes-long silences. To Laura Blizzard, Johanna Grueter, Kimi Honzaki, Ellie Lambert, Elisabeth Machua, Hadiya Mohammed, and Khala Nariman, a huge thank you for your phone calls, texts, hugs, laughter, and prayers. I love you all. To Anna Cruz and Maxine Walkes-Thompson, thank you for the catches when I fall, while climbing or otherwise.

The editorial team at Fordham University Press made the publishing process as easy and smooth as it could possibly be. A big thank you especially to Thomas Lay, Gregory McNamee, and Eric Newman. I would also like to thank Abdalla Barghash, Eric Lafforgue, and Jo Valvekens for allowing me to use their photos as illustrations in this book.

I owe my gratitude to the institutions and organizations that provided funding for my research and writing, including the Wenner Gren Foundation and the National Science Foundation, as well as the Center for the Education of Women, the Rackham School of Graduate Studies, and the

Institute for the Humanities at the University of Michigan. At the University of Toronto, I thank the Connaught Foundation and the Department of Anthropology.

Portions of Chapter 3 previously appeared in *Africa*, and material from Chapter 5 was published in *American Anthropologist*. I am grateful for the permissions to include the material here.

To my family I owe gratitude beyond words. I am grateful for their love, support, encouragement, and never-ending patience. Belgium and home, while geographically far, were brought close through calls, cards, gifts, and wonderful visits. Flore and Kato, my two beautiful nieces, bring a joy to my life that cannot be expressed in words. To my sister Liesbet, brother Maarten, and brothers-in-law David and Tim: Thank you for your support, laughter, surprises, and for your unwavering belief in my capacity to write this book. My mother, Marleen Verhelst, has been my strongest supporter and my never-ending source of comfort. Moeks, thank you for letting me find my way, many years ago, and for trusting me and my choices, even if these weren't always your own. I am forever grateful for your faith in me, your boundless encouragement, and the love and pride with which you speak of me.

Last, I want to thank a person who joined this adventure only in its final stages, but who contributed greatly to my ability to complete it. Ammar, words can never capture my gratitude to you. Your help, laughter, support, and endless patience kept me going, even at the most difficult times. Thank you for reminding me of what's most important. Thank you for always believing in me. Thank you for being my rock.

PREFACE

1. In Zanzibar, the facial veil is generally referred to as *nikabu* rather than *ninja*, with the latter often carrying a derogatory meaning. At the time of her fieldwork, Fuglesang (1994) notes the same for Lamu. In present-day Lamu, however, the facial veil is commonly referred to as *ninja* and does not have any negative connotations.

2. These are not pseudonyms. As noted in this preface, all other names given in the narrative that follows are pseudonyms, with the exception of Ustadh Mahmoud Abdulkadir (Chapter 2 and 3, and author of the poetic interludes) and Mwalim Hussein Soud (Chapter 2).

INTRODUCTION

1. KiAmu and kiBajuni are two distinct dialects of the Swahili language spoken in the Lamu Archipelago. KiAmu is the dialect spoken in Lamu Town; kiBajuni can be found on the Bajuni Islands of the archipelago, including Kizingitini, Ndau, and Kiwayu (see also the Appendix: Note on Language).

2. *Miraa* or khat is an addictive stimulant popular among Lamu residents. The fresh leaves of the khat (or qat) plant are chewed to achieve a light state of euphoria; it also has an appetite-reducing effect.

3. In fact, Ustadh Taha's repeated inquiry interestingly resembles the exchange between God and Abraham in the Hebrew Bible when Abraham is commanded to sacrifice his son Isaac. Three times God asks Abraham where he is and three times Abraham responds: *Hineni*, "Here I am." Like *hadir*, the word *hineni* states one's presence, but signals much more than a mere physical attendance; it is about the emotional and spiritual presence of a person, of their entire being. It emphasizes an awareness of one's account-ability to God but also, and importantly, comprises a mindfulness that ought to instigate action. *Hineni*. Here I am, fully present and ready. It signifies a turning point, a potentially life-changing moment requiring decision, action, and resolution. By answering God's call, the individual is therefore

interpellated as a particular kind of subject—in this case, as a Jew or Muslim—with all ensuing responsibilities (see Derrida 1995; Lambek 2010).

4. For Derrida, God's call to Abraham, and the religious obligation brought forth by the response, presupposed God's ever-present gaze; he writes that it is a gaze "that sees me without my seeing it looking at me. It knows my very secret even when I myself don't see it" (Derrida 1995, 7).

5. For critiques of such claims, see, for example, Abu-Lughod (2002, 2013).

6. Heidegger (1996) considered such a moment in which individuals are taken out of their unreflective state of being-in-the-world into a conscious-state-of-being as an instance of "moral breakdown," where individuals are caused to question the usefulness of their actions or the reasons behind their habits (Zigon 2007). Bourdieu viewed such shift from an unreflective doxa to orthodoxy as a disruption of the habitus (Bourdieu 1984).

7. The entire Lamu County (comprising the districts of Lamu West and Lamu East) has a population of about 101,000 people, according to the 2009 census.

8. The role of the Lamu Archipelago in the Indian Ocean slave trade, as well as the importance of slavery during the archipelago's golden age, has been much debated (see, for example Eastman 1988, 1994; El Zein 1974; Pouwels 1987, 1991; Romero 1983, 1986; Vernet 2009, 2013). The emphasis of these studies has generally been on East African slavery as a variant of clientship. In contrast to the Atlantic slave trade, these clients, while considered *washenzi* or "savages" of non-Swahili origin, were not considered private property (Eastman 1988; Glassman 1991, 2011; Pouwels 1987, 1991). It was only when the plantation economy expanded in the nineteenth century, in response to an increasing international demand for oil, grain, and spices, that "planters"—immigrants from Arabia and Swahili speaking, Muslim Africans from the coast itself—bought slaves, built plantations, and intensified the exploitation of labor (Cooper 1980, 3). More recent research has concentrated on East Africa's involvement in the Indian Ocean slave trade prior to the eighteenth century and describes the successful trade networks between Pate, northwestern Madagascar, the Comoros, and the Hadramawt. Vernet (2009, 2013) suggests that the Lamu Archipelago dominated the Swahili slave trade from Madagascar and the Comoros in the seventeenth century, and that city states such as Pate had been the main ports for slave traders since the end of the preceding century, with an estimated 2,000 to 3,000 slaves being exported annually to the island of Pate (Vernet 2009). He does emphasize, however, that slaves in the Swahili and Comorian communities were not laboring under harsh conditions in plantation slavery, but rather were used in a range of positions, including as

servants, concubines, sailors, agricultural laborers and even craftsmen (Vernet 2013, 2). Like Cooper (1979, 1980), Vernet underlines the fact that Swahili city-states' clientship relations with mainland communities provided such labor and that servile labor was therefore not in great demand (Vernet 2013, 2).

9. See, for example, Allen (1993); Chittick (1967); Horton and Chami (2018); Horton and Middleton (2000); LaViolette and Wynne-Jones (2018); Sutton (2018).

10. There are substantial gaps in the text, which completely fails to discuss events between the eighth and eighteenth centuries (Rollins 1983).

11. See, for example, Allen (1979, 1993); Chittick (1974); Chittick and Rotberg (1975); Horton and Chami (2018); Horton and Middleton (2000); LaViolette (2008); LaViolette and Wynne-Jones (2018).

12. Frederick Cooper (1977) considered the distinction between noblemen, savages, and slaves insurmountable, whereas Jonathon Glassman argues that the line between "free" and "slave" was fundamental only in the minds of the dominant members of society (Glassman 1991, 285). Eastman (1994) suggests that, while a distinction between nobility and barbarity has shaped life on the East African coast for centuries, the concept of *utumwa* or slavery mediated the opposition between the civilized and uncivilized over time (Eastman 1994, 87). Discussing social hierarchy structures in Zabid (Yemen), Meneley (1996) similarly notes a relational notion of personhood, whereby upper classes defined themselves in relation to other groups. Similar to Lamu, (former) slaves were viewed as having a higher status than non-Zabidi, who were perceived as lower-class based on their non-Arab origins and deficient religious observance.

13. That (former) slaves took up patricians' forms of dress and spread Islam among themselves in their striving for upward mobility, however, reflects "the extent to which the slaveholders' culture had in fact become hegemonic" (Iliffe 2005, 296). Glassman argues that in challenging their ascribed social positions through the appropriation of their patrons' practices, *watumwa* in fact, retained (and reproduced) a variant of the elites' hegemonic ideology (Glassman 1991, 292).

14. Beckerleg (2004, 26) views the introduction of maulid celebrations to Lamu as an example of the significant transformations Swahili communities historically underwent, highlighting that "the maulid movement produced new forms of religious and cultural expression that drew on Yemeni ritual and also undermined the Lamu 'patrician' elite."

15. McIntosh, for example, remarks that Swahili residents of the Kenyan coast increasingly draw upon their connection to the Middle East, not only for economic support, but also for social and political identification (2009,

9), whereas Eastman (1994, 85) refers to the "boundary work" coastal Swahili perform in everyday life, calling upon an ethnic distinctiveness associated with their Arab relations. Prestholdt (2014) draws upon Gabrielle Lynch's notion of "ethnic territoriality" to explain coastal residents' ideological association between social identity and territorial rights, whereby claims to belonging "are imagined to flow from historical, communal, and exclusive relationships to territory" (2014, 250).

16. Gearhart (2013) offers a different approach to this recognition of young people's voices. She narrates the lives of children in Lamu "through their own eyes" by providing them with a photo camera and documenting the narratives children provided about the pictures taken.

17. For additional discussion, see, for example, Abbink and van Kessel (2005); Beckerleg (1995); Burgess (2002); Caplan and Topan (2004); Diouf (2003); Dlamini, Mbembé, and Khunou (2004); Durham (2000); Fuglesang (1994); Janson (2013); Newell and Okome (2104); Weiss (2009, 2012).

18. See Newell and Okome (2014) for a broader discussion of the role of popular culture in responding to political and social transformations in the African context.

INTERLUDE I: *MILA YETU HUFUJIKA* (OUR TRADITIONS
ARE BEING DESTROYED)

1. Surah 47, Al-Ahqaf, verse 17: "But one who says to his parents, 'Uff to you; do you promise me that I will be brought forth [from the earth] when generations before me have already passed on [into oblivion]?' while they call to Allah for help [and to their son], 'Woe to you! Believe! Indeed, the promise of Allah is truth.' But, he says, 'This is not but legends of the former people'" (translated by Sahih International).

1. "THIS IS LAMU": BELONGING, MORALITY, AND MATERIALITY

1. The term *baraza* is used to refer to three interrelated but nevertheless distinct concepts in Swahili communities. It refers to actual stone benches, spread throughout town but also located at the entrance porches of traditional Swahili stone houses. At the same time, it refers to a regular gathering of a group of (older) men, generally of the same neighborhood. Such gatherings generally take place on the stone benches by the same name, but nowadays they can also happen on chairs, wooden benches provided by neighborhood residents, and so on. Last, *baraza* also stands for "council." The *Baraza la Wazee* is the "Council of Elders," a council that until Kenyan independence was in charge of governing the town. Now it fulfills mainly an advisory and ceremonial role. The three concepts are meaningfully interrelated, because *baraza* (the neighborhood gatherings on stone benches)

historically fulfilled an important social and political function as a forum for political debates and decisions. In contemporary Swahili communities, they mainly function as a space for men to socialize and philosophize (Kresse 2007).

2. Interestingly, Ustadh Mahmoud Abdulkadir explained to me that this was not the originally intended meaning of the saying. Rather, he claimed it derived from a poem written a long time ago for a competition during Lamu's yearly maulid festivals (how long ago, he couldn't say). The poem had called out to competitors from surrounding island towns (such as Pate, Siyu, or Faza) and went as follows: *Tanga lenu fungani likae baharini, musiwae wae. Hiyo ndiyo Amu atakao nae.* The translation would be "Tighten your sails properly, such that they stay (or don't loosen) when at sea, assure that you don't get seasick. This is Lamu, whoever wants to, can come." Phrased differently, those who want to participate in the competitions better prepare themselves properly. Lamu is more than ready to fight them. Contemporary Lamu residents, however, do not recall the historical origins of the saying and generally view it as a proverb signaling their historical hospitality.

3. Caplan (2004, 4), for example, emphasizes that there are many versions of history, and many histories, along the East African coast, with their writing often being not only contested but also politicized.

4. The significance of moral dispositions and proper conduct is also reflected in kiSwahili vocabulary, where a range of concepts hint at different aspects of respectful behavior, including notions such as *adabu*, *haya*, and *tabia*. *Adabu* can be translated as "manners" or "courtesy" and refers to notions of politeness and respectful composure; it concerns correct behavior toward elders in particular and refers to general comportment as well as social interactions including greeting styles (Mtoro bin Mwinyi and Allen 1981). *Haya* signifies "modesty" and pertains to women as well as to men. Someone who is described as having *haya* is considerate of the rights and sensibilities of others, displays restraints, and does not impose on others (McMahon 2006). *Tabia* refers to a range of (cultural) habits that constitute respectful behavior. Saleh (2004) adds *uaminifu* (honesty), *uadilifu* (ethics) and *ari* (honor) as attributes of moral conduct.

5. Although *heshima* was viewed as a critical component of having nobility and thus was associated with the coastal elite, McMahon emphasizes that lower classes and slaves also worked hard to obtain *heshima*: "a person's *heshima* showed their standing in the community, how fully they articulated the ideals of Islamic culture and society. People could be poor and not particularly well educated, but if they maintained their *heshima* they still had a level of respect" (McMahon 2006, 200).

6. See Meneley (1996) and Wedeen (2008) for similar discussions of social hierarchy structures in Yemen.

7. For detailed discussions of the architecture of Swahili towns, see, for example, Allen (1979); Bissell (2018); Donley-Reid (1982, 1987, 1990); Ghaidan (1975); Kamalkhan (2010); Meier (2016); Prins (1971); Wynne-Jones (2013).

8. The seemingly plain and unaccommodating interior of a Swahili house, consisting of a partition into different narrow galleries, has been the topic of many scholarly discussions. See, for example, Allen (1979); Bissell (2018); Donley-Reid (1984, 1987, 1990); Fleisher and LaViolette (2007); Gensheimer (2018); Ghaidan (1975); Horton and Middleton (2000); Kamal-khan (2010); Meier (2016); Steyn (2002); Wynne-Jones (2016).

9. See, for example, Caplan and Topan (2004); Fair (2001); Glassman (2004); LaViolette (2008); LaViolette and Wynne-Jones (2018); Horton and Chami (2018); Mazrui and Shariff (1994); Middleton (1992); Ray (2018); Salim (1984).

10. Emily Ruete's memoir *Leben im Sultanpalast* (Ruete and Nippa 1989) is full of depictions of slaves as children, uncultured and immature, who need the guiding hand that she and other aristocrats could offer.

11. http://www.lamuisland.co.ke/lamu-maulidi-festival-lamu-cultural -festivals-lamu-island-kenya-africa.html.

2. DIALECTS OF MORALITY

1. I conducted research on Sheng for a total of seven months in 2002 and 2003, with a short return visit in 2005. When I visited friends in Nairobi before leaving for Lamu in 2007, they remarked that my absence from Nairobi had caused me to miss the changes within Sheng. Like many other urban youth languages, Sheng changes rather quickly, incorporating new words almost daily. The language itself is a mix of kiSwahili, English, and other ethnic languages such as Kikuyu and Dholuo (Hillewaert 2003; see also Githinji 2005, 2006; Githiora 2002, 2018; Samper 2002).

2. For a detailed linguistic discussion of these vernaculars, see the Appendix: Note on Language.

3. William Labov similarly analyzed Martha's Vineyard speech that increased its differences from mainland dialects of American English after, and because of, increased contact with the mainland (Labov 1963).

4. The epic poems or *tendi* are typologically comparable to Western epics and sagas; they are didactic poems based on the Quran and the Prophetic Hadith and form rich material for studying the moral values of the Swahili speaking residents of the East African coast (Zhukov 2004, 7).

5. In his studies of the Bajuni, Derek Nurse (2011) suggests that kiBajuni is not merely a dialect of kiSwahili, but is distinct from it. He

argues that up until twenty years ago, "the islands were almost 100% monolingual Bajuni speakers, although male traders and fishermen who traveled to Kismayu and Kenya would have had some exposure to Swahili." He continues to say that Bajuni youth "speak poor Bajuni and lots of Swahili . . . [or] . . . a Bajuni-colored Swahili, Swahili with some Bajuni, mainly vocabulary and common phonetic features added" (Nurse 2011, 37).

6. Reports from the Portuguese, for example, mention a request from the city-state of Pate to build walls around the town as a protection against Bajuni attacks (Nurse 2011). Starting in the sixteenth century, however, raids by surrounding mainland tribes, such as the Orma and the Boni, increasingly undermined Bajuni's prominent position along the coast. In the early twentieth century, attacks by Somali tribes once again forced the Bajuni to flee from Somalia across the border into Kenya, and to the islands of the Lamu Archipelago in particular. The implosion of Somalia in 1991 resulted in a third wave of Bajuni migration. Raids by *mashifta*, or Somali bandits, forced many Bajuni villagers residing alongside the border with Somalia to flee their homes and seek shelter in Lamu. These Bajuni continue to live in Lamu as internally displaced people as they wait for their land to be reassigned to them.

7. See Irvine (2008) for a similar discussion on Wolof and Sereer.

8. I am not suggesting that Arabic was central to the development of kiSwahili. On the contrary, Nurse and Spear (1985) have long documented kiSwahili's Bantu origins (see also Glassman 2014). Rather, the argument here is that a particular racial ideology informed the standardization process, whereby presumed "foreign" elements had to be purged from the Swahili language to return to its "true," "African" form.

9. It is important to note that this distinctive aspiration can equally not be indicated using Arabic script. Swahili poets like Muhamadi Kijuma would add diacritics to the Arabic script to indicate distinctions like aspiration. This use of diacritics was never standardized.

10. Sheikh Al-Amin in Al-Islah, June 20, 1932, quoted by Mazrui (2016, 26).

11. Mwalim Hussein Soud at 2010 RISSEA Conference; from fieldnotes, translated from kiSwahili.

12. The Jaluo ethnicity does not come from Taita but lives in Western Kenya, around Lake Victoria. In many of my interview extracts, elders would refer to ethnic groups from Kenya's mainland without knowing exactly where they derived from.

13. See the Appendix: Note on Language.

INTERLUDE 2: *KISWAHILI*

1. This poem was translated in consultation with research assistants in Lamu. Another translation by Abdulkadir and Frankl (2013) was published in *Swahili Forum* 20:1–18.

2. The author refers to famous poets from the eighteenth century deriving from Mombasa as well as the Lamu Archipelago, including the islands of Lamu and Pate.

3. The Inkishafi or "Soul's Awakening" (Ibn Nasir and Hichens 1972) is considered one of the greatest epic poems in the Swahili literary tradition. It is believed to have been written between 1810 and 1820 CE by Sayyid Abdallah bin Ali Nasir.

4. The Kidani is another name for the *Utendi wa Mwana Kupona*, a poem written by Mwana Kupona binti Msham in approximately 1858. In one of the most famous works of early Swahili literature, Mwana Kupona instructs her daughter on proper conduct with regard to marriage, respectability, and wifely duties.

5. *Malenga wamvita* is a collection of poems composed by the contemporary Swahili poet Ustadh Ahmed Nassir (1971).

6. Ahmed Sheikh Nabhani (1927–2017) was a Swahili researcher and poet from Matondoni (Lamu Island) and a strong proponent of the Swahili language and its dialectal varieties.

7. These are Swahili names, recognizable as coming from the Lamu Archipelago.

8. Njoroge is a name common among people from the Kikuyu ethnicity, while Charo is common among the Giriama.

3. "YOUTH" AS A DISCURSIVE CONSTRUCT

1. I use *utumwa* and *utwana* as synonyms, both referring to local conceptions of "slavery" or servitude. Similarly, the nominal derivatives *mtumwa* (plural: *watumwa*) and *mtwana* (plural: *watwana*) are used as synonyms, both referring to "slaves" within the local context. Previous historical discussions of slavery along the East African coast suggest that *mtwana* was used to refer to a male slave, whereas *mtumwa* referred to a slave in a broader sense (and thus encompassed *mtwana*) (see, for example Eastman 1994; Lodhi 1973). Ustadh Mahmoud Abdulkadir similarly explained that *mtwana* could be used to refer to a strong man or male slave. Interestingly, he also suggested that *mtwana* was used to refer to a man who lives with a woman without marrying her. Such a man used to be referred to as *mtwanake* or *mtwana* instead of *mwanaume wake* (her man or husband). While people in Lamu are still vaguely aware of these distinctions, they tend to use the terms *mtumwa* and *mtwana* interchangeably when talking about slavery.

2. As mentioned in the Introduction, however, slave girls did not cover themselves during the time of slavery. Their lack of covering was indicative of their slave status.

3. In Islamic jurisprudence, and in the Shafi'i school of thought followed by the majority of Lamu Muslims, it is said that the area between the navel and the knee belong to a man's *'awrah*, or parts of the body that should not be shown in public. Lamu residents thus expect Muslim men to cover their bodies from below their navel up to their knees, under normal circumstances. Wearing clothing that shows a man's thighs (such as short shorts) is considered improper.

4. Local residents' inability to pass this bill speaks to the broader sociopolitical context in which we need to situate these debates. As the mainland, majority-Christian population of Lamu grows, people who are viewed as *wageni* are able to outvote locals in discussions pertaining to governance. Beach boys in particular are perceived to adhere to the behavior of outsiders to whom Lamu is increasingly losing its economic, political, and moral authority.

5. The Pokomo are one of the indigenous ethnic groups of the Lamu Archipelago.

6. *Kijoho* (pl. *Zijoho*) is a denigrating nickname used to refer to Lamu's *waungwana* families. It refers to the *joho* or robe the former merchant elites frequently wore for special events (including, weddings and official or religious functions). The robe resembles Arab or Omani dress styles and was meant to signal the Arabness of its wearer.

7. The neighborhood refers to the Balkan nation by the same name. Other areas of Lamu are called Kashmir or Kandahar, for example. Lamu residents explained these naming practices as their way of calling upon connections with Muslims in different areas of the world, who suffer equally at the hands of their governments.

8. When reading my discussion of "dot com," one of my former advisors suggested that this description must apply to young men more so than to young women, arguing that access to technology (and the spaces that provided this, like cybercafés) were bound to be gendered in the context of Lamu. I have found this to not be the case. Cybercafés were mixed-gendered spaces from the beginning, and with the popularity of mobile phones and the availability of cheap data packages, both young men and women make eager use of new technologies and social media.

4. REFRAMING MORALITY THROUGH YOUTHFUL VOICES

1. *Tudecide* could be labeled as Sheng, the urban youth slang, because it places the English verb in kiSwahili grammar. This is done more frequently nowadays and is not limited to Sheng speakers. The practice does retain a reference to familiarity with an urban context.

2. This could be translated as an imperative: "Exclaim that God is greater!"

3. This use of accents, and my analysis of it, resembles Jan Blommaert's discussion of businessmen's appropriation of American accents. He suggests that "the object of globalized commodification is accent and not language." These young men differ from Blommaert's businessmen in that the acquisition of the language does not precede the acquisition of the accent. Whereas businessmen who endeavor to "sound like an American" acquire a set of linguistic, pragmatic, and metapragmatic skills, these young men do not "buy the whole indexical package" (Blommaert 2010, 54).

5. SENSES OF MORALITY AND MORALITY OF THE SENSES

1. The subject's anticipation of both different possible audiences and the intentions they can ascribe to her—what Keane (2014a, 2016) refers to as "double reflexivity"—recalls Goffman's discussions on face-work (1955) and deference and demeanor (1956). Guarding one's "face" within social interactions equally entails adjusting one's behavior to interactants' anticipated evaluations and their expressions of such assessments (see also Keane 2014a, 13).

2. For linguistic anthropological discussions on intentionality, see Duranti (1999, 2006); Gibbs (2001); Grice (1957, 1969); Hill and Irvine (1993); Keane (2014a, 2014b); Robbins and Rumsey (2008); Searle (1983).

3. See, for example, Abu-Lughod (1998, 2013); Ahmed (1992); Deeb (2006); De Jorio (2009); De Koning (2009); Meneley (1996, 2007); Newcomb (2006); Secor (2002, 2004); Ossman (1994); Phadke (2007).

4. There are a few juice bars located along the seafront and one coffee shop, owned by Euro-Americans, in Lamu Town, next to a few locally owned restaurants. Mainly focused on tourists and highly visible to local men, one seldom finds local women in restaurants located along the seafront. Though it is secluded and shielded from views from the street, the coffee shop does not attract many local customers owing to its higher prices and evident targeting of tourists.

5. In recent years, Wahhabi discourses are also present in Lamu, with some women appropriating the *chimar* and starting to wear socks and gloves. Other Lamu women, however, often critique these practices as too conservative and restricting (see Meneley 2007 for a similar discussion on Yemen).

6. Laura Fair (1998, 2001) mentions similar practices in Zanzibar when the *abaya* was newly introduced. The meaning of the facial veil has thus been ambiguous from the onset.

7. From fieldnotes, translated from Swahili.

Abbink, Jon, and Ineke van Kessel. 2005. *Vanguard or Vandals: Youth, Politics and Conflict in Africa.* Leiden: Brill.

Abdulaziz, Mohamed H. 1979. *Muyaka: 19th Century Swahili Popular Poetry.* Nairobi: Kenya Literature Bureau.

Abdulkadir, Mahmoud Ahmad, and P. J. L. Frankl. 2003. "Kiswahili: A Poem by Mahmoud Ahmad Abdulkadir." *Swahili Forum* 20:1–18.

Abu-Lughod, Lila. 1986. *Veiled Sentiments: Honor and Poetry in a Bedouin Society.* Berkeley: University of California Press.

———. 1998. *Remaking Women: Feminism and Modernity in the Middle East.* Princeton: Princeton University Press.

———. 2002. "Do Muslim Women Really Need Saving? Anthropological Reflections on Cultural Relativism and Its Others." *American Anthropologist* 104, no. 3: 783–90.

———. 2013. *Do Muslim Women Need Saving?* Cambridge, MA: Harvard University Press.

Abungu, George Okello, and Carol Beckwith. 2009. *Lamu: Kenya's Enchanted Island.* New York: Rizzoli.

Agha, Asif. 1998. "Stereotypes and Registers of Honorific Language." *Language in Society* 27, no. 2: 151–93.

———. 2005. "Voice, Footing, Enregisterment." *Journal of Linguistic Anthropology* 15, no. 1: 38–59.

———. 2007. *Language and Social Relations.* Cambridge: Cambridge University Press.

———. 2011. "Commodity Registers." *Journal of Linguistic Anthropology* 21, no. 1: 22–53.

Ahmed, Leila. 1992. *Women and Gender in Islam: Historical Roots of a Modern Debate.* New Haven: Yale University Press.

Aldrick, J. 1990. "The Nineteenth-Century Carved Wooden Doors of the East African Coast." *Azania* 25:1–18.

Allen, James de V. 1993. *Swahili Origins: Swahili Culture and the Shungwaya Phenomenon.* Ann Arbor: University of Michigan Press.

Allen, James de V., and Thomas H. Wilson. 1979. *Swahili Houses and Tombs of the Coast of Kenya*. London: Art and Archaeology Research Papers.

Amidou, A. A. 2009. "The Role of Islam in the Political and Social Perceptions of the Waswahili of Lamu." In *Knowledge, Renewal and Religion: Repositioning and Changing Ideological and Material Circumstances among the Swahili on the East Africa Coast*, edited by K. Larsen, 236–60. Uppsala: Nordic Africa Institute.

Anderson, Leon. 2006. "Analytic Autoethnography." *Journal of Contemporary Ethnography* 35, no. 4: 373–95.

Antaki, Charles, and Sue Widdicombe, eds. 1998. *Identities in Talk*. London: Sage Publications.

Appadurai, Arjun. 1986. *The Social Life of Things: Commodities in Cultural Perspective*. Cambridge: Cambridge University Press.

Appiah, Kwame A. 2010. *The Honor Code: How Moral Revolutions Happen*. New York: Norton.

Asad, Talal. 2007. *On Suicide Bombing*. New York: Columbia University Press.

Askew, Kelly M. 1999. "Female Circles and Male Lines: Gender Dynamics along the Swahili Coast." *Africa Today* 46, nos. 3–4: 67–102.

Austin, Joe, and Michael Nevin Willard. 1998. *Generations of Youth: Youth Cultures and History in Twentieth-Century America*. New York: New York University Press.

Bakari, Mohamed. 1985. *The Morphophonology of the Kenyan Swahili Dialects*. Berlin: D. Reimer.

Bakhtin, Mikhail M. 1981. *Dialogic Imagination: Four Essays*. Austin: University of Texas Press.

Bang, Anne Katrine. 2003. *Sufis and Scholars of the Sea: Family Networks in East Africa, 1860–1925*. London: Routledge.

———. 2014. *Islamic Sufi Networks in the Western Indian Ocean (c. 1880–1940): Ripples of Reform*. Leiden: Brill Academic.

———. 2018. "Islam in the Swahili World: Connected Authorities." In *The Swahili World*, edited by Adria LaViolette and Stephanie Wynne-Jones, 557–65. London: Routledge.

Bauman, Richard, and Charles L. Briggs. 2003. *Voices of Modernity: Language Ideologies and the Politics of Inequality*. Cambridge: Cambridge University Press.

Bayat, Asef, and Linda Herrera. 2010. *Being Young and Muslim*. Oxford: Oxford University Press.

Beckerleg, Susan. 1995. "'Brown Sugar' or Friday Prayers: Youth Choices and Community Building in Coastal Kenya." *African Affairs* 94, no. 374: 23–38.

———. 2004. "Modernity Has Been Swahili-ised: The Case of Malindi." In
Swahili Modernities: Culture, Politics, and Identity on the East Coast of Africa,
edited by Pat Caplan and Farouk Topan, 19–36. Trenton, NJ: Africa
World Press.

Behar, Ruth. 1996. *The Vulnerable Observer: Ethnography That Breaks Your
Heart*. Boston: Beacon.

Benjamin, Jesse. 2013. "Legacies of Nineteenth Century Racial Forma-
tions at the Coast of East Africa: Historiography and the Academic
Suppression of Subaltern Epistemologies." In *Contesting Identities:
The Mijikenda and Their Neighbors in Kenyan Coastal Society*, edited by
Rebecca Gearhart and Linda L. Giles, 127–44. Trenton, NJ: Africa
World Press.

Bergan, Miriam Eid. 2011. "'There's No Love Here': Beach Boys in Malindi,
Kenya." University of Bergen. http://bora.uib.no/bitstream/handle/1956
/5528/84841483.pdf.

Biersteker, Ann. 1996. *Kujibizana: Questions of Language and Power in
Nineteenth- and Twentieth-Century Poetry in Kiswahili*. Lansing: Michigan
State University Press.

Biersteker, Ann, and Ibrahim Noor Shariff, eds. 1995. *Mashairi Ya Vita Vya
Kuduhu: War Poetry in kiSwahili Exchanged at the Time of the Battle of
Kuduhu*. Lansing: Michigan State University Press.

Billings, Sabrina. 2013. *Language, Globalization and the Making of a Tanzanian
Beauty Queen*. Bristol: Multilingual Matters.

Bissell, William Cunningham. 2005. "Engaging Colonial Nostalgia."
Cultural Anthropology 20, no. 2: 215–48.

———. 2018. "The Modern Life of Swahili Stonetowns." In *The Swahili
World*, edited by Stephanie Wynne-Jones and Adria LaViolette, 589–601.
New York: Routledge.

Black, Steven P. 2012. "Laughing to Death: Joking as Support amid Stigma
for Zulu-Speaking South Africans Living with HIV." *Journal of Linguistic
Anthropology* 22, no. 1: 87–108.

Blommaert, Jan. 2008. *Grassroots Literacy: Writing, Identity and Voice in
Central Africa*. London: Routledge.

———. 2010. *The Sociolinguistics of Globalization*. Cambridge: Cambridge
University Press.

Blommaert, Jan, James Collins, and Stef Slembrouck. 2005. "Spaces of
Multilingualism." *Language and Communication* 25:197–216.

Bloomfield, Leonard. 1933. *Language History*. New York: Holt, Rinehart and
Winston.

Boswell, Rosabelle. 2008. "Scents of Identity: Fragrance as Heritage in
Zanzibar." *Journal of Contemporary African Studies* 26, no. 3: 295.

Botha, Anneli. 2014. "Political Socialization and Terrorist Radicalization Among Individuals Who Joined al-Shabaab in Kenya." *Studies in Conflict and Terrorism* 37, no. 1: 895–919.

Bourdieu, Pierre. 1970. "The Berber House or the World Reversed." *Social Science Information* 9, no. 2: 151–70.

———. 1977. *Outline of Theory and Practice.* Cambridge: Cambridge University Press.

———. 1984. *Distinction: A Social Critique of the Judgment of Taste.* Cambridge, MA: Harvard University Press.

———. 1986. *Questions de sociologie.* Paris: Les Editions de Minuit.

———. 1991. *Language and Symbolic Power.* Cambridge, MA: Harvard University Press.

Brennan, James R. 2008. "Lowering the Sultan's Flag: Sovereignty and Decolonization in Coastal Kenya." *Comparative Studies in Society and History* 50, no. 4: 831–61.

———. 2012. *Taifa: Making Nation and Race in Urban Tanzania.* Athens: Ohio University Press.

Briggs, Charles L. 1988. *Competence in Performance: The Creativity of Tradition in Mexicano Verbal Art.* Philadelphia: University of Pennsylvania Press.

Bromber, Katrin. 2006. "Ustaarabu: A Conceptual Change in Tanganyikan Newspaper Discourse in the 1920s." In *The Global Worlds of the Swahili: Interfaces of Islam, Identity and Space in Nineteenth- and Twentieth-Century East Africa*, edited by Roman Loimeier and Rüdiger Seesemann, 67–82. Berlin: Lit Verlag.

Broomfield, Gerald Webb. 1930. "The Development of the Swahili Language." *Africa* 3, no. 4: 516–22.

———. 1931. "The Re-Bantuization of the Swahili Language." *Africa* 4, no. 1: 77–85.

Brown, Naomi. 1992. "Beachboys as Culture Brokers in Bakau Town, the Gambia." *Community Development Journal* 27, no. 4: 361–70.

Bryan, Margaret A. 2017. *The Bantu Languages of Africa.* London: Oxford University Press.

Bucholtz, Mary. 2002. "Youth and Cultural Practice." *Annual Review of Anthropology* 31, no. 1: 525–52.

Bucholtz, Mary, and Kira Hall. 1995. "Introduction: Twenty Years after Language and Woman's Place." In *Gender Articulated: Language and the Socially Constructed Self*, edited by Kira Hall and Mary Bucholtz, 1–24. New York: Routledge.

Burgess, Thomas. 2002. "Cinema, Bell Bottoms, and Miniskirts: Struggles over Youth and Citizenship in Revolutionary Zanzibar." *International Journal of African Historical Studies* 35, nos. 2–3: 287–313.

Caplan, Patricia. 2007. "'But the Coast, of Course, Is Quite Different': Academic and Local Ideas about the East African Littoral." *Journal of Eastern African Studies* 1, no. 2: 305–20.

———. 2009. "Understanding Modernity/ies on Mafia Island, Tanzania: The Idea of a Moral Community." In *Knowledge, Renewal and Religion: Repositioning and Changing Ideological and Material Circumstances among the Swahili on the East African Coast*, edited by Kjersti Larsen. Uppsala: Nordic Africa Institute.

———. 2011. "A 'Clash of Civilizations' on Mafia Island? The Story of a Dance Festival." *Anthropology Today* 27, no. 2: 18–21.

———. 2013. "Changing Swahili Cultures in a Globalising World: An Approach from Anthropology." *Swahili Forum* 20:31–47.

Caplan, Patricia, and Farouk Topan. 2004. *Swahili Modernities: Culture, Politics, and Identity on the East Coast of Africa.* Trenton, NJ: Africa World Press.

Caton, Steven C. 1986. "Salam Tahiyah: Greetings from the Highlands of Yemen." *American Ethnologist* 13, no. 2: 290–308.

Chimerah, Rocha. 1998. *KiSwahili: Past, Present and Future Horizons.* Nairobi: Nairobi University Press.

Chittick, Neville. 1974. *Kilwa, an Islamic Trading City on the East African Coast.* Nairobi: British Institute in Eastern Africa.

Chittick, Neville, and Robert I. Rotberg. 1975. *East Africa and the Orient: Cultural Syntheses in Pre-Colonial Times.* New York: Africana.

Chittick, William C. 1989. *The Sufi Path to Knowledge: Ibn Al-Arabi's Metaphysics of Imagination.* Albany: SUNY Press.

Comaroff, Jean, and John Comaroff. 1991. *Of Revelation and Revolution: Christianity, Colonialism, and Consciousness in South Africa.* Chicago: University of Chicago Press.

———. 2001. *Millennial Capitalism and the Culture of Neoliberalism.* Durham, NC: Duke University Press.

Cooper, Frederick. 1977. *Plantation Slavery on the East Coast of Africa.* New Haven: Yale University Press.

———. 1979. "The Problem of Slavery in African Studies." *The Journal of African History* 20, no. 1: 103–25.

———. 1980. *From Slaves to Squatters: Plantation Labor and Agriculture in Zanzibar and Coastal Kenya, 1890–1925.* New Haven: Yale University Press.

———. 1990. "The End of Slavery in Africa." *The Royal African Society* 89:457–58.

Coppola, Anna Rita. 2018. "Swahili Oral Traditions and Chronicles." In *The Swahili World*, edited by Stephanie Wynne-Jones and Adria LaViolette, 147–55. New York: Routledge.

Dahl, Bianca. 2009. "The 'Failures of Culture': Christianity, Kinship, and Moral Discourses about Orphans during Botswana's AIDS Crisis." *Africa Today* 56, no. 1: 22–43.

———. 2014. "Too Fat to Be an Orphan: The Moral Semiotics of Food Aid in Botswana." *Cultural Anthropology* 29, no. 4: 626–47.

Dane, Barbara O., and Carol Levine. 1994. *AIDS and the New Orphans.* Westport, CT: Auburn House.

De Jorio, Rosa. 2009. "Between Dialogue and Contestation: Gender, Islam, and the Challenges of a Malian Public Sphere." *Journal of the Royal Anthropological Institute* 15, no. 1: 95–111.

De Koning, Anouk. 2009. "Gender, Public Space and Social Segregation in Cairo: Of Taxi Drivers, Prostitutes and Professional Women." *Antipode* 41, no. 3: 533–56.

Deeb, Lara. 2006. *An Enchanted Modern: Gender and Public Piety in Shi'i Lebanon.* Princeton: Princeton University Press.

———. 2009. "Piety Politics and the Role of a Transnational Feminist Analysis." *Journal of the Royal Anthropological Institute* 15, no. 1: 112–26.

———. 2015. "Thinking Piety and the Everyday Together: A Response to Fadil and Fernando." *HAU: Journal of Ethnographic Theory* 5, no. 2: 93–96.

Derrida, Jacques. 1995. *The Gift of Death.* Chicago: University of Chicago Press.

Dick, Hilary Parsons. 2017. "Una Gabacha Sinvergüenza (A Shameless White-Trash Woman): Moral Mobility and Interdiscursivity in a Mexican Migrant Community." *American Anthropologist* 119, no. 2: 223–35.

Diouf, Mamadou. 2003. "Engaging Postcolonial Cultures: African Youth and Public Space." *African Studies Review* 46, no. 2: 1–12.

Dlamini, Nsizwa, J.-A. Mbembé, and Grace Khunou. 2004. "Soweto Now." *Public Culture* 16, no. 3: 499–506.

Donley-Reid, Linda W. 1984. "The Social Use of Swahili Space and Objects." PhD dissertation, University of Cambridge.

———. 1987. "Life in the Swahili Town House Reveals the Symbolic Meaning of Spaces and Artefacts Assemblages." *African Archaeological Review* 5:181–92.

———. 1990. "A Structuring Structure: The Swahili House." *Domestic Architecture and the Use of Space*, edited by S. Kent, 114–26. Cambridge: Cambridge University Press.

Dottridge, Mike. 2002. "Trafficking in Children in West and Central Africa." *Gender & Development* 10, no. 1: 38–42.

Driever, Dorothea. 1976. *Aspects of a Case Grammar of Mombasa Swahili, with Special Reference to the Relationship Between Informant Variation and Some Sociological Features.* Hamburg: Buske.

Duranti, Alessandro. 1999. "Intentionality." *Journal of Linguistic Anthropology* 9, no. 1: 134–36.

———. 2006. "The Social Ontology of Intentions." *Discourse Studies* 8, no. 1: 31–40.

Durham, Deborah. 2000. "Youth and the Social Imagination in Africa: Introduction to Parts 1 and 2." *Anthropological Quarterly* 73, no. 3: 113–20.

Eades, J. S. 2009. "Moving Bodies: The Intersections of Sex, Work, and Tourism." *Economic Development, Integration, and Morality in Asia and the Americas*, edited by Donald C. Wood, 225–53. Bingley, UK: Emerald Group.

Eastman, Carol. 1988. "Women, Slaves, and Foreigners: African Cultural Influences and Group Processes in the Formation of Northern Swahili Coastal Society." *International Journal of African Historical Studies* 21, no. 1: 1–20.

———. 1994. "Service, Slavery (Utumwa) and Swahili Social Reality." *Swahili Forum* 1, no. 1: 87–107.

El Zein, Abdul-Hamid M. 1974. *The Sacred Meadows: A Structural Analysis of Religious Symbolism in an East African Town.* Evanston, IL: Northwestern University Press.

Fabian, Johannes. 1986. *Language and Colonial Power: The Appropriation of Swahili in the Former Belgian Congo, 1880–1938.* Berkeley: University of California Press.

Fader, Ayala. 2009. *Mitzvah Girls.* Princeton: Princeton University Press.

Fadil, Nadia, and Mayanthi Fernando. 2015. "What Is Anthropology's Object of Study? A Counterresponse to Deeb and Schielke." *HAU: Journal of Ethnographic Theory* 5, no. 2: 97–100.

Fair, Laura. 1997. "Kickin' It: Leisure, Politics and Football in Colonial Zanzibar, 1900s–1950s." *Africa* 67, no. 2: 224–51.

———. 1998. "Dressing Up: Clothing, Class and Gender in Post-Abolition Zanzibar." *Journal of African History* 39, no. 1: 63.

———. 2001. *Pastimes and Politics: Culture, Community, and Identity in Post-Abolition Urban Zanzibar, 1890–1945.* Athens: Ohio University Press.

———. 2013. "Veiling, Fashion, and Social Mobility: A Century of Change in Zanzibar." In *Veiling in Africa*, edited by Elisha P Renne, 15–33. Bloomington: Indiana University Press.

Ferguson, James. 2006. *Global Shadows: Africa in the Neoliberal World Order.* Durham, NC: Duke University Press.

Fleisher, J., and Adria LaViolette. 2013. "The Early Swahili Trade Village of Tumbe, Pemba island, Tanzania AD 600–950." *Antiquity* 87, no. 338: 1151–68.

Foucault, Michel. 1976. *The Archaeology of Knowledge*. New York: Harper & Row.

Foucault, Michel. 1997. *Ethics, Subjectivity, and Truth: Essential Works of Foucault, 1954–1980*. Edited by Paul Rabinow. New York: New Press.

Fuglesang, Minou. 1994. *Veils and Videos: Female Youth Culture Along the Kenyan Coast*. Stockholm: Stockholm University.

Gal, Susan. 1995. "Language, Gender, and Power." In *Gender Articulated: Language and the Socially Constructed Self*, edited by Mary Bucholtz and Kira Hall, 169–82. New York: Routledge.

Gal, Susan, and Kathryn A. Woolard. 2001. *Languages and Publics: The Making of Authority*. Manchester: Jerome Publishing.

Gaudio, Rudolph. 2009. *Allah Made Us: Sexual Outlaws in an Islamic African City*. Malden, MA: Wiley-Blackwell.

Gearthart, Rebecca. 2013. "Seeing Life through the Eyes of Swahili Children of Lamu, Kenya: A Visual Anthropology Approach." *Anthropo Children* 3. https://popups.uliege.be/2034-8517.

Gearhart, Rebecca, and Linda L. Giles. 2014. *Contesting Identities: The Mijikenda and Their Neighbors in Kenyan Coastal Society*. Trenton, NJ: Africa World Press.

Gensheimer, Thomas. 2018. "Swahili Houses." In *The Swahili World*, edited by Stephanie Wynne-Jones and Adria LaViolette, 500–512. New York: Routledge.

Ghaidan, Usam. 1975. *Lamu: A Study of the Swahili Town*. Nairobi: East African Literature Bureau.

Gibbs, Raymond W. 2001. "Intentions as Emergent Products of Social Interactions." In *Intentions and Intentionality: Foundations of Social Cognition*, edited by Bertrand F. Malle, Louis J. Moses, and Dare A. Baldwin, 105–122. Cambridge, MA: MIT Press.

Githinji, Peter. 2005. *Sheng and Variation: The Construction and Negotiation of Multiple Identities*. Lansing: Michigan State University Press.

———. 2006. Bazes and Their Chibboleths: Lexical Variation and Sheng Speakers' Identity in Nairobi. *Nordic Journal of African Studies* 15, no. 4: 443–72.

Githiora, Chege. 2002. "Sheng: Peer Language, Swahili Dialect or Emerging Creole?" *Journal of African Cultural Studies* 15, no. 2: 159–81.

———. 2018. "Sheng: The Expanding Domains of an Urban Youth Vernacular." *Journal of African Cultural Studies* 30, no. 2: 105–20.

Glassman, Jonathon. 1991. "The Bondsman's New Clothes: The Contradictory Consciousness of Slave Resistance on the Swahili Coast." *Journal of African History* 32, no. 2: 277–312.

———. 1995. *Feasts and Riot: Revelry, Rebellion, and Popular Consciousness on the Swahili Coast, 1856–1888.* Portsmouth, NH: Heinemann.

———. 2004. "Slower Than a Massacre: The Multiple Sources of Racial Thought in Colonial Africa." *American Historical Review* 109, no. 3: 720–54.

———. 2011. *War of Words, War of Stones: Racial Thought and Violence in Colonial Zanzibar.* Bloomington: Indiana University Press.

———. 2014. "Creole Nationalists and the Search for Nativist Authenticity in Twentieth-Century Zanzibar: The Limits of Cosmopolitanism." *Journal of African History* 55:219–47.

Goffman, Erving. 1955. "On Face-Work: An Analysis of Ritual Elements in Social Interaction." *Psychiatry* 18, no. 3: 213–31.

———. 1956. "The Nature of Deference and Demeanor." *American Anthropologist* 58, no. 3: 473–502.

———. 1967. *Interaction Ritual: Essays on Face-to-Face Behavior.* Garden City, NY: Doubleday.

———. 1974. *Frame Analysis: An Essay on the Organization of Experience.* Cambridge, MA: Harvard University Press.

Gosselin, Claudie. 2000. "Feminism, Anthropology and the Politics of Excision in Mali: Global and Local Debates in a Postcolonial World." *Anthropologica* 42, no. 1: 43–60.

Gower, Rebecca, Steven Salm, and Toyin Falola. 1996. "Swahili Women Since the Nineteenth Century: Theoretical and Empirical Considerations on Gender and Identity Construction." *Africa Today* 43, no. 3: 251–68.

Gramsci, Antonio. 1971. *Selections from the Prison Notebooks of Antonio Gramsci.* Edited and translated by Quintin Hoare and Geoffrey Nowell Smith. London: Lawrence & Wishart.

Grice, H. P. 1957. "Meaning." *Philosophical Review* 66, no. 3: 377–88.

———. 1969. "Utterer's Meaning and Intention." *Philosophical Review* 78, no. 2: 147–77.

Hansen, Stig Jarle. 2016. *Al-Shabaab in Somalia: The History and Ideology of a Militant Islamist Group.* Oxford: Oxford University Press.

Hanson, Margaret, and James J. Hentz. 1999. "Neocolonialism and Neoliberalism in South Africa and Zambia." *Political Science Quarterly* 114, no. 3: 479–502.

Harb, Mona, and Lara Deeb. 2013. "Contesting Urban Modernity: Moral Leisure in South Beirut." *European Journal of Cultural Studies* 16, no. 6: 725–44.

Harrow, Kenneth W. 1991. *Faces of Islam in African Literature.* Portsmouth, NH: Heinemann.

Haviland, John B. 2003. "Ideologies of Language: Some Reflections on Language and US Law." *American Anthropologist* 105, no. 4: 764–74.

Heathcott, Joseph. 2013. "Heritage in the Dynamic City: The Politics and Practices of Urban Conservation on the Swahili Coast." *International Journal of Urban and Regional Research* 37, no. 1: 215–37.

Heidegger, Martin. 1996. *Being and Time*. Albany: State University of New York Press.

Herold, E., R. Garcia, and T. Demora. 2001. "Female Tourists and Beach Boys: Romance or Sex Tourism?" *Annals of Tourism Research* 28, no. 4: 978–97.

Hichens, William. 1938. "Khabar Al-Lamu: A Chronicle of Lamu." *Bantu Studies* 12:1–33.

Higgins, Christina. 2007. "Constructing Membership in the In-Group Affiliation and Resistance among Urban Tanzanians." *Pragmatics* 17:149–70.

———. 2014. "Constructing Identities through Literacy Events in HIV/AIDS Education." *Journal of Multilingual and Multicultural development* 35, no. 7: 709–23.

———. 2016. "Authorization and Illegitimation among Biomedical Doctors and Indigenous Healers in Tanzania." *Applied Linguistics Review* 7, no. 4: 385–407.

Hill, Jane. 1998. "Today There Is No Respect: Nostalgia, 'Respect', and Oppositional Discourse in Mexicano (Nahuatl) Language Ideology." In *Language Ideologies: Practice and Theory*, edited by Bambi Schieffelin and Kathryn Woolard, 68–86. Oxford: Oxford University Press.

———. 1995. "The Voices of Don Gabriel." In *The Dialogic Emergence of Culture*, edited by Dennis Tedlock and Bruce Mannheim, 97–147. Urbana: University of Illinois Press.

Hill, Jane H., and Judith T. Irvine. 1993. *Responsibility and Evidence in Oral Discourse*. Cambridge: Cambridge University Press.

Hillewaert, Sarah. 2003. "Sheng: Een Sociolinguistische Studie van Een Urbane Jongerencode." Unpublished thesis, Ghent University.

———. 2015. "Writing with an Accent: Orthographic Practice, Emblems, and Traces on Facebook." *Journal of Linguistic Anthropology* 25, no. 2: 195–214.

———. 2016. "Tactics and Tactility: A Sensory Semiotics of Handshakes in Coastal Kenya." *American Anthropologist* 118, no. 1: 49–66.

———. 2018. "Identity and Belonging on the Contemporary Swahili Coast: The Case of Lamu." In *The Swahili World*, edited by Stephanie Lynne-Jones and Adria LaViolette, 602–13. New York: Routledge.

Hirsch, Susan F. 1998. *Pronouncing and Persevering: Gender and the Discourses of Disputing in an African Islamic Court*. Chicago: University of Chicago Press.

Hirschkind, Charles. 2006. *The Ethical Soundscape.* New York: Columbia University Press.

Hodgson, Dorothy L. 2011. *Being Maasai, Becoming Indigenous: Postcolonial Politics in a Neoliberal World.* Bloomington: Indiana University Press.

Honwana, Alcinda. 2006. *Child Soldiers in Africa.* Philadelphia: University of Pennsylvania Press.

———. 2012. *The Time of Youth: Work, Social Change, and Politics in Africa.* Boulder, CO: Kumarian Press.

Honwana, Alcinda Manuel, and Filipe de Boeck. 2005. *Makers & Breakers: Children & Youth in Postcolonial Africa.* Oxford: James Currey.

Horton, Mark, and Felix Chami. 2018. "Swahili Origins." In *The Swahili World*, edited by Stephanie Wynne-Jones and Adria LaViolette, 135–46. New York: Routledge.

Horton, Mark, and John Middleton. 2000. *The Swahili: The Social Landscape of a Mercantile Society.* Oxford: Blackwell.

Ibn Nasir, Abdallah ibn 'Ali, and William Lionel Hichens. 1939. *Al-Inkishafi: The Soul's Awakening.* London: Sheldon Press.

Iliffe, John. 2005. *Honour in African History.* Cambridge: Cambridge University Press.

Inoue, Miyako. 2004. "What Does Language Remember? Indexical Inversion and the Naturalized History of Japanese Women." *Journal of Linguistic Anthropology* 14, no. 1: 39–56.

———. 2006. *Vicarious Language: Gender and Linguistic Modernity in Japan.* Berkeley: University of California Press.

———. 2007. "Language, Gender, and Neoliberalism." *Gender and Language* 1, no. 1: 79–92.

Irvine, Judith T. 1989. "When Talk Isn't Cheap: Language and Political Economy." *American Ethnologist* 16, no. 2: 248–67.

———. 1996. "Language and Community: Introduction." *Journal of Linguistic Anthropology* 6, no. 2: 123–25.

———. 2001. "Formality and Informality in Communicative Events." In *Linguistic Anthropology: A Reader*, edited by Alessandro Duranti, 189–207. Oxford: Wiley-Blackwell.

———. 2005. "Commentary: Knots and Tears in the Interdiscursive Fabric." *Journal of Linguistic Anthropology* 15, no. 1: 72–80.

———. 2008. "Subjected Words: African Linguistics and the Colonial Encounter." *Language & Communication* 28, no. 4: 323–43.

Irvine, Judith T., and Susan Gal. 2000. "Language Ideology and Linguistic Differentiation." In *Regimes of Language: Ideologies, Polities, and Identities*, edited by Paul Kroskrity, 35–83. Santa Fe: School of American Research Press.

Issa, Amina A. 2012. "Wedding Ceremonies and Cultural Exchanges in an Indian Ocean Port City: The Case of Zanzibar Town." *Social Dynamics* 38, no. 3: 467–78.

Jaffe, Alexandra. 2009. *Stance: Sociolinguistic Perspectives.* Oxford: Oxford University Press.

Janson, Marloes. 2013. *Islam, Youth, and Modernity in the Gambia: The Tablighi Jama'at.* Cambridge: Cambridge University Press.

Kamalkhan, Kalandar. 2010. *The Swahili Architecture Of Lamu, Kenya: Oral Tradition and Space.* Saarbrücken, Germany: Lambert Academic.

Kazungu, K. 2014a. "Dreadlock Ban Bill Opposed." http://mobile.nation.co .ke/counties/Dreadlocks-ban-Bill-opposed/-/1950480/ 2285304/-/format /xhtml/-/lg1k6sz/-/index.html.

———. 2014b. "Now Lamu Proposes to Outlaw Dreadlocks." http://www .nation.co.ke/news/Now-Lamu-proposes-to- outlaw-dreadlocks/-/1056 /2282772/-/mjxxyp/-/index.html.

Keane, Webb. 1997. *Signs of Recognition.* Berkeley: University of California Press.

———. 2003. "Semiotics and the Social Analysis of Material Things." *Language and Communication* 23, no. 3: 409–25.

———. 2007. *Christian Moderns: Freedom and Fetish in the Mission Encounter.* Berkeley: University of California Press.

———. 2010. "Minds, Surfaces, and Reasons in the Anthropology of Ethics." In *Ordinary Ethics,* edited by Michael Lambek, 64–83. New York: Fordham University Press.

———. 2011. "Indexing Voice: A Morality Tale." *Journal of Linguistic Anthropology* 21, no. 2: 166–78.

———. 2014a. "Affordances and Reflexivity in Ethical Life: An Ethnographic Stance." *Anthropological Theory* 14, no. 1: 3–26.

———. 2014b. "Rotting Bodies: The Clash of Stances toward Materiality and Its Ethical Affordances." *Current Anthropology* 55:312–21.

———. 2016. *Ethical Life: Its Natural and Social Histories.* Princeton: Princeton University Press.

Khabeer, Suad Abdul. 2016. *Muslim Cool: Race, Religion, and Hip Hop in the United States.* New York: New York University Press.

Khalid, Abdallah. 1977. *The Liberation of Swahili from European Appropriation,* volume 1. Nairobi: East African Literature Bureau.

Kibicho, Wanjohi. 2005. "Tourism and the Sex Trade in Kenya's Coastal Region." *Journal of Sustainable Tourism* 13, no. 3: 256–80.

Knappert, Jan. 1979. "The Origin and Development of Lingala." In *Readings in Creole Studies,* edited by Ian F. Hancock, 153–64. Amsterdam: John Benjamins.

———. 1999. "Loanwords in African Languages." In *African Mosaic: Festschrift for J. A. Mosaic*, edited by Rosalie Finlayson, 203–20. Pretoria: University of South Africa Press.

Kopytoff, Igor, and Suzanne Miers. 1977. *Slavery in Africa: Historical and Anthropological Perspectives*. Madison: University of Wisconsin Press.

Krapf, Johann Ludwig. 1882. *A Dictionary of the Suahili Language*. London: Trübner and Company.

Kresse, Kai. 2007. *Philosophising in Mombasa: Knowledge, Islam and Intellectual Practice on the Swahili Coast*. Edinburgh: Edinburgh University Press.

———. 2009. "Knowledge and Intellectual Practice in A Swahili Context: 'Wisdom' and The Social Dimensions of Knowledge." *Africa* 79, no. 1: 148–67.

———. 2010. "Muslim Politics in Postcolonial Kenya: Negotiating Knowledge on the Double-Periphery." In *Islam, Politics, Anthropology*, edited by Filippo Osella and Benjamin Soares, 72–90. Oxford: Wiley-Blackwell.

Kroskrity, Paul, ed. 2000. *Language Ideologies: The Cultures of Language in Theory and Practice*. Santa Fe: School of American Research Press.

Labov, William. 1963. "The Social Motivation of a Sound Change." *Word* 19, no. 3: 273–309.

Lambek, Michael. 2010. "How to Make Up One's Mind: Reason, Passion, and Ethics in Spirit Possession." *University of Toronto Quarterly* 79, no. 2: 720–41.

LaViolette, Adria. 2008. "Swahili Cosmopolitanism in Africa and the Indian Ocean World, AD 600–1500." *Archaeologies* 4, no. 1: 24–49.

LaViolette, Adria, and Stephanie Wynne-Jones. 2018. "The Swahili World." In *The Swahili World*, edited by Stephanie Wynne-Jones and Adria LaViolette, 1–14. New York: Routledge.

Lewis, Reina. 2015a. "Fashion, Shame and Pride: Constructing the Modest Fashion Industry in Three Faiths." In *The Changing World Religion Map*, 2597–2609. Berlin: Springer.

———. 2015b. *Muslim Fashion: Contemporary Style Cultures*. Durham, NC: Duke University Press.

Lodhi, Abdulaziz Y. 1973. *The Institution of Slavery in Zanzibar and Pemba*. Uppsala: Scandinavian Institute of African Studies.

———. 2003. "Aspiration in Swahili Adjectives and Verbs." *Africa & Asia* 3:155–60.

Loimeier, Roman, and Rüdiger Seesemann. 2006. *The Global Worlds of the Swahili: Interfaces of Islam, Identity and Space in 19th and 20th-Century East Africa*. Berlin: Lit Verlag.

Mahmood, Saba. 2005. *Politics of Piety: The Islamic Revival and the Feminist Subject*. Princeton: Princeton University Press.

Makoni, Sinfree. 2003. "From Misinvention to Disinvention of Language: Multilingualism and the South African Constitution." *Black Linguistics: Language, Society, and Politics in Africa and the Americas*, edited by Arnetha Ball, Arthur K. Spears, Geneva Smitherman, and Sinfree Makoni, 132–51. New York: Routledge.

Marsden, Magnus. 2005. *Living Islam: Muslim Religious Experience in Pakistan's North-West Frontier.* Cambridge: Cambridge University Press.

Marshall, Lydia Wilson, and Herman Kiriama. 2018. "The Legacy of Slavery on the Swahili Coast." In *The Swahili World*, edited by Stephanie Wynne-Jones and Adria LaViolette, 566–76. New York: Routledge.

Martin, Scott C. 1995. *Killing Time: Leisure and Culture in Southwestern Pennsylvania, 1800–1850.* Ann Arbor: University of Michigan Press.

Masquelier, Adeline Marie. 2009. *Women and Islamic Revival in a West African Town.* Bloomington: Indiana University Press.

Mazrui, Alamin M. 1992. "Conservationism and Liberalism in Swahili Poetry: The Linguistic Dimension." *Research in African Literatures* 23, no. 4: 67–76.

———. 2007. *Swahili beyond the Boundaries: Literature, Language, and Identity.* Athens: Ohio University Press.

———. 2016. *Cultural Politics of Translation: East Africa in a Global Context.* New York: Routledge.

Mazrui, Alamin M., and Ibrahim N. Shariff. 1994. *The Swahili: Idiom and Identity of an African People.* Trenton, NJ: Africa World Press.

McBrien, Julie. 2009. "Mukada's Struggle: Veils and Modernity in Kyrgyzstan." *Journal of the Royal Anthropological Institute* 15:127–44.

McIntosh, Janet. 2009. *The Edge of Islam: Power, Personhood, and Ethnoreligious Boundaries on the Kenya Coast.* Durham, NC: Duke University Press.

McMahon, Elisabeth. 2006. "'A Solitary Tree Builds Not': Heshima, Community, and Shifting Identity in Post-Emancipation Pemba Island." *International Journal of African Historical Studies* 39, no. 2: 197–219.

Meier, Prita. 2016. *Swahili Port Cities: The Architecture of Elsewhere.* Bloomington: Indiana University Press.

Meiu, George Paul. 2015. "'Beach-Boy Elders' and 'Young Big-Men': Subverting the Temporalities of Ageing in Kenya's Ethno-Erotic Economies." *Ethnos* 80, no. 4: 472–96.

Meneley, Anne. 1996. *Tournaments of Value: Sociability and Hierarchy in a Yemeni Town.* Toronto: University of Toronto Press.

———. 2007. "Fashion and Fundamentalism in Fin-de-Siècle Yemen: Chador Barbie and Islamic Socks. *Cultural Anthropology* 22, no. 2: 214–43.

Middleton, John. 1992. *The World of the Swahili: An African Mercantile Civilization.* New Haven: Yale University Press.

———. 2004. *African Merchants of the Indian Ocean: Swahili of the East African Coast*. Long Grove, IL: Waveland Press.

Moyer, Eileen. 2004. "Popular Cartographies: Youthful Imaginings of the Global in the Streets of Dar Es Salaam, Tanzania." *City & Society* 16, no. 2: 117–43.

———. 2005. "Street-Corner Justice in the Name of Jah: Imperatives for Peace among Dar Es Salaam Street Youth." *Africa Today* 51, no. 3: 31–58.

Mtoro bin Mwinyi, Bakari, and J. W. T. Allen. 1981. *The Customs of the Swahili People*. Berkeley: University of California Press.

Newcomb, Rachel. 2006. "Gendering the City, Gendering the Nation: Contesting Urban Space in Fes, Morocco." *City & Society* 18, no. 2: 288–311.

Newell, Sasha. 2012. *The Modernity Bluff: Crime, Consumption, and Citizenship in Côte d'Ivoire*. Chicago: University of Chicago Press.

Newell, Sasha, and Onookome Okome, eds. 2014. *Popular Culture in Africa: The Episteme of the Everyday*. New York: Routledge.

Nurse, Derek. 1980. *Bantu Expansion into East Africa: Linguistic Evidence*. Nairobi: Institute of African Studies.

———. 1982. "A Tentative Classification of the Primary Dialects of Swahili." *SUGIA: Sprache & Geschichte in Afrika* 4:165–205.

———. 1985. "The 'Indigenous versus Foreign' Controversy about the Sources of Swahili Vocabulary." *Studies in African Linguistics* 9:245–50.

———. 2011. *Bajuni: People, Society, Geography, History, Language*. Department of Linguistics, Memorial University of Newfoundland. http://www.ucs.mun.ca/~dnurse/bajuni_database/general_document.pdf

———. 2011. Bajuni Database. http://www.faculty.mun.ca/dnurse/Database/Bajuni.pdf.

Nurse, Derek, and Thomas J. Hinnebusch. 1993. *Swahili and Sabaki: A Linguistic History*. Berkeley: University of California Press.

Nurse, Derek, and Thomas T. Spear. 1985. *The Swahili: Reconstructing the History and Language of an African Society, 800–1500*. Philadelphia: University of Pennsylvania Press.

Nyanzi, Stella, Ousman Rosenberg-Jallow, Ousman Bah, and Susan Nyanzi. 2005. "Bumsters, Big Black Organs and Old White Gold: Embodied Racial Myths in Sexual Relationships of Gambian Beach Boys." *Culture, Health & Sexuality* 7, no. 6: 557–69.

Ogechi, Nathan Oyori. 2003. "On Language Rights in Kenya." *Nordic Journal of African Studies* 12, no. 3: 277–95.

Oppermann, Martin. 1999. "Sex Tourism." *Annals of Tourism Research* 26, no. 2: 51–66.

Osella, Filippo, and Benjamin Soares. 2010. *Islam, Politics, Anthropology.* Oxford: Wiley-Blackwell.

Ossman, Susan. 1994. *Picturing Casablanca: Portraits of Power in a Modern City.* Berkeley: University of California Press.

Peel, J. D. Y. 2003. *Religious Encounter and the Making of the Yoruba.* Bloomington: Indiana University Press.

Peterson, Derek R. 2006. "Language Work and Colonial Politics in Eastern Africa: The Making of Standard Swahili and Kikuyu." In *The Study of Language and the Politics of Community in Global Context*, edited by David L. Hoyt and Karen Oslund, 185–214. Lanham, MD: Lexington Books.

———. 2012. *Ethnic Patriotism and the East African Revival: A History of Dissent, c. 1935–1972.* New York: Cambridge University Press.

Phadke, Shilpa. 2007. "Dangerous Liaisons: Women and Men: Risk and Reputation in Mumbai." *Economic and Political Weekly* 42, no. 17: 1510–18.

Polomé, Edgar C. 1967. *Swahili Language Handbook.* Washington, DC: Center for Applied Linguistics.

Pouwels, Randall L. 1987. *Horn and Crescent.* Cambridge: Cambridge University Press.

———. 1991. "The Battle of Shela: The Climax of an Era and a Point of Departure in the Modern History of the Kenya Coast." *Cahiers d'Études Africaines* 31, no. 123: 363–89.

Praxides, Chedi. 2014. "Lamu IDPs Not Genuine, Says Miiri." *The Star* (Nairobi), 26.

Prestholdt, Jeremy. 2004. "On the Global Repercussions of East African Consumerism." *American Historical Review* 109, no. 3: 755–81.

———. 2008. *Domesticating the World: African Consumerism and the Genealogies of Globalization.* Berkeley: University of California Press.

———. 2009. "Phantom of the Forever War: Fazul Abdullah Muhammad and the Terrorist Imaginary." *Public Culture* 21, no. 3: 451–64.

———. 2011. "Kenya, the United States, and Counterterrorism." *Africa Today* 57, no. 4: 2–27.

———. 2014. "Politics of the Soil: Separatism, Autochthony and Decolonization at Kenya's Coast." *Journal of African History* 55, no. 2: 1–22.

Prins, A. H. J. 1961. *The Swahili-Speaking Peoples of Zanzibar and the East African Coast: Arabs, Shirazi and Swahili.* London: International African Institute.

———. 1971. *Didemic Lamu, Social Stratification and Spatial Structure in a Muslim Maritime Town.* Groningen: Instituut voor Culturele Antropologie der Rijks-universiteit.

Ranger, Terence O. 1975. *Dance and Society in Eastern Africa 1890–1970: The Beni Ngoma.* Berkeley: University of California Press.

Ray, Daren. 2018. "Defining the Swahili." In *The Swahili World,* edited by Stephanie Wynne-Jones and Adria LaViolette, 67–80. New York: Routledge.

Renne, Elisha P. 2013. *Veiling in Africa.* Bloomington: Indiana University Press.

Richter, Linda, Craig Higson-Smith, and Andrew Dawes. 2004. *Sexual Abuse of Young Children in Southern Africa.* Cape Town: HSRC Press.

Robbins, Joel, and Alan Rumsey. 2008. "Introduction: Cultural and Linguistic Anthropology and the Opacity of Other Minds." *Anthropological Quarterly* 81, no. 2: 407–20.

Roehl, Karl E. 1930. "The Linguistic Situation in East Africa." *Africa* 3, no. 2: 191–202.

Rollins, Jack Drake. 1983. *A History of Swahili Prose, Part 1: From Earliest Times to the End of the Nineteenth Century.* Leiden: Brill Archive.

Romero, Patricia W. 1983. "Laboratory for the Oral History of Slavery: The Island of Lamu on the Kenya Coast." *American Historical Review* 88, no. 4: 858–82.

———. 1986. "'Where Have All the Slaves Gone?': Emancipation and Post-Emancipation in Lamu, Kenya." *Journal of African History* 27, no. 3: 497–512.

———. 1997. *Lamu : History, Society, and Family in an East African Port City.* Ann Arbor: University of Michigan Press.

Ruete, Emily, and Annegret Nippa. 1989. *Leben im Sultanspalast.* Frankfurt: Athenäum.

Ryan, Chris, and Colin Michael Hall. 2001. *Sex Tourism: Marginal People and Liminalities.* London: Psychology Press.

Sacks, Harvey. 1972. "Notes on Police Assessment of Moral Character." In *Studies in Social Interaction,* edited by David Sudnow, 280–93. New York: Free Press.

Saleh, Mohamed Ahmed. 2004. "'Going with the Times': Conflicting Swahili Norms and Values Today." In *Swahili Modernities: Culture, Politics, and Identity on the East Coast of Africa,* edited by Pat Caplan and Topan Farouk,145–55. Trenton, NJ: Africa World Press.

Salim, Ahmed Idha. 1970. "The Movement of 'Mwambao' or Coast Autonomy in Kenya, 1956–1963." In *Hadith 2,* edited by B. A. Ogot, 212–28. Nairobi: East African Publishing House.

———. 1984. "The Elusive 'Mswahili': Some Reflections on His Identity and Culture." In *Swahili Language and Society,* edited by J. Maw and

D. J. Parkin, 215–27. Vienna: Institut für Afrikanistik und Ägyptologie der Universität Wien.

Samper, David. 2002. "Talking Sheng: The Role of a Hybrid Language in the Construction of Identity and Youth Culture in Nairobi, Kenya." PhD dissertation, University of Pennsylvania.

Sands, Kristin Zahra. 2006. *Sufi Commentaries on the Quran in Classical Islam.* New York: Routledge.

Saritoprak, Zeki. 2017. *Spirituality: Theology and Practice for the Modern World.* New York: Bloomsbury.

Schieffelin, Bambi, Kathryn Woolard, and Paul Kroskrity, eds. 1998. *Language Ideologies: Practice and Theory.* Oxford: Oxford University Press.

Schielke, Samuli. 2009. "Being Good in Ramadan: Ambivalence, Fragmentation, and the Moral Self in the Lives of Young Egyptians." *Journal of the Royal Anthropological Institute* 15:40.

———. 2015. "Living with Unresolved Differences: A Reply to Fadil and Fernando." *HAU: Journal of Ethnographic Theory* 5, no. 2: 89–92.

Schielke, Samuli, and Liza Debevec. 2012. *Ordinary Lives and Grand Schemes: An Anthropology of Everyday Religion.* New York: Berghahn Books.

Schiffrin, Deborah. 1974. "Handwork as Ceremony: The Case of the Handshake." *Semiotica* 12, no. 3: 189–202.

Schottman, Wendy. 1995. "The Daily Ritual of Greeting among the Baatombu of Benin." *Anthropological Linguistics* 37, no. 4: 487–523.

Searle, John R. 1983. *Intentionality: An Essay in the Philosophy of Mind.* New York: Cambridge University Press.

Secor, Anna J. 2002. "The Veil and Urban Space in Istanbul: Women's Dress, Mobility and Islamic Knowledge." *Gender, Place and Culture: A Journal of Feminist Geography* 9, no. 1: 5–22.

———. 2004. "Feminizing Electoral Geography." In *Mapping Women, Making Politics: Feminist Perspectives on Political Geography*, edited by Lynn A. Staeheli, Eleonore Kofman, and Linda Peake, 261–72. London: Psychology Press.

Seesemann, R. 2005. "The Quotidian Dimension of Islamic Reformism in Wadai (Chad)." In *L'Islam politique au sud du Sahara: Identités, discours et enjeux*, edited by M. Gomez-Perez, 327–46. Paris: Karthala.

Seidel, A. 1895. "Beitrage zur Kenntnis des Lamu-Dialektes der Suaheli-Sprache." *Zeitschrift für Afrikanische und Ozeanische Sprachen* 1:169–83.

Selim, Samah. 2010. "Review of Politics of Piety: The Islamic Revival and the Feminist Subject." http://www.jadaliyya.com/Details/23539/Politics -of-Piety-The-Islamic-Revival-and-the-Feminist-Subject.

Silverstein, Michael. 1979. "Language Structure and Linguistic Ideology." In *The Elements: A Parasession on Linguistic Units and Levels*, 193–247. Chicago: Chicago Linguistic Society.

———. 1981. "Case Marking and the Nature of Language." *Australian Journal of Linguistics* 1:227–44.

———. 2003. "Indexical Order and the Dialectics of Sociolinguistic Life." *Language and Communication* 23, no. 3: 193–229.

Silverstein, Michael, and Greg Urban. 1996. *Natural Histories of Discourse*. Chicago: University of Chicago Press.

Smart, Devin. 2017. "Developing the Racial City: Conflict, Solidarity, and Urban Traders in Late-Colonial Mombasa." *Journal of Eastern African Studies* 11, no. 3: 425–41.

Soares, B., and R. Otayek. 2007. *Islam and Muslim Politics in Africa*. New York: Palgrave Macmillan.

Southall, Aidan. 1970. "The Illusion of Tribe." *Journal of Asian and African Studies* 5, nos. 1–2: 28–50.

Spitulnik, Debra. 1996. "The Social Circulation of Media Discourse and the Mediation of Communities." *Journal of Linguistic Anthropology* 6, no. 2: 161–87.

Steere, Edward. 1919. *A Handbook of the Swahili Language as Spoken at Zanzibar*. 3rd ed. London: Society for Promoting Christian Knowledge.

Stigand, C. H. 1915. *A Grammar of Dialectal Change in the Swahili Language*. Cambridge: Cambridge University Press.

Stiles, Erin E., and Katrina Daly Thompson, eds. 2015. *Gendered Lives in the Western Indian Ocean: Islam, Marriage, and Sexuality on the Swahili Coast*. Athens: Ohio University Press.

Strand, Thea R. 2012. "Winning the Dialect Popularity Contest: Mass-Mediated Language Ideologies and Local Responses in Rural Valdres, Norway." *Journal of Linguistic Anthropology* 22, no. 1: 23–43.

Tarlo, Emma. 2010. *Visibly Muslim: Fashion, Politics, Faith*. London: Berg.

Thompson, Katrina. 2015a. "Discreet Talk about Supernatural Sodomy, Transgressive Gender Performance, and Male Same-sex Desire in Zanzibar Town." *GLQ: A Journal of Lesbian and Gay Studies* 21:4.

———. 2015b. "Learning to Use Profanity and Sacred Speech: The Embodied Socialization of a Muslim Bride in Zanzibar." In *Gendered Lives in the Western Indian Ocean: Islam, Marriage, and Sexuality on the Swahili Coast*, edited by Erin Stiles and Katrina Daly Thompson, 168–208. Athens: Ohio University Press.

———. 2017a. "Beginnings and Endings: An Authethnographic Account of Two Zanzibari Marriages." *Anthropology and Humanism* 42, no. 1: 149–55.

———. 2017b. *Popobawa: Tanzanian Talk, Global Misreadings*. Bloomington: Indiana University Press.

Topan, Farouk. 1992. "Swahili as a Religious Language." *Journal of Religion in Africa* 22, no. 4: 331–49.

Van de Veer, Peter. 2008. "Embodiment, Materiality, and Power: A Review Essay." *Comparative Studies in Society and History* 50, no. 3: 809–18.

Vernet, Thomas. 2009. "Slave Trade and Slavery on the Swahili Coast (1500–1750)." In *Slavery, Islam and Diaspora*, edited by Ismael Musah Montana and Paul Lovejoy, 37–76. Trenton, NJ: Africa World Press.

———. 2013. *East Africa: Slave Migrations*. Wiley Online Library. https://onlinelibrary.wiley.com/doi/abs/10.1002/9781444351071.wbeghm188.

Vierke, Clarissa. 2011. *On the Poetics of the Utendi: A Critical Edition of the Nineteenth-Century Swahili Poem "Utendi wa Haudaji" Together with a Stylistic Analysis*. Berlin: Lit Verlag.

———. 2014. "Akhi Patia Kalamu: Writing Swahili Poetry in Arabic Script." In *Arabic Script in Africa: Studies in the Use of a Writing System*, edited by Meikal Mumin and Kees Versteegh, 319–42. Leiden: Brill.

———. 2017. "Poetic Links across the Ocean: On Poetic 'Translation' as Mimetic Practice at the Swahili Coast." *Comparative Studies of South Asia, Africa, and the Middle East* 37, no. 2: 321–35.

Wald, Benji. 1985. "Vernacular and Standard Swahili as Seen by Members of the Mombasa Swahili Speech Community." In *Language of Inequality*, edited by Nessa Wolfson and Joan Manes, 123–44. Berlin: Mouton.

Walley, Christine J. 2004. "Modernity and the Meaning of Development within the Mafia Island Marine Park, Tanzania." In *Swahili Modernities: Culture, Politics, and Identity on the East Coast of Africa*, edited by Pat Caplan and Farouk Topan, 61–81. Trenton, NJ: Africa World Press.

Walsh, Martin. 2018. "The Swahili Language and Its Early History." In *The Swahili World*, edited by Stephanie Wynne-Jones and Adria LaViolette, 121–30. New York: Routledge.

Wedeen, Lisa. 2008. *Peripheral Visions: Publics, Power, and Performance in Yemen*. Chicago: University of Chicago Press.

Weiss, Brad. 2002. "Thug Realism: Inhabiting Fantasy in Urban Tanzania." *Cultural Anthropology* 17, no. 1: 93–124.

———. 2004. *Producing African Futures: Ritual and Reproduction in a Neoliberal Age*. Leiden: Brill.

———. 2009. *Street Dreams and Hip Hop Barbershops: Global Fantasy in Urban Tanzania*. Ann Arbor: University of Michigan Press.

Whiteley, Wilfred Howell. 1969. *Swahili: The Rise of a National Language*. London: Methuen.

Williams, Raymond. 1977. *Marxism and Literature*. Oxford: Oxford University Press.

Willis, Justin, and George Gona. 2013. "Pwani C Kenya? Memory, Documents and Secessionist Politics in Coastal Kenya." *African Affairs* 112, no. 446: 48–71.

Woolard, Katheryn A. 2016. *Singular and Plural. Ideologies of Linguistic Authority in 21ˢᵗ Century Catalonia*. Oxford: Oxford University Press.

Wortham, Stanton E. F. 1996. "Mapping Participant Deictics: A Technique for Discovering Speakers' Footing." *Journal of Pragmatics* 25, no. 3: 331–48.

Wynne-Jones, Stephanie. 2013. "The Public Life of the Swahili Stonehouse, 14th–15th Centuries AD." *Journal of Anthropological Archaeology* 32, no. 4: 759–73.

Yahya-Othman, Saida. 1995. "Aren't You Going to Greet Me? Impoliteness in Swahili Greetings." *Text & Talk* 15, no. 2: 209–27.

Ylvisaker, Marguerite. 1979. *Lamu in the Nineteenth Century: Land, Trade, and Politics. Boston University*. Boston: African Studies Center.

Zhukov, Andrey. 2004. "Old Swahili-Arabic Script and the Development of Swahili Literary Language." *Sudanic Africa* 15:1–15.

Zigon, Jarrett. 2007. "Moral Breakdown and the Ethical Demand." *Anthropological Theory* 7, no. 2: 131–50.

Sarah Hillewaert is Associate Professor of Linguistic Anthropology at the University of Toronto.

www.ingramcontent.com/pod-product-compliance
Lightning Source LLC
Chambersburg PA
CBHW022138020426
42334CB00015B/945